Hands-On Cloud Administration in Azure

Implement, monitor, and manage important Azure services
and components including IaaS and PaaS

Mustafa Toroman

Packt>

BIRMINGHAM - MUMBAI

Hands-On Cloud Administration in Azure

Commissioning Editor: Gebin George
Acquisition Editor: Shrilekha Inani
Content Development Editor: Dattatraya More
Technical Editor: Sayali Thanekar
Copy Editor: Safis Editing
Project Coordinator: Kinjal Bari
Proofreader: Safis Editing
Indexer: Tejal Daruwale Soni
Graphics: Jisha Chirayil
Production Coordinator: Jyoti Chauhan

First published: October 2018

Production reference: 2061118

Published by Packt Publishing Ltd.
Livery Place
35 Livery Street
Birmingham
B3 2PB, UK.

ISBN 978-1-78913-496-4

www.packtpub.com

Mapt

Mapt is an online digital library that gives you full access to over 5,000 books and videos, as well as industry leading tools to help you plan your personal development and advance your career. For more information, please visit our website.

Why subscribe?

- Spend less time learning and more time coding with practical eBooks and Videos from over 4,000 industry professionals

- Improve your learning with Skill Plans built especially for you

- Get a free eBook or video every month

- Mapt is fully searchable

- Copy and paste, print, and bookmark content

Packt.com

Did you know that Packt offers eBook versions of every book published, with PDF and ePub files available? You can upgrade to the eBook version at www.packt.com and as a print book customer, you are entitled to a discount on the eBook copy. Get in touch with us at customercare@packtpub.com for more details.

At www.packt.com, you can also read a collection of free technical articles, sign up for a range of free newsletters, and receive exclusive discounts and offers on Packt books and eBooks.

Foreword

I've been alive for more than 40 years, and I can tell you that we are lucky to live in these technologically exciting times. In a plastic or magnesium alloy, school notebook-sized box, weighing less than a bottle of juice, we have more portable power than a secret government data center would have had a few decades ago. We can run multiple operating systems on one computer at once, connect to a zillion devices wirelessly in an instant, and send messages and stream videos in a blink of an eye. Optical cables and even the air around us gives us access to an unfathomable amount of worldwide information and resources.

Around our wrists today, we wear millions of times more computing power and data storage than would have been in a computer not so long ago. What was once a huge block of buildings, connected to power plants, operating with the help of hundreds of engineers, is today a tiny piece of silicon in your pocket, with a processing power a billion times greater.

Technology is saving people's lives, allowing surgeries to be performed at a distance, empowering people with knowledge that is now more accessible than ever at just few clicks away—in the air, at sea, in the middle of nowhere.

Years ago, we waited 5 to 10 minutes for a program of just 48 kilobytes to load from a tape we got in the mail. Not email, folks—yes, you have read it right—in the mailbox, the actual box that holds the papers and stuff your postman delivers. Once we got the internet, we waited minutes, often hours, just to connect to the internet because access points were rare. You reached them by dialing—turning a ring or pushing plastic buttons. And once you got in, you patiently waited again to download that huge 1 megabyte document or a picture through a telephone wire. Yes, we also had operating systems that were upgraded or replaced with a new version every 5, 10, or 15 years.

Yeah, right, we were not in a hurry and had every minute between two operating system version upgrades available to learn the nuts and bolts of how that particular operating system worked and behaved.

Now… well, today we attend university classes from our homes with a lecturer on a different continent; we watch condensed and fast-paced computer technology classes on a train on our way home from work. Operating systems and applications are upgraded every six months, with feature upgrades and fixes coming out every week. Microsoft Azure is evolving and getting new features, upgrades, services, and capabilities on a weekly basis.

Today, we live with an abundance of technology but march through a scarcity of time.

Mustafa and I met on one of the numerous conferences we attended and became friends through a mutual passion and love for technology, particularly Microsoft Azure. A database professional with more than 30 technical certifications, Mustafa is currently a cloud architect and system engineer responsible for architecting and managing thousands of Azure services and workloads for some of the largest Fortune 500 companies.

Through this book, *Hands-On Cloud Administration in Azure*, Mustafa effortlessly explains the most important pieces of the Azure puzzle, giving you grab-and-go concepts without losing so much valuable time. Beginning with cloud administration models, the book explains the pillars of Azure: virtual networks and the Infrastructure-as-a-Service model. In the second part of the book, you will make an efficient start on building advanced solutions in Azure. The book then closes with an exploration of the essential security solutions and administration tools, looking at the best tips and tricks for them.

Each Microsoft Azure service or feature could have a whole book written on it. The chapters in this book could be expanded to fill their own books as well; there is simply a lot to cover. What this book offers is a straightforward and practical approach that you can follow in the Azure portal as you are going through chapters—you'll see the results right away, without wasting your valuable time. Jumpstarting your experience in Microsoft Azure has never been easier or more efficient, thanks to *Hands-On Cloud Administration in Azure*.

Backed up with Mustafa's extensive hands-on experience, this unique and practical book will give you nuggets of Azure knowledge in an efficient, practical, and timely way.

Sasha (Sasa) Kranjac, MVP, MCT, CEI

Contributors

About the author

Mustafa Toroman is a program architect and senior system engineer with Authority Partners. He has years of experience in designing and monitoring infrastructure solutions, and has lately been focused on designing new solutions in the cloud and migrating existing solutions to the cloud. He is very interested in DevOps processes and he's also an Infrastructure-as-Code enthusiast. Mustafa has over 30 Microsoft certificates and has been a **Microsoft Certified Trainer (MCT)** for the last 6 years. He often speaks at international conferences (such as MS Ignite, European Collaboration Summit, and IT/Dev Connections) about cloud technologies, and has been named an MVP for Microsoft Azure for the last three years in a row.

About the reviewer

Sasha (Sasa) Kranjac is a security and Azure specialist and instructor with more than two decades of experience in the field. He can be spotted speaking at numerous conferences or delivering Microsoft, EC-Council, and his own Azure and security courses internationally.

He is a **Microsoft MVP**, MCT, MCT Regional Lead, Certified EC-Council Instructor (CEI), and holds a few other certifications as well. He is a real security and Azure otaku!

Sasha owns a small training and consulting company, and his clients include some of the world's largest enterprises.

He is currently writing *MCSA Windows Server 2016 – Certification Guide*, for Packt Publishing, and has a few titles in the pipeline on top of that.

> *I would like to thank the great people at Packt Publishing for producing this title, as well the author for the huge amount of effort and hours invested in writing this book.*

Packt is searching for authors like you

If you're interested in becoming an author for Packt, please visit `authors.packtpub.com` and apply today. We have worked with thousands of developers and tech professionals, just like you, to help them share their insight with the global tech community. You can make a general application, apply for a specific hot topic that we are recruiting an author for, or submit your own idea.

Table of Contents

Preface   1

Chapter 1: Key Concepts of Cloud Computing   7
  Cloud computing concepts   7
    Types of cloud computing   8
    A brief history of Azure (from ASM to ARM)   12
  Cloud services models   15
    Pros and cons of cloud service models   18
    Other benefits of the cloud   18
  Understanding the Azure subscription model   22
    Azure subscription types   24
    Deciding between IaaS or PaaS   27
    Understanding the pricing of Azure resources   29
    ARM revolution   31
  Summary   32
  Questions   33

Chapter 2: Azure Networking - Foundation of Azure IaaS   35
  Technical requirements   35
  Azure networking basics   36
    Creating your first virtual network in Azure   36
    Azure virtual network options   39
  Connected devices   45
    Creating an Azure virtual machine   45
  IP address types   50
    Private IP addresses   51
    Network security groups   53
    Public IP address   57
    Other Azure network services   59
  ARM templates   59
  Summary   69
  Questions   70

Chapter 3: Infrastructure as a Service - the First Layer of Cloud Computing   73
  Technical requirements   73
  Deploying Azure Virtual Machines   74
    Creating a new Azure Virtual Machine   74
    Basic Azure Virtual Machine information   75
    Azure Virtual Machine sizes   76

Advanced VM options   78
Managing Azure Virtual Machines   82
VM settings   82
Azure Virtual Machine operation and monitoring   84
Azure Load Balancers   91
Creating an Azure Load Balancer   92
Configuring the Azure Load Balancer   94
Azure Load Balancer ARM template   100
Azure Virtual Machine Scale Set   102
Creating an Azure Virtual Machine Scale Set   102
Managing Azure Virtual Machine Scale Sets   107
Azure Virtual Machine Scale Set ARM template   109
Summary   114
Questions   115

**Chapter 4: Azure App Service - Hosting Web Applications without a
Server**   117
Technical requirements   117
Azure App Service Plan and Azure Web Apps   118
Creating an App Service Plan   119
Creating an Azure Web App   121
Managing Azure Web App   123
Azure Web App deployment settings   123
Azure Web App general settings   127
Custom domains, certificates, and scaling   131
Azure Web App Tools   135
Monitoring a Web App in Azure   137
Application Insights   138
Azure App Service Plan   143
Azure Web App high availability   145
Creating a Traffic Manager   146
Traffic Manager configuration and settings   148
Running Azure Web Apps in a dedicated environment   151
Summary   152
Questions   152

Chapter 5: The Azure Data Platform   155
Technical requirements   155
Azure Database options   155
SQL Server as IaaS   156
Creating an Azure Virtual Machine with a SQL image   156
Managing SQL Server in the Azure Virtual Machine   162
High availability for SQL Server in Azure Virtual machine   164
SQL Server as PaaS   165
Creating the Azure SQL Database   165

Managing the Azure SQL Database   169
Creating highly available Azure SQL Database   173
Azure SQL Database security   177
Monitoring and troubleshooting Azure SQL Database   183
Azure SQL Database backup   186
Other data services in Azure   187
Summary   188
Questions   189

**Chapter 6: Azure Storage, Backup, and Site Recovery - Moving your
Data to Azure**   191
Technical requirements   191
Azure Storage   192
Creating an Azure Storage account   192
Azure Storage settings   196
Migrating a database to the cloud   198
Backing up a database to storage   199
Migrating a database to Azure SQL   202
Database assessment   207
Azure Recovery Service   211
Creating a recovery service vault   212
Enabling Azure Backup   213
Backing up on-premises resources   215
Azure Site Recovery   222
Configuring ASR for on-premises resources   222
Using ASR as a migration tool   234
Failover and migrating the VM   236
Other options   238
Summary   239
Questions   239

**Chapter 7: Hybrid Cloud with Azure - Extending Local Workloads to
the Cloud**   241
Technical requirements   241
Hybrid clouds   242
Connecting the local network and Azure Virtual Network   243
Creating a S2S Connection   243
Configuring Azure settings for S2S   249
Configuring a local firewall for S2S   251
Configuring services in a hybrid environment   252
Connecting virtual networks across Azure   253
On-premises data gateway   255
Local installation   256
Cloud service   258
Azure Stack   260

Summary 262
Questions 263
Chapter 8: Azure Active Directory - Identity in the Cloud 265
Technical requirements 265
The Azure Active Directory 266
Creating a new directory 267
Customizing your domain 269
Syncing AAD with on-premises AD 271
Installing Azure AD Connect 273
Managing AAD 277
Creating a new user 278
Managing user options and permissions 280
Registering an application in AAD 282
Role-based access control 286
Summary 289
Questions 289
Chapter 9: Azure Security and Administration 291
Technical requirements 291
Demystifying cloud security 292
Securing your identity 292
Enabling multi-factor authentication 293
Other identity security options 295
Securing the network 295
Azure Firewall 295
Preparing the environment 295
Creating an Azure Firewall 297
Azure Route Table 300
Configuring Azure Firewall 303
Other network security options 304
Encryption 305
Azure Key Vault 305
Creating an Azure Key Vault 306
Adding keys and secrets 309
Encrypting the storage account 311
Encrypting databases 312
Installing Azure PowerShell 312
Using your own key for Azure SQL Database encryption 313
Encrypting VM disks 314
Azure Security Center 315
Azure Security Center overview 316
Azure Security Center recommendations 317
Enabling endpoint protection 319
Azure Security Center Alerts 320
Just-in-Time access 322

Summary   325
Questions   326

Chapter 10: Best Practices   329
  Technical requirements   329
  Azure best practices   330
    Naming convention   330
    Public endpoints   331
    Other things to consider   335
  Infrastructure as code   337
    Installing tools   338
      ARM templates   338
      Azure PowerShell   338
      Azure CLI   339
    Creating Azure resources with IaC   342
      Creating an Azure Web App with ARM templates   342
      Creating an Azure Web App with Azure PowerShell   345
      Creating an Azure Web App with Azure CLI   347
      Deploying multiple resources   348
  Configuration as code   350
    Apply DSC with Azure Automation   351
  Summary   356
  Questions   356

Assessments   359

Other Books You May Enjoy   367

Index   371

Preface

Welcome to *Hands-On Cloud Administration in Azure*. This book is designed to help you start with Azure and guide you on your cloud journey. We will start with cloud concepts that will help you to understand the difference between cloud and local infrastructure. Basic **Infrastructure as a Service (IaaS)** and **Platform as a Service (PaaS)** services will be explained, to help you understand how to leverage cloud to your advantage. Next, we'll move to migration and then hybrid cloud, and explain how to move your services to the cloud and how to combine them with on-premises resources. Identity and security will be covered in order to explain how to secure and protect your cloud resources. Finally, we'll go over some best practices and Infrastructure-as-Code to help you administer and monitor your resources.

Everything will be covered with real-world examples and a step-by-step approach that will help you to understand cloud principles and apply them in your environment.

Who this book is for

This book targets IT pros, system engineers and administrators, DevOps practitioners, and anyone who wants to understand Azure and cloud concepts. You should have a basic understanding of cloud computing, and intermediate knowledge of networking and server administration.

What this book covers

Chapter 1, *Key Concepts of Cloud Computing*, introduces you to cloud computing and basic cloud concepts and models. The focus will be on the differences between IaaS and PaaS. We'll also explain Azure subscriptions and tenant.

Chapter 2, *Azure Networking - Foundation of Azure IaaS*, covers the basic Azure networking concepts that will help you get started with IaaS services and set the foundation for your environment.

Chapter 3, *Infrastructure as a Service - the First Layer of Cloud Computing*, explains how to set up and configure an Azure **Virtual Machine (VM)**. We'll also cover how to monitor and administer VMs.

Chapter 4, *Azure App Service - Hosting Web Applications without a Server*, deals with the basics of PaaS services and how to host your application with Azure App Service. We'll cover how to set up PaaS and monitor your websites.

Chapter 5, *The Azure Data Platform*, covers databases in Azure, focusing both on IaaS and PaaS services. We'll explain the differences and when to use which approach.

Chapter 6, *Azure Storage, Backup, and Site Recovery - Moving Your Data to Azure*, explains Azure Storage services and how to set up backup and DR in Azure. After we have our data in Azure, we'll explain how to use backup and DR to move to Azure from on-premises systems.

Chapter 7, *Hybrid Cloud with Azure - Extending Local Workloads to the Cloud*, looks at how hybrid clouds are in use for most organizations and how we increasingly need to use a combination of cloud-based and on-premises resources. We'll cover how to set up a hybrid cloud with Azure and how to securely connect cloud-based and on-premises services.

Chapter 8, *Azure Active Directory - Identity in the Cloud,* covers identity, which is a very important part of any IT system. We'll explain how to set up Azure Active Directory for authentication and authorization for cloud services. We'll also cover how to connect your local Active Directory and use the same identities for local and cloud-based resources.

Chapter 9, *Azure Security and Administration*, goes into how, for many organizations, security is the most important thing to consider before moving to the cloud. In this chapter, we'll explain how secure Azure really is and how we can harden our security in the cloud to make it more secure than a local data center.

Chapter 10, *Best Practices*, covers some best practices and real-life scenarios, from setting up your subscription and naming resources, to Infrastructure-as-Code and monitoring.

To get the most out of this book

A basic understanding of cloud computing is recommended. Intermediate knowledge of server and network administration is required to better understand key differences between locally-based and cloud-based infrastructures. The following tools will be used during this book:

- Windows Server 2016
- MS SQL Server 2016
- Hyper-V
- Active Directory
- PowerShell

- Microsoft Azure
- Azure PowerShell
- Azure CLI

Download the example code files

You can download the example code files for this book from your account at www.packt.com. If you purchased this book elsewhere, you can visit www.packt.com/support and register to have the files emailed directly to you.

You can download the code files by following these steps:

1. Log in or register at www.packt.com.
2. Select the **SUPPORT** tab.
3. Click on **Code Downloads & Errata**.
4. Enter the name of the book in the **Search** box and follow the onscreen instructions.

Once the file is downloaded, please make sure that you unzip or extract the folder using the latest version of:

- WinRAR/7-Zip for Windows
- Zipeg/iZip/UnRarX for Mac
- 7-Zip/PeaZip for Linux

The code bundle for the book is also hosted on GitHub at https://github.com/PacktPublishing/Hands-On-Cloud-Administration-in-Azure. In case there's an update to the code, it will be updated on the existing GitHub repository.

We also have other code bundles from our rich catalog of books and videos available at https://github.com/PacktPublishing/. Check them out!

Download the color images

We also provide a PDF file that has color images of the screenshots/diagrams used in this book. You can download it here: https://www.packtpub.com/sites/default/files/downloads/9781789134964_ColorImages.pdf.

Conventions used

There are a number of text conventions used throughout this book.

CodeInText: Indicates code words in text, database table names, folder names, filenames, file extensions, pathnames, dummy URLs, user input, and Twitter handles. Here is an example: "Basic-tier VMs are intended for dev/test environments, and even though they have a similar performance to standard tier VMs, there are a few limitations."

A block of code is set as follows:

```
{
  "$schema":
"http://schema.management.azure.com/schemas/2015-01-01/deploymentTemplate.j
son#",
  "contentVersion": "1.0.0.0",
  "parameters": {
    "name": {
```

Any command-line input or output is written as follows:

```
Connect-AzureRmAccount
```

Bold: Indicates a new term, an important word, or words that you see on screen. For example, words in menus or dialog boxes appear in the text like this. Here is an example: "To create a new Azure VM, we need to select **New resource** and then select **New Virtual Machine**."

Warnings or important notes appear like this.

Tips and tricks appear like this.

Get in touch

Feedback from our readers is always welcome.

General feedback: If you have questions about any aspect of this book, mention the book title in the subject of your message and email us at customercare@packtpub.com.

Errata: Although we have taken every care to ensure the accuracy of our content, mistakes do happen. If you have found a mistake in this book, we would be grateful if you would report this to us. Please visit www.packt.com/submit-errata, selecting your book, clicking on the Errata Submission Form link, and entering the details.

Piracy: If you come across any illegal copies of our works in any form on the internet, we would be grateful if you would provide us with the location address or website name. Please contact us at copyright@packt.com with a link to the material.

If you are interested in becoming an author: If there is a topic that you have expertise in and you are interested in either writing or contributing to a book, please visit authors.packtpub.com.

Reviews

Please leave a review. Once you have read and used this book, why not leave a review on the site that you purchased it from? Potential readers can then see and use your unbiased opinion to make purchase decisions, we at Packt can understand what you think about our products, and our authors can see your feedback on their book. Thank you!

For more information about Packt, please visit packt.com.

Key Concepts of Cloud Computing

1

Cloud has been a buzzword for quite some time and is a big trend in IT. More and more companies are starting their cloud journeys but starting these journeys can be hard. Different skills and a different mindset are needed when compared to on-premises IT, and cloud administrators are in demand. In this book, we'll start our cloud journey together and help you to get a grasp on cloud administration and to understand Microsoft Azure services and architecture. Become an Azure expert and help your company have a safe and pleasant journey to Azure.

The topics we're going to cover include the following:

- Cloud computing concepts
- Cloud services models
- Azure subscription model

Cloud computing concepts

As we are going to use Microsoft Azure, it's important that we understand the key concepts of cloud computing and especially the concept of the public cloud, as Azure is exactly that: a public cloud.

In the past, we have seen many trends in the IT industry; some of them were short-term and some of them stayed for quite some time. Many consider cloud computing to be a trend that will not be here for a long time, but they don't really understand the concept of the cloud and where it all begins.

Cloud computing didn't just starting with public cloud offerings, but it began in the 1990s. Obviously, the cloud didn't have a form like it does today but started more as something that companies implemented internally, offering their employees the option to create virtual machines on demand. At this stage, the cloud included a virtualization platform that allowed employees to create development/test environments composed of virtual machines based on preprepared images when needed. Two components are part of the foundation of cloud computing: virtualization and on-demand resources. None of this would be possible without server virtualization, an option that allows us to create many virtual machines on a single physical server. Cloud takes virtualization to another level beyond just simple server virtualization, but we'll get to that a bit later.

The ability to get resources on demand, when we need them, is the foundation of what cloud computing is about. As mentioned before, it all started with virtualization platforms and companies creating platforms that would enable their employees to create virtual machines on demand. Today, we call this the private cloud.

Types of cloud computing

There are different types of cloud computing and different opinions on how they should be categorized. Personally, I find four types most logical:

- **Private**: Everything hosted internally, in our own data center.
- **Hosted**: Something between a private and public cloud; the service provider creates a separate environment in their data center and offers us an isolated cloud for our use only.
- **Public**: The service provider offers a service available to everyone—publicly available. There is still tenant isolation but we'll talk about this later.
- **Hybrid**: A combination of private and public cloud. Some services are used in the public cloud but some stay in our local data center with direct connection between two or more environments. From my experience, this is the most common form of cloud computing. Again, we'll explain more about this later.

In the private cloud, all resources are located on-premises, in our local data center, and no internet access is needed to access resources. The internet and resources are accessed separately as shown in the following diagram. Building your own private cloud previously required large-scale investment, both materially and in terms of knowledge. First, you needed space and needed to consider other elements like cooling and power. Then, you needed to invest in hardware like firewalls, routers, network switches, servers, and storage.

You needed licenses for a virtualization layer, operating system licenses for virtual machines, and then licenses for different kinds of software. In the end, all material investment was in vain if you didn't have the right people to set everything up and maintain it in the years to come. Once everything was in place and you had your private cloud running, it required new investment every few years as you needed new versions of software (virtualization, operating systems, and other software) and hardware needed to be replaced as well:

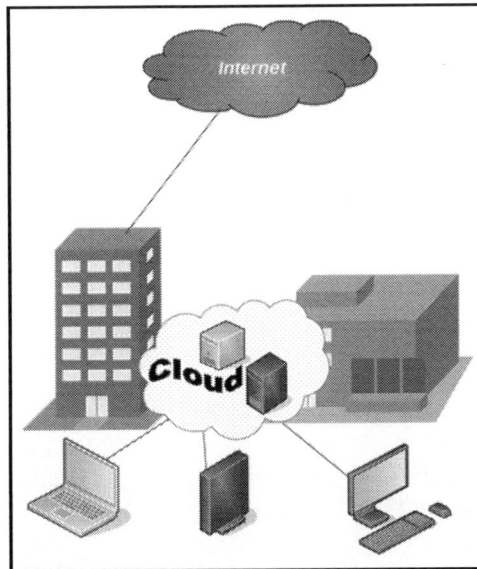

The hosted cloud came as the first step in the transition from the private cloud to the public. As creating and maintaining your own private cloud demanded large-scale investment, some companies took advantage and started offering services where you could rent part of their data center and use it as your own private cloud. They specialized in this kind of offer; it was cheaper for them to buy hardware and software as vendors offered discounts on mass purchases. So, creating an environment in the hosted cloud was cheaper then creating an identical environment in the private cloud.

There is also the question of upfront investment; using the private cloud requires that all hardware and most software licenses be paid for upfront, so many companies have decided to use the hosted cloud as they don't have to make an upfront investment but monthly or yearly subscriptions instead. Also, it's easier for data centers to provide experts to maintain systems as a single expert can take care of multiple customer environments. For the private cloud, you need a network engineer, a storage specialist, a virtualization specialist, and so on, and this is for a single data center.

In the case of a hosted cloud, all personnel are still required but a single specialist can set up and maintain environments for multiple customers and the price of maintenance is lower than for a private cloud. Note that to access the hosted cloud, usually some sort of **Virtual Private Network (VPN)**, either site-to-site or point-to-site, is required. We access resources located outside our own network and located in another hosted network as shown in the following diagram:

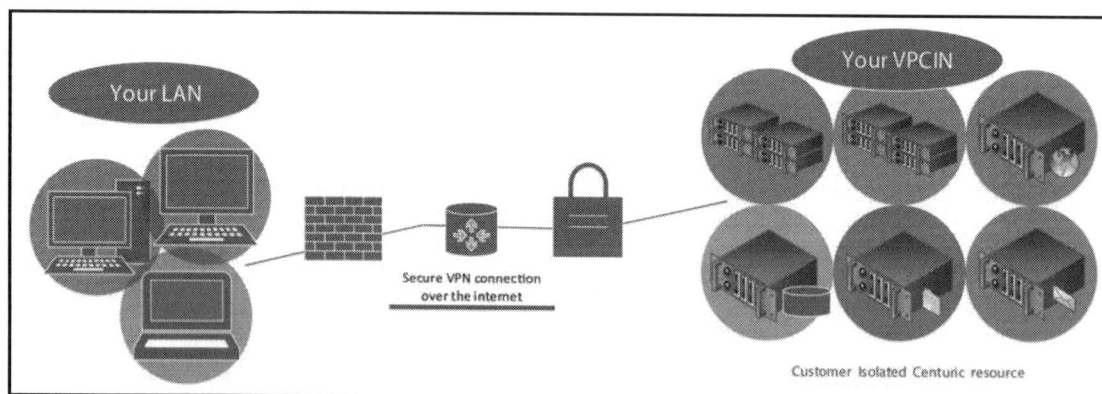

In the next step of cloud evolution, the public cloud emerged. Large service providers offered large amounts of resources for on-demand use. Similar to the hosted cloud, resources you used were still outside your local infrastructure and hosted by service providers who specialized in this kind of offer.

There are two key differences. The first difference is that in a hosted data center the amount of resources available I usually predetermined and to get more resources you need to wait for new resources to be configured, if this becomes available at all. In the public cloud, providers have a large amount of resources available for on-demand requests and you can get them whenever you need them. You can create any kind and any amount of resources when needed. All you need is to create a subscription and access to the internet to start deploying. This also means you have highly scalable environments and you are not limited by the initial size of the resources created. For example, if you create a virtual machine with four CPUs and 16 GB of RAM and find out over time that the virtual machine can't handle the workload you have, you don't need to create a new virtual machine; you can use a scale-up option to change size. Scaling up is explained later in more detail. This works other way around: If you find out that the size of the virtual machine initially created is too large for your workload, you don't need to keep that size and pay for something you don't need. Simply scaling down will do the trick. In this case, we access resources over the internet as shown in the following diagram:

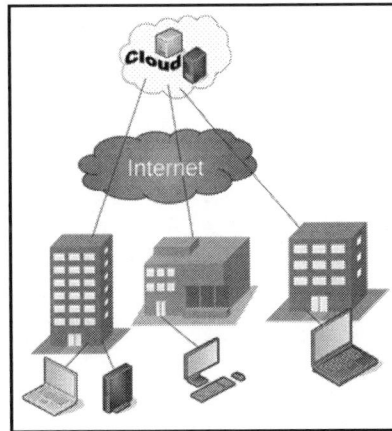

The other difference between a hosted cloud and a private cloud is pricing. In a hosted cloud, you would get an agreed amount of resources and pay a monthly or yearly subscription no matter in what capacity these resources are used, whether 10% or 100%. In the public cloud, pricing is based on usage and the model of payment is such that you pay for only things that are used. So, in the public cloud, if you create a virtual machine, you will be paying for that virtual machine for the time you actually use it. If you stop or delete this virtual machine, you will not be paying for it. The payment model is different for different cloud providers and can vary by per-day, per-hour, or per-minute usage. As we'll talk about Microsoft Azure, it's important to mention that Azure is using a per-minute billing system. So, for example, if you create a virtual machine in Microsoft Azure and delete it after 12 days, 11 hours and 13 minutes, the amount you pay will be calculated for that exact amount of time. In a per-hour billing system, you would pay for 12 days and 12 hours. In a per-day billing system, you would pay for 13 days.

Another difference is multitenancy. Even the public cloud is available to everyone; creating your own subscription creates your own tenant. By using special fabric, this tenant separates your resources from other tenants, and resources created in that tenant are available only to people with access to that specific tenant.

To sum up, the key concepts of the public cloud are:

- Access over the internet
- Multitenancy
- Resource pooling
- On-demand consumption
- Highly scalable

The term cloud or public cloud wasn't forged with modern IT but the term started in the 1960s with the concept of resources being time shared. The concept did evolve in the 1990s with the private cloud. However, the cloud did evolve and shift further to a modern form in the 2000s.

It all started with Amazon Web Services, a subsidiary of Amazon, when they released their **Elastic Cloud Compute (EC2)** in 2006. Google followed with Google App Engine in 2008. Microsoft announced their version of the cloud in October 2008 and it was publicly available in February 2010. Other service providers followed and many companies such as IBM or Oracle have their own public cloud offering. Looking at market shares and the pace at which they evolve, we can put only two cloud providers at the top of this list: Amazon Web Services and Microsoft.

A brief history of Azure (from ASM to ARM)

We already said that Microsoft announced their version of the public cloud in 2008 and public release was in 2010. At this time, the official name for Microsoft's public cloud platform was Windows Azure. The name was changed in April 2014 to Microsoft Azure. The reason for the change was never publicly announced but there were many guesses. One of the theories was that Microsoft needed to change its name due to embracing open source software. As Microsoft added a Linux virtual machine to their offering, the name convention became too confusing. A virtual machine running Linux on a Microsoft public cloud would initially be Windows Azure Linux virtual machine, and having Windows and Linux in same name was confusing indeed. Changing it to Microsoft Azure Linux virtual machine made more sense. Now, this is only one of the theories that you can find and not an official reason for the name change.

Not only the name changed over the years. The first version of Azure, Windows Azure, had completely different specifications and a different type of portal. The first Azure portal was accessed at the address `https://manage.windowsazure.net` and was based on Silverlight. This portal was later referred to as a **classic** portal and the model of management for resources created in the **classic** portal was referred to as **Azure Standard Management (ASM)**. The classic portal layout is shown in the following screenshot:

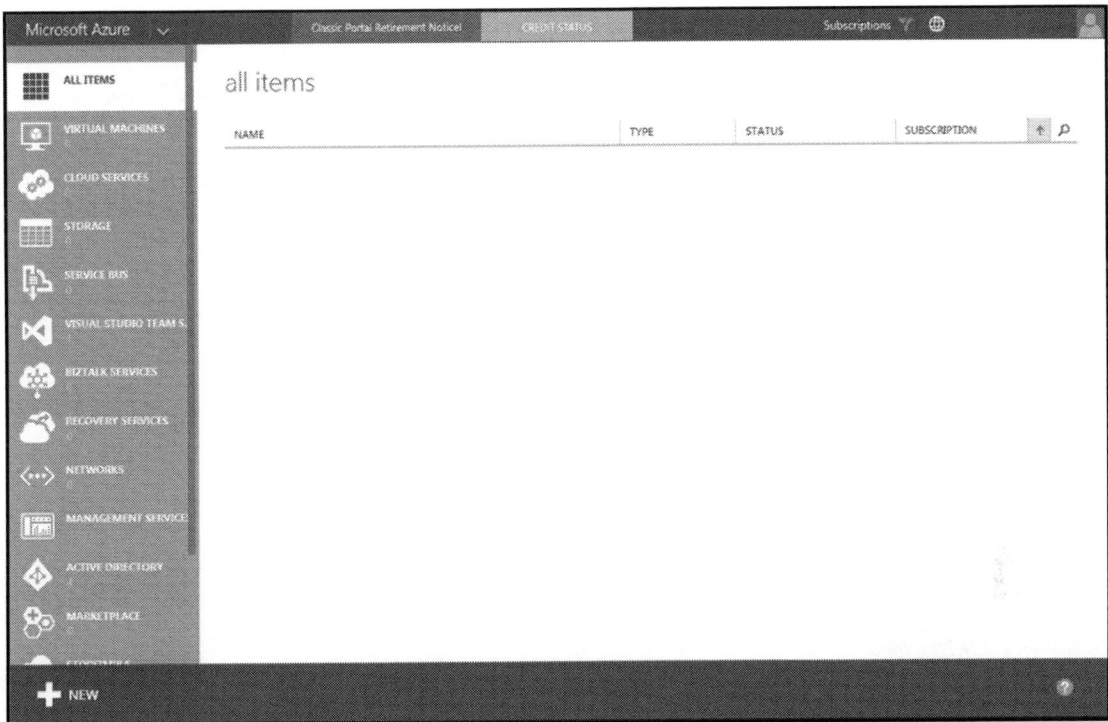

At this time, Microsoft realized there were issues with their cloud model and started working on completely new fabric. In 2014, a new Azure portal was announced. Along with a new portal, we got a new model of management called **Azure Resource Manager (ARM)**. ARM brought new features like **role-based access control (RBAC)** and resource groups.

These features changed how we managed resources in the cloud. In ASM, the only way to allow someone to administrate Azure resources was to add this person as a co-administrator to the Azure subscription. This person would have total access and control over the subscription in question. With RABC, we got the option to give different permission levels to users such as reader or contributor, without giving them full access to the subscription.

Resource groups went even further. Resource groups in Azure represent logical containers where you can place resources depending on the convention of your choosing. For example, you can place all resources that are used by a single application in a single resource group. This would allow you to give user access to a single resource group with the option to manage or access only that specific resource group. When that user logs in to the tenant, he will be able to see only the resource group that was assigned to him even if you have other resource groups under the same subscription or tenant. You could go further with RABC and assign only users to a specific resource but that is too granular and hard to manage. Assignment based on resource groups is considered best practice and the best way to manage Azure resources.

The new Azure portal was considered a preview version until December 2015. At that time, it became an official portal and could be accessed at the address `https://portal.azure.com`. This portal became available in April 2014, when it was announced, but it was a preview version. The new portal layout is shown in the following screenshot:

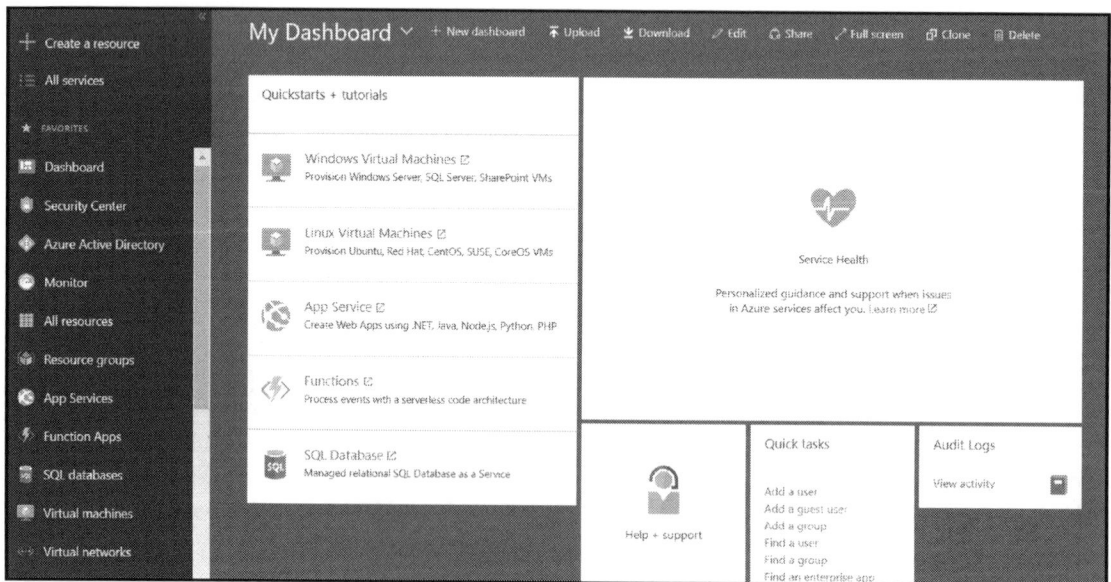

The classic portal was announced to be retired and this eventually happened in January 2018. Along with RBAC and resource groups, ARM brought us another amazing feature—ARM templates. ARM templates are JSON files that hold information about Azure resources and can be used to deploy new resources or edit existing resources.

With the ARM model and ARM templates, Microsoft stepped up and really changed cloud business. In the cloud and in DevOps, the **Infrastructure as code (IaC)** concept is very important and that was exactly what ARM templates were. You are able to create an ARM template and reuse it multiple times to create similar environments. By doing so, you automated your infrastructure deployment steps and removed possible mistakes in the deployment and configuration process.

Cloud services models

Speaking of IaC, we have lot of terms something as something in cloud world. The main types of services in Microsoft Azure (and cloud in general) are:

- **Infrastructure as a Service (IaaS)**
- **Platform as a Service (PaaS)**
- **Software as a Service (SaaS)**

Each type represents a different kind of service level and our control over that resource. To explain each one and how they relate, it's best to compare them to services in our local data center. A service layer for all models is shown in the following diagram and we'll use this to explain the relationship between cloud models:

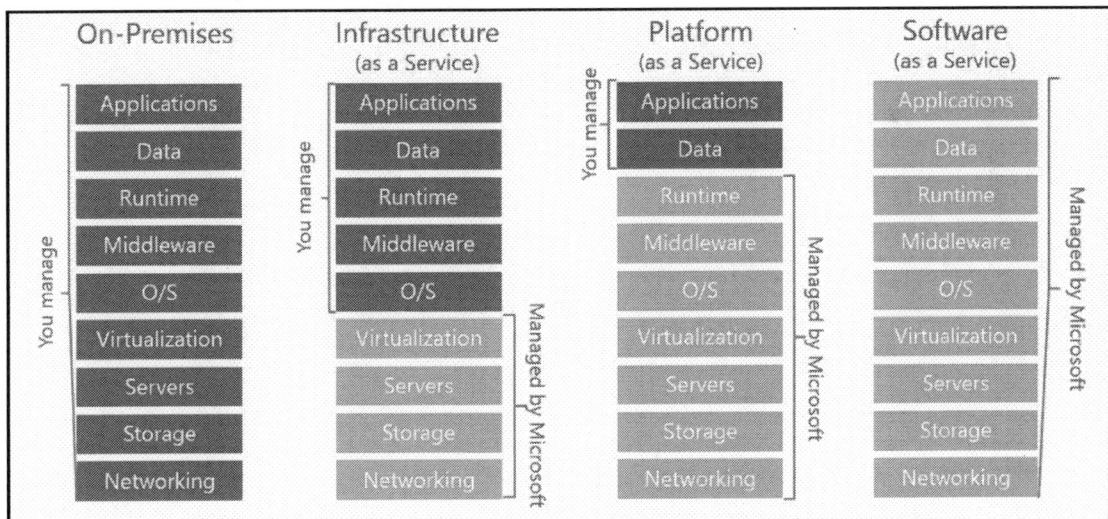

In a private data center, we are responsible to set up and maintain everything. We need to set up a networking stack, prepare and configure storage, buy and prepare hardware, install software, and configure the virtualization host. Then we need to configure images and servers, and deploy and manage databases. Security is also our concern in all aspects—physical security, network security, host and OS security, and finally application security for all application software running on our servers.

With IaaS, it gets easier. We don't have to prepare anything anymore; all we need to do is sign up for a subscription and create a virtual machine when needed and start using it. The part where we must buy, prepare, configure, and maintain is no longer our concern and the cloud service provider takes care of that, in our case Microsoft with Azure. Preparing images and deployments is also no longer our responsibility. Security is getting easier and physical, network, and host security are handled by Microsoft. We still have a responsibility in the security corner in order to keep our operating system up to date, patched, and secure. Application security is also our responsibility and we need to keep applying the best security practices in order to stay safe and secure. Many people forget that when migrating to the cloud we need to step up security. As the cloud service provider takes care of a big part of security, many get comfortable and relaxed and they neglect the part of security they need to take care of. When moving to the cloud, we need to remember that our resources and applications are publicly exposed and will experience significantly more "attacks" compared to when using on-premises infrastructure. Attacking resources on-premises usually means getting behind a firewall, then breaching the server and getting some data out. Now, many services are accessible over the internet and you need to take care of security better than ever before. The best examples of IaaS, when talking about Microsoft Azure, are Azure virtual machines. Both Windows Server and Linux virtual machines are available in Microsoft Azure. An interesting fact is that, according to information Microsoft released in October 2017, more than 40% of virtual machines in Azure are running Linux.

PaaS is getting even easier to use than IaaS. Everything that we said the cloud service provider is taking care of applies, plus some more. In this type of service, Microsoft is taking care of the operating system, additional software needed, and an additional layer of security. We still need to maintain everything we place there (depending on the PaaS service) and the part of security that remains our problem. Again, people forget that security part very quickly as even more responsibility is on Microsoft. However, IaaS is often used with VPN connections (either point-to-site or site-to-site) and endpoints are not publicly exposed in this case. This is not the case with PaaS, which is more often accessed over the internet. Because of this, we need to take security very seriously unless we want to lose our data or access to our services. The best examples of PaaS in Azure are Azure app service or Azure SQL databases.

Finally, we have SaaS. In SaaS, the cloud service provider is taking care of almost everything, from end to end. In this case, we have a complete solution prepared and all we have to do is create a subscription and assign users different kinds of access. Usually, SaaS has to have modules, an administrator, and a user. The administrator module is used to manage users and access levels; the user module is used to actually use the software feature we subscribed to. Security is also our responsibility, only on the user level, and we need to make sure users are aware that they need to keep their credentials safe and their password strong enough to prevent accounts being brute-forced into. The best example of SaaS in Microsoft Cloud is Office 365.

This diagram explaining Pizza as a Service is very often used to describe how cloud services relate to real-life situations and to better understand what cloud computing offers:

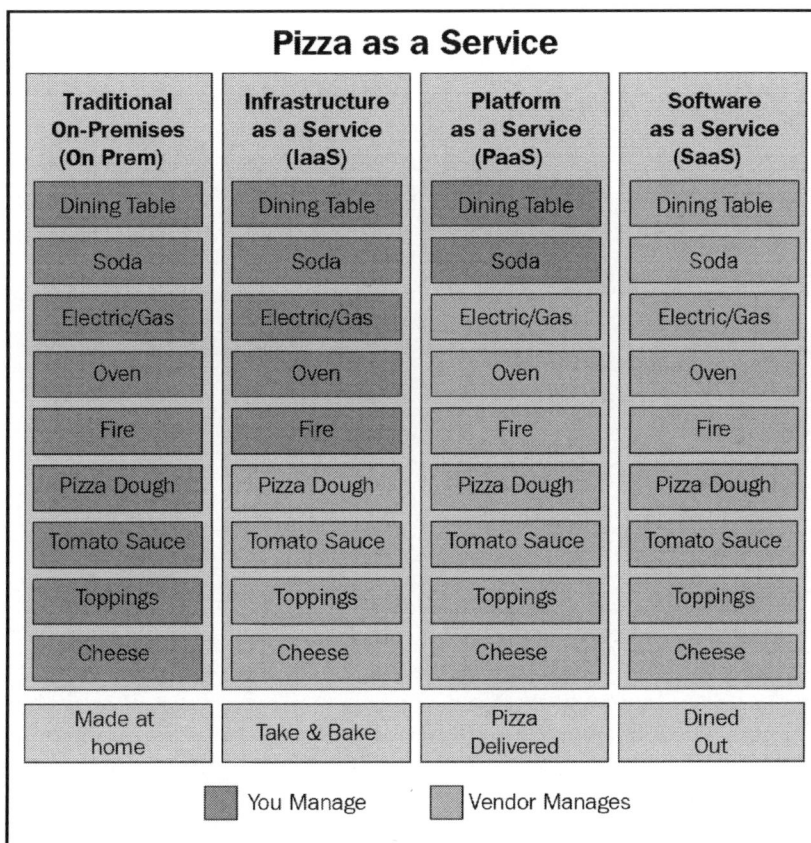

Pizza as a Service

Traditional On-Premises (On Prem)	Infrastructure as a Service (IaaS)	Platform as a Service (PaaS)	Software as a Service (SaaS)
Dining Table	Dining Table	Dining Table	Dining Table
Soda	Soda	Soda	Soda
Electric/Gas	Electric/Gas	Electric/Gas	Electric/Gas
Oven	Oven	Oven	Oven
Fire	Fire	Fire	Fire
Pizza Dough	Pizza Dough	Pizza Dough	Pizza Dough
Tomato Sauce	Tomato Sauce	Tomato Sauce	Tomato Sauce
Toppings	Toppings	Toppings	Toppings
Cheese	Cheese	Cheese	Cheese
Made at home	Take & Bake	Pizza Delivered	Dined Out

■ You Manage   ■ Vendor Manages

In this case, we can compare pizza to all four types we have in the previous diagram that explains IaaS, PaaS, and SaaS as well as on-premises computing.

When compared to on-premises computing, pizza would be the homemade option. We need to buy all ingredients, mix everything, bake it, buy sodas, and serve. Comparing pizza to IaaS, we would buy frozen pizzas and bake them, set up the table, and serve. Pizza, compared to PaaS, would be home delivery—we just order our pizza and need to buy sodas and serve. Lastly, the SaaS version of pizza would be dining in a restaurant: we go out and order and everything is done for us. We get our pizza, get our sodas, and everything is served.

Pros and cons of cloud service models

We already discussed some of the features and benefits that each cloud service model brings to us. IaaS needs more enrolment and more maintenance than PaaS. SaaS needs even less of a human touch than PaaS and almost no maintenance except for user administration.

But there is an other side of that as well. SaaS asks for minimum maintenance and administration, but gives you a minimum amount of customization too. If you need something changed in SaaS, you'll probably need to contact your cloud service provider who can make the changes.

In PaaS, you have more freedom in terms of administration, maintenance, and customization. However, these changes are usually a preconfigured set of options you can choose from, but there are still more options than in SaaS.

IaaS requires the most administration and maintenance but gives you the best customization options as well. As you are controlling everything from the operating system upwards (you can select different preconfigured images or even bring in your own OS image), you have the best control as well. You can select what features you are going to configure, what server roles you are going to have on that server, and even install any type of software on that virtual machine.

The bottom line is you need to decide what kind of feature is best suited for you in a given situation. In some cases, the simplest solution would be SaaS, as that product offers everything you need. If you need the latest settings and features, you'll probably use the PaaS model. If you have some legacy dependencies, IaaS would be the way to go. This way, you would be able to configure and install everything related to that dependency.

Other benefits of the cloud

The first benefit of cloud computing is obvious from all things previously written: it's easier to maintain and manage.

With the cloud there are many areas of expertise you don't need to provide yourself; the cloud service provider manages these thing for you. But this can be kind of a trap—cloud resources are not self-managed and you still need IT professionals who will manage and maintain your resources and keep them in good health. These are different kinds of IT professionals than in a local data center, but we still need people who understand core IT. If you are using IaaS, you still need a Windows Server Administrator (or Linux Server Administrator, depending on your preferences). If you are using databases, you are still going to need a database administrator. IT professionals need to adjust their skills and roles to cloud computing and leave on-premises behind them, but we still need them very much.

The financial benefit is also one of the obvious pros. In an on-premises environment you needed to buy and pay for all resources upfront, before you started using them. There are many different hardware components that we need to prepare for a local data center such as a firewall, network switches, storage, servers, a power supply that cannot be interrupted, and so on. We need to prepare infrastructure that can handle this kind of hardware, such as a proper server room. Cooling that will keep our hardware at the optimum temperature or provide enough electrical power that we can keep this running without overloading our electrical grid. And when we have everything in place, we need to have proper licenses for the virtualization host, operating system licenses for each virtual machine you want to run, and licenses for any additional software you plan to use such as SQL Server, endpoint protection, or any other software needed. In a local data center, you need to buy and prepare everything in advance. This can be a significant financial hit for any organization.

And after this initial cost, we have to pay upkeep. We are paying for electricity, for a cooling system, the required spare parts, and someone to maintain all of this.

After a few years, our hardware and software becomes obsolete and we need to repeat everything again. It can be hard to keep up and stay relevant in these conditions.

In the cloud, we don't have to pay upfront for anything; we are using services in a pay-as-you-go model where you pay for resources you are using on a per-minute basis. We don't have to invest heavily in anything—you create resources when you need them, for the amount of time you need them for, and delete them once you're done.

If we need a new server, we can have that in a matter of minutes in the cloud. There is no need to contact different resellers, no filling in orders and waiting for deliveries. In Azure, you just spin up a virtual machine (or any other resource) whenever you need it. Once you don't need it anymore, you can delete it and from that moment on you don't need to pay for it anymore. This is also one of the differences between the cloud and on-premises: you are not stuck with what you buy. In a local data center, you need to buy resources in order to use them. Once you don't need them, they don't magically disappear from your server room. And even if it did somehow disappear, you still invested money.

Assessment in terms of how many resources we need for a specific service can also be a big issue. Let's say we are creating a new web application that we are going to offer to end users. The application is completed and we need to host it somewhere in order for users to start signing up and using that application. The application is probably going to need servers, a web server and a database server. We need to buy new hardware and licenses for these servers. The problem here is that we need to buy hardware that is going to be able to handle our workload. The workload needs to be estimated for an initial number of users and growth over time but this can be very hard to estimate. If we guess the initial workload, it's very easy to make mistakes with growth numbers. If we overestimate, we are stuck with something we don't actually need but have paid for. If we underestimate, we need to upgrade very quickly. Upgrading can bring us to two problems: time and money.

It can take some time to order upgrades and resolve issues with workload. And in this time, while we're waiting on upgrade components, users experiencing bad performance caused by high workload may leave. Losing users due to the bad performance of our application is something we definitely want to avoid but may be out of our hands because it takes time to get permission (especially in large companies) to order upgrade components, to have them delivered, and to upgrade our servers. Upgrading servers will also cause some downtime because we need to shut down servers in order to add new components. Again, we have something that we want to avoid.

The second thing about upgrades is that they cost money. It can take a significant amount of money in order to increase server workload. In some cases, if we need to upgrade memory, we are not able to do that unless we upgrade the CPU. Sometimes, upgrading a CPU requires the upgrading of the motherboard first in order to continue. But that is if servers can be upgraded, because sometimes we are limited with what we get and are not able to upgrade at all. In such cases, we need to buy brand-new hardware and we have an old server that we don't need but already paid for.

The cloud keeps these issues much more simple and easier to resolve. We will create either two servers (in case we decide to use IaaS) or two other services (in case we decide on PaaS; we have multiple options there). Managing workloads and the amount of resources is simple, fast, and easy.

If time shows that we overestimated ourselves, we can simply scale down resources and the issue is resolved. We are not stuck with something we don't need and we are not paying for it. We simply scale down the server/resources and from that moment forward, we are paying for a **smaller** server that we actually do need.

In case we underestimated ourselves, we can scale up and increase the amount of resources just as easily and quickly. We don't have to wait for parts and don't need to lose time until upgrade components are finally delivered. We just increase the amount of resources and the issue is resolved.

Another benefit of the cloud is also tied to resource amounts. In some cases, we have **spikes** in our applications. Spikes are sudden increases in workload and can be predictable or unpredictable. For example, if we are hosting a web shop application, we can predict spikes in workload if we have offer discounts on popular items or increased workloads during holidays. If we have some kind of news portal, we can experience unpredicted spikes in workload caused by some breaking news or something similar.

In both cases—unpredicted or predicted spikes—we need to account for them when setting up resources we are going to use. Even if our resources are sitting idle and underused most of the time, we need to buy hardware that is going to handle these kinds of workloads. So, if we are having 10,000 users on a normal day and 1,000,000 during spikes, we need to buy resources that can handle a workload for 1,000,000. Otherwise, during spikes, users are going to experience high workload and an unresponsive application. As a result, we will lose users once again. But, buying a server that will be underused 90% of the time is something we would like to avoid as it is expensive. We have a choice: either pay or lose customers.

The cloud lets us handle this issue very quickly as well. We can scale up and down very easily, simply, and quickly. Two approaches can be taken, depending on if we have unpredicted or predicted spikes.

In case of predictable spikes, we can increase and decrease the amount of resources on demand. By doing so, we are no longer paying for a large amount of resources outside of the period we actually need them. In a normal period, we are paying only for a normal workload and in the case of increases we are paying for a high workload but only for the period we have a higher workload before we scale down back to normal.

In the case of unpredictable spikes, we can set performance counters and alerts that will trigger a scale-up (or scale-down) as needed. For example, we can set up a trigger that will monitor the CPU. Once the CPU hits 90%, we can schedule automatic scaling out and increase the amount of resources assigned to that service. This way, users don't experience any issues caused by high workload and increased usage of our application. We need to be careful of automatic scaling out as this will create an increase in pricing and unless we scale back down, we will pay the increased price. Scaling down can be done manually but it can be done automatically as well. We can create another trigger that will perform scaling down in case the CPU drops below 50%. This way, we can always use only the resources that we actually need and use.

Understanding the Azure subscription model

Most of the cloud service providers have similar subscription models but have some unique features. We are going to concentrate on Microsoft Azure as this is the cloud service we are going to cover in this book. From now on, all features we are going to discuss are going to be Azure-specific.

For Microsoft Azure subscription, the highest level of administration is that of a tenant. Azure is a public cloud with data centers all over the world that are available to everyone. There are a few exceptions such as the US government's data center that is available only to US government institutions, the Chinese government's data center for Chinese official institutions, or the German data center only available to companies registered in Germany.

As a public cloud provider, Microsoft has to keep data separate for each user. Azure fabric is used to separate resources in the data center and tie them to a specific customer. So, even if you are sharing physical resources such as network, servers, and storage, your services can be accessed and managed only by you.

As the highest level of Azure, a tenant is created by default when you create your first Azure subscription. Many people don't realize that they already have an Azure tenant if they use Office 365. Office 365 requires Azure Active Directory and creates your first Azure tenant. I have seen many people making the mistake of creating a new Azure tenant even when they had Office 365 in use. The issue is that the tenant is tied to Azure Active Directory and creating a new tenant creates a new copy of Azure Active Directory. This makes Azure Active Directory hard to manage as you have two copies and differences appearing over time.

Creating your first Azure subscription creates a new Azure tenant and a new Azure Active Directory. There are multiple options for managing Azure Active Directory but we'll discuss that in `Chapter 8`, *Azure Active Directory – Identity in the Cloud*. Creating an additional Azure Active Directory creates a new Azure tenant as well.

The next level under tenant is Azure subscription. You can have multiple Azure subscriptions under a single tenant. Creating a new tenant will result in an empty tenant with only an Azure Active Directory without subscriptions. As Azure Active Directory has multiple tiers, you will not be able to change Azure Active Directory from Basic (that is free) to another tier without a valid subscription. A subscription is needed in order to collect usage information, generate a billing report, and finally issue an invoice for service usage.

An Azure subscription can be used to separate Azure environments by financial and administration logic. This can be done in many ways and you can design it to fit your needs. One example would be to have a single tenant at the company level and an Azure subscription for each department. This way you can assign a different administrator to each subscription/department and keep track of how much each department is spending. Another example for subscription separation would be to have different stage environments. I've seen many companies dividing their subscriptions into development, testing, and production environments and having different Azure subscriptions for each of these environments. This approach gives you the ability to administer and manage each environment separately but provides insight into how much you are spending on each environment as well.

The third part of separating resources would be using resource groups. Resource groups were introduced with the ARM model and bring many benefits. As with subscriptions, you can use resource groups to separate resources in terms of logical or billing level. An example would be to have a different resource group for each department or development/test/production environment. You can then assign different administrators to each resource group and track billing for each resource group. Note that for billing, you will still receive a single invoice at the end of the month and need to manage and track spending manually. Billing separation is much easier on a subscription level. If you need to separate invoices per department/environment, you should go with subscription separation.

Every resource in Azure can be tracked using hierarchy. Resource belongs to a resource group, resource group belongs to subscription, and subscription belongs to tenant. Logging in to the Azure portal will connect you to the default tenant. You can manage which tenant is going to be the default one as a single account can be in multiple tenants. For example, my corporate account is by default in my corporate tenant but I'm a guest user in multiple client tenants. By default, I connect to my company tenant but can select client tenants from a drop-down list. I can change my default tenant as well and select in which tenant I want to be logged in by default when I sign in to my Microsoft Azure account.

To look at this from a Microsoft Azure perspective, when you log in to Microsoft Azure with your account, Azure fabric determines to which tenant you have access, signs you in to your default tenant, and you have access to subscriptions that are in that tenant. From there you can manage all subscriptions, resource groups, and resources that belong to that tenant. By switching tenants, you have access to different subscriptions, resource groups, and resources that belong in that tenant. All this is handled by Azure fabric in order to separate client environments.

This approach is much better since the ARM model was introduced as things were much different in ASM. In ASM, after login you would have access to all subscriptions that were under that single account. Azure Active Directory wasn't tied to a specific tenant and you could have multiple Azure Active Directories in a single tenant. It was difficult to keep track of resources as there were no resource groups and the only thing separating them was the subscription level.

A similar hierarchy can be applied to resources administration too. You can assign a user to have certain access to your resources as well. The access level can have different kinds of permissions such as owner, contributor, reader, and so on. You can build custom permissions to achieve your own rules and policies. User roles can be assigned on the level of tenant, subscription, resource group, or single resource. Managing user access at the resource level can be hard and time-consuming and I wouldn't recommend this approach.

On the other hand, access to the tenant level is something you will often want to avoid because in most cases you don't want users to have same access to all resources. A few administrators can be exceptions, but this approach is something you want to avoid in general. The best and most common option is to assign users access at the subscription or resource group level. Subscription-level access can be used if you have different departments or environments for each subscription and you can assign an administrator for that department or environment as a subscription administrator. Access to the resource group level can be applied if you have a single application or environment in the resource group and assign an application/environment administrator for corresponding resource groups. These aren't the only options or models you can use but you can adjust and create whatever option best fits your needs. For example, I have seen where organizations have placed similar resources in a single resource group and assigned an administrator based on their on-premises role. All network resources would be in a single resource group and network engineers assigned to a network resource group. All databases would be placed in another resource group and a database administrator assigned as administrator for that resource group and so on.

Azure subscription types

To create your first Azure subscription, you need a few things. The first thing is to provide an email address that needs to be either a Microsoft Live account or an Office 365 account. You need to provide a phone number. Finally, you need to provide credit or debit card information along with a billing address. Credit card information is needed even for free subscriptions because Microsoft uses it to verify your identity.

When talking about Azure subscriptions, we can divide them into three different types:

- Sponsored subscriptions
- Pay as you go
- Enterprise subscriptions

There are a few different sponsored subscriptions in Azure: trial, Azure pass, MSDN subscription, Azure sponsorship, and so on. What all of them have in common is that they have a certain amount of resources available to you free of charge. Another thing they have in common is that not all services are available in all regions. For example, you may be able to create an A2 standard virtual machine only when selecting the North Europe region, but you will not be able to create this virtual machine in any other region.

The Azure trial offers you $200 of service for 30 days. Subscription will expire whatever comes first: either you spend $200 or it expires at the end of the month. You need to provide credit/debit card information for this type of subscription. You can convert subscription from a trial to a pay-as-you-go model at any time using that card or by providing details of a new one. Credit card information must be provided—it's used only for identity verification, and you will not be charged any amount of money unless you specify that you want to remove the spending limit and start billing after the trial is over. What Microsoft is trying to achieve is to prevent you using Azure for anything illegal. Without credit card information, anyone could set up a trial subscription and use it to host illegal things for 30 days. At the end of a trial, a person would need to set up a new trial and continue to use Azure services for illegal content. In this case, Microsoft wouldn't be able to provide information on who was conducting illegal activities using Azure and they would be held accountable by the respective authorities.

Azure pass is offered as another type of trial subscription and offers a limited amount of credit for 30 days. This type of subscription is tied to Microsoft's official courseware and the amount of credit is determined by the course, each type having a different amount of credit. This type of subscription doesn't require a credit card as you need to register for a course and information from that registration can be used to verify your identity if needed. As with a trial, you are limited in the type of resources you can create, the amount of resources available, and the region resources can be created in.

MSDN Azure subscription is tied to a user's MSDN subscription and has a different credit amount based on the MSDN subscription level (a different amount per MSDN level, such as professional and enterprise). The amount of credit given is on a per-month basis and you get a certain amount at the beginning of each billing period (the billing period depends on the date of activation, the date of activation will be the beginning of your billing period, and the end of the billing period will be in 30 days).

The Azure subscription will be active as long as the MSDN subscription is active as well. Credit card information isn't needed as another way of identifying verification can be used (MSDN payment information). If you reach your spending limit in a single month, your resources will be deactivated and stopped until the end of the billing period.

To use these services again, you need to wait for the beginning of a new billing period or provide credit card information that will be used to charge any use over the sponsored amount. Removing the limit can be specified to apply to single months or for subscriptions. Single-month removal will remove the spending limit only for that month while subscription removal will the remove spending limit permanently and start billing every time the spending limit is reached. In the case of a single-month limit removal, the limit will be removed only for a specified month and if the issue happens again in the following month, it will disable your service. If the limit is removed from the subscription, once you reach the spending limit, it will automatically start to charge your usage.

Note that in every case, first the sponsored amount will be spent and only then will the credit card be activated. An Azure subscription for MSDN is limited for development and testing; it should never be used for commercial or production purposes. You also have a limit on the amount of resources and regions available. MSDN subscription also applies different pricing for resources. You are not charged for software licensing as this is a dev/test environment and prices of resources are much cheaper as a result.

Azure sponsorship is very similar to an MSDN subscription. It should not be used for commercial or production purposes. Azure sponsorship also has spending limits but in this case, it is not per-month but per-year. The billing period is one out of two differences between Azure sponsorship and Azure MSDN subscription, where sponsorship is billed per-year and MSDN per-month. The limit can be removed; there is a limit for resources and regions. The second difference is in that normal prices apply and you will be charged for software licenses.

Pay as you go is the most simple and most common type of Azure subscription. You sign up for an Azure subscription, provide credit card information, and this credit card is used for billing at the end of each month. The name tells you almost everything in this case: there are no limitations and you are billed for only what you use. If you don't have a single resource in your subscription, Microsoft will not charge you for only having a subscription. If you have resources in your subscription, you will be charged only for those resources. If you add some resources, you will be charged additionally. If you delete some of them, you will be charged only for those still active. There is no minimum or maximum limit on your subscription; you can spend nothing or millions per month.

Enterprise subscription requires a contract that determines a minimum amount you will spend on Azure resources. You receive a certain discount for resource prices as you commit that you will be spending a certain amount of money at a yearly level. You are charged on a monthly basis, based on the amount in the contract. Any amount that is over the minimum amount determined in the contract is billed separately at end of the year. With an enterprise subscription, there is also an option to bring your own licenses to Azure, enabling you to reuse existing licenses you have for on-premises resources.

Additionally, there is a reserved instances discount. It can be applied to both pay-as-you-go and enterprise subscriptions. You determine the number and type of virtual machines that you are going to use in the next period. The period can be 1 or 2 years. One year gives you a discount on these virtual machines and 2 years gives you an additional discount (for a longer time, and a bigger discount as you are obliged to use the service for longer). You can edit the reserved instances agreement at any time by adding or removing virtual machines. An increase in number can provide an additional discount and a decrease will result in penalties.

Deciding between IaaS or PaaS

Once a subscription is in place, you can start creating resources in order to use them and deploy your application. Choosing what to use and when can be overwhelming in terms of the broad choice Microsoft Azure has to offer. There are different approaches and different architectures we need to consider before even starting.

We have already talked about IaaS, PaaS, and SaaS. An example of Microsoft SaaS is Office 365 and, as a cloud software, it is available under a subscription model. Office 365 even runs in Azure data centers (it was the initial purpose of these data centers along with identity management—we now call this Azure Active Directory), but we will not discuss this product further as it isn't directly connected to Azure subscriptions. Our goal will be to distinguish Microsoft Azure's offerings when it comes to IaaS and PaaS.

IaaS is the first step in migration to the cloud. It's natural for traditional IT professionals to accept this as a first step in the cloud journey. Creating an Azure virtual machine is simple and from a VM level there isn't much difference between a local VM and a cloud VM. You don't have access to hardware or host components, which makes maintenance easier and cheaper. But administering and managing VM in Azure isn't much different form on-premises versions, no matter what host we used locally—Hyper-V, VMWare or something else (Microsoft Azure uses a modified version of Hyper-V hosts that are different than the version used on-premises).

You select an image for the operating system, select the size of the VM, and some other parameters. From there forward, you connect to your VM and install features and software as you see fit. You can control access, frameworks, and data for all software installed on your VM; you'll need to pay for it as part of a subscription or provide a valid license of you own. If your create a VM with Windows Server 2016 and SQL Server 2016, you will be charged extra for both licenses.

Creating a PaaS resource is even simpler than IaaS. It's easier to administer and manage as well. But, on the other hand, control is no longer completely in your hands. You can edit some key features that are predefined to have different values or to be turned on and off. But, some things are default and you are no longer able to edit them. All licenses are included in the price of resources by default.

Let's consider a simple scenario where you have a web application running on IIS in the frontend and a database on SQL Server in the backend.

For IaaS, you'll need to create two virtual machines, a web server, and a database server. In order to host your application, you'll need to set up IIS on a web server that will be running Windows Server 2016. A database server can be a VM with SQL Server 2016 running on Windows Server 2016. By now, added to our computing prices, we have two licenses for Windows Server and one license for SQL Server (price also varies in the version of SQL Server if we choose web, standard, or enterprise edition). Once we have installed and configured IIS, we need to create firewall and network security group rules that will allow us to access our application over the internet. We need to set up communication between the web server and database server and create similar rules in order to allow communication between our application and database. We already have our hands full enabling a simple scenario with IaaS.

For IaaS, we will set up the app service plan in order to host our web application and Azure SQL database for the backend. All licenses are already configured and we don't have to do anything else in terms of configuration. The process is much simpler and easier.

Note that pricing is cheaper for PaaS in most cases.

But on the other hand, PaaS doesn't always allow us to have everything we need to run our applications. If we need to use an older version of some framework, PaaS will not work. PaaS already has a preconfigured set of frameworks that you can use but you can't install anything additionally. In the case that you have some features for the database that are not supported in Azure SQL or compatibility issues, you need to use SQL Server in VM.

Overall, PaaS is usually cheaper and needs less attention than IaaS, but IaaS gives better control and better legacy support.

Service offerings are growing by the day and every few weeks we have new services and new features in Microsoft Azure. A couple of services that we mentioned are only examples for a simple scenario. IaaS does give us control as to what is going to be on our VM and offers better combinations compared to a single resource, but the PaaS list doesn't stop there. For Azure PaaS, we can create an app service, content delivery network, Azure SQL database, traffic manager, service bus, Azure functions, Azure CosmosDB, Azure storage, and Redis cache just to name a few.

Azure data platform has over 50 different services that are PaaS. The same goes for other platforms such as web, media, compute, and so on. Choosing the right service can be beneficial both when we look at the solution from a financial perspective and a performance perspective. We need to consider if some service has some limitation that will make us use another service just to cover that limit. And there could be another service that will cover both aspects and there will be no need to use an additional service. Limitations can cause performance issues if we don't look at all aspects and try to anticipate all possible scenarios. Luckily, with Azure, we are not stuck with a single solution, even if we see that we have made a mistake and the service we chose doesn't really cover our needs—we can always scale out or switch to another service completely.

Understanding the pricing of Azure resources

There are few things you need to consider regarding pricing in Microsoft Azure. There are resources that have fixed pricing and resources that have consumption pricing. Also, fixed-price resources sometimes have service level limits included in the basic price. Once you reach that limit, you will be charged extra based on consumption. This potentially turns fixed-priced resources into consumption-priced ones. There are also exceptions that have different uses applied.

Resources that have fixed pricing will be added to your bill as soon as you create them. Fixed-pricing resources are billed on a monthly basis, have a fixed price, and are added to your bill as soon as you create them. Examples of these services would be OMS or Azure Active Directory on higher tiers. A reserved public IP address is also one of the fixed-cost resources. After you delete this type of resource, it will be added to your bill for the current billing period.

Azure storage is based on consumption and you pay for the amount of data you have in your storage account. But the amount of data varies every month and there could be less data at the beginning or end of the month, but more data in the middle of the month. In this case, average consumption is calculated and you are billed on the average consumption of Azure Storage.

An example of a service that has performance-level restrictions would be bandwidth. Inbound data transfer is free of charge and you don't pay anything as long as data is going towards an Azure data center. Outbound data is free for the first 5 GB per month and you are charged extra for everything over those 5 GB. Another example of a service limit would be Azure container registry, where you have 100 minutes of CPU included but pay extra when exceeding that limit. Azure function is also an example of this type of resource where you get the first 1,000,000 executions for free and you are charged for additional executions.

Resources based on computing are calculated on a per-minute basis. If you have a virtual machine or app service running, billing will stop as soon as you delete these resources. This also applies to resources being stopped in some cases. Azure SQL database can't be stopped but pricing will be calculated on a per-minute basis. If you delete Azure SQL database, you stop paying for it the same minute it's deleted. For virtual machines and app services, you can stop these resources and you will not pay for compute hours any longer. Note that there are a few pricing details related to a virtual machine. Virtual machine price information, that you can find in Azure portal when creating virtual machine or shown in Azure calculator, is only for compute hours. A virtual machine also uses Azure storage that you pay for, separately from computing, and you will pay for storage no matter if the virtual machine is running or stopped. Some network components can create additional charges for virtual machines. For example, you can reserve a public IP address that is charged separately.

It is very important to keep track of your resources in Azure and to know what you are using, if resources are utilized, and what the limits are for current resources. If you are not using something correctly or not using it at all, you are still paying for it. This is different from a traditional IT environment where you have resources prepaid and it doesn't really matter if a single virtual machine is being used or not as long as you don't reach the resource limit at the host level. In Azure, you are paying for everything you created (or have running in some cases) so you need to keep track of active resources and what you actually need. Otherwise, the cloud can become a very expensive solution and bills will start to pile up. Financial benefits can be great but if you are not careful, it can go the other way as well. I've seen many companies using a development and test environment without control and many resources where no one knows who created them and why, let alone if there is someone actually using them. This is not as often a problem with production environments, but can happen in some cases.

Be smart and Azure will help you, but if you don't keep track of usage and billing, it can go the other way. It's your choice: you can get either promoted or fired!

ARM revolution

In April 2014, Microsoft announced a new approach to Azure with a new portal and ARM model. We already discussed how ARM and RBAC changed the administration of Azure resources and made life in the cloud much easier.

But another option ARM brought to the table was ARM templates. ARM templates are files in JSON format that contain information on all resources in a single resource group. We can use ARM templates to deploy new resources, update resources, or remove resources from a resource group. Every resource group in Azure portal has an automation blade that allows us to save an ARM template for that resource group, redeploy resources, or download a template locally. This allows us to replicate resources from a resource group quickly and simply.

This is why placing resources for a single application is common practice in Azure. If we have a complicated environment that takes some time to deploy, it can be very useful. For example, let's say that we have a SharePoint farm with Windows Server running a domain controller role, two servers for SharePoint farm, and two additional servers running SQL Server. This requires us to create a virtual network, create five servers, and add them to the virtual network. Doing this manually in the Azure portal requires some time to create. But with ARM templates we can do this in a matter of seconds.

Deploying infrastructure with ARM templates is only one option for infrastructure as a code. We can achieve similar things with PowerShell and Azure CLI as well. Using infrastructure as a code allows us to deploy infrastructure needed to run our application in a fast and reliable way. It's a more consistent option as well because we are excluding manual tasks from deployment, creating an automated process, and eliminating human error in deployment.

Another great thing about ARM templates is that they can be added to our application project and stored in a repository, and we can keep track of versions of our environment. Different versions of an application may require changes in environment and with ARM templates and code repositories we can keep track of these changes and make sure that the correct environment is deployed for the version of the application we are deploying.

To sum everything up, ARM templates are a fast, reliable, and consistent way to deploy Azure resources that allow us to keep track of environment versioning and automate deployment processes. This is especially interesting and useful if we are trying to implement DevOps in our software delivery. In combination with configuration as a code (we'll talk about this in later chapters), we can build or replicate any environment with all resources required and apply the configuration needed for everything to run correctly.

A sample of an empty ARM template is shown here:

```
{
  "$schema":
"https://schema.management.azure.com/schemas/2015-01-01/deploymentTemplate.
json#",
  "contentVersion": "1.0.0.0",
  "parameters": {
  },
  "variables": {
  },
  "resources": [
  ],
  "outputs": {
  }
}
```

An ARM template contains information on parameters, variables, resources, and outputs. Using this information we define what resources need to be deployed, using which parameters, and which of these parameters can be variables that can be changed. Finally, we define the output as a replay, but this part is optional.

Summary

In this chapter, we explained cloud computing types and the evolution of cloud computing over time with a focus on the public cloud and Microsoft Azure. The next step was to explain the public cloud service model and how IaaS, PaaS, and SaaS work and the basic concepts of these public cloud types. You should also understand how Azure subscription works, how prices of resource are calculated, and basic administration concepts in relation to Azure subscriptions and the ARM model. We provided more information on ARM in general, and how it's connected to RBAC and ARM templates.

Understanding Azure subscriptions and ARM templates along with IaaS and PaaS in Azure is very important, as we'll use this knowledge in chapters to come.

The next step will be IaaS, as the first step toward cloud computing. The foundation for IaaS (and all other Azure services) is the Azure networking stack, and we'll start with this.

Questions

1. Which type of cloud requires an internet connection and allows anyone to sign up for service?
    1. Private cloud
    2. Hosted cloud
    3. Public cloud

2. Which cloud service model allows us most control over resources?
    1. IaaS
    2. PaaS
    3. SaaS

3. Which cloud service model requires the least management and administration?
    1. IaaS
    2. PaaS
    3. SaaS

4. Which cloud service model always gives us the latest features and updates?
    1. IaaS
    2. PaaS
    3. SaaS

5. What is responsible for separating the client environment from other clients in Azure?
    1. Azure fabric
    2. Azure tenant
    3. Azure subscription

6. What is the first access layer in Microsoft Azure?
    1. Azure fabric
    2. Azure tenant
    3. Azure subscription

7. What is the lowest granularity at which you can assign access to Azure resources?
    1. Azure resource
    2. Azure resource group
    3. Azure subscription

8. What is the recommended access level that should be assigned for Azure resources?
    1. Azure resource
    2. Azure resource group
    3. Azure subscription

9. How is pricing calculated for Microsoft Azure?
    1. Per year
    2. Per month
    3. Per minute

10. ARM templates are part of what?
    1. Infrastructure as a code
    2. IaaS
    3. Configuration as a code

Azure Networking - Foundation of Azure IaaS

2

The next step in our cloud journey is Azure networking. This step will lay the foundation for our Azure infrastructure and will be used by both IaaS and PaaS in chapters to come. It's important to design and implement your Azure network with consideration for all Azure services that will be used in the future. This will save you a lot of headaches, and keep your cloud journey safe and without turbulence.

The areas that we'll cover in this chapter are the following:

- Azure VNet
- Address ranges
- Subntets
- IP address types and reservations
- DNS
- **Network security groups (NSGs)**
- Azure virtual machine networking

Technical requirements

For this chapter, you'll need an Azure subscription.

Azure networking basics

The networking stack in Microsoft Azure is very important and is the foundation for other services, especially when we talk about IaaS. Setting up Azure networking correctly is very important, as it will be key to setting up your IaaS infrastructure and allowing your virtual machines to communicate. The networking stack in Azure is composed of two components, external and private. External is used to access service endpoints over the internet and private is used for communication between Azure services internally.

Almost all Azure services have external endpoints configured by default, but we have some special cases when we don't want to enable access over the internet. In these cases, we can disable external endpoints and set up these services to use private traffic only. This applies to PaaS as well, even though these services usually don't have private network access configured by default (except for some PaaS services that are designed for this, for example, app service isolated). In this chapter, we'll discuss basic networking features and will continue to explore networking options for specific services when the time comes.

IaaS usually has external endpoints configured as well, but we have the option to disable these and not allow access over the internet. On the other hand, IaaS always comes with a private network configured. Every virtual machine in Azure has to be assigned to a virtual network and have a private IP address assigned. Even if we have a single virtual machine configured and want to use it only for public access over the internet, a virtual network will be created in the background, and this VM will have a private IP address assigned.

Azure networking also extends to VPN options, which allow you to access services only over a private network and private IP addresses. This allows you to secure resources further and disable any kind of public access. We will explore these features and options when we discuss hybrid cloud with Microsoft Azure.

Creating your first virtual network in Azure

Azure virtual network (**Azure VNet**) is created in two cases, when you create a new VNet or when you create a new Azure virtual machine. Options are similar in both cases, but I recommend creating Azure VNet in advance and joining virtual machines to an existing VNet because this gives you a few more options.

To create a new Azure Vnet, open the Azure portal, select **Create a resource** and choose **Virtual network** in **Networking** services (or search for Virtual network in the search bar), as shown in the following screenshot:

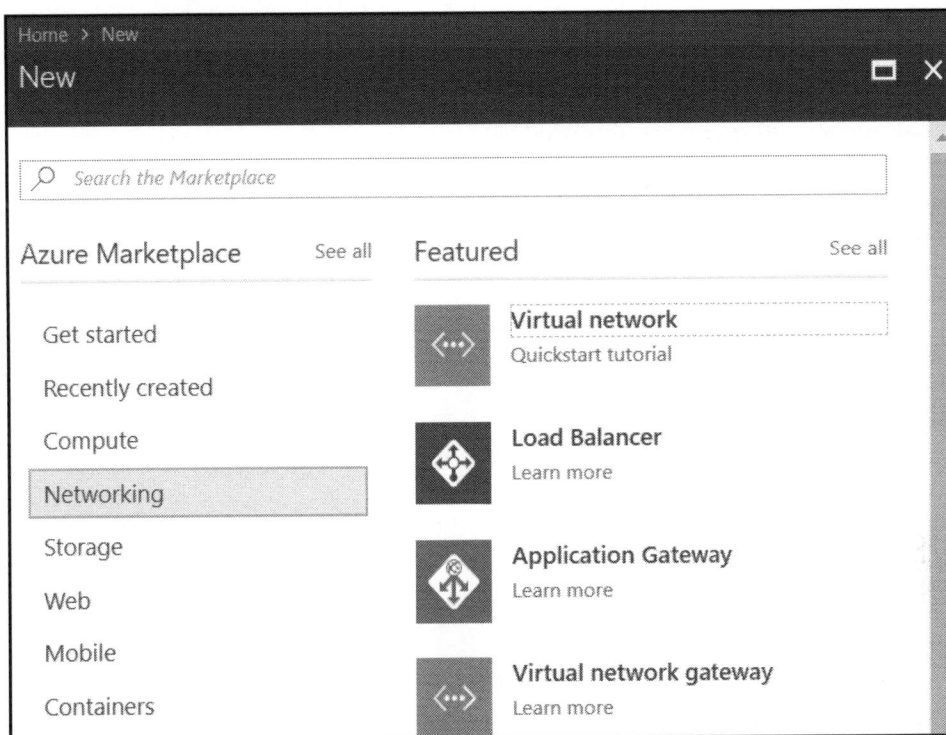

You need parameters for your virtual network. The resource name must be unique on the resource group level and must be one string, with no spaces allowed. My resource **Name** is PacktVNet, but it could be Packt_VNet if I wanted to separate the words. The next parameter we need to provide is **Address space**. This will define how many IP addresses will be available in this VNet and uses CIDR format. The biggest address space is /8 and smallest is /29. In this case, I'll use /16, which will give me plenty of address space to use. We need to select the subscription where we want to place our resource (only if we have multiple subscriptions; one will be selected by default in the case of a single subscription). Two options are available for **Resource group** name, either a new one or to select an existing resource group. As I usually configure virtual network prior to any other resource, a new resource group is created along with VNet. The next step is to select the region where we want to create the resource. I recommend to select the Azure data center closest to you geographically, as this will provide the least network latency in the future. If you selected an existing resource group, this option will be preselected as the same region in which the resource group is located. You need to name the default subnet and provide an address space for that subnet. The address range for the subnet must be inside the address range of your VNet address space.

Basic DDoS protection is provided by default for free, but you can select the standard tier, which is charged separately. We will discuss DDoS further when we reach `Chapter 9`, *Azure Security and Administration*. Examples of the information needed for virtual network deployment are shown in the following screenshot:

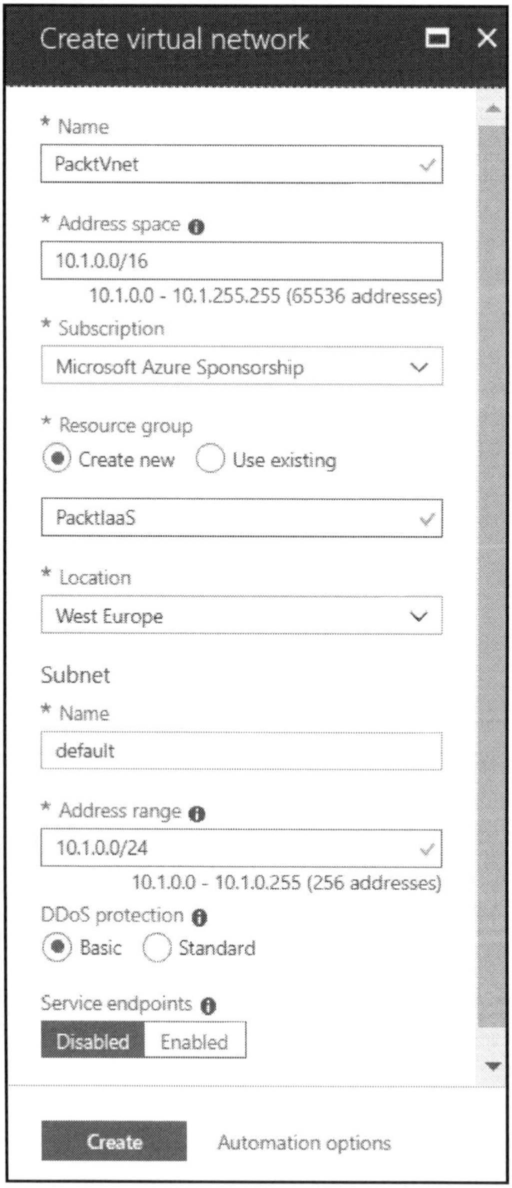

The final option is related to service endpoints. If we enable this, new windows will be shown, as in the following screenshot. This option enables you to attach PaaS services to your VNet. You can select between Azure Cosmos DB, event hub, key vault, service bus, SQL, and storage, or you can select all of them. At this time, I'll disable endpoints and we'll discuss them later:

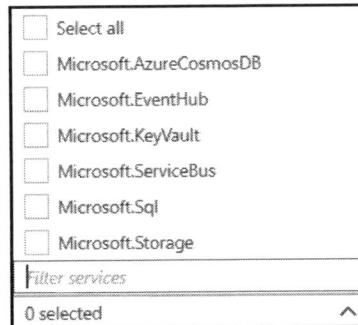

```
  Select all

  Microsoft.AzureCosmosDB

  Microsoft.EventHub

  Microsoft.KeyVault

  Microsoft.ServiceBus

  Microsoft.Sql

  Microsoft.Storage

  Filter services

  0 selected                              ^
```

The last step is to confirm options and start the process of creating a resource. Azure virtual network works relatively fast and a resource should be created in less than a minute. This can depend on data center workload and the number of requests but should be completed relatively quickly, even in high-demand situations.

Azure virtual network represents your own network in the cloud. It has similar features to your local network, such as IP address range and subnets. If you're familiar with networking in on-premises scenarios, it will be very easy to understand Azure networking.

Azure virtual network options

Once deployment is finished, you have different management options available. Locate your resource group and open the VNet blade. In the **Overview** tab, you can see different information about your VNet, such as resource group, subscription location, and so on.

In settings, we have multiple options that are available for configuration: **Address space**, **Connected Devices**, **Subnets**, **DDoS protection**, **DNS servers**, **Peering**, and **Service endpoints**. Properties, locks, and automation scripts are available for every resource in Azure and aren't limited only to Azure VNet. Properties have read-only information about your resource, and locks point out if there are any services in dependency to this service. The automation script will generate an ARM template for resource redeployment. Note that this option generates an ARM template for a complete resource group, not only for a specific resource. The automation script can be used for future redeployment, in case we need to replicate resources for a new client or a new environment.

In address space, we can edit an existing address space or add additional ones. There are two restrictions: address spaces can't overlap and you can't change an address space to be smaller than the subnets using that address space. For example, if you created address space `10.1.0.0/16` and subnet `10.1.0.0./16`, the address space can't be changed to less than `10.1.0.0/16` unless the subnet is changed first. It's important, how you use an address space; in terms of future VPN connection, you cannot connect Azure VNet to a network (Azure or physical) using the same address space. Adding a new address space can be seen in the following screenshot. Make sure the new address space doesn't overlap with the existing one:

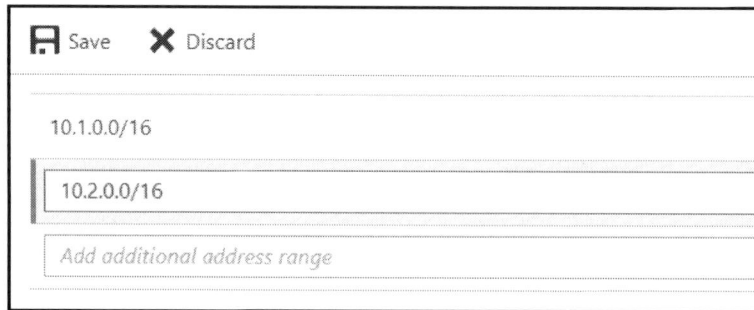

In the subnet blade, you have two options: to change the existing subnet or to add a new one. For both options, you have to use existing address spaces, and subnets can't overlap. An existing subnet can't be changed to use less address space than already in use. For example, if you have an address space of `10.1.0.0/24` and have 200 VMs on the subnet already, then you can't change to anything less than `/24`, as `/25` has only 128 addresses available.

Another thing to note is that you don't have the complete IP range available on your subnet; five IP addresses are reserved for Azure-provided network roles such as DNS or DHCP. Speaking of DHCP, having a custom DHCP solution in Azure is not supported, you have to use an Azure-provided DHCP. This is not the case with DNS; by default, you use the Azure DNS service, but can use a custom solution as well.

To add a new subnet, you need to provide similar information to when you created the default one during VNet deployment, but you have a couple of additional options. Again, you need to provide a name for your subnet and IP address range that must use the existing IP address range of your VNet and must not overlap with other subnets on your VNet. Note that here you get information about the reservation of five IP addresses for Azure networking services. A similar VNet deployment is the service endpoint option, which allows you to add PaaS services to your subnet. You can assign a **Network security group** to the subnet level and assign **Route table**.

NSGs are your main tool to control traffic on Azure Vnets, and we'll discuss them in more detail later. Azure routes traffic automatically between all subnets on the same VNet, but you can create custom route tables to override the default options. This can be useful in cases when you have VPN or virtual appliance (third-party firewalls in Azure). An example of adding a new subnet to VNet is shown in the following screenshot:

The DNS blade allows us to add a custom DNS solution to our VNet. As mentioned before, this is Azure-provided by default but you can use your own DNS, either a VM with DNS or public DNS.

If you have a Site2Site connection to your local network, this can be DNS for your local network. If this is the case, I would recommend using a replica of your DNS in Azure. This will make the response faster and DNS available on your Azure VNet in case the VPN connection or your local network is down for some reason. The option to provide custom DNS is shown in the following screenshot. You need to provide the IP address of the DNS server, the public IP in case you choose public DNS, or a private one if you deploy DNS on your VNet:

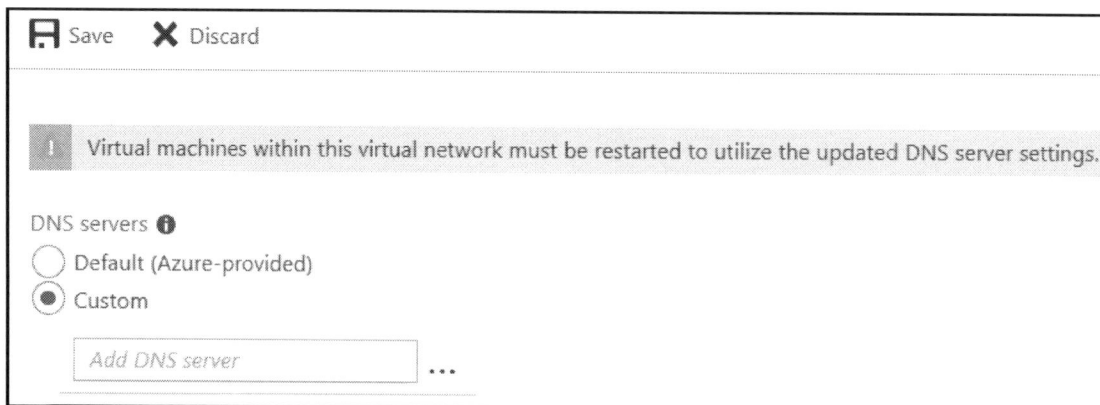

Save ✕ Discard

Virtual machines within this virtual network must be restarted to utilize the updated DNS server settings.

DNS servers ⓘ
○ Default (Azure-provided)
● Custom

Add DNS server ...

We had the option to add service endpoints to our VNet during deployment, but we can add them at any time using the service endpoint blade, shown in the following screenshot. As adding these services starts a provisioning process that will set up routing and rules, it can take up to 15 minutes for the process to complete. The service endpoint option is available on at the VNet and subnet levels, so you can enable endpoints either for a complete network or on a single subnet. Using a single subnet gives you more control and the ability to separate the PaaS service from rest of your virtual network:

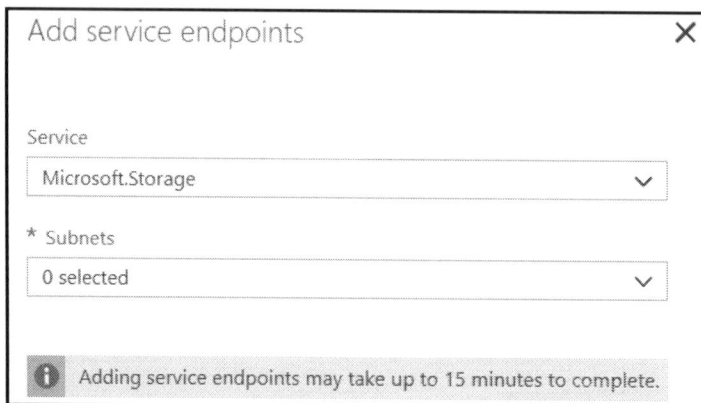

Add service endpoints ✕

Service
Microsoft.Storage ∨

* Subnets
0 selected ∨

ⓘ Adding service endpoints may take up to 15 minutes to complete.

Peering allows you to connect your VNet to other VNets in order to exchange traffic. This is available only for VNets in a single Azure tenant (but available across subscriptions in that tenant). You need to give a name to the connection and then select the appropriate subscription and virtual network. You have some additional options to define if needed, like if you want traffic forwarding, allowing gateway transit, and use of remote gateways. By default, only traffic coming from one VNet will go to the second VNet. Traffic coming from outside VNets that are connected by peering (coming from a second peer, only one of the VNets is involved in or coming over gateways) will not be forwarded unless you specify these options.

For example, let's say we have three VNets: A, B, and C. A is connected to B, and C is connected to B, but there is no direct connection between A and C. By default, traffic would be allowed for A to B, from B to A, from B to C, and C to B. No traffic would go from A to C or from C to A. If we enable traffic forwarding, traffic from A to C and C to A would go through.

A similar thing goes for virtual gateways. Let's say we have networks A and B and peering between these VNets. VNet A has a virtual gateway and is connected to our on-premises network. By default, traffic would be allowed from A to B, B to A, from the on-premises network to A and from A to on-premises network. No traffic would be allowed from on-premises network to B and from B to on-premises network, unless we allow this traffic using extra options that allow gateway transit and the use of remote gateways.

Another way to achieve this is to create a virtual gateway for each VNet and create a Site2Site connection, the same one that you would use in case you wanted to connect to your on-premises network (we'll discuss this in the hybrid cloud chapter). The big difference between the two approaches is that peering is free and you pay for a virtual gateway. If you want to connect two VNets that are located on different tenants, you need to use a virtual gateway; peering is available only for VNets on the same tenant.

To connect different networks, either VNet to VNet or VNet to local network, IP address spaces/subnets must not overlap. If you have the same subnet for both networks, you won't be able to create this connection as this would create confusion and make routing impossible. It would be impossible to distinguish which device is on which network and where traffic should go. How to connect your VNet to another VNet in your subscription is shown in the following screenshot:

Where we have multiple networks connected either by peering or Site2Site, it's recommended to use route tables. Custom route tables allow us to create and forward traffic in specific cases and define rules concerning where traffic should go in each situation.

Connected devices

We have our VNet configured and ready but we need resources in there to actually start using it. The first step is to add a new Azure virtual machine to our VNet in order to start using the Azure networking stack.

Creating an Azure virtual machine

In order to create a new Azure virtual machine through the portal, we have to take three steps. We need to select **New resource** and select a new virtual machine. We have hundreds of images available and we'll discuss that in chapters to come:

1. In this case, we need a single VM only, to show networking options for it, and we'll set all default parameters in order to get there quickly. I selected the **Windows Server 2016** image and started providing the basic information needed: **Name**, **VM disk type**, **Username**, **Password**, **Subscription**, **Resource group**, and **Location**. Note that under **Location**, you have the options to create a new resource group and select an existing one. I selected to **Use existing**, the same one where our VNet is located.

An example of basic VM creation is shown in the following screenshot:

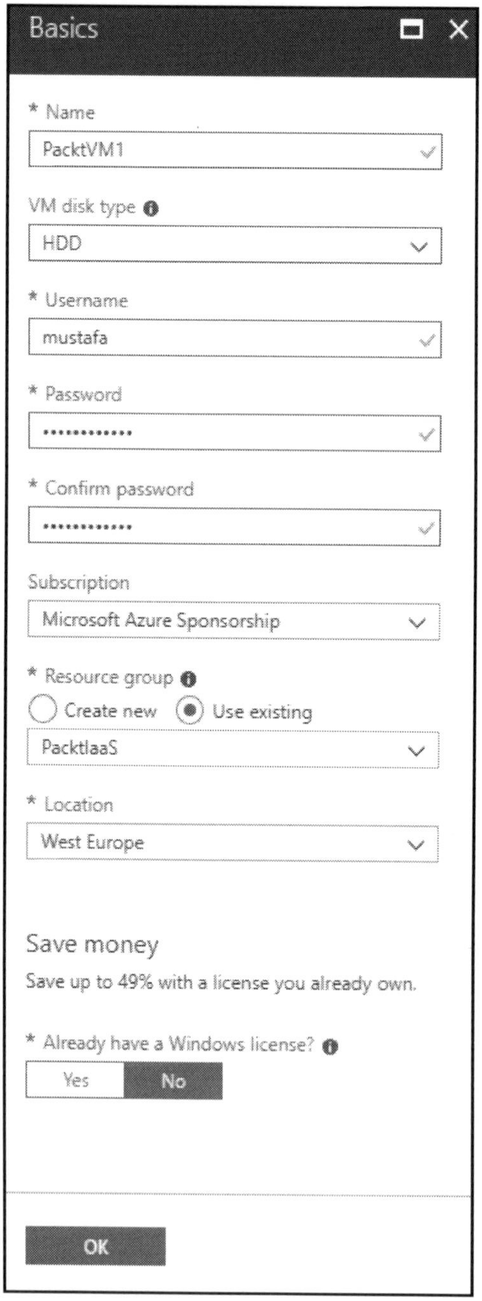

2. The next step is to choose virtual machine size. This again is not relevant to the networking part and I'll select the first one offered, **B1s**, shown in the following screenshot:

RECOMM...	SKU	TYPE	COMPUT...	VCPUS	GB RAM	DATA DIS...	MAX IOPS	LOCAL SSD	PREMIU...	ADDITIO...	ZONES	EUR/MO...
Available												
	B1s	Standard	General purpc 1	1	2	800	4 GB	SSD			1,2,3	€10.73
	B1ms	Standard	General purpc 1	2	2	1600	4 GB	SSD			1,2,3	€20.33
	B2s	Standard	General purpc 2	4	4	3200	8 GB	SSD			1,2,3	€40.66
	B2ms	Standard	General purpc 2	8	4	4800	16 GB	SSD			1,2,3	€76.80
	B4ms	Standard	General purpc 4	16	8	7200	32 GB	SSD			1,2,3	€145.12
	B8ms	Standard	General purpc 8	32	16	10800	64 GB	SSD			1,2,3	€278.95
	D2s_v3	Standard	General purpc 2	8	4	4000	16 GB	SSD			1,2,3	€133.01
	D4s_v3	Standard	General purpc 4	16	8	8000	32 GB	SSD			1,2,3	€266.02
	D8s_v3	Standard	General purpc 8	32	16	16000	64 GB	SSD			1,2,3	€532.05
	D16s_v3	Standard	General purpc 16	64	32	32000	128 GB	SSD			1,2,3	€1,064.10
	D32s_v3	Standard	General purpc 32	128	32	64000	256 GB	SSD			1,2,3	€2,128.19
	D64s_v3	Standard	General purpc 64	256	32	128000	512 GB	SSD			1,2,3	€4,256.38
	E2s_v3	Standard	Memory optin 2	16	4	4000	32 GB	SSD			1,2,3	€158.11

Prices presented are estimates in your local currency that include only Azure infrastructure costs and any discounts for the subscription and location. The prices don't include any applicable software costs. Recommended sizes are determined by the publisher of the selected image based on hardware and software requirements.

Select

3. In the final step, we are getting to the part where we have some networking options. I'll leave all other options at their defaults and concentrate on the network part.

First, we need to choose the **Virtual network** our VM will be connected to. We can choose either an existing one or create a new VNet. If no VNet is found, new VNet parameters will be automatically provided. If there is already a virtual network in the resource group where we place our VM, that VNet will be automatically selected. In our case, the **PacktVNet** created in the first step is shown in the following screenshot:

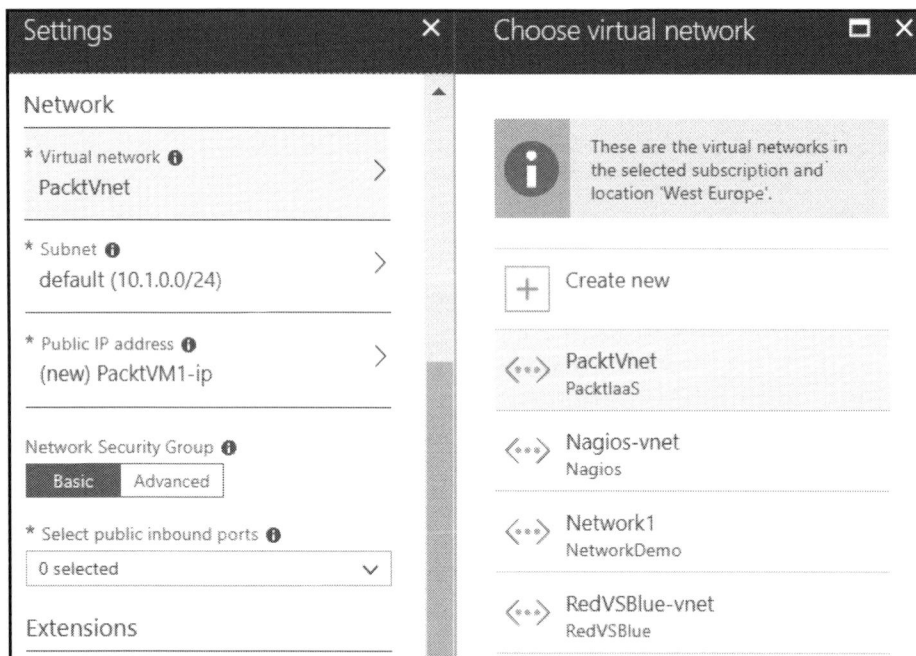

The second option we have is to choose the **Subnet** for our VM. If we are creating a new VNet along with the VM, this option will not be available; only the default subnet will be created. To be able to choose between subnets, a virtual network needs to be created prior to the VM, along with the subnet you want to use. In this case, I'll choose to join the VM to the DMZ subnet I created before. Selecting the **Subnet** option is shown in the following screenshot:

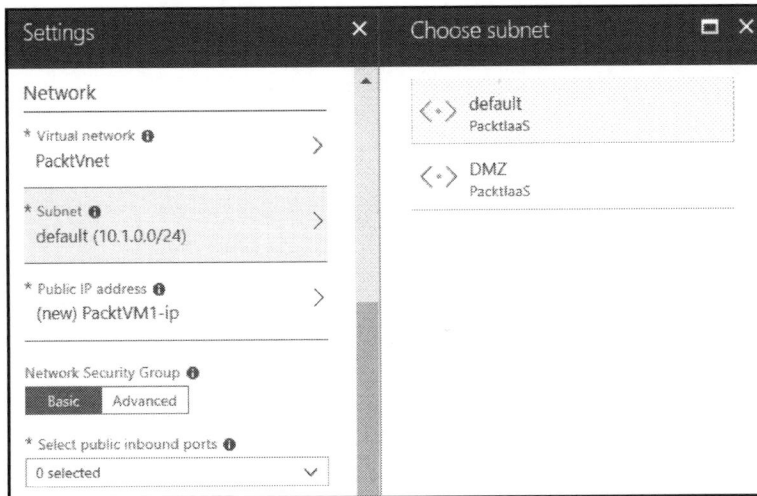

We also have options to choose the **Public IP address** for our VM. We can choose from an existing one (a reserved IP address no longer in use) or create a new public IP address. Same goes for **Network Security Groups**: we can choose an existing one or create a new one. I'll select to create a new **Public IP address** and a new **Network Security Group** for my VM, as shown in the following screenshot:

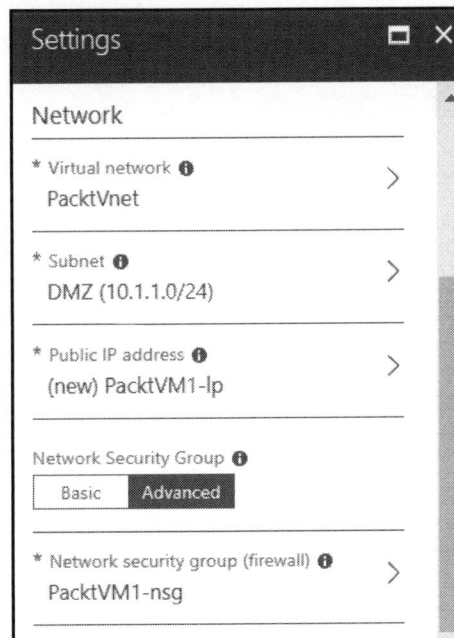

After this, the deployment of the VM starts and it takes a few minutes until the process is complete. The time required to deploy a new Azure virtual machine depends on the VM size, screenshot, and number of requests against the data center.

IP address types

Once the deployment of the VM is finished, we can see the device in **Connected devices** under the virtual network blade. An example of what the connected device blade looks like is shown in the following screenshot. Information shown here includes the device name, type of device connected, private IP address, and subnet the device is assigned to. IP address information is related to a private IP address, one that was assigned to our VM on the VNet level and is used only for internal traffic. Note that type of device is **Network interface**. Every VM has a **network interface card** (**NIC**) that is used to communicate with the network and one is automatically created with your VM. A virtual machine can have more than one NIC if you need to connect to multiple subnets or make sure that the VM is available, even when one NIC fails. The number of NICs depends on VM size, it can be from 1 for basic tier VMs to 8 for higher tiers:

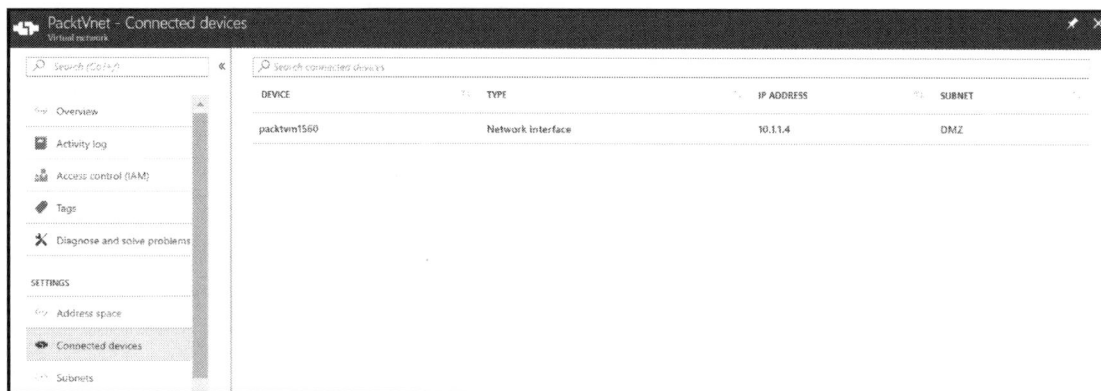

If we click on the device, it will take us to the NIC blade, as illustrated in the following screenshot. We can get to the same blade if we select NIC in the resource group. In IP configuration, we can enable or disable **IP forwarding**, change the **Subnet** that the NIC is connected to, and see the **IP configurations** for both private and public IP addresses:

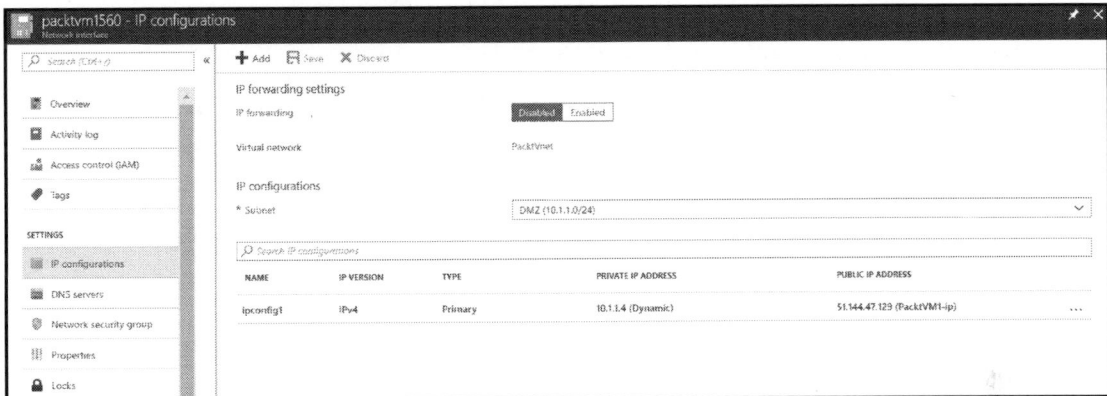

Private IP addresses

If we select IP configuration, we have further options for IP addresses. An example is show in the following screenshot.

By default, a public IP address is enabled but we can disable it if needed. This is often used when the VM is in the backend and now public exposure is needed. In this case, we need to make sure that we have other options to connect to this VM, usually through a VPN. Disabling a public IP address is often in hybrid cloud scenarios when no access over the internet is needed. Beside using the public IP address assigned, we can create a new one as well here.

A private IP address is by default dynamic and can change over time. A change of IP address will not happen out of thin air but in the case of a VM restart or shutdown. If we use a private IP address for communication with other VMs on our VNet, we may want to keep this address. This can be done by setting IP address assignment from **Dynamic** to **Static**. This will reserve our IP for this NIC even if the VM is kept turned off for a long period of time:

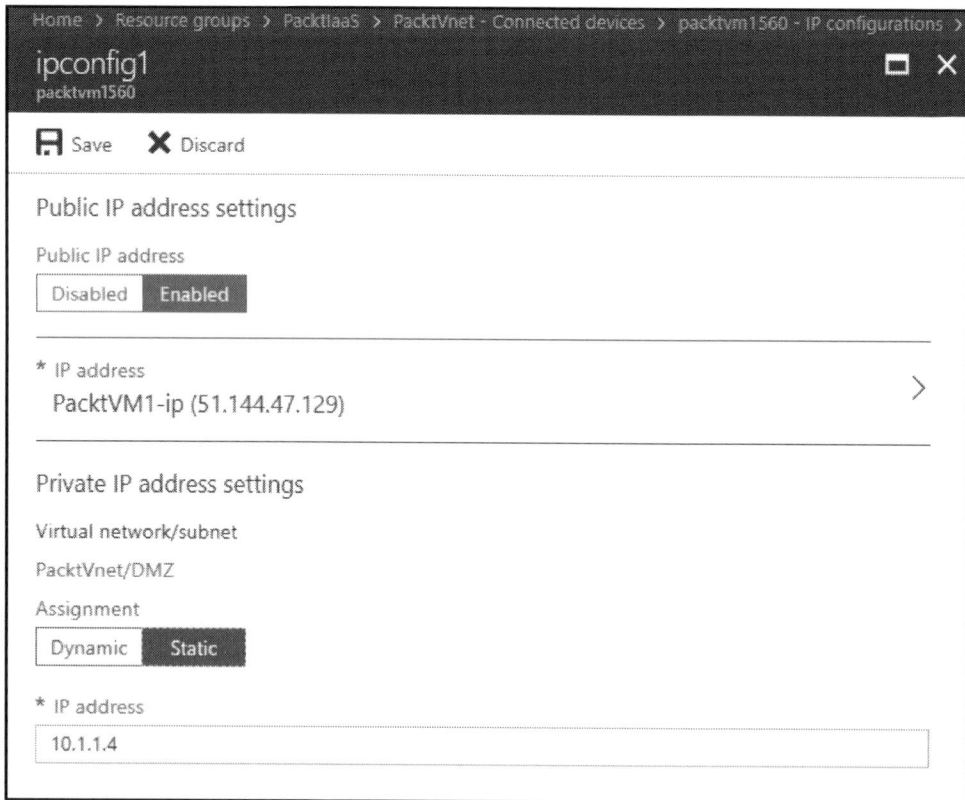

DNS is another option that is available on both the Vnet and VM levels. We can assign **Custom** DNS that will apply only for this specific NIC. If we assign DNS to the VNet level, that DNS will be applied to all VMs connected to that VNet. The default option for NIC DNS is to inherit the setting from the virtual network. In this case, it will be either Azure DNS or custom DNS, depending on VNet settings. If we selected **Custom** DNS for VNet, we can no longer choose Azure DNS as an option on the NIC level. Our only option available is to use **Inherit from virtual network** or **Custom** DNS. The DNS blade on the NIC level is shown in the following screenshot:

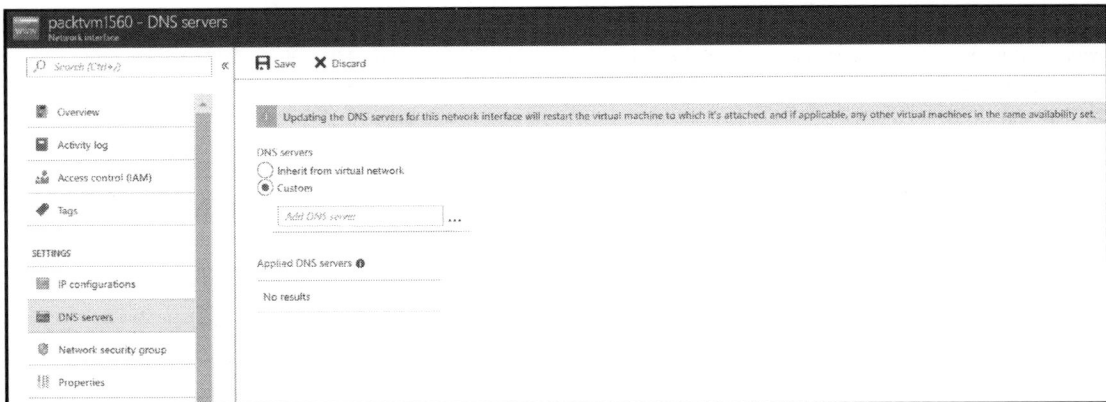

Network security groups

NSGs are a set of security rules applied on your Azure network resources. They are the main tool to enforce and control network traffic rules for your resources. NSGs can be applied to two types of resources: subnets and NICs. If an NSG is applied to a subnet, the rules will be applied to all devices that are connected to that subnet. When an NSG is applied to an NIC, the rules will be applied only for that device.

In the overview of the NSG blade, we can see all the rules that are currently applied, both inbound and outbound. By default, all inbound traffic from outside is disabled, except port 3389, which allows us to connect to the VM remotely. All inbound traffic coming from inside the virtual network or Azure load balancers is allowed. These rules can be edited and more added as needed.

Outbound traffic is by default allowed on all levels, going to the virtual network or outside. These rules can be edited as well, but there is usually no need to restrict outbound traffic.

All rules have a priority assigned to them; a lower number represents a rule with a higher priority. For example, we have the RDP rule with priority 1000 and the DenyAllInBound rule (which will block all inbound traffic) with priority 65500. Even though the DenyAllInBound rule to block all incoming traffic is enforced, the rule to allow RDP has a higher priority and will be enforced first. As a result, we have all inbound traffic blocked with the exception of RDP, which is allowed due to being a higher priority rule.

NSG settings can be opened either through the NIC blade or by selecting NSG in the list of resources in the resource group. The overview of the NSG blade is shown in the following screenshot:

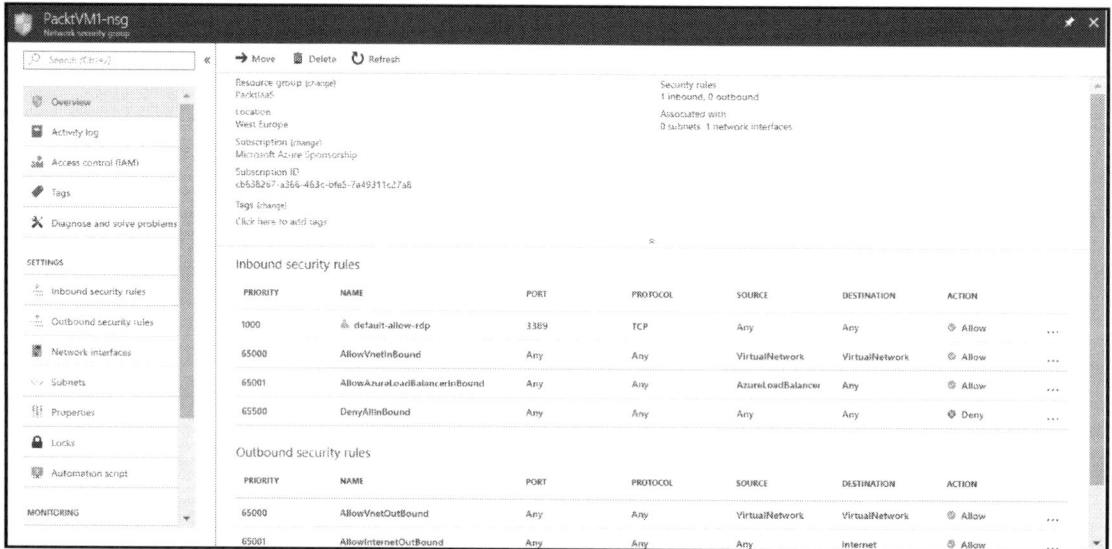

To add a new rule, go to **Inbound security rules** and select **Add new rule**. You can choose basic or advanced. If you choose basic, only a few options will be available to choose from. I recommend using advanced, as this will give you more control over rules:

- **Source**: For **Source**, you can select between several options. **Any** will allow traffic from any source. **IP addresses** will allow traffic only from named addresses; you can enter either a single IP or a range of IP addresses in the CIDR format. This can be very useful for restricting access over port 3389 and to secure your virtual machines. **Service tag** will allow traffic coming from a specific service. For example, using the **Service tag** option, you can allow traffic coming from Azure storage but block everything else.
  The last option for source is an **Application Security Group** (**ASG**). An ASG allows you to create rules and allow traffic only to a certain group of resources on your network. For example, we have multiple servers in our VNet, web servers and database servers. Allowing traffic over port 1433 to database servers should be enabled for web servers but not over the internet. Placing web servers in an ASG and creating a rule would allow only web servers to access our databases over port 1433 and stop any other traffic.

- **Source port ranges**: With **Source port ranges**, we can also restrict traffic and allow it only if it's coming from a specific port or port range.
- **Destination port ranges**: The **Destination port ranges** option is similar to the source option; we have the same set of options available. An ASG is something that can be useful to allow traffic only to a certain type of VM on your network. For example, placing web servers in an ASG and allowing traffic over ports 443 or 80 would allow only these servers to be accessed over these ports and block traffic to any other type of VM.
The **Destination port ranges** allow us to specify over which ports traffic is allowed, restricting it to a single port or a range.
- **Protocol**: It helps us define which protocols are allowed, choosing from either TCP or UDP.
- **Action**: It defines whether this rule is used to allow traffic or block it. An NSG can be used either way, it can help us define if certain traffic is allowed, but can be used to deny traffic as well and help us secure our resources in Azure.
- **Priority**: This option is very important as it allows us to define which rules are applied first and which rules have the advantage. As mentioned before, the lower the priority number assigned to the rule, the higher priority the rule has. The rules are processed in order, from the highest priority rule (the lowest number) to the lower priority rule (higher number) until the condition is met. Once the condition is met, the rule is processed, and the rule processing stops. For example, let's create a rule that will block all traffic over port 1433 and give it priority 1000, and then create a rule that will allow certain sources to have traffic over port 1433 with priority 2000. No traffic over port 1433 will ever go through, as a rule with a higher priority is blocking this traffic.
- **Name**: The last options are to **Name** the rule and enter a **Description**. The **Description** is optional, but I encourage you to fill this in, as it will help you later to keep track and understand why something was created in the first place.

Example settings for advanced options in an NSG are shown in the following screenshot:

NSGs can be applied on two levels, to NICs and to subnets. If an NSG is applied to an NIC, the rules defined in that NSG will be enforced only for the virtual machine attached to that NIC. If an NSG is applied to a subnet, the rules will be enforced on all VMs on that subnet.

You can have an NSG applied both on a subnet and an NIC in some cases. Be careful with configuration in that case, as only traffic that is allowed on both levels will go through. If we have traffic over port 80 allowed on the subnet level but blocked on the NIC level, nothing will pass over port 80. Same goes the other way around, if allowed on the NIC but blocked on the subnet, nothing will pass. If you want to block something on the VM that has NSG applied on both the subnet and NIC levels, it's enough to block traffic over the named port on one of the NSGs.

Using NSGs in combination with ASGs is the best possible way to protect and secure your resources.

Let's create a scenario where we have three groups of servers: web, application, and database.

We need web servers to have a connection to application servers and application servers to have a connection to the database server. The only connection allowed over the internet would be to web servers and we don't want a connection over internet to database servers under any circumstances. The first step would be to create three Azure security groups, one ASG for each server role. The next step would be to configure NSG rules with the use of ASGs.

Connection over the internet would be allowed only to servers that are in the web ASG. Connection to application servers would be allowed only in the case that traffic is coming from servers placed in the web ASG. This would be achieved by setting a rule that would allow traffic to the application ASG from the web ASG, blocking everything else. Finally, we create a rule that allows traffic to database servers (the database ASG) only in cases when the traffic is coming from the application ASG.

This approach makes administration and maintenance easier and more consistent. If you are adding a server to any of the three pools, you need to set proper rules and all apply the settings needed. It's easy to make a misstep that would result in that server not having all the needed connections or, in the worst case, being a security issue. When using an NSG and ASG to keep track of all the rules, all we need to do is add a new server to the proper ASG and all the rules and settings will automatically apply.

Public IP address

Public IP address settings are available through NSG settings or by selecting **Public IP address** from the resources in the **Resource group** blade.

Settings for public IP addresses are similar to private IP addresses. By default, they are **Dynamic**, so the IP can change in the case of a restart or shutdown, but we can change this setting to **Static**. **Static** will keep the reservation of our IP but there is a difference between public and private IP addresses in this case. Private IP reservation is free of charge as this is an internal IP, so you can choose the range and even set an IP address from that range to be reserved for a specific VM. Public IP addresses are assigned and there isn't the option to choose which IP address you want. The other difference is that public IP address reservation is not free; the first five public IP address reservations are free per subscription, but every reservation over that number is charged. The price of a reservation over the initial five public IP addresses is not much (around $3 per month), but it's good to know what you're paying for.

A public IP address can be removed from your NIC if you want to restrict access (private IP addresses can't be removed). If you choose to use a public IP address, you'll probably need it either to connect to your VM remotely or to use it for applications. If you don't want to create a reservation, there is another option, to use a DNS name label. This option will assign a DNS name to your NIC and you can use it to access your VM. Any change of public IP address, which may happen as result of a restart or shutdown of your VM, will be handled by Azure DNS. Options for public IP address configuration are shown in the following screenshot:

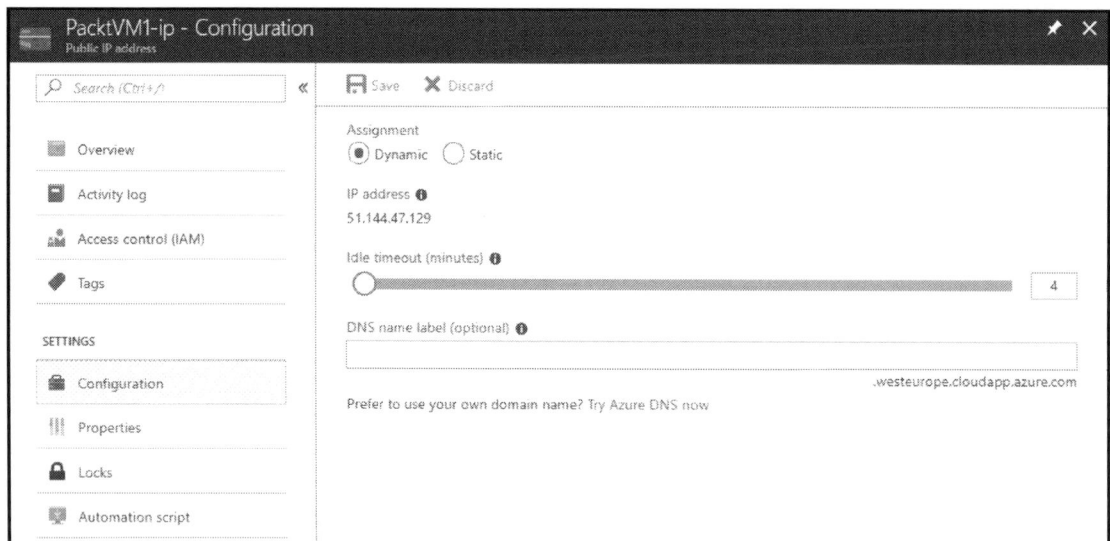

Other Azure network services

The Azure services that we have covered so far are just part of the Azure networking stack. The Azure networking stack doesn't stop here and there are many other Azure services that are network-related, such as traffic manager, load balancers, or virtual gateways. Some of them will be covered in chapters to come.

For example, we'll discuss load balancers with virtual machine high availability. A similar case will be with traffic manager when we discuss high availability for PaaS. Virtual gateways will be our topic in the chapter about hybrid cloud with Microsoft Azure.

Hybrid scenarios and security can be managed with a virtual appliance. Virtual appliances are Azure virtual machines with third-party firewall software. Most leading industry firewalls are supported and available (such as Barracuda, CheckPoint, Cisco, and PaloAlto). Virtual machine images for virtual appliances are available through Azure marketplace, and you can easily configure and set up a virtual appliance and use it to manage and secure your Azure network.

However, Microsoft Azure is evolving daily and more services are becoming available. It would be impossible to cover all services and features. Each chapter in this book is potentially a standalone book.

ARM templates

We already talked about ARM templates and how they can help us automate things. For this chapter, I created a virtual network and joined one virtual machine to that network.

If you move to automation, you can find an ARM template in JSON format that you can use to redeploy my resources. The ARM template will contain all the resources and all the settings: a virtual network and parameters, a virtual machine with information about the image and size, NSG rules, and so on. It will contain information on all dependencies and information on what needs to be created first. For example, in order to create a VM, a subnet needs to be created in order to join the VM to that subnet, and a subnet can't be created until a VNet is created.

Note that some `parameters`, such as passwords, are not provided as a password isn't allowed to be shown in clear text, but only as a secure string, so you need to provide these `parameters` manually:

```
{
  "$schema":
"https://schema.management.azure.com/schemas/2015-01-01/deploymentTemplate.
json#",
  "contentVersion": "1.0.0.0",
  "parameters": {
  "virtualMachines_PacktVM1_name": {
  "defaultValue": "PacktVM1",
  "type": "String"
  },
  "virtualNetworks_PacktVNet_name": {
  "defaultValue": "PacktVNet",
  "type": "String"
  },
  "networkInterfaces_packtvm1240_name": {
  "defaultValue": "packtvm1240",
  "type": "String"
  },
  "publicIPAddresses_PacktVM1_ip_name": {
  "defaultValue": "PacktVM1-ip",
  "type": "String"
  },
  "networkSecurityGroups_PacktVM1_nsg_name": {
  "defaultValue": "PacktVM1-nsg",
  "type": "String"
  },
  "subnets_DMZ_name": {
  "defaultValue": "DMZ",
  "type": "String"
  },
  "subnets_default_name": {
  "defaultValue": "default",
  "type": "String"
  },
  "securityRules_default_allow_rdp_name": {
  "defaultValue": "default-allow-rdp",
  "type": "String"
  },
  "adminUsername": {
  "type": "string",
  "metadata": {
  "description": "Default Admin username"
  }
  },
```

```
"adminPassword": {
"type": "securestring",
"metadata": {
"description": "Default Admin password"
}
}
},
"variables": {},
"resources": [
{
"type": "Microsoft.Compute/virtualMachines",
"name": "[parameters('virtualMachines_PacktVM1_name')]",
"apiVersion": "2017-12-01",
"location": "westeurope",
"scale": null,
"properties": {
"hardwareProfile": {
"vmSize": "Standard_B1s"
},
"storageProfile": {
"imageReference": {
"publisher": "MicrosoftWindowsServer",
"offer": "WindowsServer",
"sku": "2016-Datacenter",
"version": "latest"
},
"osDisk": {
"osType": "Windows",
"name":
"[concat(parameters('virtualMachines_PacktVM1_name'),'_OsDisk_1_b6ae3bba44e
f491f8c2acd7bfb5aa975')]",
"createOption": "FromImage",
"caching": "ReadWrite",
"managedDisk": {
"storageAccountType": "Standard_LRS"
},
"diskSizeGB": 127
},
"dataDisks": []
},
"osProfile": {
"computerName": "[parameters('virtualMachines_PacktVM1_name')]",
"adminUsername": "[parameters('adminUsername')]",
"adminPassword": "[parameters('adminPassword')]",
"windowsConfiguration": {
"provisionVMAgent": true,
"enableAutomaticUpdates": true
},
```

```
"secrets": []
},
"networkProfile": {
"networkInterfaces": [
{
"id": "[resourceId('Microsoft.Network/networkInterfaces',
parameters('networkInterfaces_packtvm1240_name'))]"
}
]
},
"diagnosticsProfile": {
"bootDiagnostics": {
"enabled": true,
"storageUri": "https://nagiosdiag316.blob.core.windows.net/"
}
}
},
"dependsOn": [
"[resourceId('Microsoft.Network/networkInterfaces',
parameters('networkInterfaces_packtvm1240_name'))]"
]
},
{
"type": "Microsoft.Network/networkInterfaces",
"name": "[parameters('networkInterfaces_packtvm1240_name')]",
"apiVersion": "2018-02-01",
"location": "westeurope",
"scale": null,
"properties": {
"provisioningState": "Succeeded",
"resourceGuid": "2d51720b-041b-4248-ab04-8dd9fd3fa7d9",
"ipConfigurations": [
{
"name": "ipconfig1",
"etag": "W/\"b681e202-2d98-4d28-a30d-aaf93b9f1243\"",
"properties": {
"provisioningState": "Succeeded",
"privateIPAddress": "10.1.1.4",
"privateIPAllocationMethod": "Static",
"publicIPAddress": {
"id": "[resourceId('Microsoft.Network/publicIPAddresses',
parameters('publicIPAddresses_PacktVM1_ip_name'))]"
},
"subnet": {
"id": "[resourceId('Microsoft.Network/virtualNetworks/subnets',
parameters('virtualNetworks_PacktVNet_name'),
parameters('subnets_DMZ_name'))]"
},
```

```
"primary": true,
"privateIPAddressVersion": "IPv4"
}
}
],
"dnsSettings": {
"dnsServers": [],
"appliedDnsServers": [],
"internalDomainNameSuffix":
"gbyhmwrx0mmutogdwlxg2i521c.ax.internal.cloudapp.net"
},
"macAddress": "00-0D-3A-2E-EA-03",
"enableAcceleratedNetworking": false,
"enableIPForwarding": false,
"networkSecurityGroup": {
"id": "[resourceId('Microsoft.Network/networkSecurityGroups',
parameters('networkSecurityGroups_PacktVM1_nsg_name'))]"
},
"primary": true
},
"dependsOn": [
"[resourceId('Microsoft.Network/publicIPAddresses',
parameters('publicIPAddresses_PacktVM1_ip_name'))]",
"[resourceId('Microsoft.Network/virtualNetworks/subnets',
parameters('virtualNetworks_PacktVNet_name'),
parameters('subnets_DMZ_name'))]",
"[resourceId('Microsoft.Network/networkSecurityGroups',
parameters('networkSecurityGroups_PacktVM1_nsg_name'))]"
]
},
{
"type": "Microsoft.Network/networkSecurityGroups",
"name": "[parameters('networkSecurityGroups_PacktVM1_nsg_name')]",
"apiVersion": "2018-02-01",
"location": "westeurope",
"scale": null,
"properties": {
"provisioningState": "Succeeded",
"resourceGuid": "11b65174-a94e-44e1-947c-dd140c45a6c8",
"securityRules": [
{
"name": "default-allow-rdp",
"etag": "W/\"9b7736d4-5a76-4804-a63f-6cd1875f1d5c\"",
"properties": {
"provisioningState": "Succeeded",
"protocol": "TCP",
"sourcePortRange": "*",
"destinationPortRange": "3389",
```

```
"sourceAddressPrefix": "*",
"destinationAddressPrefix": "*",
"access": "Allow",
"priority": 1000,
"direction": "Inbound",
"sourcePortRanges": [],
"destinationPortRanges": [],
"sourceAddressPrefixes": [],
"destinationAddressPrefixes": []
}
}
],
"defaultSecurityRules": [
{
"name": "AllowVnetInBound",
"etag": "W/\"9b7736d4-5a76-4804-a63f-6cd1875f1d5c\"",
"properties": {
"provisioningState": "Succeeded",
"description": "Allow inbound traffic from all VMs in VNET",
"protocol": "*",
"sourcePortRange": "*",
"destinationPortRange": "*",
"sourceAddressPrefix": "VirtualNetwork",
"destinationAddressPrefix": "VirtualNetwork",
"access": "Allow",
"priority": 65000,
"direction": "Inbound",
"sourcePortRanges": [],
"destinationPortRanges": [],
"sourceAddressPrefixes": [],
"destinationAddressPrefixes": []
}
},
{
"name": "AllowAzureLoadBalancerInBound",
"etag": "W/\"9b7736d4-5a76-4804-a63f-6cd1875f1d5c\"",
"properties": {
"provisioningState": "Succeeded",
"description": "Allow inbound traffic from azure load balancer",
"protocol": "*",
"sourcePortRange": "*",
"destinationPortRange": "*",
"sourceAddressPrefix": "AzureLoadBalancer",
"destinationAddressPrefix": "*",
"access": "Allow",
"priority": 65001,
"direction": "Inbound",
"sourcePortRanges": [],
```

```
"destinationPortRanges": [],
"sourceAddressPrefixes": [],
"destinationAddressPrefixes": []
}
},
{
"name": "DenyAllInBound",
"etag": "W/\"9b7736d4-5a76-4804-a63f-6cd1875f1d5c\"",
"properties": {
"provisioningState": "Succeeded",
"description": "Deny all inbound traffic",
"protocol": "*",
"sourcePortRange": "*",
"destinationPortRange": "*",
"sourceAddressPrefix": "*",
"destinationAddressPrefix": "*",
"access": "Deny",
"priority": 65500,
"direction": "Inbound",
"sourcePortRanges": [],
"destinationPortRanges": [],
"sourceAddressPrefixes": [],
"destinationAddressPrefixes": []
}
},
{
"name": "AllowVnetOutBound",
"etag": "W/\"9b7736d4-5a76-4804-a63f-6cd1875f1d5c\"",
"properties": {
"provisioningState": "Succeeded",
"description": "Allow outbound traffic from all VMs to all VMs in VNET",
"protocol": "*",
"sourcePortRange": "*",
"destinationPortRange": "*",
"sourceAddressPrefix": "VirtualNetwork",
"destinationAddressPrefix": "VirtualNetwork",
"access": "Allow",
"priority": 65000,
"direction": "Outbound",
"sourcePortRanges": [],
"destinationPortRanges": [],
"sourceAddressPrefixes": [],
"destinationAddressPrefixes": []
}
},
{
"name": "AllowInternetOutBound",
"etag": "W/\"9b7736d4-5a76-4804-a63f-6cd1875f1d5c\"",
```

```json
"properties": {
"provisioningState": "Succeeded",
"description": "Allow outbound traffic from all VMs to Internet",
"protocol": "*",
"sourcePortRange": "*",
"destinationPortRange": "*",
"sourceAddressPrefix": "*",
"destinationAddressPrefix": "Internet",
"access": "Allow",
"priority": 65001,
"direction": "Outbound",
"sourcePortRanges": [],
"destinationPortRanges": [],
"sourceAddressPrefixes": [],
"destinationAddressPrefixes": []
}
},
{
"name": "DenyAllOutBound",
"etag": "W/\"9b7736d4-5a76-4804-a63f-6cd1875f1d5c\"",
"properties": {
"provisioningState": "Succeeded",
"description": "Deny all outbound traffic",
"protocol": "*",
"sourcePortRange": "*",
"destinationPortRange": "*",
"sourceAddressPrefix": "*",
"destinationAddressPrefix": "*",
"access": "Deny",
"priority": 65500,
"direction": "Outbound",
"sourcePortRanges": [],
"destinationPortRanges": [],
"sourceAddressPrefixes": [],
"destinationAddressPrefixes": []
}
}
]
},
"dependsOn": []
},
{
"type": "Microsoft.Network/publicIPAddresses",
"sku": {
"name": "Basic",
"tier": "Regional"
},
"name": "[parameters('publicIPAddresses_PacktVM1_ip_name')]",
```

```
"apiVersion": "2018-02-01",
"location": "westeurope",
"scale": null,
"properties": {
"provisioningState": "Succeeded",
"resourceGuid": "972b3091-fe6e-49cc-bd06-22d260608254",
"ipAddress": "40.74.60.181",
"publicIPAddressVersion": "IPv4",
"publicIPAllocationMethod": "Dynamic",
"idleTimeoutInMinutes": 4,
"ipTags": []
},
"dependsOn": []
},
{
"type": "Microsoft.Network/virtualNetworks",
"name": "[parameters('virtualNetworks_PacktVNet_name')]",
"apiVersion": "2018-02-01",
"location": "westeurope",
"scale": null,
"properties": {
"provisioningState": "Succeeded",
"resourceGuid": "5a767030-d337-4919-b8c3-b2ee6e23fcda",
"addressSpace": {
"addressPrefixes": [
"10.1.0.0/16",
"10.2.0.0/16"
]
},
"subnets": [
{
"name": "default",
"etag": "W/\"98f91850-e7b2-40b6-8043-1caa5bf4865a\"",
"properties": {
"provisioningState": "Succeeded",
"addressPrefix": "10.1.0.0/24",
"serviceEndpoints": []
}
},
{
"name": "DMZ",
"etag": "W/\"98f91850-e7b2-40b6-8043-1caa5bf4865a\"",
"properties": {
"provisioningState": "Succeeded",
"addressPrefix": "10.1.1.0/24",
"serviceEndpoints": []
}
}
```

```
],
"virtualNetworkPeerings": [],
"enableDdosProtection": false,
"enableVmProtection": false
},
"dependsOn": []
},
{
"type": "Microsoft.Network/networkSecurityGroups/securityRules",
"name": "[concat(parameters('networkSecurityGroups_PacktVM1_nsg_name'),
'/', parameters('securityRules_default_allow_rdp_name'))]",
"apiVersion": "2018-02-01",
"scale": null,
"properties": {
"provisioningState": "Succeeded",
"protocol": "TCP",
"sourcePortRange": "*",
"destinationPortRange": "3389",
"sourceAddressPrefix": "*",
"destinationAddressPrefix": "*",
"access": "Allow",
"priority": 1000,
"direction": "Inbound",
"sourcePortRanges": [],
"destinationPortRanges": [],
"sourceAddressPrefixes": [],
"destinationAddressPrefixes": []
},
"dependsOn": [
"[resourceId('Microsoft.Network/networkSecurityGroups',
parameters('networkSecurityGroups_PacktVM1_nsg_name'))]"
]
},
{
"type": "Microsoft.Network/virtualNetworks/subnets",
"name": "[concat(parameters('virtualNetworks_PacktVNet_name'), '/',
parameters('subnets_default_name'))]",
"apiVersion": "2018-02-01",
"scale": null,
"properties": {
"provisioningState": "Succeeded",
"addressPrefix": "10.1.0.0/24",
"serviceEndpoints": []
},
"dependsOn": [
"[resourceId('Microsoft.Network/virtualNetworks',
parameters('virtualNetworks_PacktVNet_name'))]"
]
```

```
    },
    {
     "type": "Microsoft.Network/virtualNetworks/subnets",
     "name": "[concat(parameters('virtualNetworks_PacktVNet_name'), '/',
parameters('subnets_DMZ_name'))]",
     "apiVersion": "2018-02-01",
     "scale": null,
     "properties": {
     "provisioningState": "Succeeded",
     "addressPrefix": "10.1.1.0/24",
     "serviceEndpoints": []
     },
    "dependsOn": [
    "[resourceId('Microsoft.Network/virtualNetworks',
parameters('virtualNetworks_PacktVNet_name'))]"
    ]
    }
   ]
   }
```

This can be particularly helpful once we have multiple resources deployed in our resource group. Using these templates, we can provision identical environments automatically, quickly, and with precision. Redeploying a resource group to recreate an environment by hand can lead to inconsistencies and missing steps. Using ARM templates produces the same result each and every time.

Summary

We covered the basic features of Azure networking with virtual networks, IP address types, and NSGs. This basic knowledge of Azure networking will be the foundation for chapters to come.

It's also very important to understand ARM templates, as they will be very helpful once our infrastructure becomes more complex.

From here, we'll advance to Azure IaaS, which will use Azure networking as the backbone and the service that holds everything together. We'll see how to create advanced VM scenarios that will use Azure networking, private for communication between VMs and public for external access. We'll explain in more detail options for creating new Azure virtual machines, availability groups, and high-availability for IaaS in Azure.

Questions

1. Which services are depended on the Azure network in Microsoft Azure?
    1. IaaS
    2. PaaS
    3. Both

2. What defines the IP address range in Azure?
    1. Subnet mask
    2. CIDR
    3. RIP

3. Service endpoints are used to connect which services to your virtual network?
    1. Virtual machines
    2. PaaS
    3. SaaS

4. The default DNS service in Microsoft Azure is...?
    1. Azure DNS
    2. Public DNS
    3. Custom DNS

5. When can service endpoints be added?
    1. When creating a virtual network
    2. After a virtual network is created
    3. At any time

6. Private IP addresses in Azure can be...?
    1. Dynamic
    2. Static
    3. Both

7. Public IP addresses in Azure can be...?
    1. Dynamic
    2. Static
    3. Both

8. NSGs are...?
    1. Security rules that define traffic flow
    2. Rules on IP address reservations
    3. Both

9. What does an NSG define?
   1. Outbound traffic rules
   2. Inbound traffic rules
   3. Both

10. To what can an NSG not be assigned to?
    1. Virtual network
    2. NIC
    3. Subnet

Infrastructure as a Service - the First Layer of Cloud Computing

3

The next step in our cloud journey is to leverage the Azure Virtual Machines offering as part of Azure IaaS. This is the first logical step when moving our workloads to the cloud, as managing Azure Virtual Machines is not much different from managing local VMs. We no longer have access to the virtualization host and hardware, but administrating and managing Azure VMs is no different from administrating and managing local servers or VMs.

We'll show you how to achieve high availability of your services and how to scale out workloads as one of the main benefits that Microsoft Azure offers.

Areas that we'll cover in this chapter are:

- Creating Azure Virtual Machines
- Managing Azure Virtual Machines
- Creating Azure Load Balancers
- Configuring Azure Load Balancers
- Creating Azure Virtual Machines scale sets

Technical requirements

For this chapter, you'll need:

- An Azure subscription

Deploying Azure Virtual Machines

Deployment of any Azure resource can be done in several ways and it's no different with Azure Virtual Machines. We can use the Azure portal, ARM templates, Azure PowerShell, or Azure CLI. We will discuss all these methods but for the time being we'll stick to the Azure portal and occasionally use ARM templates. This is to gain better knowledge of Azure services and what is created in each deployment. Other tools can help us in the long run, especially when we talk redeployment and automation, but we'll get to that part later.

We already did a quick create of an Azure VM, but this time we'll look more closely for options that are available as last time we only considered the Azure networking part as the important one.

Creating a new Azure Virtual Machine

To create a new Azure VM, we need to select **New resource** and select **New Virtual Machine**.

The first step is to select the operating system for our VM. There are hundreds of images available to select from both Windows and Linux. It's important to mention that more and more Linux VMs are deployed to Azure daily. Information from the end of 2017 tells us that more than 40% of all Azure Virtual Machines are running Linux, and that percentage is probably up since then.

Supported versions of Windows Server in Azure are:

- Windows Server 2008 R2 SP1
- Windows Server 2012
- Windows Server 2012 R2
- Windows Server 2016

For Linux, there are too many versions to name but supported distributions are:

- Ubuntu
- CentOS
- RHEL
- Kali
- Oracle

All images can be selected as a minimum installation or preconfigured with additional software installed. For example, we can select Windows Server 2016 with all settings at default or select an image that has SQL Server installed and ready to use. We can choose the same for Linux, choose minimum installation, or choose an already configured image with software such as Chef, Puppet, Jenkins, and so on.

There is also an option to choose your custom image with the configuration and software of your choosing. This can be an image of your on-premises VM that is uploaded to Azure or an image created from another Azure VM.

After we choose the OS, we start a new blade that will take us through three stages.

Basic Azure Virtual Machine information

The first step is to provide basic information for our VM. A name needs to be provided for any type of resource in Azure. It's useful to give names based on procedures and roles as this will help in later management. It's easier when the name of your VM gives you a hint about what its purpose is. As I intend to use this one as a web server, I'll name it `WebSrv1`.

VM disk type lets us choose between two values—**HDD** and **SSD**. This can be critical for our VM as the disk type can significantly impact performance. As this impacts the price of the VM as well, we need to find a balance and choose based on expected workloads. Choosing **HDD** may be good enough if we create a web server but if you're going to deploy a database server, **SSD** is the recommended option.

The **Username** option doesn't allow us to use most common server usernames such as `Admin`, `Administrator`, `SysAdmin`, and similar. This is in order to protect your cloud resources. As most Azure VMs with a public IP address can be accessed through RDP, it's critical to limit that access as much as possible. I have multiple VMs that are attacked daily and the most common attempts are made using these exact usernames. We can apply additional security to VMs and usernames, but we'll discuss that in later chapters.

Similar to any other resource, we need to provide information for the **Subscription**, the **Resource group**, and **Location** where the VM will be deployed. An example of basic information can be seen in the screenshot shown here:

Azure Virtual Machine sizes

The second step in the Azure Virtual Machine creation blade is to choose the size of your VM. The size of the VM will determine three things—the number of CPUs, the amount of memory, and the type of OS disk. As you choose the type of disk in step one as well, this will narrow down the options that are available. VM sizes have three different pricing tiers:

- Basic
- Standard
- Low priority

Basic-tier VMs are intended for `dev/test` environments and, even though they have a similar performance to VMs on the standard tier, there are a few limitations. They have lower IOPS than standard-tier VMs and don't support load balancing or auto-scaling.

Standard-tier VMs are intended to be used in a production environment and have better CPUs and IOPS performance.

Low-priority VMs are allocated based on free and unused resources in Azure Datacenter. They come with a lower price but can be unavailable at any time, as Microsoft Azure may claim these resources to satisfy requests with a higher priority. They are intended to be used for batch processing and random jobs.

But the pricing tier isn't the only thing to determine the price of your VM. Each tier has different sizes that provide a certain amount of CPU and memory; a higher amount equals a higher price.

The standard tier has additional categories based on the VM purpose:

- General-purpose
- Compute-optimized
- Memory-optimized
- Storage-optimized
- GPU
- High-performance compute

Most of these are self-explanatory as general-purpose has a balanced CPU-to-memory ratio, compute-optimized has more CPU, memory-optimized has more RAM, and storage-optimized has the best IOPS. GPUs are specialized VMs for heavy graphic rendering and video editing. High-performance VMs have at least eight vCPUs and use DDR4 RAM.

The size of the VM also determines the number of NICs that can be attached to your VM.

This can be from one to eight depending on purpose and size.

Options for selecting the VM size can be seen in the following screenshot:

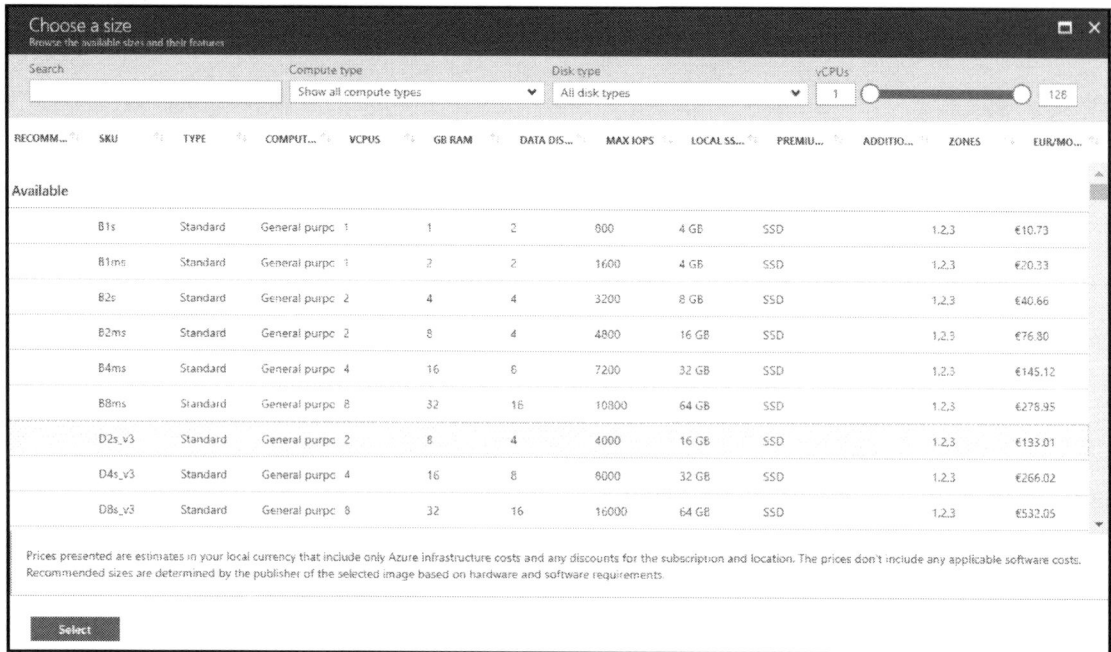

Advanced VM options

The third blade gives us the option to configure a lot of additional settings. In the previous chapter, we focused only on the networking part, but this time we'll explore these options more closely.

The high availability section gives us two options—**Availability zone** and **Availability set**.

The **Availability zone** determines the zones inside the Azure Datacenter. These zones have an independent power source, networking, and cooling, and protect your VM against failures inside the Datacenter. If you have a critical service that will run on multiple VMs, you want to place these VMs in different availability zones so, if there is a failure on the Datacenter level, there is less chance that all your VMs will be impacted.

Availability set does similar things on a host level, ensuring that your VMs are placed across multiple physical servers, compute racks, storage units, and network switches. If hardware failure occurs, there is less chance that all your VMs will be impacted.

Note that these availability options can't be changed later. You need to define the **Availability zone** and **Availability set** during the creation process. This is important to remember if you plan to design highly available solutions and services.

I'll place this VM in an **Availability set** named **(new) WebSet** as I intend to use it later.

Storage options allow us to choose between **Disk type** and **Use managed disks**. The **Disk type** option is the same as we had before; we can choose between **HDD** and **SSD**. Depending on the size of VM chosen, all types of disk may not be available to choose here. If you want to choose a different option that is not available, you need to go back and choose a different size of VM.

Use managed disks are there to make our lives a little easier. This option was available from February 2017 and, prior to this, we need to manage storage on our own. Creating a disk actually creates a storage account and we needed to manage that storage. With a managed disk, we don't have to be concerned with this and it's managed automatically. Storage is still created but, if we choose **Use managed disks**, everything is handled in the background and no user action is required. This can be especially useful when scaling our VM (or VM Scale Sets). Managed disks also introduced a few very useful features such as snapshots and backups. I strongly recommend using a managed disk as this helps you get better performance with less management.

Setting for high availability and disks can be seen in the screenshot shown here:

Networking options were covered in the previous chapter but let's quickly review what our options are here. We can select our VNet, subnet on that VNet, and public IP address for our VM. The last networking option is to select the **network security group** (**NSG**) for our VM. In the following screenshot, you can see that I selected **PacktVNet** and the **DMZ (10.1.1.0/24)** subnet. A new public IP address is created for my new VM as I intend to use it as a web server. As I have the NSG rule applied on the DMZ subnet, I don't want to separate the NSG on the VM level. This will help me simplify management and keep standardized rules across all my VMs, so I'll leave the NSG field blank as shown here:

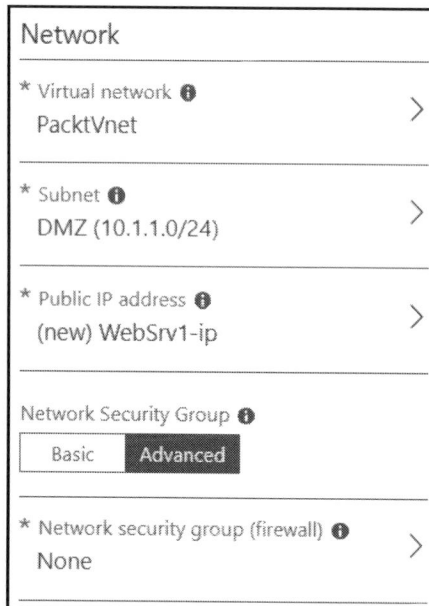

```
Network

  * Virtual network ❶                          >
    PacktVnet

  * Subnet ❶                                    >
    DMZ (10.1.1.0/24)

  * Public IP address ❶                         >
    (new) WebSrv1-ip

  Network Security Group ❶
  ┌─────────┬─────────────┐
  │  Basic  │  Advanced   │
  └─────────┴─────────────┘

  * Network security group (firewall) ❶         >
    None
```

Extensions gives us the option to add additional features to our VM. You can choose from set predefined software or execute a custom script that will install additional software or features.

Auto-shutdown can help you save on computing hours if you don't need the VM to run 24/7. For example, if this is a dev environment and no one is using it after work hours, you can set **Auto-shutdown** to shut down your VM every day at 5 p.m. so you don't pay for it overnight. Of course, if this web or database server is in production, this isn't an option you really want to use.

Monitoring can be **Enabled** for boot diagnostics and guest OS monitoring. This is beside the basic monitoring options that are available by default. Both of these options will require a storage account where logs will be stored. Avoid using storage that is used for a VM disk as this can cause performance issues. If your VM is having performance issues on a disk level, this will generate more logs, and these logs will increase the load on storage on top of that. This will cause more disk issues and you will be in an infinite loop where you won't be able to see if the issue is caused by disk or by logs.

The last options are **Managed service identity** and **Backup**. **Managed service identity** allows you to use your Azure Active Directory with your VM, and **Backup** will create an additional backup service (Azure Backup). Both of these services will be covered in more depth later.

Options for **Extensions**, **Auto-shutdown**, **Monitoring**, **Managed service identity**, and **Backup** can be seen in the following screenshot:

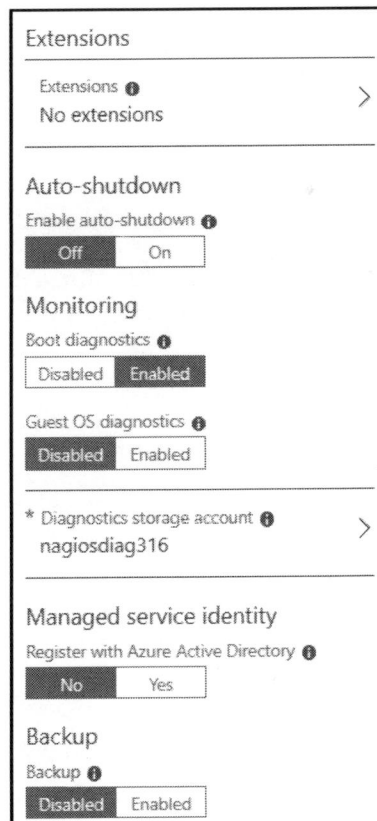

Finally, we can start deployment and after a few minutes we can start using our VM. As I mentioned before, the time taken to create a new VM can depend on the size of the VM and the availability of resources in the Azure Datacenter.

Managing Azure Virtual Machines

After deployment is completed, we can see four different resources have been created—`Virtual machine`, `Disk`, `Network interface` and `Public IP address`. A `Public IP address` is optional and doesn't need to be created if you intend to use and manage the VM only using private IP addresses with the use of VPN. If a managed disk wasn't chosen, there would be a storage account where the disk would be placed here as well, as shown:

NAME	TYPE	LOCATION	
WebSrv1	Virtual machine	West Europe	...
WebSrv1_OsDisk_1_d731d762891146c6bd4983d5c4a0ba69	Disk	West Europe	...
websrv1700	Network interface	West Europe	...
WebSrv1-ip	Public IP address	West Europe	...

Every one of these resources has different options for management. We have already seen options for IP addresses and NICs; we'll explore disk and storage in later chapters. For now, let us focus on the VM and what options are available to us for administration and management.

VM settings

Under the **Virtual Machine** blade, we have various options such as **SETTINGS, OPERATIONS, MONITORING,** and **SUPPORT**. Under **SETTINGS**, we have multiple choices as well: **Networking, Disks, Size, Security, Extensions, Availability set** and **Configuration. Properties, Locks** and **Automation script** are available as for all other Azure resources as well. Note that we have **Continuous delivery (Preview)** here as well. Preview features are still in development and they aren't intended for production purposes. It's fine to test but avoid depending on these features until they are officially released. In this instance, **Continuous delivery (Preview)** allows us to connect to VSTS projects and make easier CI/CD.

Some options here are similar to options in the VM creation process. **Size** will allow us to open the blade to choose a different size for our VM at any time. Note that to complete this process, a restart of the VM is required. **Extensions** can be used to add software or execute custom scripts, the same as before. **Availability set** is only for information purposes as this setting needs to be defined during VM creation. **Security** and **Configuration** will be our focus in chapters to come and we'll leave these settings as defaults for now.

The **Networking** option gives us an overview of all network information regarding our VM. We can see NIC information, what addresses are associated with our VM, the network security group associated with the VM and all NSG rules. We can attach additional NICs here and add additional NSG rules. Note that in the following screenshot, the NSG is applied on the subnet level. If changes are made to the NSG, these will be applied to all VMs on this subnet so you need to be careful. For example, if this subnet had multiple VMs and we wanted to allow RDP access to a single one, creating this rule would result in all VMs being accessible over RDP:

Network Interface: websrv1700   Effective security rules   Topology
Virtual network/subnet: PacktVnet/DMZ   Public IP: **13.80.42.85**   Private IP: **10.1.1.4**   Accelerated networking: **Disabled**

APPLICATION SECURITY GROUPS ⓘ

✎ Configure the application security groups

INBOUND PORT RULES ⓘ

Network security group DMZ (attached to subnet: DMZ)
Impacts 1 subnets, 0 network interfaces

Add inbound port rule

PRIORITY	NAME	PORT	PROTOCOL	SOURCE	DESTINATION	ACTION	
100	⚠ Port_3389	3389	Any	Any	Any	⊘ Allow	...
110	Port_80	80	Any	Any	Any	⊘ Allow	...
120	Port_443	443	Any	Any	Any	⊘ Allow	...
65000	AllowVnetInBound	Any	Any	VirtualNetwork	VirtualNetwork	⊘ Allow	...
65001	AllowAzureLoadBalancerInBound	Any	Any	AzureLoadBalancer	Any	⊘ Allow	...
65500	DenyAllInBound	Any	Any	Any	Any	⊘ Deny	...

OUTBOUND PORT RULES ⓘ

Network security group DMZ (attached to subnet: DMZ)
Impacts 1 subnets, 0 network interfaces

Add outbound port rule

Under the disk blade, we can see all disks associated with our VM. The OS disk can't be changed, data disks can be added or removed. An example of the disk blade can be seen in the following screenshot:

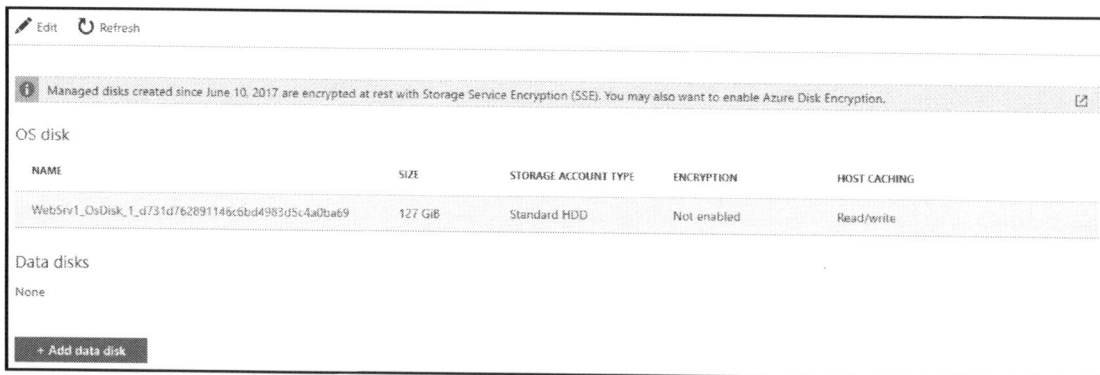

Azure Virtual Machine operation and monitoring

OPERATIONS and **MONITORING** give us more administration and managing options for our Azure Virtual Machines. In **OPERATIONS**, we have **Auto-shutdown, Backup, Disaster recovery, Update management, Inventory, Change tracking,** and the **Run command**. We will explain **Auto-shutdown** and the **Run command** now but the rest of these features require additional services that we'll cover later.

We have a similar situation with **MONITORING** , we'll cover **Metrics** and **Alerts (classic)** now and the rest of the services will be explained in the chapters to come.

The **Auto-shutdown** option enables you to schedule the shutdown of your VM in Azure. As I mentioned before, this option allow us to save money if we don't need the VM to run all the time. The feature is intended to be used in dev/test environments and isn't for production.

However, I've seen people using it for applications that are needed only during working hours. In that case, **Auto-shutdown** is used to turn the VM off at specific times and use Azure Automation for starting it before work hours begin. Other than for scheduled time, we have options to send a notification when the VM is going to be turned off. This allows us to notify people using the VM that shutdown will occur. We can use email or webhooks for these notifications. The following screenshot shows the `run` script option. We can use various prepared scripts such as `EnableAdminAcount`, `SetRDPPort`, `ResetAccountPaasword`, and so on. Or we can execute a custom script against our VM. Options for script execution can be seen in following screenshot:

NAME	DESCRIPTION
RunPowerShellScript	Executes a PowerShell script
EnableAdminAccount	Enable administrator account
EnableRemotePS	Enable remote PowerShell
IPConfig	List IP configuration
RDPSettings	Verify RDP Listener Settings
ResetAccountPassword	Reset built-in Administrator account password
ResetRDPCert	Restore RDP Authentication mode to defaults
SetRDPPort	Set Remote Desktop port

The running command can be done directly through the portal. This can be really useful when we can't access the VM any other way (for example, from a mobile device or machine that doesn't have PowerShell). An example is shown in the following screenshot where the script to enable `PSRemoting` is executed:

```
Output

Name                   : Allow WinRM HTTPS
DisplayName            : WinRM HTTPS
Description            :
DisplayGroup           :
Group                  :
Enabled                : True
Profile                : Any
Platform               : {}
Direction              : Inbound
Action                 : Allow
EdgeTraversalPolicy    : Block
LooseSourceMapping     : False
LocalOnlyMapping       : False
Owner                  :
PrimaryStatus          : OK
Status                 : The rule was parsed successfully from the store.
                         (65536)
EnforcementStatus      : NotApplicable
PolicyStoreSource      : PersistentStore
PolicyStoreSourceType  : Local

ResourceCreated
    Address = http://schemas.xmlsoap.org/ws/2004/08/addressing/role/anonymous
    ReferenceParameters
        ResourceURI = http://schemas.microsoft.com/wbem/wsman/1/config/listener
        SelectorSet
```

Here is also the script to enable `PSRemote` on the Azure Virtual Machine:

```
Enable-PSRemoting -Force
New-NetFirewallRule -Name "Allow WinRM HTTPS" -DisplayName "WinRM HTTPS" -
Enabled True -Profile Any -Action Allow -Direction Inbound -LocalPort 5986
-Protocol TCP
$thumbprint = (New-SelfSignedCertificate -DnsName $env:COMPUTERNAME -
CertStoreLocation Cert:\LocalMachine\My).Thumbprint
$command = "winrm create winrm/config/Listener?Address=*+Transport=HTTPS
@{Hostname=""$env:computername""; CertificateThumbprint=""$thumbprint""}"
cmd.exe /C $command
```

Monitoring your Azure resources is important on many levels. It gives you the ability to see your resource consumption and plan the pricing tier accordingly. If monitoring shows that your resources are under a certain percentage of workload, it's probably a good idea to lower the resource tier. If it's another way around and you have a high percentage all the time, it's probably a good idea to change to a higher tier. A lot of different metrics are available but not for CPU and memory monitoring, you need to enable guest-level monitoring. Metrics gives us the option to change different metrics over different time periods. An example is show in the screenshot here where you can see graphs on disk read and write operations over the last hour:

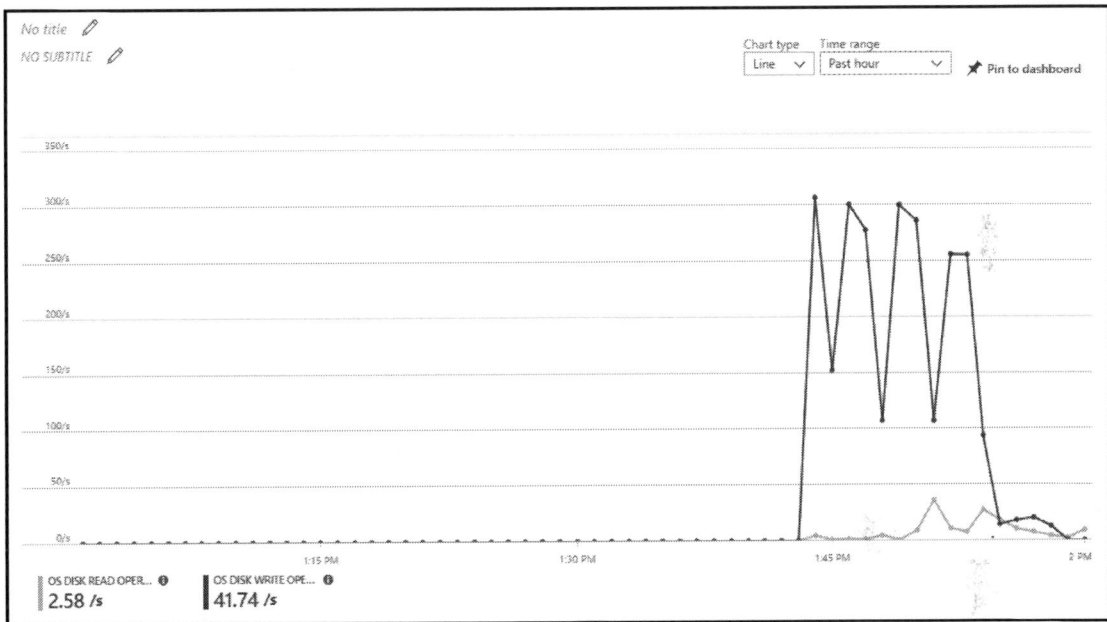

Alerts are an essential part of your Azure resource management and can be real lifesavers. In alerts, you can create custom rules that will notify you if a defined trigger is activated. For example, you can set up alerts that will notify you if the CPU reaches a threshold of 90% utilization over a period of more than 5 minutes. Similar to auto-shutdown, you can send notifications via email or webhooks.

This example is shown in the following screenshot:

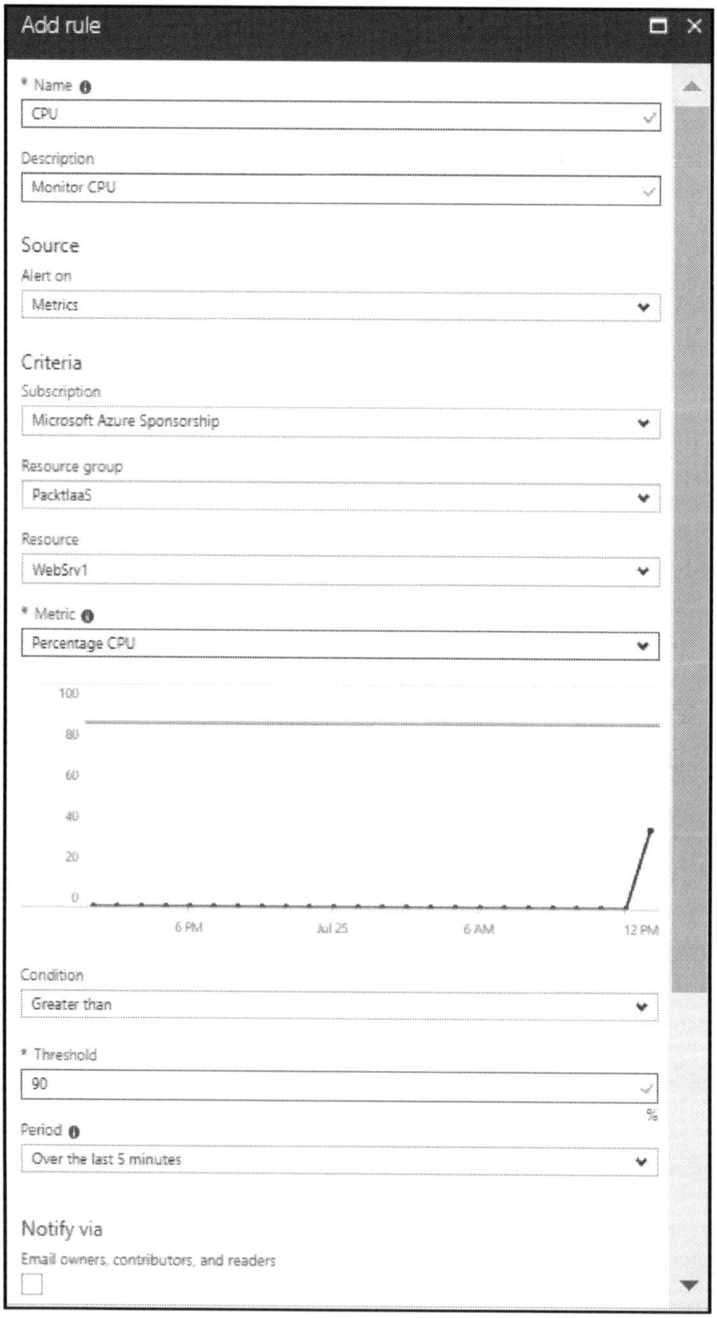

Beside sending a notification, alerts can be set to trigger a custom action with the use of runbooks or logic apps. Both are powerful tools to perform custom actions when needed. The logic app is easy to use with workflow diagrams that enable you to drag and drop actions that need to be taken, in order to perform some maintenance tasks or resolve issues. Runbooks require an Azure Automation account and can perform actions based on predefined plans or use custom scripts. Most administrators find runbooks more useful as they allow you to perform any type of action using PowerShell. In my opinion, both are very useful but administrators find runbooks more familiar as they can use PowerShell, which is the tool they used for on-premises administration:

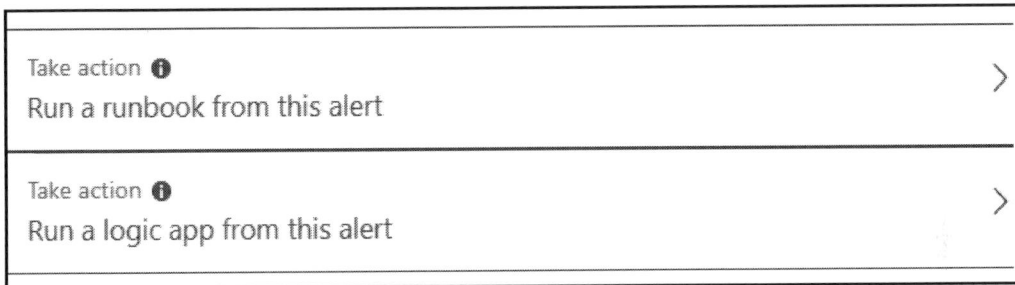

Take action **ⓘ**

Run a runbook from this alert 〉

Take action **ⓘ**

Run a logic app from this alert 〉

If we select to perform an action via runbooks, we can select either a user-defined or built-in action. With a user-defined action, you need to select an automation account and select a custom runbook in that account to be executed. This can be any type of script that will be executed on your Azure VM.

Built-in action offers you five options: **Restart VM**, **Stop VM**, **Scale Up VM**, **Scale Down VM**, and **Remove VM.** An example of a runbook configuration is shown here with **Built-in** runbooks listed:

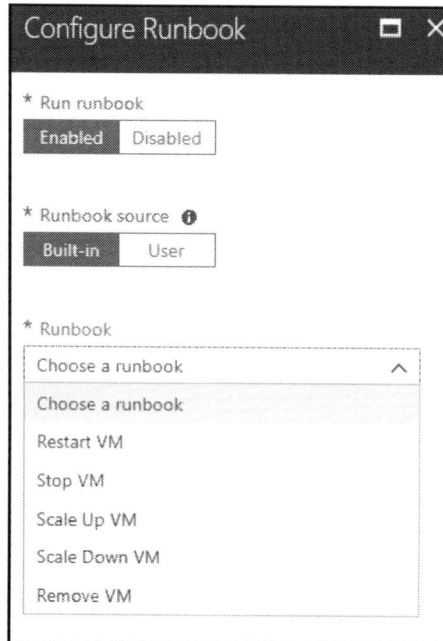

Most of these actions are self-explanatory, but note that you have **Scale Up VM** and **Scale Down VM**. This allows us to create a scaling up or scaling down of our resources based on demand. One of the cloud's benefits is to pay for what you use, when you use it. So, if our VM can handle workloads 90% of the time but we have peaks in workload only occasionally, we try to avoid paying more to satisfy only peaks. If we scale up permanently only to handle peak workloads, we pay more and now have a VM that isn't fully utilized 90% of the time, as a lower price VM could handle everything but peak periods. Setting up a **Scale Up VM** rule allows you to change your VM size to a higher tier in case 90% CPU is reached. This will enable your VM to handle workloads when the threshold is reached and increase the VM size on demand. To make the most out of what Microsoft Azure is offering, you need to create a similar rule in the other direction, to scale down once workload decreases. Having only a rule to scale up will increase the price of your VM and you will end up paying more. To prevent this, you can create a rule that when the CPU falls below 40%, a **Scale Down VM** action is performed and the VM is reverted to its original size. This way you will pay for more only when workload demands, and pay less for periods when workload isn't high.

The **SUPPORT + TROUBLESHOOTING** section give us a few additional options. **Resource health** and **New support request** are options present for all Azure resources. The first one gives you information if there is an issue with your VM on the Azure Datacenter level, and the second one takes you to the form to submit an Azure support ticket. **Resource health** can be useful to check when your resource isn't performing as usual. This can save you time troubleshooting and trying to figure out what went wrong when in fact there is a large issue at the Datacenter level you can't do anything about. Luckily, this isn't a common occurrence.

Boot diagnostics gives you the ability to see the current screen of your VM and serial log. It can be very helpful when the VM is unresponsive in order to check the current state.

With the **Reset password** option, you can reset the password for the VM but only if you know the correct username. Once you log in to the VM, you'll need to reset the password again as the password used here is only temporary. **Reset password** also has the option to reset the remote desktop service configuration.

Serial console (Preview) gives you access to Windows serial console through your browser. However, this feature is still in preview so you shouldn't rely on it too much.

Redeploy is a very interesting feature. If your VM is unresponsive and you can't connect, you can use this feature. Redeploying the VM will migrate your VM to a new host in the Azure Datacenter to try to fix your issue. Migration will cause the reboot of your VM, which is unresponsive to begin with, so this isn't really an issue and may resolve the problem you have.
Features and options listed here are management options specific to Azure Virtual Machines. Managing the VM continues with the use of standard administrator tools. We can connect to the VM via RDP and perform any kind of task we want. We can install roles and features to our VM, add any kind of third-party software or our custom software. Other administration tools such as **Remote Server Administration Tools (RSAT)** or PowerShell are also options.

Azure Load Balancers

Deploying Azure Virtual Machines is the first step but what about business critical services and applications. For these, we'll probably want to design highly available solutions that will have the best possible **service level agreement (SLA)** and uptime.

Infrastructure as a Service - the First Layer of Cloud Computing

The first step for this must be performed during VM creation with the setting up of an **Availability zone** and **Availability set**. Then we add another VM to our solution with a different **Availability zone** and the same **Availability set**. This will ensure that the VMs are placed in different zones in the Azure Datacenter and don't depend on the same power source, networking, and cooling. If there is an issue within the Azure Datacenter, there is less chance that both VMs will be impacted.

Setting up the same **Availability set** will insure that VMs are placed on different physical servers, compute racks, storage units, and network switches. If hardware failure occurs, there is less chance both VMs will be affected. Another thing availability set takes care of is that Microsoft will never perform maintenance that will impact both VMs at the same time. To keep Azure Datacenters secure and performing in the best possible way, maintenance tasks must be performed periodically to install updates to hosts, or upgrade firmware on hardware. Placing VMs in an availability set informs Microsoft that these VMs are set up to achieve high availability, and maintenance will be performed keeping this in mind and never affecting all VMs at the same time.

So, to achieve high availability, we need at least two VMs set up. But what about traffic? How do we direct whether something goes to the first or the second VM? If the first VM isn't available, how do we direct traffic to the second one?

This is where Azure Load Balancers come into play. This is one of Azure's network services that we skipped before and will explain when the time is right. We will have similar situations in later chapters as well. Azure Load Balancers distribute incoming traffic from frontend to backend pool instances. They can support both inbound and outbound scenarios with low latency and high throughput. In this scenario, incoming traffic would come to the Load Balancer IP and the Load Balancer would distribute traffic to VMs configured in the backend pool. Azure Load Balancer can be internal or public, depending on what kind of traffic we need to distribute. For web server roles, we probably want public Load Balancers. But in the case of a database server, we probably want to use an internal one as we don't want databases exposed over the internet.

Creating an Azure Load Balancer

To create a new Azure Load Balancer, we need to select to create a new resource and select Azure Load Balancer from the list. This will open the create load Balancer blade where we need to provide basic information.

The information that is the same for all resources are **Name**, **Subscription**, **Resource group**, and **Location**.

Options specific to Azure Load Balancer are **Type**, **SKU**, and **Public IP address**.

The **Type** of Load Balancer can be internal or external, depending on what kind of traffic you want to route. A **Public** type must have the public IP address configured and I recommend you place static for this IP address. Optionally, you can enable Public IPv6 for your Azure Load Balancer while Public IPv4 is the default.

The **stock keeping unit (SKU)** can be **Basic** or **Standard**. **Standard** has more options and features available but comes at a price that is formed based on the number of load-balancing rules. On the other hand, **Basic** is free of charge and the only fee associated with it comes from reserving public IP addresses and outbound traffic.

An example of the information needed to create a new Azure Load Balancer is shown in the following screenshot:

Deployment of most Azure Network features is done in under one minute. Azure Load Balancer is no different and deployment should complete very quickly.

Configuring the Azure Load Balancer

After the deployment of the Azure Load Balancer is completed, we can go to the resource and find different options. **SETTINGS** is of most interest to us and we'll need it to configure our Load Balancer. We can find standard Azure resource settings such as **Properties**, **Locks**, and **Automation script** that can be found for all Azure resources. Frontend IP configuration gives us the ability to manage IP addresses associated with our Load Balancer, add new IP addresses, or remove existing ones. Other settings will be needed to configure our Load Balancer to distribute incoming traffic and to configure where that traffic should be directed to.

First, we need to configure the **Backend pools** for our Load Balancer. I'll select my Load Balancer to be associated to an **Availability set**. Previously in this chapter, I created a VM named WebSrv1 with an **Availability set** named WebSet. Then I added an identical VM named WebSrv2 and added it to the same **Availability set**. So, I have two identical VMs in the same **Availability set** and I have associated my Azure Load Balancer to this set. Finally, we have to define the network IP configuration that will be used and set it up to use both VMs in this availability set. If we had more VMs in this **Availability set**, we could set up more IP configurations to be targeted. An example of how to set up a backend pool is shown in this screenshot:

Add backend pool
WebLB

* Name

WebLBPool ✓

IP version

| IPv4 | IPv6 |

Associated to ❶

Availability set ∨

Availability set ❶

WebSet
number of virtual machines: 2 ∨

Target network IP configurations

Only VMs within the current availability set can be chosen. Once a VM is chosen, you can select a
network IP configuration related to it.

🗑

* Target virtual machine ❶

WebSrv1
size: Standard_D2s_v3, network interfaces: 1 ∨

* Network IP configuration ❶

ipconfig1 (10.1.1.4) ∨

OK

The second step is to set up health probes. We need to define the **Protocol, Port, Interval,** and **Unhealthy threshold. Protocol** and **Port** will define what needs to be monitored. As I intend to use `WebSrv1` and `WebSrv2` as web servers, I'll set up monitoring on port 80. **Interval** will define how often a check needs to be performed in order to make sure the server is responsive. The threshold defines how many consecutive intervals must probe and fail to contact the server in order to declare it unresponsive. An example of how to set up a health probe on port 80 is shown in this screenshot:

As I want to use the web server role, I'll repeat the same thing for port 443. In the screenshot here, we can see both probes are created but the **USED BY** information is empty:

NAME	PROTOCOL	PORT	USED BY	
WebProbe1	TCP	80	-	...
WebProbe2	TCP	443	-	...

In the third step, we create a load-balancing rule. We need to provide a **Name**, **IP Version**, **Frontend IP address**, **Protocol**, **Frontend port**, **Backend port**, **Backend pool**, **Health probe**, **Session persistence**, and **Idle timeout (minutes)**. **Name** and **IP Version** are self-explanatory options, so let's jump on the rest of them.

For the **Frontend IP address**, you can choose any of the Load Balancer IP addresses as it can be associated with multiple IP addresses. There is a restriction on what IP address you can choose based on the IP version selected. If the **IP Version** is set to **IPv4**, you can select only the **IPV4** IP address. If **IPv6** is selected, only the IP addresses of the same version associated with the Load Balancer can be selected.

Protocol and **Port** are connected, with this option you select what protocol needs to be forwarded from the defined port to the defined **Backend port**. For example, TCP on port 80 should be forwarded to port 80.

With the **Backend pool**, we define where traffic is forwarded to. As you can have multiple backend pools in a single Azure Balancer, you can select any of these pools.

Health probe needs to be selected in order to have a check on the VM state. You need to select the probe that performs a check on the backend port used in the rule you are creating.

Options for **Sessions persistence** and **Idle timeout (minutes)** are related to how client connections should be handled. As you have at least two VMs in your **Backend pool**, you need to set traffic to be handled by the same VM for the duration of one session. If you select that traffic coming from the same client IP over the same protocol, this should keep the session alive. The client will be directed to the same VM as long as the session is active.

Idle timeout (minutes) determines how long the session will stay active if no action is taken. The default value is **4** minutes but it can be changed to up to **30** minutes. With this setting, you determine how long the session will be active if the client isn't using the application, and isn't sending any messages in order to keep the session alive.

The option for a Floating IP (direct server return) address is **Disabled** by default and should only be used with **SQL AlwaysOn Availability Listener**.

In the screenshot here, you can see the options to set up the load-balancing rule, **HTTP**:

I'll create another rule named **HTTPS** for port 443. Note in the screenshot here, that probes created earlier are now used by load-balancing rules:

NAME	PROTOCOL	PORT	USED BY	
WebProbe1	TCP	80	HTTP	...
WebProbe2	TCP	443	HTTPS	...

The last option in the Load Balancer settings is the inbound NAT rule. It has similar options as the load-balancing rule with one exception. Traffic, in this case, isn't forwarded to the backend pool but to a single VM. In the screenshot here, you can see how to set up an inbound NAT rule that will forward traffic coming over port 5589 (**WinRM**) to **WebSrv1**:

So, let's review what was achieved with setting the Load Balancer and availability set. We have two VMs acting as web servers in the backend pool. VMs are placed in different availability zones and the same availability set in order to increase the chance that at least one of the VMs is running. Health probes are checking if VMs are available on the defined port. If any of the VMs is unresponsive to two consecutive checks, it will be declared as failed. A load-balancing rule is set up to forward traffic that is coming over the Load Balancer public IP address to the backend pool. If both VMs in the backend pool are healthy, traffic will be forwarded on the round-robin rule. If the health probe declares any of the VMs unresponsive, all traffic will be forwarded to the VM that is in a healthy state. Sessions are kept alive based on the client IP, protocol, and idle timeout. Sessions from the same IP address over the same protocol will be forwarded to the same VM as long as a keep-alive signal is sent at least every 4 minutes.

This will ensure our application is up and running, even if a single VM fails. Failures can be caused by hardware or network errors in the Azure Datacenter (the availability zone and availability set ensure that both VMs are not affected). Placing more VMs in the availability set and backend pool increases the chances that at least one VM is up and running.

Azure Load Balancer ARM template

Here is the ARM template for creating a new Azure Load Balancer:

```
{
"$schema":
"http://schema.management.azure.com/schemas/2015-01-01/deploymentTemplate.j
son#",
"contentVersion": "1.0.0.0",
"parameters": {
"name": {
"type": "string"
},
"location": {
"type": "string"
},
"sku": {
"type": "string"
},
"publicIPAddressName": {
"type": "string"
}
},
"resources": [
{
"apiVersion": "2017-08-01",
```

```
"name": "[parameters('name')]",
"type": "Microsoft.Network/loadBalancers",
"location": "[parameters('location')]",
"sku": {
"name": "[parameters('sku')]"
},
"dependsOn": [
"[concat('Microsoft.Network/publicIPAddresses/',
parameters('publicIPAddressName'))]"
],
"properties": {
"frontendIPConfigurations": [
{
"name": "LoadBalancerFrontEnd",
"properties": {
"publicIPAddress": {
"id": "[resourceId('test', 'Microsoft.Network/publicIPAddresses',
parameters('publicIPAddressName'))]"
}
}
}
]
}
},
{
"apiVersion": "2017-08-01",
"type": "Microsoft.Network/publicIPAddresses",
"name": "[parameters('publicIPAddressName')]",
"location": "[parameters('location')]",
"sku": {
"name": "[parameters('sku')]"
},
"properties": {
"publicIPAllocationMethod": "Dynamic",
"publicIPAddressVersion": "IPv4"
}
}
]
}
```

Azure Virtual Machine Scale Set

Elasticity is one of the big benefits of cloud computing. We have the ability to scale up and down based on our workloads and demand. If we have increased workload, we scale up. If workload decreases, we scale back down. With a pricing model of paying for what you use and billing by the minute, this allow us to save money.

We have already explained how to set up scale up and scale down VMs in Microsoft Azure. Scaling up and down means to change the size of the VM to a bigger or smaller instance. This is called vertical scaling. This can be very useful, but this approach has one consequence—every time a VM size is changed, reboot occurs. So, vertical scaling can be helpful as it can increase the size of the VM to handle more workload, but it will always cause downtime in the period when the VM is rebooting.

The solution for this is horizontal scaling, and for Azure Virtual Machines we can use Azure Virtual Machine Scale Set. Instead of changing the size of the VM, scale set creates additional instances of the VM and spreads the workload across instances using Azure Load Balancer. This is called horizontal scaling. The approach is similar to the high availability scenario but, instead of having multiple VMs in the availability set, scale set starts VMs based on workload and starts them only when needed. Another difference is that in the availability set, VMs are independent and an issue on one VM will not cause an issue on others. In scale set, all VMs take a copy of the primary VM, and if the primary VM is compromised, the issue will reflect across the scale set. We need to outline that the scale set is not a high availability solution but horizontal scaling based on workloads.

Creating an Azure Virtual Machine Scale Set

Let's create a new Azure Virtual Machine Scale Set and explain all the details as we go.

To create a new Azure Virtual Machine Scale Set, all information is provided in a single screen. In order to make it more visible, I have separated the screen into three images—basic and instances, autoscale, and networking.

The basic information for Scale Set is very similar to the basic information for VMs. This is only logical as scale set creates a primary VM and then clones this VM in order to scale out. We need to provide a **Virtual machine scale set name**, **Operating system disk image**, **Subscription**, **Resource group**, **Location**, **Username**, **Password**, and optionally add an **Availability zone**.

Next, we create the instance rules. This will determine the size of VMs in Scale Set and how many instances scale set is allowed to create. The maximum number of instances allowed is 1,000 for Azure-provided OS images and 300 for custom OS images. If you have an issue on the application and the application itself is causing high CPU or memory, it will cause scale set to scale out and create new instances. As new instances are an identical replica of the primary VM, the issue will persist on these VMs and scaling out will continue until you reach the maximum instance count. It's important to set up an instance count to something you are actually ready to pay for, as spinning 1,000 VMs can cause significant financial impact, even for a short period of time.

Deploying scale set VMs as low-priority can save you up to 80% in prices. Low-priority VMs are created using allocated and unused resources in the Azure Datacenter but these resources can be claimed by higher priority resources and can be unavailable at any time. So, even if this option can help you save a lot of money, resources may not be available when needed. This option shouldn't be used for services that are required to be available at any time, or for critical services. The recommendation is to use lower priority only for low-priority services or batch processing.

Scale Set creates multiple instances of a VM and all these VMs have a separate disk. Managing these disk and storage accounts in a scale-out process, especially when we spin up 1,000 instances, can prove to be very challenging. I recommend using a managed disk that will be managed by Azure automatically so you don't need to worry about this part.

An example of basic and instance settings is shown in the following screenshot:

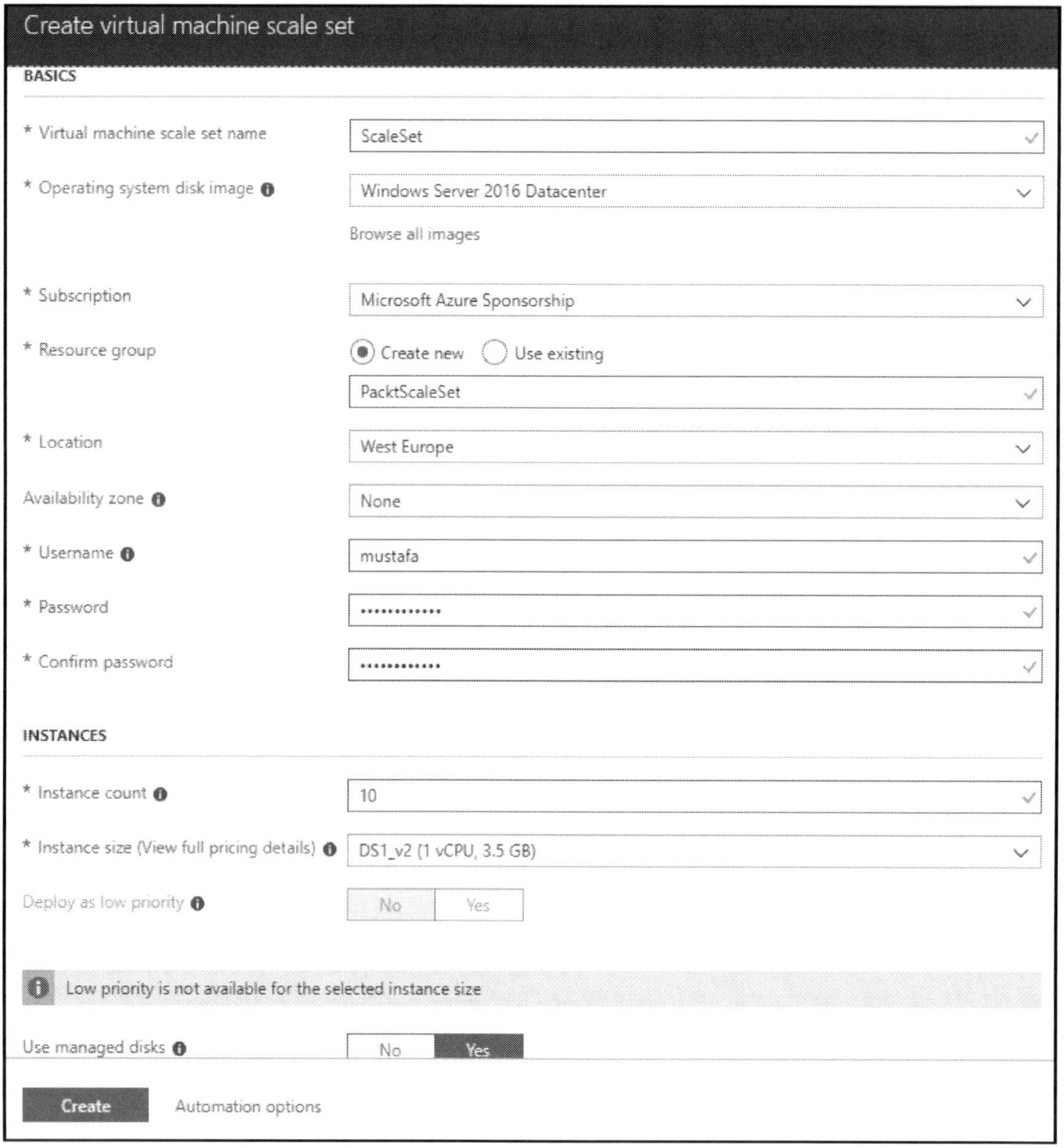

Auto-scale creates a set of rules on how your scale set is going to scale in and out. We need to set a minimum and maximum number of VMs in our scale set. A maximum number is automatically collected from the instance count previously set, but it doesn't have to be the same. The **Instance count** determines how many VMs are going to be created initially but the maximum number determines how many VMs can be created in total.

We create scale-out and scale-in rules that will increase and decrease the number of VMs in our scale set. For example, if the threshold reaches 75% of CPU utilization, it will spin up additional VM(s). If utilization falls below 25%, it will decrease the number of VM(s) in the scale set. The number of VMs that will be added/removed can be set as a separate value.

Let's say that we set a minimum number of VMs to 1, the instance count to 10 and the maximum number of VMs to 100. When the scale set is created, it will create 10 copies of the VM and start only one of them, the primary copy. When the scale-out threshold is reached, it will add a new VM to Scale Set. This VM is one of 10 initially created. If utilization continues to rise, it will add new VMs until we reach 10 VMs. If the maximum number of VMs is different from the instance count, new VMs will be created and started. The difference between the first 10 VMs and later ones is that initial VMs are already created and only need to be started. Additional VMs need to be provisioned before being started and this makes the process of scaling out slower. However, initial VM comes with a cost even when not running, as you pay for the disk even when the VM is turned off. It's good to find a balance between the initial number and maximum number of VMs . **AUTOSCALE** is shown in the following screenshot:

AUTOSCALE	
Autoscale ❶	Disabled **Enabled**
* Minimum number of VMs ❶	1
* Maximum number of VMs ❶	10
Scale out	
* CPU threshold (%) ❶	75
* Number of VMs to increase by ❶	1
Scale in	
* CPU threshold (%) ❶	25
* Number of VMs to decrease by ❶	1

The **NETWORKING** part gives us the option to choose between the **Application Gateway** and **Load balancer**. Whatever you choose, this will be used as the endpoint for your users and it will automatically disperse traffic across the Azure Virtual Machine Scale Set. The **Load balancer** in Azure Virtual Machines is free and **Application Gateway** is billed per hour but supports many additional features. **Application Gateway** supports SSL termination, URL-based routing, multisite routing, cookie-based session affinity, web application firewalls, and routable IP addresses.

When using the **Load balancer**, the difference between one used in the availibility set and scale set is that for scale set no additional management is needed (you have the option to set additional rules and settings, but it's not required). Load-balancing rules and adding VMs to the backend pool is done automatically and no user action is required. An example of network settings with the Azure Load Balancer is shown in the screenshot here:

NETWORKING

Microsoft Azure Application Gateway is a dedicated virtual appliance providing application delivery controller (ADC) as a service.
Azure Load Balancer allows you to scale your applications and create high availability for your services.
Learn more about load balancer differences

RESOURCES	OPTIMAL FOR	SUPPORTED PROTOCOLS	SSL OFFLOADING	RDP TO INSTANCE
Application Gateway	Web-based traffic	HTTP/HTTPS/WebSocket	Supported	Not supported
Load balancer	Stream-based traffic	Any	Not supported	Supported

Choose Load balancing options   ◯ Application Gateway   ⦿ Load balancer

* Public IP address name ❶
ScaleSetIP   ✓

* Domain name label ❶
packtscaleset   ✓
.westeurope.cloudapp.azure.com

Deployment of Azure Virtual Machine Scale Set depends on many different parameters. Network services needed for scale set must be deployed prior to the VMs, but this process is done very quickly. Then, VMs are deployed and this can take time depending on the instance count and VM size. Deploying a few large instances can be done relatively quickly, but if we deploy hundreds of small VMs, it can take up to an hour.

Managing Azure Virtual Machine Scale Sets

After deployment is finished, multiple resources are created in our resource group and we can see **Virtual machine scale set** and a set of network-related resources. Network resources created are a **Load balancer**, **Public IP address** (used by the Load Balancer), **Virtual network**, and **Network security group**. NSG is applied on the subnet level and NSG rules will be effective on all VMs in scale set. This makes sense as all VMs are identical, are used by the same application, and have the same purpose. We can see in the screenshot here all the resources created for our scale set:

NAME	TYPE	LOCATION	
ScaleSet	Virtual machine scale set	West Europe	...
ScaleSetIP	Public IP address	West Europe	...
ScaleSetlb	Load balancer	West Europe	...
ScaleSetnsg	Network security group	West Europe	...
ScaleSetVnet	Virtual network	West Europe	...

As we have already discussed all the networking features in question, we are going to concentrate on Virtual Machine Scale Set and options that are provided to manage it. A lot of options are identical to the VM settings such as **Size**, **Continuous delivery (Preview)**, **Configuration**, **Properties**, **Locks**, and **Automation script**. SETTINGS that are unique to scale set are **Instances**, **Scaling**, **Storage**, and **Operating system**. **Operating system** is only informational and we can see only information such as the image and OS version used to create a scale set.

Storage settings also gives us information on the type of storage and disks used with only one option to choose—**Caching**. Options available are **None**, **Read-only**, and **Read/write**.

The **Instance** blade shows us all VMs in our scale set and their state. We can see which VMs are running and perform different operations such as **Start**, **Stop**, **De-allocate** and **Delete**. Specially interesting options are **Reimage** and **Upgrade**. **Reimage** will reset all settings on a selected VM and restore it to the default version. **Upgrade** will perform a manual upgrade for a selected VM to the latest changes. All VMs in scale set are an identical replica of the primary VM and, if changes are made on the primary, they will be replicated to all instances in time. The **Upgrade** option gives us the ability to perform upgrades manually and force changes immediately. This can be useful when we have a large number of VMs in scale set, as replicating changes will take time and change might be critical to be applied as soon as possible. However, both the **Reimage** and **Upgrade** options will reboot the VM in the process, so take that into consideration as well. The last option unique to the Azure Virtual Machine Scale Set is scaling, but it will take time to explain this option further.

The scaling blade shows us all the rules for scaling out and scaling in that are effective on our scale set. If rules are created during the deployment process, they will be shown here and we can edit them or delete them. Additional rules can be created as well and we can monitor multiple parameters for our VMs. For example, we can create separate rules for CPU, memory, and disk utilization. If any of these rules are triggered, it will perform scaling out or scaling in processes, accordingly. Creating more scale rules gives us better flexibility and performance as we don't depend on a single point. If we monitor CPU but have issues with memory, scaling out will not happen and performance will decrease. If we monitor memory but have high disk utilization, again we don't have automatic scaling out and performance will decrease:

Default Profile1 ✎	⊘

Delete warning	ⓘ The very last or default recurrence rule cannot be deleted. Instead, you can disable autoscale to turn off autoscale.	
Scale mode	◉ Scale based on a metric ◯ Scale to a specific instance count	

Rules	**Scale out**		
	When	ScaleSet	(Average) Percentage CPU > 75	Increase instance count by 1
	Scale in		
	When	ScaleSet	(Average) Percentage CPU < 25	Decrease instance count by 1
	＋ Add a rule		

	Minimum ⓘ	Maximum ⓘ	Default ⓘ
Instance limits	1	10	1

Schedule	**This scale condition is executed when none of the other scale condition(s) match**

＋ Add a scale condition

It's important to outline two things when speaking about Azure Virtual Machine Scale Set. A scale set is very different to an availability set. In an availability set, we have a constant number of VMs in order to increase the chances of at least one VM being available at all times and achieving high availability. Scale set monitors workload and increases the number of VMs based on demand, but all VMs are replicas and an issue can cause all VMs to replicate issue.

Another thing we need to outline is scenarios where we can use Azure Virtual Machine Scale Set. As all VMs in scale set are replicas of the initial image, changes are made from the initial image to all other VMs. But the process is not done the other way around, and changes on additional instances are not applied anywhere. For this reason, Azure Virtual Machine Scale Set is not good for roles like SQL Server or Exchange Server where changes must be applied across all instances. Rather use scale set for application scenarios where changes are not made by user sessions and data persists over time.

Azure Virtual Machine Scale Set ARM template

In addition, here is the ARM template to deploy a new Azure Virtual Machine Scale Set:

```
{
 "$schema":
"http://schema.management.azure.com/schemas/2015-01-01/deploymentTemplate.j
son",
 "contentVersion": "1.0.0.0",
 "parameters": {
 "vmSku": {
 "type": "string",
 "defaultValue": "Standard_D1",
 "metadata": {
 "description": "Size of VMs in the VM Scale Set."
 }
 },
 "vmssName": {
 "type": "string",
 "metadata": {
 "description": "String used as a base for naming resources. Must be 3-61
characters in length and globally unique across Azure. A hash is prepended
to this string for some resources, and resource-specific information is
appended."
 },
 "maxLength": 61
 },
 "instanceCount": {
 "type": "int",
 "metadata": {
 "description": "Number of VM instances (100 or less)."
 },
 "defaultValue": 2,
 "maxValue": 100
 },
 "adminUsername": {
 "type": "string",
```

```
"metadata": {
"description": "Admin username on all VMs."
}
},
"adminPassword": {
"type": "securestring",
"metadata": {
"description": "Admin password on all VMs."
}
}
},
"variables": {
"vnetName": "vnet",
"subnetName": "subnet",
"subnetRef": "[resourceId('Microsoft.Network/virtualNetworks/subnets',
variables('vnetName'), variables('subnetName'))]",
"publicIPAddressName": "pip",
"loadBalancerName": "loadBalancer",
"loadBalancerFrontEndName": "loadBalancerFrontEnd",
"loadBalancerBackEndName": "loadBalancerBackEnd",
"loadBalancerProbeName": "loadBalancerHttpProbe",
"loadBalancerNatPoolName": "loadBalancerNatPool"
},
"resources": [
{
"type": "Microsoft.Compute/virtualMachineScaleSets",
"name": "[parameters('vmssName')]",
"location": "[resourceGroup().location]",
"apiVersion": "2017-03-30",
"dependsOn": [
"[concat('Microsoft.Network/virtualNetworks/', variables('vnetName'))]",
"[resourceId('Microsoft.Network/loadBalancers',
variables('loadBalancerName'))]"
],
"sku": {
"name": "[parameters('vmSku')]",
"capacity": "[parameters('instanceCount')]"
},
"properties": {
"overprovision": "true",
"upgradePolicy": {
"mode": "Manual"
},
"virtualMachineProfile": {
"storageProfile": {
"osDisk": {
"createOption": "FromImage",
"caching": "ReadWrite"
```

```
    },
    "imageReference": {
    "publisher": "MicrosoftWindowsServer",
    "offer": "WindowsServer",
    "sku": "2016-Datacenter",
    "version": "latest"
    }
    },
    "osProfile": {
    "computerNamePrefix": "[parameters('vmssName')]",
    "adminUsername": "[parameters('adminUsername')]",
    "adminPassword": "[parameters('adminPassword')]"
    },
    "networkProfile": {
    "networkInterfaceConfigurations": [
    {
    "name": "nic",
    "properties": {
    "primary": true,
    "ipConfigurations": [
    {
    "name": "ipconfig",
    "properties": {
    "subnet": {
    "id": "[variables('subnetRef')]"
    },
    "loadBalancerBackendAddressPools": [
    {
    "id": "[concat('/subscriptions/',
    subscription().subscriptionId,'/resourceGroups/', resourceGroup().name,
    '/providers/Microsoft.Network/loadBalancers/',
    variables('loadBalancerName'), '/backendAddressPools/',
    variables('loadBalancerBackEndName'))]"
    }
    ],
    "loadBalancerInboundNatPools": [
    {
    "id": "[concat('/subscriptions/',
    subscription().subscriptionId,'/resourceGroups/', resourceGroup().name,
    '/providers/Microsoft.Network/loadBalancers/',
    variables('loadBalancerName'), '/inboundNatPools/',
    variables('loadBalancerNatPoolName'))]"
    }
    ]
    }
    }
    ]
    }
```

```
        }
    ]
    }
    }
    }
    },
    {
    "type": "Microsoft.Network/virtualNetworks",
    "name": "[variables('vnetName')]",
    "location": "[resourceGroup().location]",
    "apiVersion": "2017-04-01",
    "properties": {
    "addressSpace": {
    "addressPrefixes": [
    "10.0.0.0/16"
    ]
    },
    "subnets": [
    {
    "name": "[variables('subnetName')]",
    "properties": {
    "addressPrefix": "10.0.0.0/24"
    }
    }
    ]
    }
    },
    {
    "type": "Microsoft.Network/publicIPAddresses",
    "name": "[variables('publicIPAddressName')]",
    "location": "[resourceGroup().location]",
    "apiVersion": "2017-04-01",
    "properties": {
    "publicIPAllocationMethod": "Dynamic",
    "dnsSettings": {
    "domainNameLabel": "[toLower(parameters('vmssName'))]"
    }
    }
    },
    {
    "type": "Microsoft.Network/loadBalancers",
    "name": "[variables('loadBalancerName')]",
    "location": "[resourceGroup().location]",
    "apiVersion": "2017-04-01",
    "dependsOn": [
    "[concat('Microsoft.Network/publicIPAddresses/',
    variables('publicIPAddressName'))]"
    ],
```

```
"properties": {
"frontendIPConfigurations": [
{
"name": "[variables('loadBalancerFrontEndName')]",
"properties": {
"publicIPAddress": {
"id": "[resourceId('Microsoft.Network/publicIPAddresses',
variables('publicIPAddressName'))]"
}
}
}
],
"backendAddressPools": [
{
"name": "[variables('loadBalancerBackendName')]"
}
],
"loadBalancingRules": [
{
"name": "roundRobinLBRule",
"properties": {
"frontendIPConfiguration": {
"id": "[concat(resourceId('Microsoft.Network/loadBalancers',
variables('loadBalancerName')), '/frontendIPConfigurations/',
variables('loadBalancerFrontEndName'))]"
},
"backendAddressPool": {
"id": "[concat(resourceId('Microsoft.Network/loadBalancers',
variables('loadBalancerName')), '/backendAddressPools/',
variables('loadBalancerBackendName'))]"
},
"protocol": "Tcp",
"frontendPort": 80,
"backendPort": 80,
"enableFloatingIP": false,
"idleTimeoutInMinutes": 5,
"probe": {
"id": "[concat(resourceId('Microsoft.Network/loadBalancers',
variables('loadBalancerName')), '/probes/',
variables('loadBalancerProbeName'))]"
}
}
}
],
"probes": [
{
"name": "[variables('loadBalancerProbeName')]",
"properties": {
```

```
"protocol": "Tcp",
"port": 80,
"intervalInSeconds": "5",
"numberOfProbes": "2"
}
}
],
"inboundNatPools": [
{
"name": "[variables('loadBalancerNatPoolName')]",
"properties": {
"frontendIPConfiguration": {
"id": "[concat(resourceId('Microsoft.Network/loadBalancers',
variables('loadBalancerName')), '/frontendIPConfigurations/',
variables('loadBalancerFrontEndName'))]"
},
"protocol": "Tcp",
"frontendPortRangeStart": 50000,
"frontendPortRangeEnd": 50019,
"backendPort": 3389
}
}
]
}
}
]
}
```

Summary

We have covered the basic IaaS concepts and how to set up Azure Virtual Machines. The logical step to expand IaaS scenarios was to cover high availability and we succeeded in achieving this goal with Azure Load Balancers and availability sets.

One of the key concepts of cloud computing is elasticity and on-demand resources. We showed how to achieve both vertical scaling (with alerts and custom actions) and horizontal scaling (with Azure Virtual Machine Scale Sets).

In the next chapter, we will progress to the PaaS model and explore the Azure App Service as a more abstract model compared to Azure Virtual Machines. The app service gives us some unique options that will help us progress in our cloud journey but gives us less control over infrastructure than VMs. We'll compare how IaaS features relate to PaaS and how we can achieve scaling and high availability with app service.

Questions

1. What is the oldest Windows Server version supported for Azure VMs?
    1. Windows Server 2003
    2. Windows Server 2008 R2 SP1
    3. Windows Server 2012 R2

2. What do basic-tier VMs support?
    1. Lower IOPS
    2. Load Balancers
    3. Auto-scaling

3. What are low-priority VMs intended to be used for?
    1. High availability
    2. Batch processing
    3. Balanced workloads

4. Size setting in the Azure Virtual Machine blade is used to...?
    1. Scale up
    2. Scale down
    3. Both

5. Runbooks can be used to perform?
    1. Maintenance tasks
    2. Scaling up and down VMs
    3. Both

6. Azure Load Balancer is used...?
    1. To distribute traffic across VMs in the backend pool
    2. To isolate traffic and stop attacks on the VM
    3. Both

7. Placing VMs in the same availability set will result in...?
    1. VMs will be created in different Azure Datacenters
    2. VMs will be placed in a different rack
    3. VMs will be placed in the same rack

8. Scaling by creating additional instances of VM is called...?
    1. Scaling up
    2. Scaling down
    3. Scaling out

9. Scaling out is an example of...?
   1. Vertical scaling
   2. Horizontal scaling
   3. Diagonal scaling

10. For scaling out of Azure VMs we use...?
   1. Availability zone
   2. Availability set
   3. Scale set

4
Azure App Service - Hosting Web Applications without a Server

The next step in our cloud journey is PaaS, and we'll introduce Azure App Service. Azure App Service is the simplest example of Azure PaaS, and is intended to host web applications. We'll see how different hosting applications in IaaS and PaaS is.

In this chapter, we will cover the following:

- Azure App Service Plans
- Azure Web Apps
- Traffic Manager
- App service environment

Technical requirements

For this chapter, you'll need an Azure subscription.

Azure App Service Plan and Azure Web Apps

PaaS in Azure (or in any public cloud) is more abstract than IaaS. It's simple to understand the IaaS model because it's not much different from on-premises: we create a virtual machine, we configure it any way we want, we install anything we want (of course, limited by the OS itself; we can't install something that wouldn't run on-premises either).

After we create our Azure VM, we have complete control over everything on that VM. For example, the VMs created in the previous chapter were intended to be used as web servers. We can connect to that VM and install all the required roles, features, and software in order to start hosting our application.

But what if we want to do a similar thing with PaaS?

An Azure App Service Plan is used to host our web applications in Azure. We need to create an Azure App Service Plan and then add Azure Web Apps for our applications. A single App Service Plan can host multiple Azure Web Apps. If we install IIS on our web server, we can host multiple applications as well. An App Service Plan can be compered very much to IIS, but with one big difference: with IIS, we have complete control over configuration and with App Service Plan we have a limited set of options. This is essentially the difference between IaaS and PaaS.

With less control comes less maintenance, as many tasks that we needed to perform in an on-premises environment are now automated and we don't need to worry about them. For example, installing updates in a local environment must be performed regularly in order to keep everything up to date and secure. With PaaS, we don't need to install any updates as this is done automatically on the host level.

Creating an App Service Plan

Let's start by creating a new App Service Plan. Similar to all Azure resources, we need to provide a name, **Subscription**, **Resource Group**, and **Location**. The other options available are **Operating System** and **Pricing tier**. The options available for OS are Windows and Linux. An example of all the information needed to create a new App Service Plan is shown in the following screenshot:

The default value for App Service Plan **Pricing tier** is **S1 Standard** or **Standard 1**. If we change this value, a new blade will open with more options. The App Service Plan pricing blade is shown in the following screenshot:

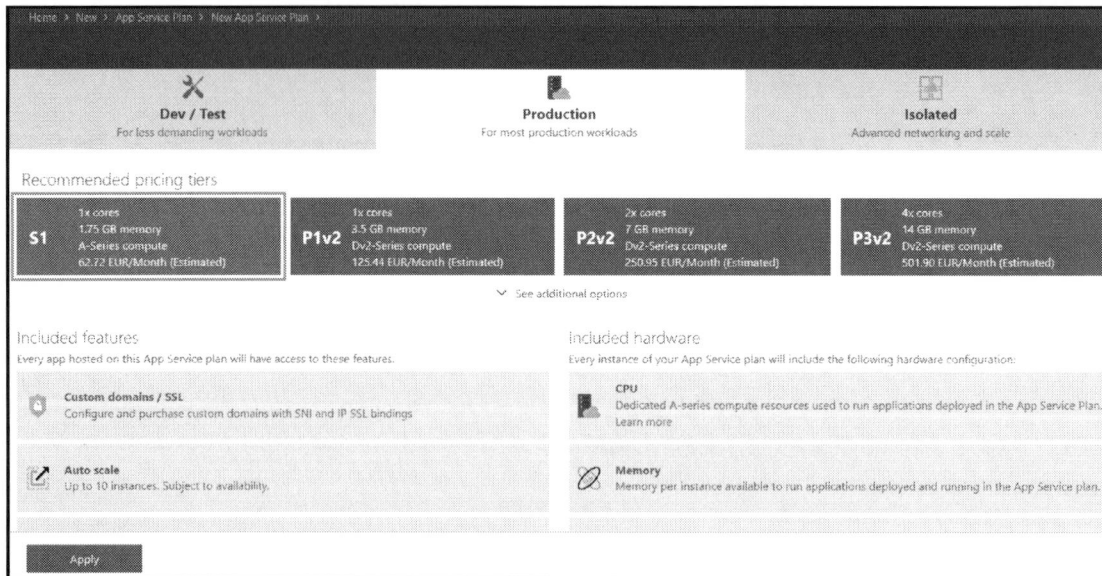

App Service Plan pricing is divided into three sections:

- **Dev/Test**
- **Production**
- **Isolated**

Dev/Test is intended for small workloads in dev/test environments. It has different sizes: **F1**, **D1**, and Basic (**B1**, **B2**, and **B3**). **F1** is free on shared infrstructure, has limited compute time per day, and doesn't support custom domains. **D1** has more compute hours per day and support for custom domains. The Basic tier has dedicated infrastructure and has support for custom domains, SSL, and manual scaling.

Production is intended for bigger workloads in a production environment. It comes with Standard and Premium tiers, which each have additional sizes (**S1**, **S2**, **S3**, **P1**, **P2**, **P3**, **P1v2**, **P2v2**, and **P3v2**). All sizes in the production section bring additional features, like autoscale, slots, backup, and Traffic Manager support. The amount of resources available to an App Service Plan depends on size, as each size comes with a different amount of memory and number of cores. This also applies to the Basic tier, even though it's not intended for production. The main difference between the standard and premium tiers is disk type, as standard uses standard storage (HDD) and premium uses premium storage (SSD). Premium can also be **v1** and **v2**, where **v2** has a different processor type and more memory.

After an App Service Plan is created, you can start adding Web Apps. It's important to say that you can add multiple Web Apps to a single App Service Plan. Billing is done on the App Service Plan level and you pay for the entire App Service Plan, not for each individual app. The number of apps that can be added to each App Service Plan depends on tier and size.

Creating an Azure Web App

To create a new Azure Web App, the standard values that need to be provided are **App name**, **Subscription**, **Resource Group**, and **Application Insights Location**. The other required values are **OS**, **App Service plan/Location**, and **Application Insights**. The available options for OS are **Windows**, **Linux**, and **Docker**. Values will depend on the type of application you want to run. In **App Service plan/Location**, you can create a new App Service Plan or use an existing one.

App Service plan/Location will determine the location of your Web App, as it needs to be in the same location as the App Service Plan it's associated with. Finally, I encourage enabling **Application Insights**, as this will allow you better monitoring and reporting regarding your application usage and performance.

An example of all the information needed to create a Web App is shown in the following screenshot:

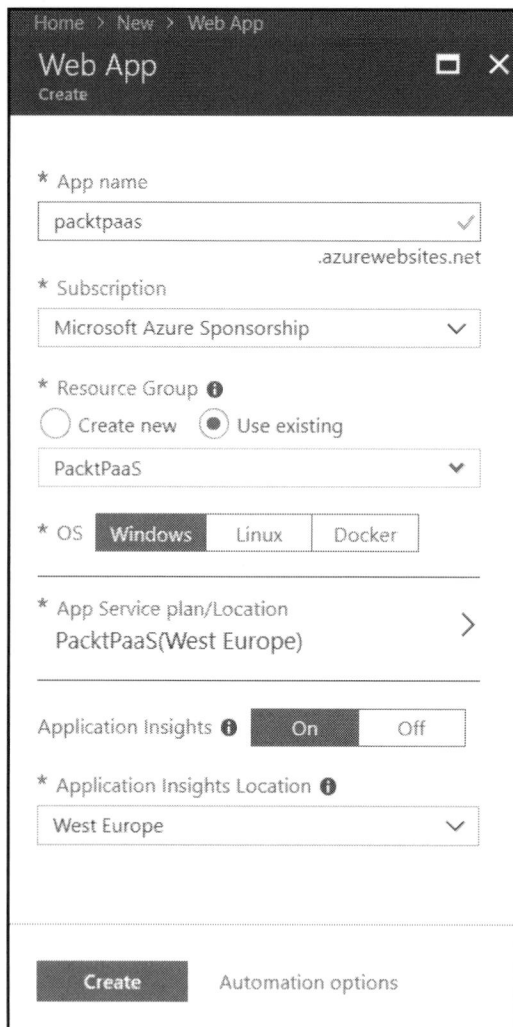

After deployment completes, we can see the following resources created: **App Service plan**, **App Service**, and **Application Insights**. This can be a bit confusing because different names are used when creating resources and after they are actually created. App Service Plan is App Service Plan in both cases.

In the case of Web App, the name is different. When you want to create a new Web App, the blade will show the name Web App, but after it's created you will see it as App Service. To sum up, App Service Plan is referred as App Service Plan and Web App is referred to as both Web App and App Service:

NAME	TYPE	LOCATION	
packtpaas	Application Insights	West Europe	•••
PacktPaaS	App Service plan	West Europe	•••
packtpaas	App Service	West Europe	•••

Managing Azure Web App

After the deployment of resources is completed, we need to configure them. As we don't have direct access and can't install software, roles, or features, we have an extended set of preconfigured settings that we can edit. There are more options in the App Service blade than in the Virtual Machine Blade, but overall we have fewer options as direct configuration isn't available.

Let's start with the Azure Web App and continue with configuration.

Azure Web App deployment settings

The first set of options available for an Azure Web App is deployment. **Quickstart** offers us links to various documents and guides.

We can set the **Deployment credentials** that will be used for deployment and FTP access:

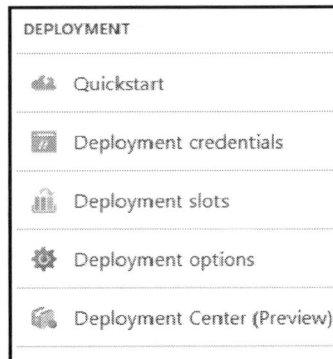

DEPLOYMENT

Quickstart

Deployment credentials

Deployment slots

Deployment options

Deployment Center (Preview)

Deployment slots is a very interesting feature which allows us to create multiple environments for our application. Slots are separate environments, but they can be used to swap application versions as well. To create a new slot, we select **Add a slot** and then provide a **Name** and a **Configuration Source**. The **Configuration Source** can be one of the existing slots (the configuration of the selected slot will be cloned), or we can select not to clone and leave the default values. A example of adding a new slot is shown in the following screenshot:

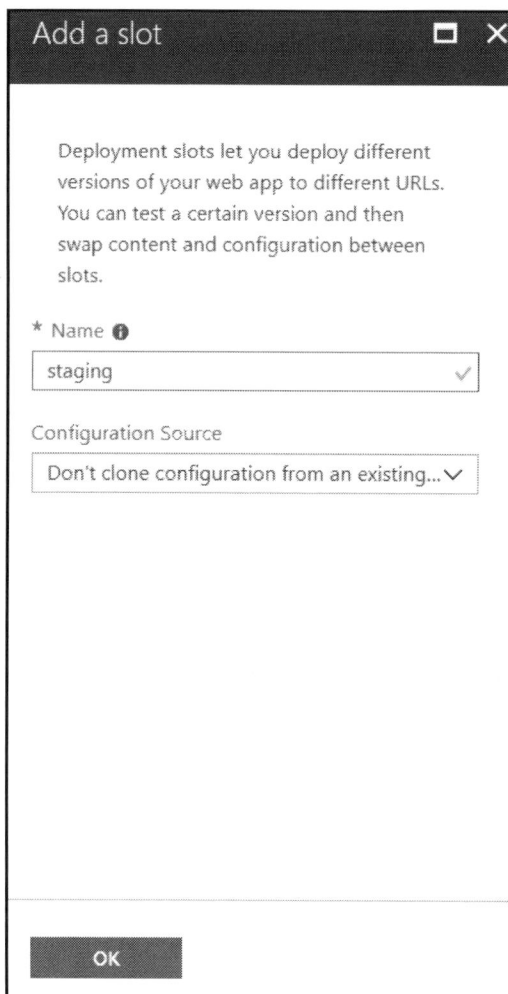

Add a slot ⬜ ✕

Deployment slots let you deploy different versions of your web app to different URLs. You can test a certain version and then swap content and configuration between slots.

* Name ℹ

staging ✓

Configuration Source

Don't clone configuration from an existing... ⌄

OK

The slot's name will be formed from the application name with the slot name added. For example, I created two slots: staging and test. This is shown in the following screenshot:

NAME	STATUS	APP SERVICE PLAN
packtpaas-staging	Running	PacktPaaS
packtpaas-test	Running	PacktPaaS

A great feature is the option to swap slots. For example, we can have a production slot running and have all users pointed to this slot when using the application. We can deploy and test on different slots, and this will have no impact on the production version of the application that users are currently using. Once we have tested everything, we can deploy the new version to the staging slot. The option to swap slots allows us to switch between the old production version and the new version in a matter of seconds with minimal impact on our users. When we hit swap, everything in staging becomes production and the old production becomes staging. Settings between slots are not changed, so staging can use a different database than production, for example. Another great thing is that we can swap back as well. Even when we test and validate, users may experience problems and bugs in new versions of applications. In this case, we can simply switch back and return to the previous production version, moving it from staging to production and the new version from production to staging. This will allow users to continue using the last stable version of the application, while we can examine and troubleshoot in staging in order to resolve the issue. Once we resolve the issue, simply swap again and the new version is back in production.

An example of slot swapping is shown in the following screenshot:

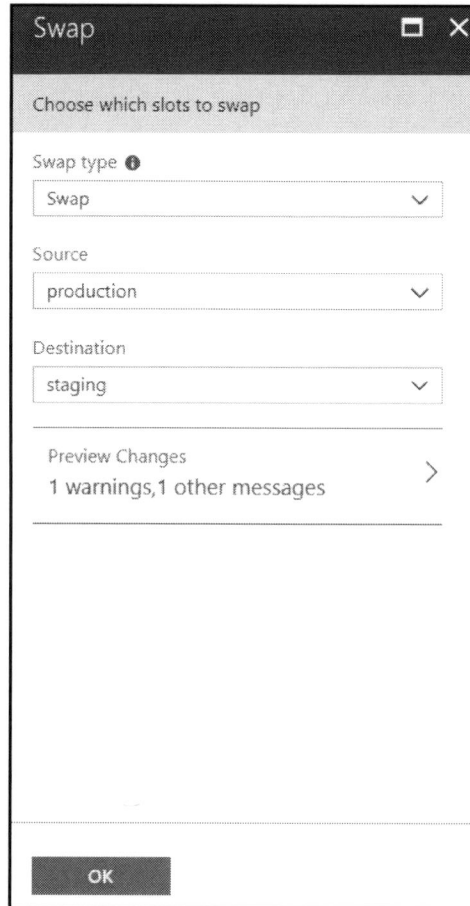

Deployment option and **Deployment Center (Preview)** give you options to connect to a code repository. Most common repositories are default options, such as **Visual Studio Team Services**, **GitHub**, or **Bitbucket**. File shares like **OneDrive** or **Dropbox** are also an option and you can link to a custom external repository as well, like **Local Git Repository** or **Team Foundation Server**. The difference is that besides connecting a repository, **Deployment Center (Preview)** gives you the option to establish a continuous integration/continuous delivery pipeline. **Deployment option** sources are shown in the following screenshot:

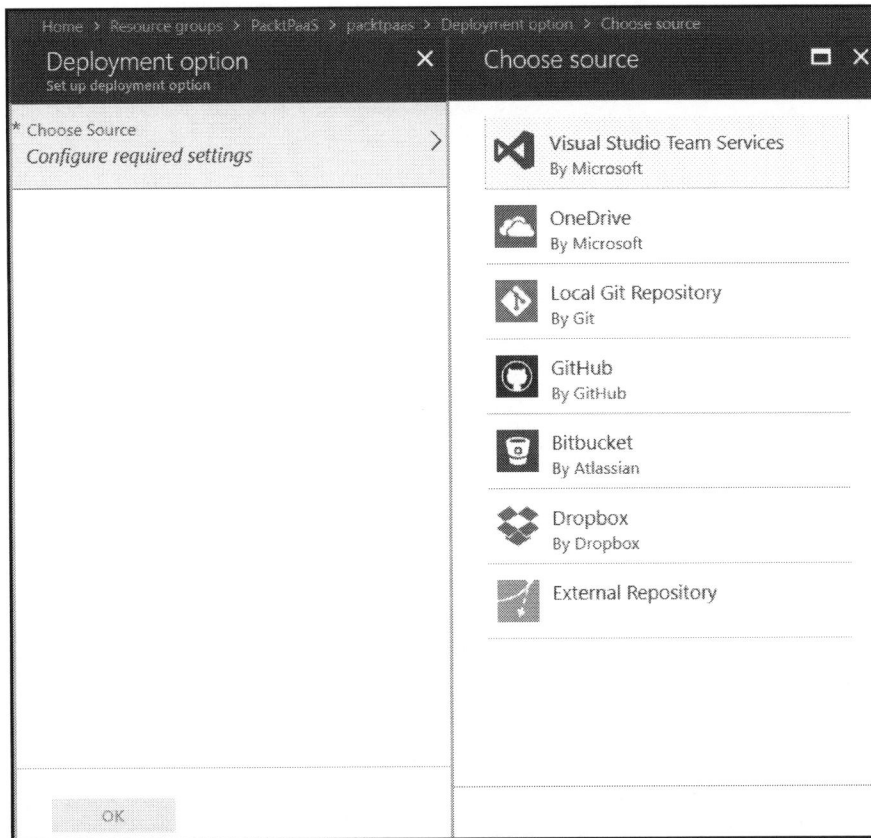

Azure Web App general settings

Azure Web App settings have some similar features to other Azure services, such as properties and locks. Also, most Azure services have a **Scale up (App Service plan)** and/or **Scale out (App Service plan)** option. Some unique settings are **Application settings**, **Authentication/Authorization**, **Application Insights**, **Managed service identity**, **Backups**, **Custom domains**, **SSL settings**, **Networking**, **WebJobs**, **Push** notifications, and **MySQL In App**. The **Networking** option allows us to connect a Web App to an Azure VNet, or even create a hybrid connection to our on-premises environment. **WebJobs** allow us to create background processes that can be executed on a schedule or triggered by an event. **Push** notifications are usually used for mobile applications in order to send various notifications to the mobile device where the application is running, like news, updates, and so on. **MySQL In App** creates a MySQL instance that your application can use.

However, this is for small workloads and I don't recommend using this other than for development and testing. A list of all settings is shown in the following screenshot:

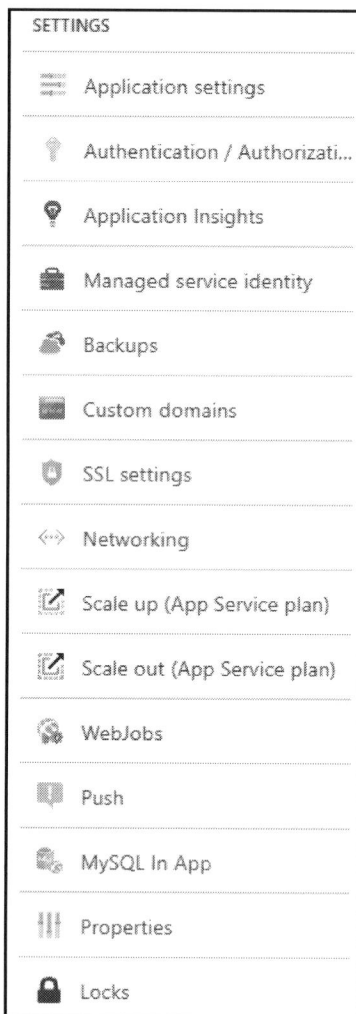

General settings have a preconfigured set of options which allow us to change framework versions and other settings needed for our application. For example, we can switch between different versions of .NET, PHP, Python, or Java. We can also switch between 32-bit and 64-bit platforms, turn Websockets on or off, set a managed pipeline version to classic or integrated, and so on.

One very important option is always on, and I strongly recommend you set this to **On**. If the application isn't used for a period of time, it can take some time to establish the first connection. For example, if the application is used during working hours, it can take some time for first users to connect in the morning because the application wasn't used during the night. Setting **Always On** will ping the application from time to time and keep it active. This way, whenever users try to connect, the application will be ready and there will be no wait time:

The **Authentication/Authorization** option allows us to set up a user login for our application. The default option is anonymous access, but we can set up **Azure Active Directory**, a **Microsoft** Live account, **Facebook**, **Google**, and **Twitter**. **Managed Service Identity** allows the application to be registered in **Azure Active Directory** and use the registration to communicate with other applications in **Azure Active Directory**. A list of **Authentication Providers** in the **Authentication/Authorization** blade is shown here:

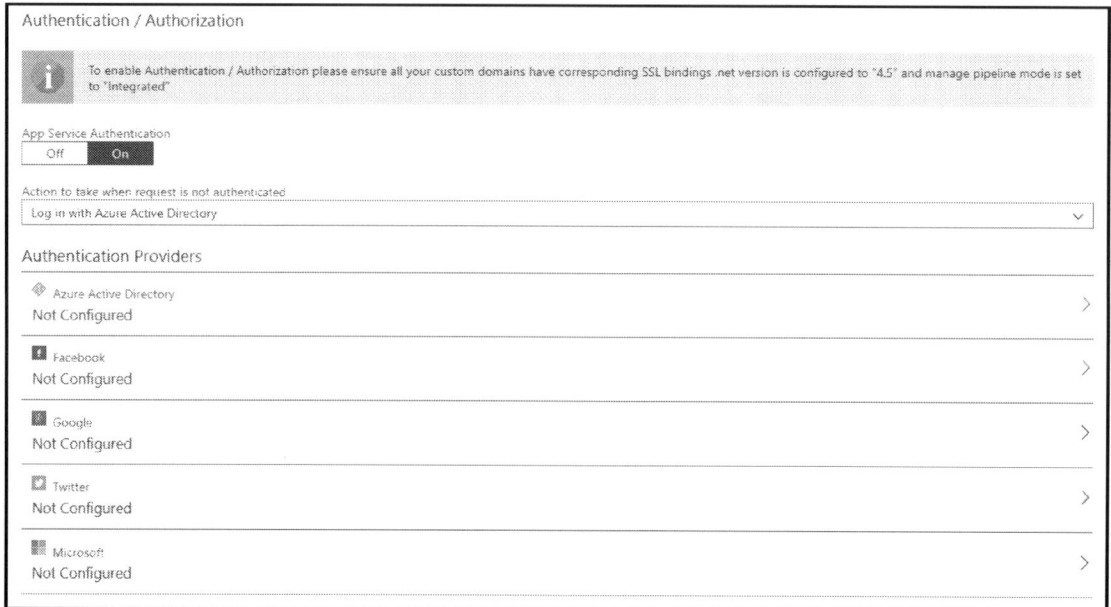

The **Backup** option allows us to create a backup for our application. We need to provide **Storage Settings** (the storage account where the backup will be stored), backup schedule, and retention period. The default retention period is 30 days and the default schedule is daily, but you can change these settings. If you set up a connection to a code repository, this option is not really necessary as you can redeploy the application at any time, but it's a useful feature if you want a quick restore or if you don't use a code repository:

Backup Configuration

Backup Storage

Select the target container to store your app backup.

Storage Settings
backup   >

Storage Account: nagiosdiag316.blob.core.windows.net

Backup Schedule

Configure the schedule for your app backup.

Scheduled backup | On | Off |

* Backup Every
| 1 | | Days | Hours |

* Start backup schedule from | 2018-07-28 📅 | 12:28:58 PM |
                                 | (UTC+02:00) --- Current Time... ▾ |

* Retention (Days) ⓘ | 30 |

Keep at least one backup | No | Yes |

| Save | Discard

Custom domains, certificates, and scaling

Custom domains and SSL settings allow us to customize the URL for our application and
apply certificates to encrypt connections and increase security. These are directly connected
as you can't apply a valid SSL certificate without a custom domain for your Web App.

An Azure Web App, by default, has the URL `customname.azurewebsites.net` (where in `customname` is the name you provided while creating the Web App). In order to simplify access, you can use a custom URL that you already own or you can buy a new domain. There is even the option to buy a new domain through the Azure portal, but the offer is not provided by Microsoft, but by partners. If you buy a new domain through the Azure portal, this will be added to your Azure bill.

In order to set up a custom domain, domain ownership needs to be verified. This is done by adding ether CNAME (`customname.azurewebsites.net`) or a record (Azure Web App IP address) on your DNS which will point your custom domain to the Azure Web App. Once verification is done, you just need to confirm that you want to use that domain for your Azure Web App. Also, you can set up your website to use HTTPS only to increase security, especially if you are using SSL. Information on CNAME and the IP addresses that need to be added to verify ownership, and later to be used to point to your website, can be found on this page:

SSL Configuration allows us to set **HTTPS Only** again. I strongly advise you to use this whenever possible. Another security option is **Minimum TLS Version**, wherein you can choose between **1.0**, **1.1** and **1.2**. It is recommended to use TLS **1.2** as it may be reported insecure otherwise. The **Bindings** option allows you to pair up a custom domain and available certificates. As you can have more custom domains point to a single website, all available domains with SSL will be shown in the list, as shown here:

The **Certificates** section under SSL settings allows you to manage certificates for your website. You can either **Import App Service Certificate** or **Upload Certificate**. An App Service certificate is an option that allows you to buy a certificate through the Azure portal and use that certificate for your applications. This certificate will be available to all apps in the tenant. The **Upload Certificate** option allows you to upload an existing certificate that you already have or have bought from an external source. Certificates will show under the public or private list, depending on the type of certificate you uploaded or imported. You can also request **Client Certificates** if needed. All certificate options are shown in the following screenshot:

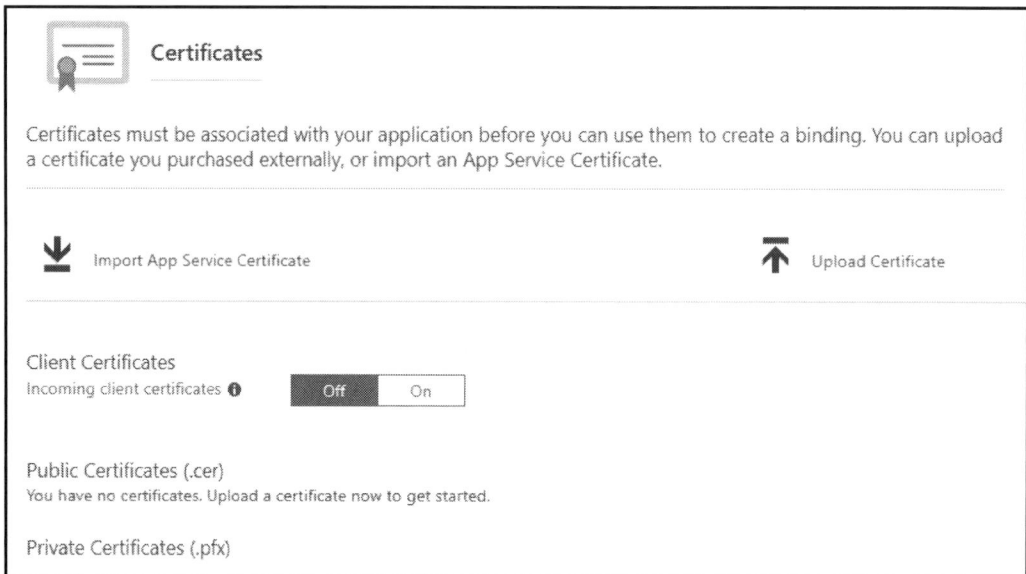

Automatic scaling for Azure Web Apps is done similarly to a **virtual machine scale set** (**VMSS**). Under the **Scale out** section, you can find a blade that is identical to the scale out blade in VMSS. In order to configure scale out rules, you need to set up scale out and scale in parameters. For example, you can set up a web app to add an additional instance whenever the CPU goes over 70%, and then decrease the number of instances if the CPU goes under 25%. You can set up the minimum, maximum, and default number of instances. Additional scale out and scale in rules can be added that will perform a scale in/out depending on different metrics. This will allow you to save money and run the minimum number of instances needed without suffering performance issues. An example of scale conditions is shown in the following screenshot:

Default Auto created scale condition 🖉	⊘

Delete warning	ⓘ The very last or default recurrence rule cannot be deleted. Instead, you can disable autoscale to turn off autoscale.
Scale mode	⦿ Scale based on a metric ◯ Scale to a specific instance count

Scale out

When	PacktPaaS	(Average) CpuPercentage > 70	Increase instance count by 1

Rules

Scale in

When	PacktPaaS	(Average) CpuPercentage > 25	Decrease instance percent by 1

➕ Add a rule

	Minimum ⓘ	Maximum ⓘ	Default ⓘ
Instance limits	1	5 ✓	1

Schedule	**This scale condition is executed when none of the other scale condition(s) match**

Azure Web App Tools

Azure Web Apps have some unique tools that are specific to this service: **DEVELOPMENT TOOLS**, **MOBILE**, and **API**.

DEVELOPMENT TOOLS start with the **Clone app** option, which allows us to create a new instance of the Web App that will be an identical replica of the existing app. However, this option is limited only to the **Premium tier**, and if you are using any other tier, this option will not be available unless you upgrade. Console gives you web access to the console, where you can browse files and perform actions on the command line.

Advanced Tools opens an additional window that contains a few different options, like debug console, process explorer, resource explorer, and different information for debugging and deployment. We can also add extensions to our Web App and choose hundreds of different extensions from the gallery in the site extensions section.

App Service Editor (Preview) allows you web access to the code editor, wherein you can make live changes to application code without any additional tools. **Performance test** allows you to perform load tests on your app and see how it would handle any amount of concurrent users. **Resource explorer** and **Extensions** are the options available in the advanced tools that we talked about.

A very interesting option is **Testing in production**. It requires the use of slots and allows you to redirect a percentage of users to a different slot for user testing. For example, we deployed a new version of the application to the staging slot. Using this feature, we can point 10% of users to this slot in order to verify that the application is working as expected. Once we verify that 10% of the users don't have any issues, we can increase this to 25%, then to 50%, and then finally switch all users to the new version. A list of all development tools is shown in the following screenshot:

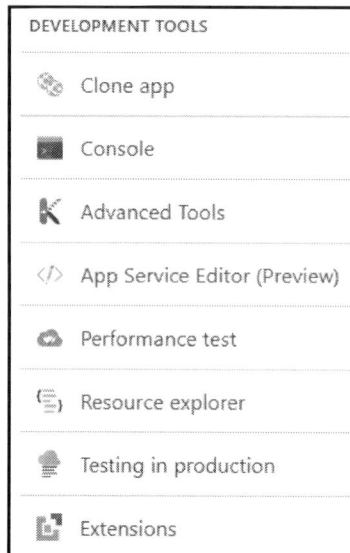

The other sections available are **MOBILE**, **API**, and **MONITORING**:

- **MOBILE**: This has three options which are intended to be used for mobile applications. These options are **Easy tables**, **Easy APIs**, and **Data connections**. **Data connections** defines a connection to the Azure SQL database and is also a requirement for **Easy tables** and **Easy APIs**. Both **Easy tables** and **Easy APIs** require mobile extension to be installed on your Web App.
- **API**: The **API** section contains API Definitions and CORS. **API definition** lets you configure the location of the Swagger 2.0 metadata describing your API. This makes it easy for others to discover and consume your API. Note that the URL can be a relative or absolute path, but must be publicly accessible. **Cross-Origin Resource Sharing** (CORS) allows JavaScript code running in a browser on an external host to interact with your backend.

- **MONITORING**: This is available for other resources, and we already covered most of these options. The options available for monitoring are **Alerts (Classic)**, **Diagnostic logs**, **Log stream**, and **Process explorer**. In **Diagnostic logs**, you can set the level of logs you want to save. **Log stream** gives you the option to observe logs live. The list of options in the **MOBILE**, **API**, and **MONITORING** sections is shown in the following screenshot:

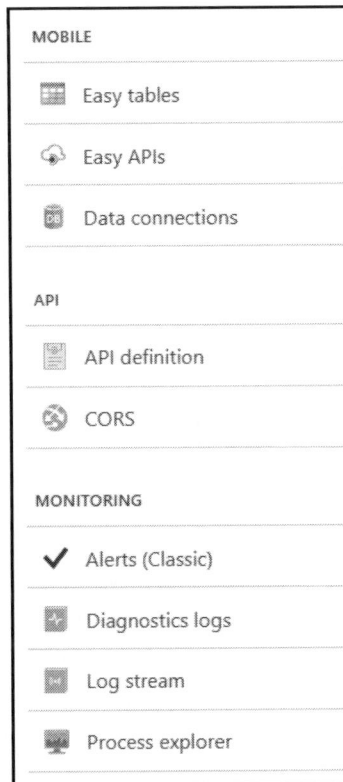

Monitoring a Web App in Azure

The default options for monitoring Azure Web Apps can be useful, but it's only the beginning of the Web App monitoring options. If you want a really powerful tool for monitoring and alerting with dashboards and analytics, Application Insights is the tool you want to use. Application Insights can be created and linked to a Web App while creating the Web App or later.

Also, you can use a single Application Insight to monitor multiple Azure Web Apps. It's interesting that Application Insights is not limited to Azure Web Apps, but can be used with an application hosted anywhere, including other cloud providers or an on-premises data center.

Application Insights

A first look at Application Insights gives you a few dashboards that show basic information on requests, response time, and availability for your application in the last two hours. These dashboards can be customized with different time frames and to show different metrics altogether. An example of **App Insights** dashboards is shown in the following screenshot:

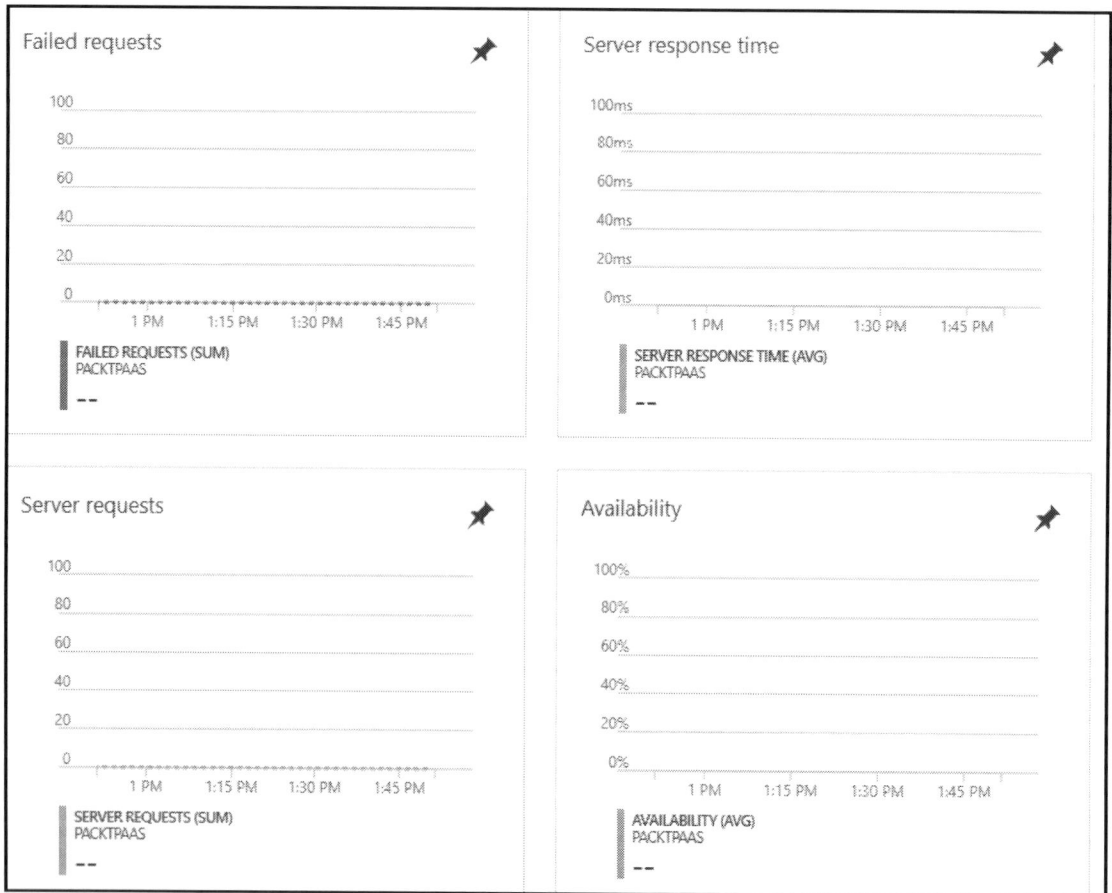

The first set of options under **Application Insight**s is under the **INVESTIGATE** section. In this section, we have multiple metric options which allow us to track different performance counters and dependencies. Most of these options can be edited and we can extract specific information, as well as create custom dashboards and alerts. Some of these metrics can be collected only if the Application Insight SDK is installed on your application. A list of all options under the **INVESTIGATE** section is shown in the following screenshot:

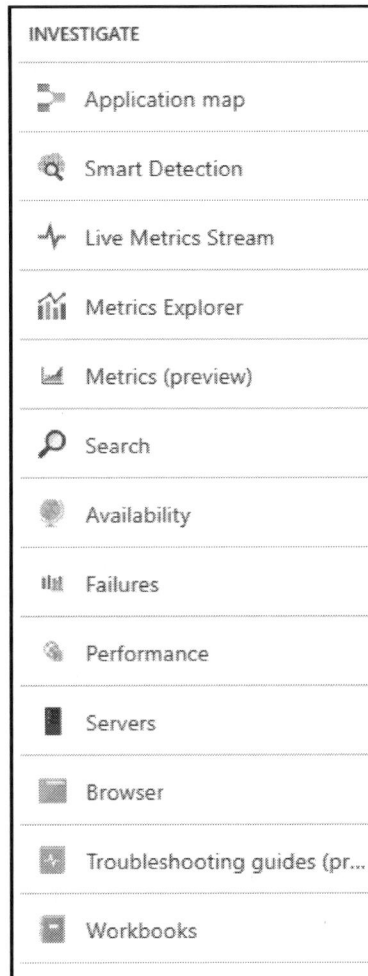

An example of one of these alerts is availability. We can create a test that will continuously test our application from different locations in order to confirm that the application is available.

We can edit test frequency, test locations, success criteria, and alerts. If the default settings are used, the application will be pinged every 5 minutes from five different locations. In case three or more locations fail to contact the application, an alert will be triggered and a notification will be sent. An example of an availability test is shown in the following screenshot:

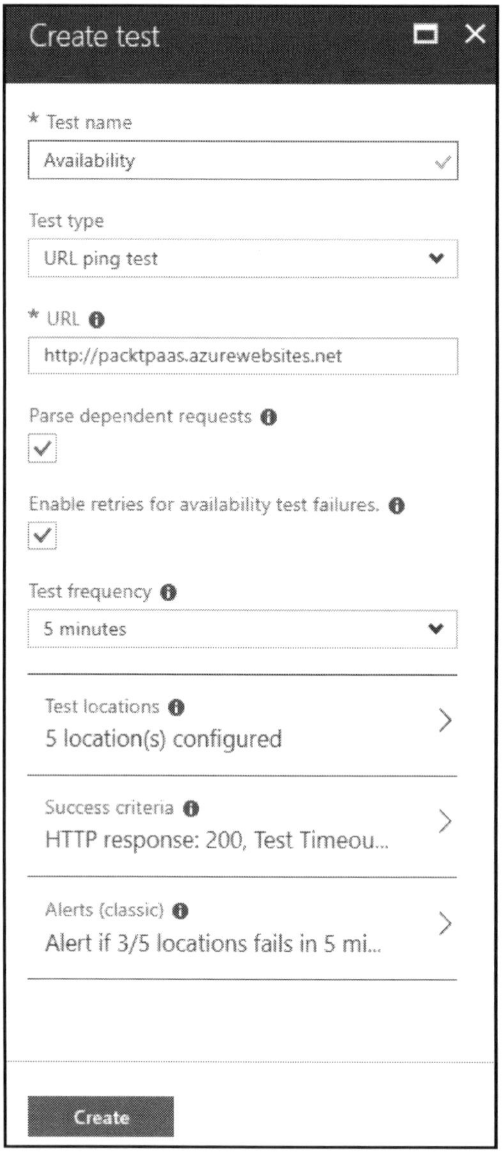

The **USAGE** section contains various information on **Users**, **Sessions**, **Events**, and **User Flows**. To get metrics in this section, you need to use the Application Insight JavaScript SDK and add JavaScript code snippets to your application. A list of all options under users is shown in the following screenshot:

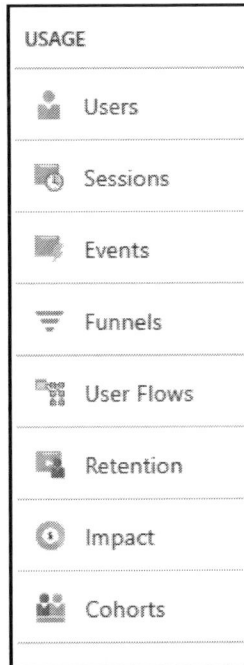

Here is an example of a code snippet that needs to be added to an application in order to collect usage information:

```
<!-- To collect end-user usage analytics about your application, insert the
following script into each page you want to track. Place this code
immediately before the closing </head> tag, and before any other scripts.
Your first data will appear automatically in just a few seconds. -->
<script type="text/javascript"> var
appInsights=window.appInsights||function(a){ function
b(a){c[a]=function(){var
b=arguments;c.queue.push(function(){c[a].apply(c,b)})}}var
c={config:a},d=document,e=window;setTimeout(function(){var
b=d.createElement("script");b.src=a.url||"https://az416426.vo.msecnd.net/sc
ripts/a/ai.0.js",d.getElementsByTagName("script")[0].parentNode.appendChild
(b)});try{c.cookie=d.cookie}catch(a){}c.queue=[];for(var
f=["Event","Exception","Metric","PageView","Trace","Dependency"];f.length;)
b("track"+f.pop());if(b("setAuthenticatedUserContext"),b("clearAuthenticate
dUserContext"),b("startTrackEvent"),b("stopTrackEvent"),b("startTrackPage")
```

```
,b("stopTrackPage"),b("flush"),!a.disableExceptionTracking){f="onerror",b("
_"+f);var g=e[f];e[f]=function(a,b,d,e,h){var
i=g&&g(a,b,d,e,h);return!0!==i&&c["_"+f](a,b,d,e,h),i}}return c }({
instrumentationKey:"ebfab75c-e0ea-4d45-8aa9-ac11e656e644" });
window.appInsights=appInsights,appInsights.queue&&0===appInsights.queue.len
gth&&appInsights.trackPageView(); </script>
```

The **CONFIGURE** section has a lot of settings that are already included in other Application Insights settings (such as **Smart Detection settings**) and Azure Web Apps settings (such as **Performance Testing**). The most interesting features are **API Access** (which allows you to manage API keys that allow other applications to access APIs on your Azure Web App) and **Work Items** (which allow you to connect to Visual Studio Team Services and link work items directly to your application). A list of settings under the configuration section in Application Insights is shown in the following screenshot:

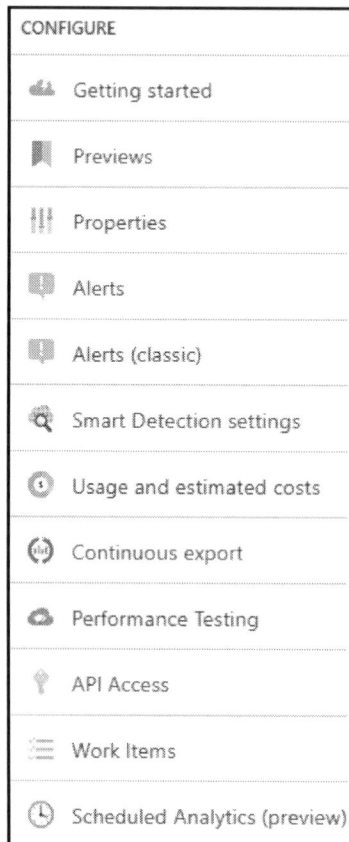

APPLICATION INSIGHTS logs a lot of different metrics. You can create custom queries to get different kinds of information in **Application Insights Analytics**. The results of these queries can be displayed as a table or as a chart. A screenshot of **Application Insight Analytics** is shown here:

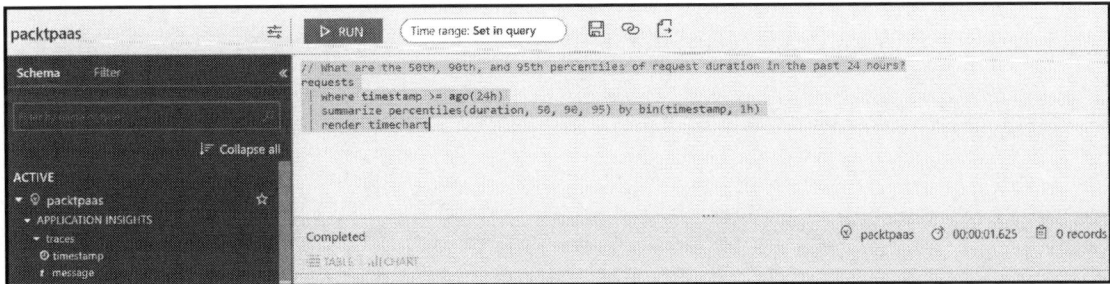

Here is an example of an Application Insights query:

```
requests
| where timestamp >= ago(24h)
| summarize percentiles(duration, 50, 90, 95) by bin(timestamp, 1h)
| render timechart
```

Azure App Service Plan

In the process of creating an Azure Web App, we needed to create an Azure App Service Plan. Let's take a step back and go over the settings available in the Azure App Service Plan.

Under **SETTINGS**, we have some options that are available in Azure Web Apps, such as **Networking, Scale up (App Service plan)**, and **Scale out (App Service plan)**. **Properties, Locks**, and an **Automation script** are available as well, as in all other Azure resources. Note that an App Service Plan can host multiple Azure Web Apps. Billing is done for an Azure App Service Plan; you don't pay per Web App. So, tier changes on an Azure Web App are directly connected to tier changes in the Azure App Service Plan. Scale up/down and scale in/out operations done in the Web App blade will be shown here as the tier will not change for the Azure Web App, but for the Azure App Service Plan.

A list of all options under settings in the Azure App Service Plan is shown in the following screenshot:

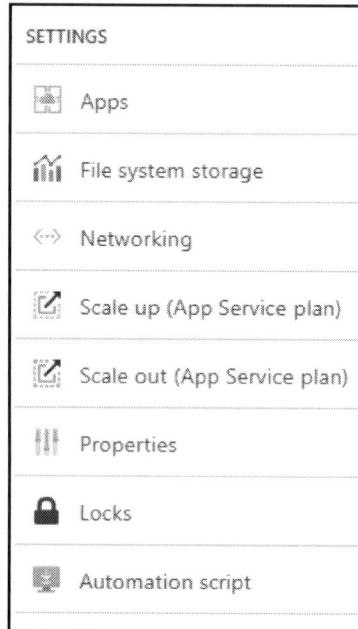

SETTINGS
🖼 Apps
📶 File system storage
⟨⋯⟩ Networking
📝 Scale up (App Service plan)
📝 Scale out (App Service plan)
ᛁᛁᛁ Properties
🔒 Locks
🖥 Automation script

On of the things that is different and unique for an Azure App Service Plan is Apps. As already mentioned, more Azure Web Apps can be hosted on a single Azure App Service Plan. The Apps option under settings has all these Web Apps listed, along with any slots that are created under these Web Apps. An example of an app list is shown in the following screenshot:

NAME	TYPE	RESOURCE GROUP	STATUS
packtpaas	Web app	PacktPaaS	Running
packtpaas-staging	Slot	PacktPaaS	Running
packtpaas-test	Slot	PacktPaaS	Running

Another different option is file system storage. Every Azure App Service Plan has resource limitations. Under **File system storage**, we have information on how much total and free space is available. A screenshot of **File system storage** is shown here:

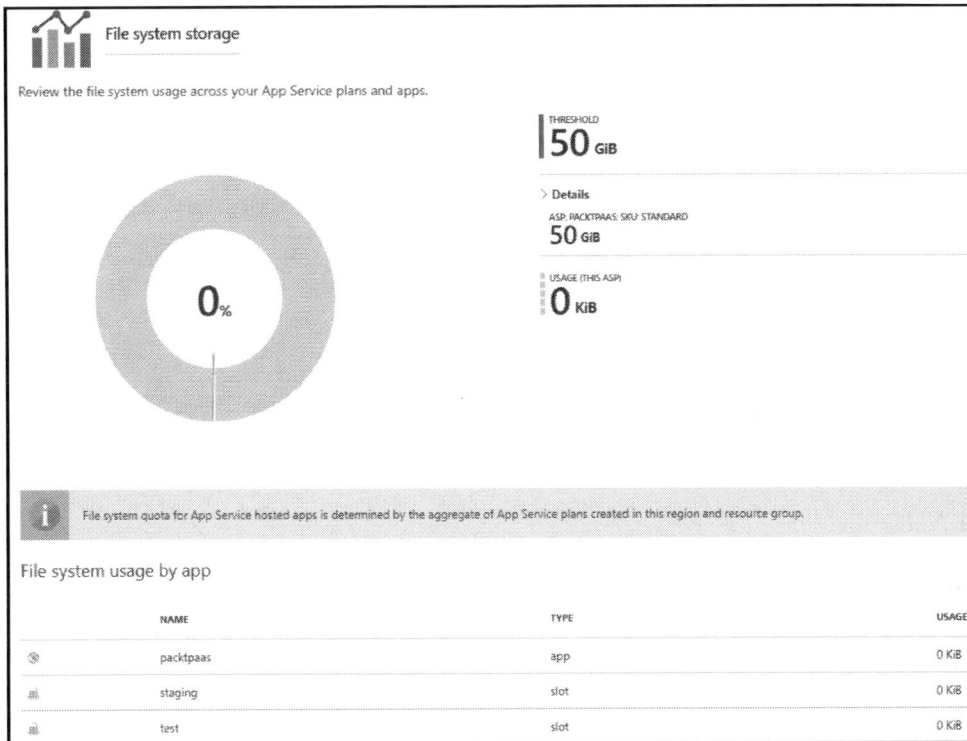

Azure Web App high availability

We have already seen how to set up automatic scaling for Azure Web Apps and how to create scale in and out rules. But scaling can improve performance and keep the application up if there is an increase in requests and doesn't really secure the high availability of the application. If there is an issue in the Azure Data Center where the application is located, or maintenance on the host is in progress, the application will be unavailable if hosted in a single location.

In order to achieve high availability, we need to introduce another Azure service: Traffic Manager. Azure Traffic Manager operates on the DNS level to direct incoming requests to endpoints based on custom routing rules.

Let's start with creating a new Azure Traffic Manager and go through the configuration to show how to set up high availability for Azure Web Apps.

Creating a Traffic Manager

To create a new Azure Traffic Manager, we need to provide the name, routing method, subscription resource group, and location. The location will be automatically chosen if an existing resource group is used. One option that is specific to Traffic Manager is the routing method, and the available options are performance, weighted, priority, and geographical.

The **Performance** option is used when you want to point a user to a location that will provide the best performance based on response time, network latency, and so on.

Weighted will distribute requests evenly or according to weight rules. For example, the default rule will distribute it evenly, and if we have two endpoints defined then half the requests will go to one endpoint and the other half to the second endpoint. But weight rules can be defined to have one endpoint receive 70% (or any other number) of requests, and the rest will be sent to the second endpoint. Of course, you can have more than two endpoints defined (two is the minimum) and create rules to weight any ratio you want.

The **Geographical** option will point users to the closest geographical location. For example, we can have two endpoints which are located in West Europe and East US. If the geographical routing method is used, users coming from Europe will be pointed to the endpoint in West Europe and users coming from the USA will be pointed to East US.

Finally, the priority routing method is usually used when high availability is the goal. One endpoint will be used as the primary endpoint, so all traffic will be pointed only to the primary endpoint. In case the primary endpoint becomes unavailable, all traffic will be pointed to the secondary instance. Of course, you can have more than only two endpoints. More endpoints ensures a bigger chance that at least one endpoint will be available and this increases the high availability percentage.

In some cases, the performance method can be used to achieve a similar goal to endpoint tracking, and users are pointed to the one that will perform best in a given situation. If the endpoint is unavailable, this will be reflected as a drop in performance and users will be directed to another endpoint that is giving better results. An issue with this approach is that the performance drop can take time to be detected, and users may experience issues until the performance of the endpoint is recognized to be down and they are redirected to a different endpoint. With the priority method, the availability of the endpoint is monitored, an issue is detected much faster, and users are pointed to a healthy instance faster and with lesser chance of experiencing issues.

An example of a filled template used to create a new Azure Traffic Manager is shown in the following screenshot:

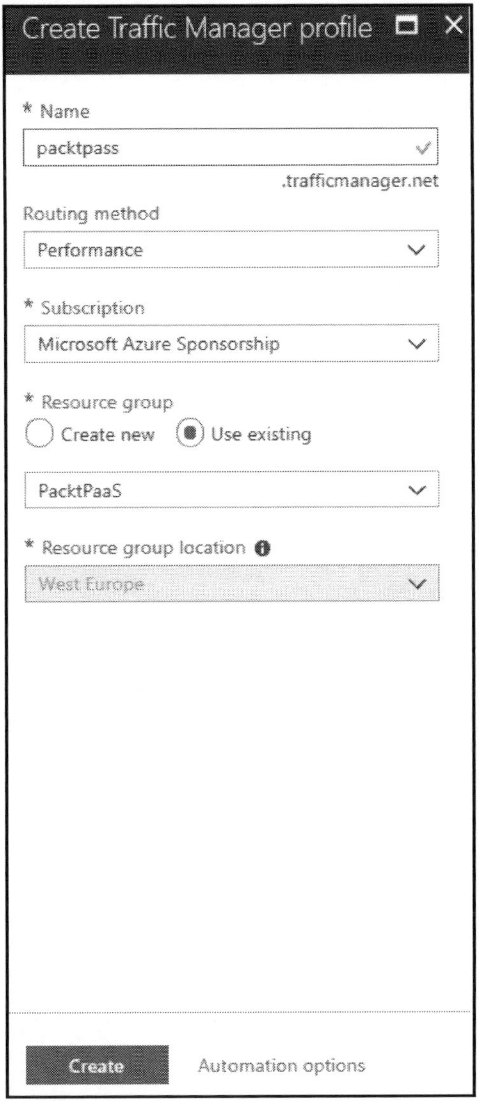

Traffic Manager configuration and settings

Once an Azure Traffic Manager is created, we can proceed with configuration. The **SETTINGS** specific to Traffic Manager are **Configuration**, **Real user measurements**, **Traffic view**, and **Endpoints**.

Real user measurements and **Traffic view** allow you to monitor behavior and see where users are pointed and how traffic is flowing. **Traffic view** will give you insights into where requests are coming from, using a map and pointing to request origins geographically. **Real user measurements** can give you more insight into requests and traffic, but requires a measurement key and JavaScript snippet to be embedded in the application code:

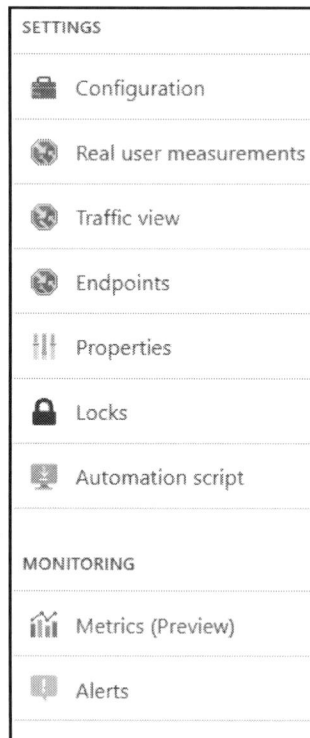

SETTINGS

Configuration

Real user measurements

Traffic view

Endpoints

Properties

Locks

Automation script

MONITORING

Metrics (Preview)

Alerts

The **Endpoint** option allows you to register endpoints toward which traffic will be directed. These can be either Azure endpoints or external endpoints. In the case of external endpoints, only **fully qualified domain name** (**FQDN**) is allowed. For **Azure endpoints**, it can be **Cloud Service**, **App Service**, **App Service slot**, or **Public IP address**. This is another example of naming that creates confusion. **App Service** and the **App Service slot** are actually Web App and the Web App slot in this case. An example of adding an Azure Web App (**App Service**) is shown in the following screenshot:

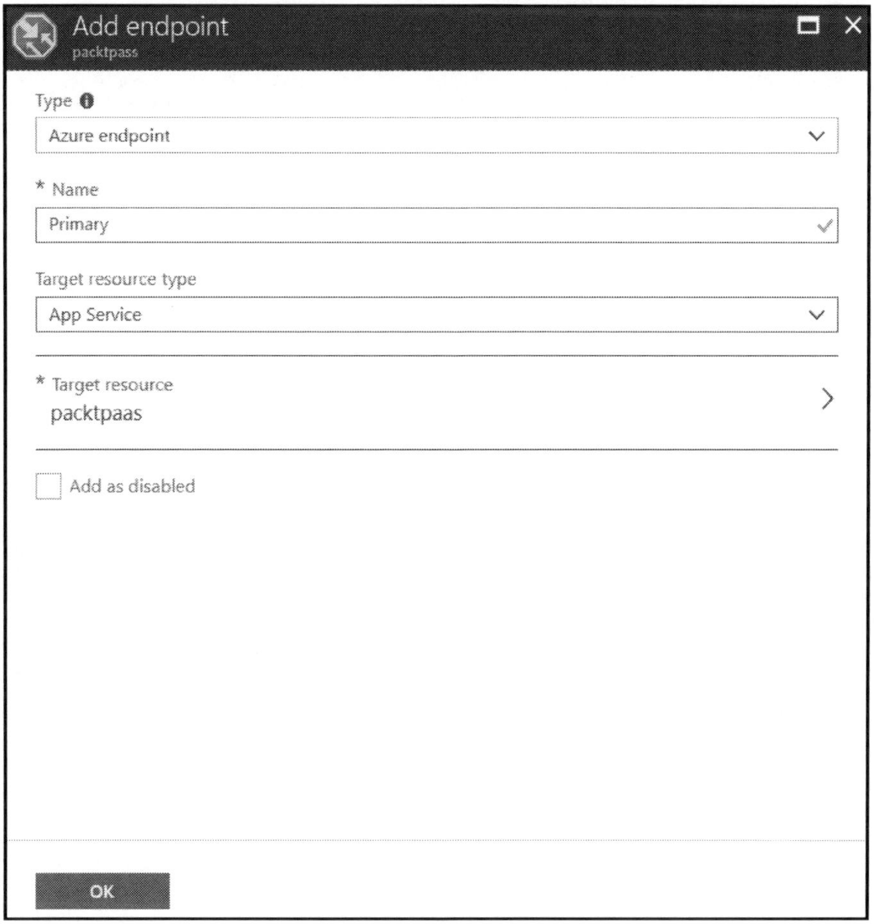

Having only one endpoint doesn't really help us to achieve high availability, and we need at least one more endpoint. I recommend that the second endpoint is located in a different region to resolve possible issues with maintenance or service in a single data center. A list of all available endpoints is located under **Endpoints**, with **NAME, STATUS, TYPE**, and **LOCATION**. An example is shown in the following screenshot:

NAME	STATUS	MONITOR STATUS	TYPE	LOCATION
Primary	Enabled	Checking endpoint	Azure endpoint	West Europe
Secondary	Enabled	Checking endpoint	Azure endpoint	East US

The last step is to create rules under configuration. Note that we can change the routing method here, and this option can be changed after creating a Traffic Manager. This isn't the case with all Azure resources, and some settings can't be changed once you create them. For example, no resource in Azure can be renamed: the only option is to delete it and create a new one if a name change is required. Under the **Endpoint monitoring settings**, you can choose the **Protocol**, **Port**, and **Path** that you want to monitor.

Finally, the **Fast endpoint failover settings** need to be configured. The **Probing interval** can be set to **10** or **30** seconds, and this determines how often endpoint status will be checked. **Tolerated number of failures** can be set to 0-9, and this determines how many times a check can fail before the endpoint is declared failed. **Probe timeout** determines the time needed before the probe times out. This value needs to be at least 5, and less than the probing interval time. Lower numbers for these settings mean that issues will be detected faster and failover will occur before an issue is detected by users. However, you need to be careful, as pinging the application more often than needed and declaring too few tolerated failures can cause the application to switch between instances too often and create additional issues. An example configuration is shown in the following screenshot:

Routing method ❶

| Performance | ⌄ |

* DNS time to live (TTL) ❶

| 60 |

seconds

Endpoint monitor settings ❶

Protocol

| HTTPS | ⌄ |

* Port

| 80 |

* Path

| / | ✓ |

Fast endpoint failover settings

Probing interval ❶

| 30 | ⌄ |

* Tolerated number of failures ❶

| 3 |

* Probe timeout ❶

| 10 |

seconds

Running Azure Web Apps in a dedicated environment

Azure Web Apps use public endpoints and are usually accessed over the internet without any restrictions. In a case where more isolated access is needed, there is another option: **Azure App Service Environment (ASE)**. Azure ASE offers a fully isolated and dedicated environment for secure applications at high scale. Azure ASE is usually used with workloads that require very high scale, isolated and secure network access, and high memory utilization. As ASE comes as a dedicated environment, this eliminates the problem of noisy neighbors (performance issues that may result from another application sharing the same host) and allow you to fully utilize all resources.

An Azure App Service Plan can be connected to an Azure VNet, but this requires additional work. On other hand, ASE comes automatically connected to a VNet and can be accessed only over private connections and private IP addresses.

Summary

An Azure App Service Plan is the best example of the PaaS model in Microsoft Azure. It allows us to host applications without servers and virtual machines. Even though management options are simplified and cut down to the minimum, we still have a lot of configuration options. Legacy support is next to nothing, but the PaaS model is intended for modern applications that require the latest features and frameworks. If you need to run legacy software, IaaS is the best choice.

We introduced IaaS and PaaS in Azure from the application perspective. But the application is nothing without data. In the next chapter, we'll move to Data Platform in Azure and show how to create and manage databases in the cloud.

Questions

1. Azure App Service is...
    1. IaaS
    2. PaaS
    3. SaaS

2. How much control do we have with an App Service Plan compared to virtual machines?
    1. More
    2. Less
    3. The same

3. How much administration do we have with an Azure App Service Plan compared to virtual machines?
    1. More
    2. Less
    3. The same

4. An App Service Plan is used to host...
    1. Web applications
    2. Databases
    3. Both

5. Slots are used to...
    1. Host different version of the application
    2. Host the application in different regions
    3. Handle increased workload

6. An Azure App Service Plan's increased workload is handled by...
    1. Scaling up
    2. Scaling out
    3. WebJobs

7. The best monitoring tool for Azure Web Apps is...
    1. Splunk
    2. Log analytics
    3. Application Insights

8. High availability for Azure Web Apps is achieved by...
    1. Scaling up
    2. Scaling out
    3. Traffic Manager

9. Traffic Manager supports...
    1. Azure endpoints
    2. External endpoits
    3. Both

10. An isolated and dedicated environment for Azure Web Apps is an...
    1. Azure App Service Plan
    2. Azure ASE
    3. Azure Virtual Machine

The Azure Data Platform

5

The most important part of any IT system is data. Without data, applications and IT systems don't mean a thing. We discussed how to set up our applications in the IaaS and PaaS models, but how do we set up our databases?

In this chapter, we'll discuss database options and how to create environments that will host our databases.

We will cover the following topics:

- SQL Server in Azure Virtual Machine
- **Database as a Service (DaaS)**
- Azure SQL Database
- Azure data and analytics platform

Technical requirements

For this chapter, you'll need the following:

- An Azure subscription
- SQL Server Management Studio

Azure Database options

Understanding database options in Azure is a very important part of our cloud journey. All services that we use must, in the end, store information somewhere. Microsoft Azure offers extensive data platforms and multiple services in which we can store data. We'll start with the **relational database management system (RDBMS)** as the most traditional database model, and we'll discuss cloud options for SQL Server as Microsoft's on-premises solution for RDBMS.

To run SQL Server in Azure we have two different options—IaaS and PaaS. Database in PaaS is often referenced as DaaS. We'll explain both approaches and examine other services in Azure data platform.

SQL Server as IaaS

Running SQL Server as IaaS requires creating an Azure Virtual Machine that will host our SQL Server. We can either create a clean VM with an OS image and install SQL Server ourselves, or we can create a VM with SQL Server already included. Managing databases in both cases is not much different from managing databases in an on-premises environment. You have the full version of SQL with all options you would have in the on-premises version.

Let's begin with creating a VM for our SQL Server and explain everything.

Creating an Azure Virtual Machine with a SQL image

As mentioned, you can either create a VM and install SQL Server later, or you can choose an image that already has SQL Server included. In this case, I'm going to choose an image named SQL Server 2016 SP1 Enterprise Edition which already has SQL Server included. This VM is based on Windows Server 2016, and this is going to be our OS.

Most options are very similar to options that we had when SQL Server wasn't included in the image used to create a virtual machine. We start with basic information, where we have to provide a **Name**, **VM disk type**, **Username**, **Password**, **Subscription**, **Resource group**, and **Location**. I strongly recommend you use **SSD** as the VM disk type when creating a VM that will run SQL Server.

Disk speed has big impact on SQL Server performance, and selecting a faster disk type will help you get the best performance. A list of all basic settings and an example is shown in the screenshot:

Our next step is to select the size of the VM. Based on the disk type, the list will be limited to sizes that support only the disk type selected. When selecting the size for the VM that will run SQL Server, I recommend selecting more CPU and memory. SQL Server requires resources, and selecting the right size is beneficial for performance. Luckily, if you select a size that is too big or too small, you can change it later. This is one of the cloud computing perks, and you are not stuck with the initial size. A list of VM sizes based on SSD are shown in the following screenshot:

Choose a size
Browse the available sizes and their features

Search		Compute type			Disk type			vCPUs		
		Current generation			SSD only			1		128

RECOMM...	SKU	TYPE	COMPUT...	VCPUS	GB RAM	DATA DIS...	MAX IOPS	LOCAL SS...	PREMIU...	ADDITIO...	ZONES	EUR/MO...
Available												
	B2s	Standard	General purpc	2	4	4	3200	8 GB	SSD		1,2,3	€40.66
	B2ms	Standard	General purpc	2	8	4	4800	16 GB	SSD		1,2,3	€76.80
	B4ms	Standard	General purpc	4	16	8	7200	32 GB	SSD		1,2,3	€145.12
	B8ms	Standard	General purpc	8	32	16	10800	64 GB	SSD		1,2,3	€278.95
	D2s_v3	Standard	General purpc	2	8	4	3200	16 GB	SSD		1,2,3	€133.01
	D4s_v3	Standard	General purpc	4	16	8	6400	32 GB	SSD		1,2,3	€266.02
	D8s_v3	Standard	General purpc	8	32	16	12800	64 G8	SSD		1,2,3	€532.05
	D16s_v3	Standard	General purpc	16	64	32	25600	128 GB	SSD		1,2,3	€1,064.10
	D32s_v3	Standard	General purpc	32	128	32	51200	256 GB	SSD		1,2,3	€2,128.19

Prices presented are estimates in your local currency that include only Azure infrastructure costs and any discounts for the subscription and location. The prices don't include any applicable software costs. Recommended sizes are determined by the publisher of the selected image based on hardware and software requirements.

Select

The **Settings** blade has all the options we have used before and we can set a default for everything. If you intend to set up high availability for your SQL Server, make sure you select **Availability zone** and **Availability set** now, as this cannot be done later. Also, take note of the **Network**, **Subnet**, and **Network Security Group** that the VM is going to be connected to. If multiple subnets are in use, you probably don't want SQL Server to end up in DMZ. The same goes with NSG—you probably want different security settings for SQL Server than Web Server. Luckily, these settings can be changed later. An example of the **Settings** is shown in the screenshot:

Settings

High availability

Availability zone ⓘ

None	⌄

* Availability set ⓘ
None   >

Storage

Use managed disks ⓘ

No	Yes

Network

* Virtual network ⓘ
PacktVnet   >

* Subnet ⓘ
default (10.1.0.0/24)   >

* Public IP address ⓘ
(new) DBserver-ip   >

Network Security Group ⓘ

Basic	Advanced

OK

Finally, we have a set of settings which are specific to images with SQL Server and can't be found when creating VMs that don't have SQL Server included. In **SQL Server settings** we can configure **SQL connectivity**, **SQL Authentication**, **Storage configuration**, **Automated patching**, **Automated backup**, **Azure Key Vault integration**, and **R Services (Advanced analytics)**.

SQL connectivity allows us to set up the connectivity level and port. For the connectivity level, we can allow connection to the SQL Server only from within the VM: **Private (from Virtual Network)** and **Public (over internet)**. I strongly recommend not using public access to SQL Server. This will expose your databases to access over the internet; anyone can try to gain access and you're exposing the database to brute force attacks. Access to SQL Server only from within the VM may not be an option either, unless you run everything on a single VM and intend to run the application on the same server. Most often the scenario will be private access from within the virtual network, allowing other VMs on the same network to access the database. The default **Port** for SQL Server will be 1433 but can be changed if needed.

Default authentication for SQL Server will be Windows authentication, but you can **Enable SQL Authentication** if needed. If **SQL Authentication** is enabled, the username and password used for the VM will be added as the SQL login as well.

Storage configuration is **Not available** at this time and this setting will be used after the VM is created.

Automated patching is set to **Sunday at 2:00** by default. This setting can be changed to another time, or it can be **Disabled**. I recommend not disabling it, as this will ensure your SQL Server is up to date and patched with the latest updates, including security updates. However, in some cases, you need to test updates before installing them, so in this case you want to disable them. Note that, in this case, you are responsible for keeping the server up to date.

Automated backup is **Disabled** by default. If **Enabled**, you have multiple options available. You can select the storage account in which backups will be placed; the retention period is 30 days by default, and it can be set to a lower value (minimum 1 and maximum 30 days). Backup encryption can be set to on or off; system database backup can be included if needed. The last option is to configure the backup schedule. Automatic backup, set by default, will perform backup operations weekly. You can change this setting to daily. You can set up a time for backup, as well as the frequency. (This can be configured to back up the database from every 5 minutes to once a day.)

The last two options are **Azure Key Vault integration** and **R Services (Advanced analytics)**, and these allow you to **Enable** these features if needed. Azure Key Vault will require Key Vault information that will be used, and R service will simply install additional analytics features.

An example of **SQL Server settings** is shown in the following image:

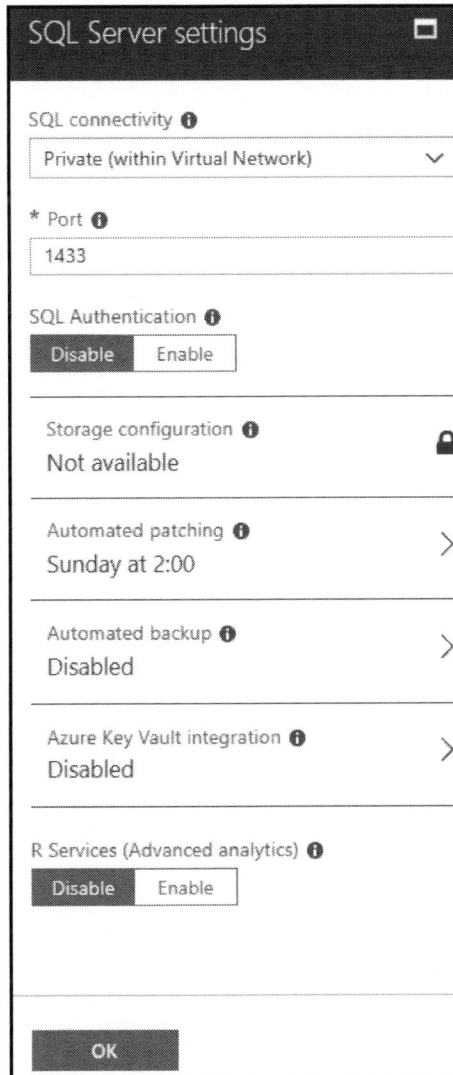

Deploying Azure Virtual Machine with SQL Server takes a little longer than deploying a similar VM without SQL Server. This is due to passing additional information and configuring the SQL Server instance inside the VM.

Managing SQL Server in the Azure Virtual Machine

Once the VM with SQL Server is deployed, you can find settings very similar to settings of other Azure Virtual Machines. The only difference is in the SQL Server configuration that can be found here.

Under **SQL Server configuration** is a new blade which has the same options as the **SQL Server settings** in the last step of creating a new VM with SQL Server.

The first option in this blade is **Storage**; the option that was **Disabled** previously. Here we can find storage usage and performance.

Next are **SQL connectivity** settings, in which we can change the access level and SQL Server **Port** and turn on **SQL Authentication** (or turn it off if previously enabled).

A screenshot showing the storage and connectivity part of the blade is shown here:

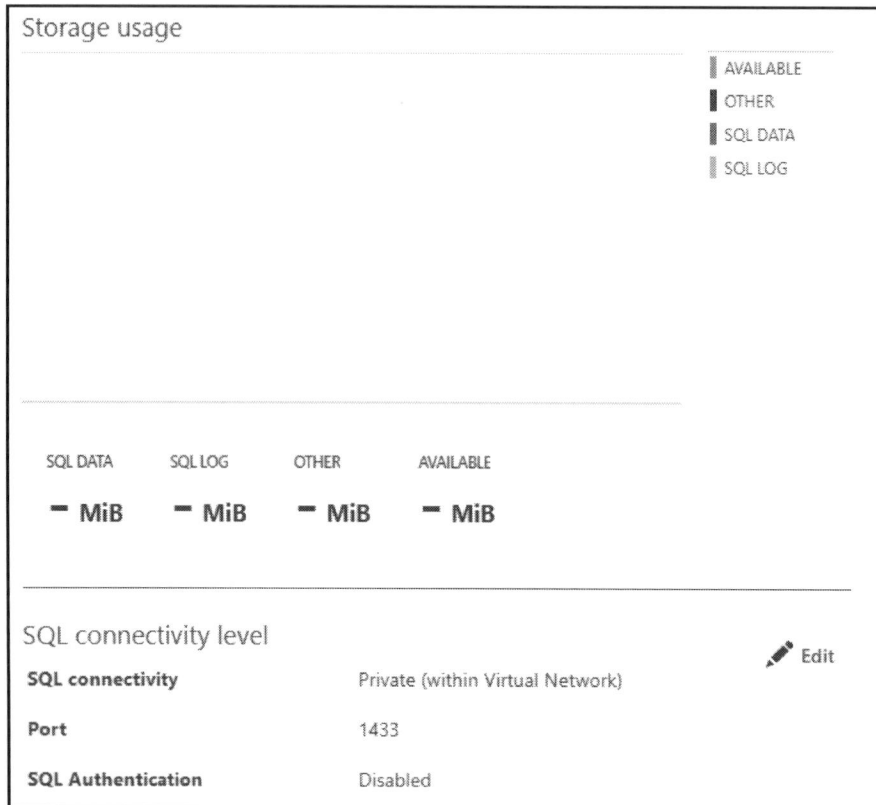

Other settings available under SQL Server configuration are **Automated patching,
Automated backup, Azure Key Vault integration** and **R Services (Advanced analytics)**.
All settings for these features are the same as those available while creating the VM. A
screenshot with other settings follows:

Automated patching		Edit
Automated patching	Enabled	
Maintenance schedule	Sunday	
Maintenance start hour (local time)	02:00	
Maintenance window duration (minutes)	60	
Automated backup		Edit
Automated backup	Disabled	
Automated Backup is currently disabled due to a change in backup settings via SQL Server Managed Backup. When you enable automated backup, your managed backup settings will be overridden.		
Azure Key Vault integration		Edit
Status	Disabled	
Additional features		Edit
R Services (Advanced analytics)	Disabled	

We can connect to the VM and use SQL Server Management Studio to connect to SQL
Server. Alternatively, you can do the same from your computer if SQL Server access is set
to public. As you can see, when connected to SQL Server, you have all the options and
features that are available when accessing SQL Server in a local on-premises environment.
From this point, managing and administrating your databases in the cloud is no different
than doing the same on the local server or VM.

We can perform any operation and make any change that we could do in the local environment. The following screenshot shows us that all options available for the local SQL Server are available for SQL Server in the Azure Virtual Machine:

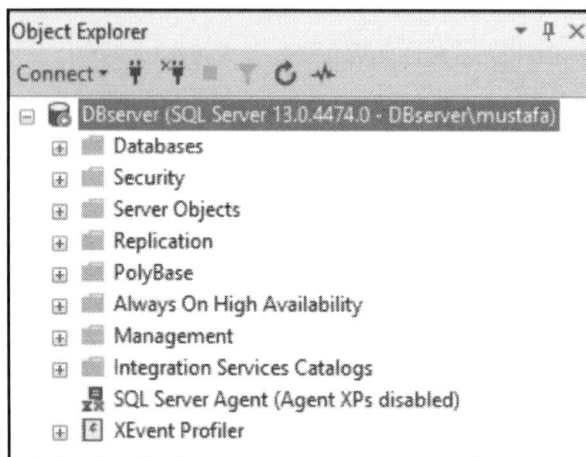

Administering and maintaining the VM itself is no different than managing any other Azure Virtual Machine. All settings are identical; the only difference is that the VM with SQL has additional features such as SQL Server configuration.

Now we'll move to SQL Server as PaaS and try to compare what each option is offering us and which choices are available.

High availability for SQL Server in Azure Virtual machine

The administration and management of SQL Server in Azure Virtual Machine is not much different from SQL Server on-premises. A similar thing can be said about creating a high-availability solution.

There are several options available to create high availability for SQL Server in Azure VM:

- Always on failover cluster instances
- Always on availability groups
- Database mirroring
- Log shipping

Note that in order to create such a solution, the VM must be placed in the availability zone and/or availability set.

SQL Server as PaaS

Running databases as PaaS (or DaaS) allows us to leverage PaaS advantages. This means that we have fewer settings available, but there is less maintenance as well. We don't have direct access to SQL Server and can't perform many operations, but we can still manage with preconfigured options that are available.

Let's begin creating Azure SQL Database and explain all the options.

Creating the Azure SQL Database

To create a new Azure SQL Database, we need to provide a standard set of information such as **Database name**, **Subscription**, and **Resource group**. Additional information is specific to Azure SQL Database; we need to **Select source**, provide **Server**, and **Pricing tier**. There is the option to select whether we **want to use SQL elastic pool?** which is directly connected to the **Pricing tier**, and we'll get to that in a moment. For the database source, we can select blank (empty database), sample (`AdventureWorkLT`, standard Microsoft sample database), and from backup (if this option is selected, we need to provide the storage information of where the backup is located).

The **Collation** of the database is always `SQL_Latin1_General_CP1_CI_AS` and cannot be changed. A list of settings is shown in the following screenshot:

A database can not exist without a server, so during Azure SQL Database creation, we need to provide the server. If there isn't an existing server, we need to create a new one. We need to provide a name (a unique name that will be used as a public endpoint), username, password, and location.

Pricing for Azure SQL Database can be confusing as there are multiple approaches. The first approach is single database pricing. In this pricing model, you are charged per database and the server is free. You can have multiple databases on single or multiple servers; the price is based on database count, and server count doesn't impact pricing. For example, we can have 10 Azure SQL Databases. The price will be same for these if the databases are located on one server or on 10 different servers. Where it really gets complicated is the pricing unit, **database transaction unit** (**DTU**). This is a blend measure of a CPU, memory, data I/O, and transaction log I/O. Traditionally, in an on-premises environment, we would monitor the CPU, memory, and disk IOPS and translate this to DTU, but it is not that simple. Luckily, we have the ability to change this over time so that any size selected can be changed if we determine that the database performance is impacted or not utilizing current resources. Tiers available in the DTU model are **Basic**, **Standard**, and **Premium**, each coming with a different DTU value. **Basic** comes with five DTUs and it goes up to 4,000 for Premium P15. Available space is also influenced by tier and can go from 2 GB for basic and up to 4 TB for P15. A screenshot of the DTU tier selection is shown here:

As the DTU model turned out to be complicated, Microsoft recently decided to introduce a new Azure SQL Database pricing model based on vCores. This model allows you to select how many vCores will be assigned to your database and how much memory will be available. The number of vCores can go from **2** to **80**. Memory depends on the number of vCores, and can go from **5.5** to **408** GB. A screenshot of vCore tier selection is shown here:

We mentioned that an elastic pool is also an option connected to pricing. This is a completely different model based on resource pooling. If elastic pool is selected as the pricing model for Azure SQL Database, the price isn't determined by the number of databases but by the size of the pool. Both pricing models available for a single database are available for elastic pool, and we can select whether elastic pool resources will be based on DTUs or vCores. The difference between an elastic pool and a single database pricing model is that selected amount of resources are available to the pool and resources are shared between databases located in the elastic pool. So, if we select 4,000 DTUs for the elastic pool, these will be shared between all databases located in the pool. In a scenario in which all your databases are highly utilized at the same time, this is not ideal and single database pricing should be selected. But if you have databases that have a high workload during different times of the day, this is the ideal scenario.

Let's say that you are hosting applications for clients located all over the world. This will peak database workload differently for each client and at different times based on their time zones. One database will have a high workload during work hours in Europe and have a low workload during work hours in the USA. The database for a client in the USA will have a low workload during work hours in Europe but a high workload during work hours in the USA. Placing these databases in the elastic pool allows you to share resources, and databases can use more of the resources available in different time periods.

Deployment time of Azure SQL Database can depend on tier and source. The source determines the size of the database and what kind of operations need to be performed. It's logical that it takes less time to create a blank database than restoring a backup that has a couple of GBs or TBs of data.

Once deployment is finished, we can see two resources: **SQL server** and **SQL database**:

NAME	TYPE	LOCATION
packt	SQL server	West Europe
Demo (packt/Demo)	SQL database	West Europe

Managing the Azure SQL Database

Managing an Azure SQL Database starts with **Firewall settings**. By default, only Azure services are allowed to connect to your database. To allow any other connection, you need to set up a firewall rule that will accept a connection from an allowed IP addresses. To add your IP address, select **Add client IP**. Azure portal will automatically detect your current IP address and add firewall rules. Note that you always need to select the **Save** option when performing changes. Adding the new IP address in firewall rules means nothing if you don't save the new settings.

This has happened to me on more than one occasion—I added a new IP address and spent some time trying to figure out why I couldn't connect, only to realize I forgot to click on **Save**. **Firewall settings** are shown in the following screenshot:

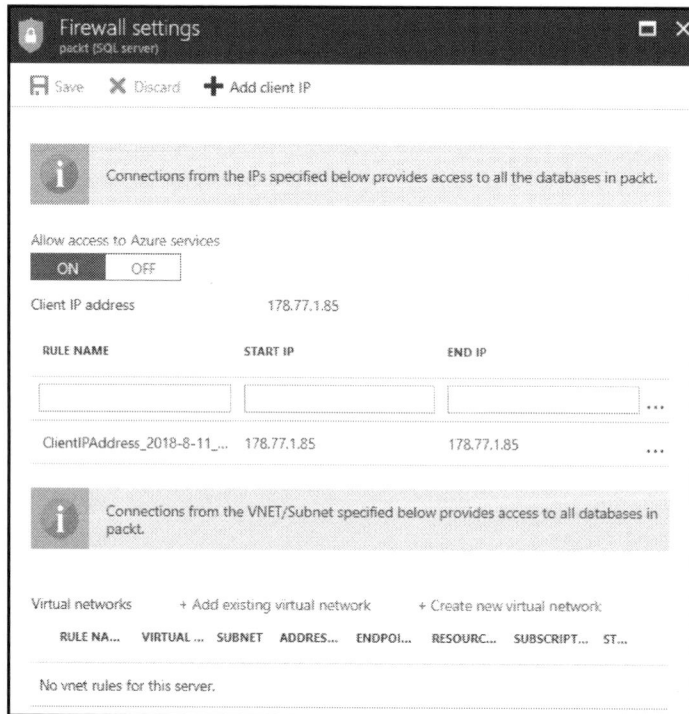

Once we add our IP address, we can connect to Azure SQL Server with **SQL Server Management Studio** (**SSMS**). Note that we have a limited set of options compared to the local instance of SQL Server. Beside databases and security, all other options are gone and we cannot manage databases as we did on-premises. A comparison between SQL Server and Azure SQL is shown in the following screenshot:

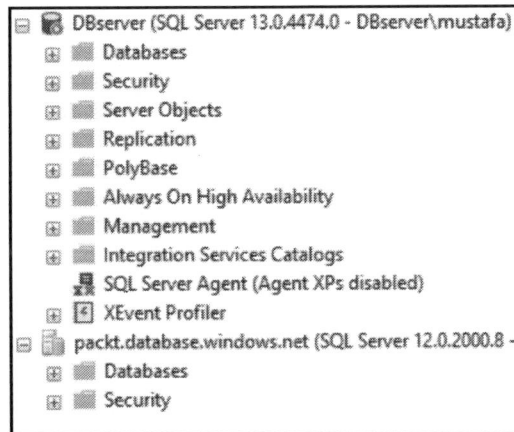

Luckily, there are plenty of options available to us in Azure to manage databases, and most features won't be missed. Database administration and maintenance has never been so easy as with Azure SQL.

The first option unique to Azure SQL is the **Query Editor**. This means that we no longer need SSMS; we can run any query from a browser. Some other task, performed in SSMS can be done in the Azure portal as well. A screenshot of a web query editor is shown here:

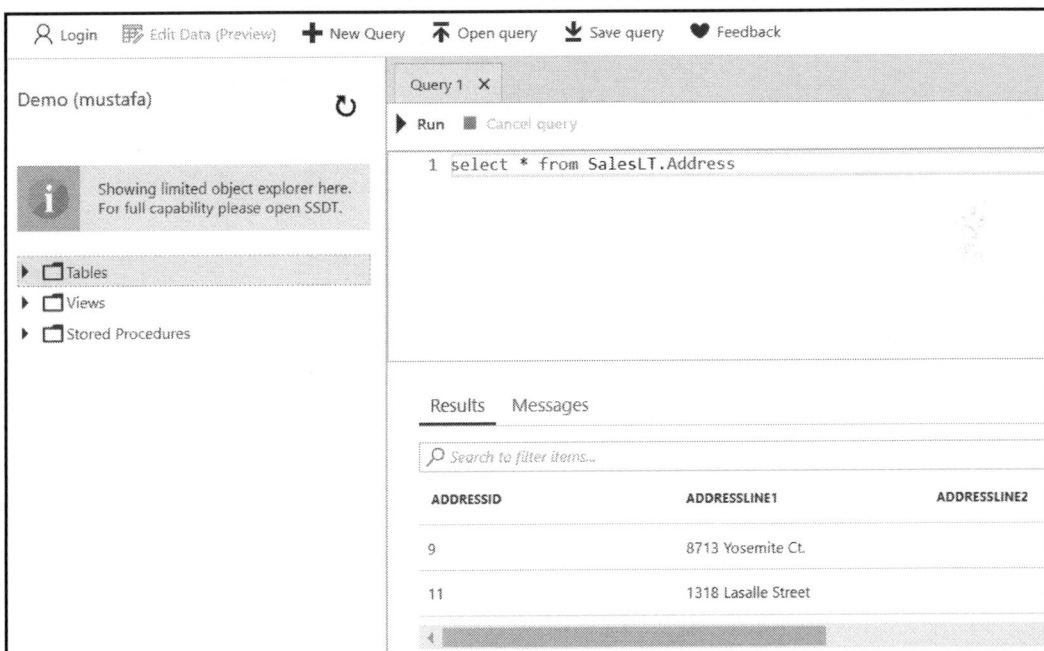

SETTINGS for Azure SQL Database have the usual options such as **Properties**, **Locks**, and **Automation script**. **Configure** is also an option often found in Azure resources settings, but unique options are **Geo-Replication**, **Connection strings**, **Sync to other databases**, and **Add Azure Search**. Syncing to other databases allows you to create a sync group and set up group of databases that will automatically be synchronized. Adding an Azure search option allows you to connect the database to a search service which allows you to perform full-text search without any additional coding or configuration.

The **Configure** option under **SETTINGS** allows you to change database tier. This will open a new blade that is identical to selecting the database tier while creating a database. A screenshot of the database tier change is shown here:

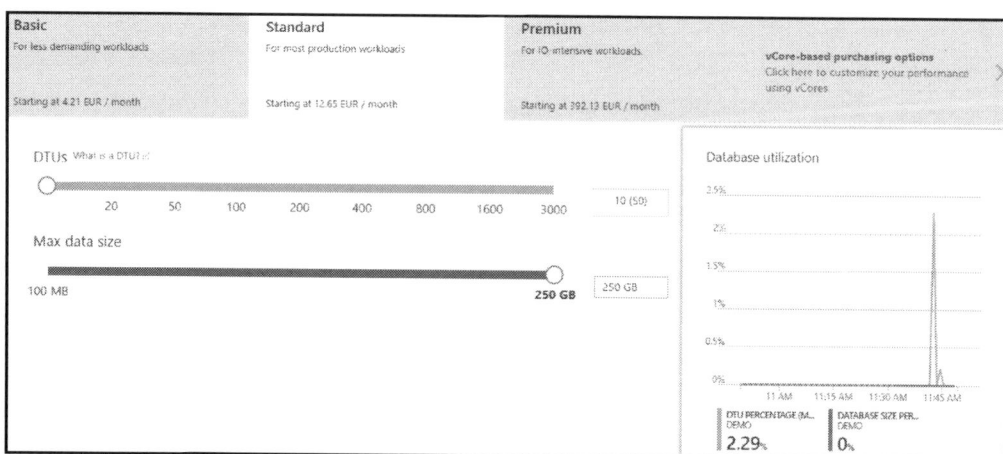

Connection strings allow you to find connection strings for your database for various programming languages.

Here is an example of a connection string for ADO.NET:

```
Server=tcp:packt.database.windows.net,1433;Initial Catalog=Demo;Persist
Security Info=False;User
ID={your_username};Password={your_password};MultipleActiveResultSets=False;
Encrypt=True;TrustServerCertificate=False;Connection Timeout=30;
```

Creating highly available Azure SQL Database

Creating SQL Server high availability solutions can be complicated, hard to configure, and even harder to maintain and manage. Azure SQL Database high availability is much easier to create and requires almost no maintenance.

The option we need to start with is **Geo-Replication**. The geo-replication blade shows the world map with marks showing data centers in which databases are currently located and all data centers available for replication. The current data center, in which the database is located, is marked in blue. The data center recommended for replication is marked in purple (this will be the data center closest to the current data center) and all other available data centers are marked green. On the map, you can see information about the current database that will be our primary database. An image of a geo-replication blade is shown in following image:

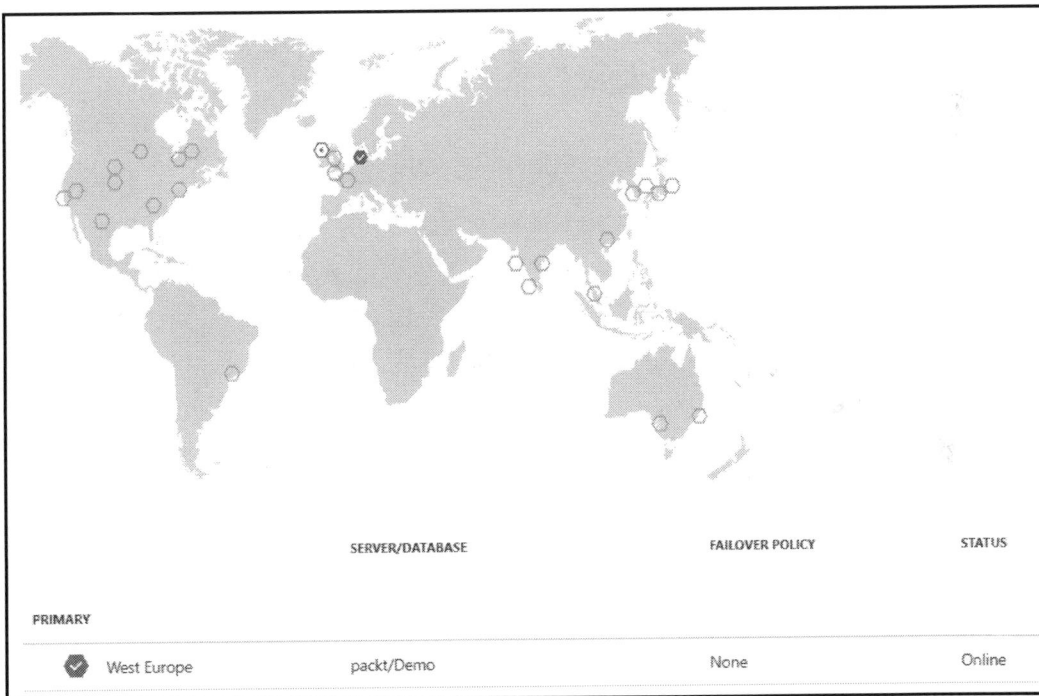

	SERVER/DATABASE	FAILOVER POLICY	STATUS
PRIMARY			
West Europe	packt/Demo	None	Online

To create a new database replica, we can select any data center on the map to start a new blade. The **Create secondary** blade will open, in which we need to provide a target SQL Server (create a new server if it doesn't exist in location selected). The **Database name** will be the same as the original one, and the database the will be in read-only mode. The **Pricing tier** will be same as the original, but you can change the tier to another value. An example of the settings needed to create a secondary database is shown here:

After deployment is finished, the map will change, showing the connection between the primary and secondary database. Deployment time depends on the database size.

During deployment, the empty database is created in the secondary data center, and then the data is copied from primary to secondary. A map with the replication in place is shown here:

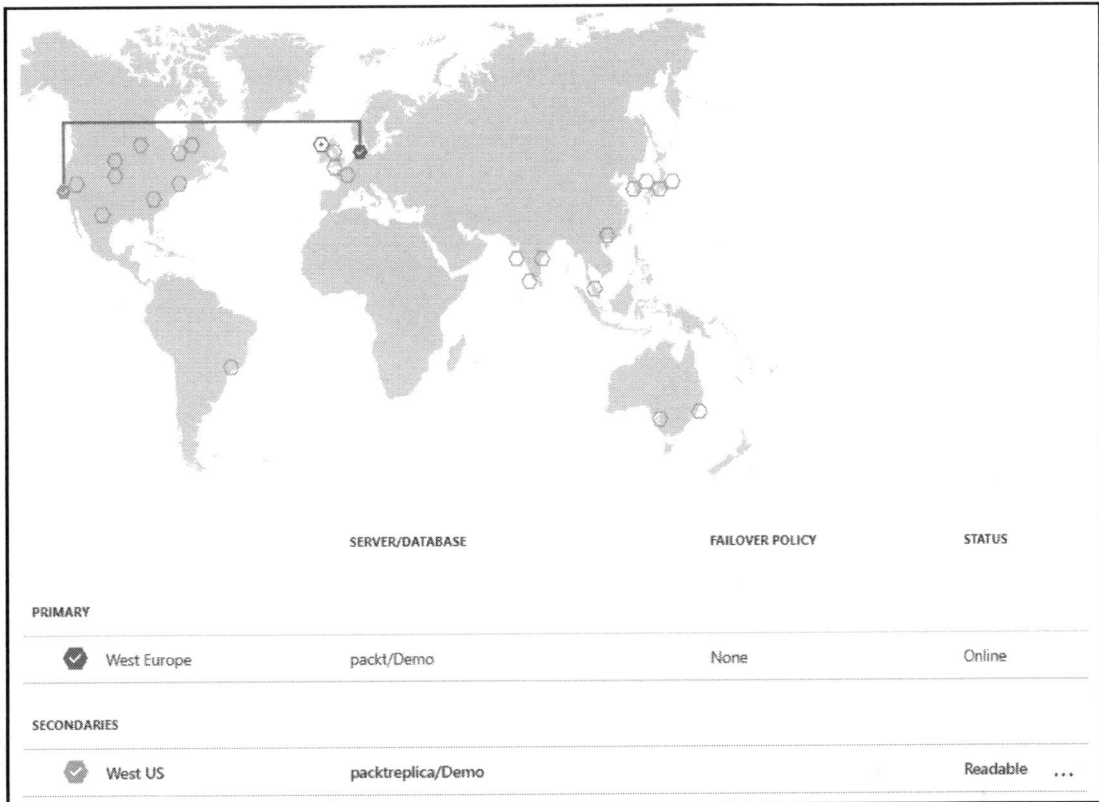

	SERVER/DATABASE	FAILOVER POLICY	STATUS
PRIMARY			
✔ West Europe	packt/Demo	None	Online
SECONDARIES			
✔ West US	packtreplica/Demo		Readable ...

However, notice that this is only creating a readable copy of the primary database. In the case of disaster or if the primary database is unavailable, the secondary database must be manually changed from read-only to read/write and all connection strings to the database must be changed manually. This doesn't really represent a high availability solution, so we need to take an additional step by creating a failover group.

In the **Failover group** blade, we need to provide a **Primary server**, **Secondary server**, **Failover group name**, **Read/Write failover policy**, and **Read/Write grace period (hours)**. The failover group name must be unique, and this will be the new endpoint for the connection to our database. Connecting to the failover group name will automatically point us to the primary server whenever the primary server is available.

If that primary server isn't available, all connections to the failover group name will be pointed to the secondary server. All failover and failback happens automatically and requires no user action. A screenshot of the **Failover group** options is shown here:

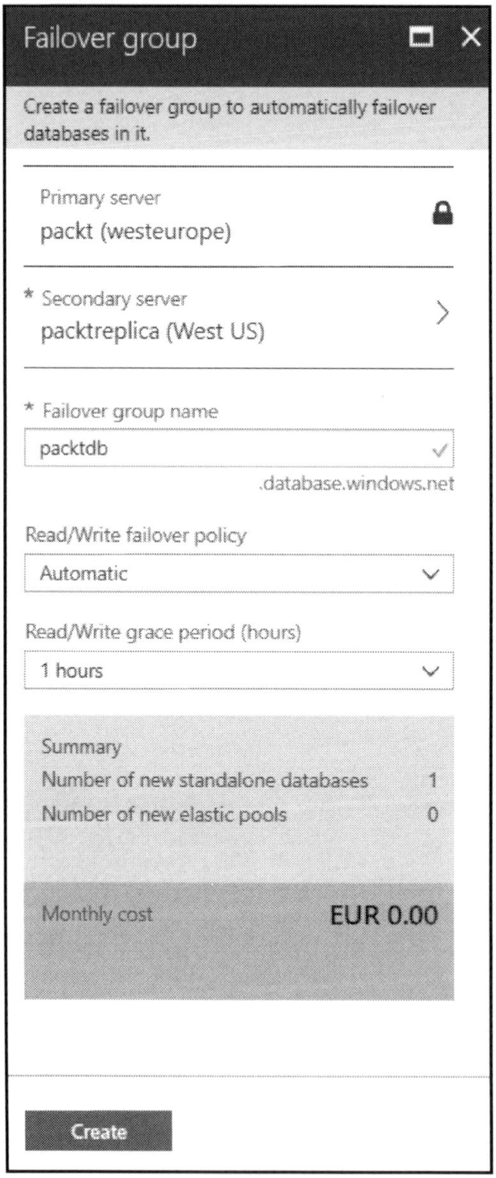

As you can see, creating the Azure SQL Database high availability solution is simple and fast. It requires no user action once it's created, and failover and failback happen automatically. If you have ever created a similar solution in an on-premises environment, you probably know how complicated a failback process can be.

Azure SQL Database security

When it comes to data, security is very important (not that other resources should be left unsecured). Under the **Azure SQL Database** blade, we have a set of options related to security. **SECURITY** options include **Advanced Threat Protection, Auditing, Dynamic Data Masking,** and **Transparent data encryption. Advanced Threat Protection** and **Auditing** can be applied on the server level (for all databases on the server) or for a single database.

Advanced Threat Protection contains three subsections:

- **Data Discovery & Classification (preview)**
- **Vulnerability Assessment**
- **Threat Detection**

The **Data Discovery & Classification (preview)** feature is still in beta but can be very useful. A scan of the database will be performed, and recommendations will be provided on which columns in your database should be marked as classified. This can be especially useful when considering data that should be considered regarding the **general data protection regulation (GDPR)**.

Vulnerability Assessment will perform a security scan and provide security recommendations for your database. Examples of recommendations would be to to track firewall rules or to classify sensitive data.

Threat Detection applies machine learning to your security. This feature analyzes normal behavior and alerts you to any action that is out of the ordinary. For example, if one of the SQL logins always accesses the database in work hours and suddenly tries to log in during other periods, you will be alerted. Or, if one of the logins is always coming from a specific IP address and tries to access the database from the other side of the world, action will be detected and you will be alerted.

A screenshot of advanced threat protection is shown here:

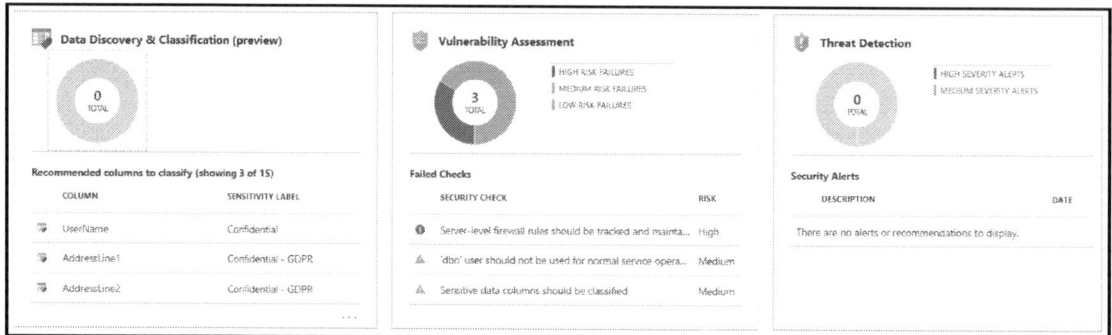

Auditing allows us to track events and log them to the storage account. We can define the log retention period, and whether events are logged on the database or server level. As auditing is often a requirement for many organizations, especially in order to be compliant to different standards, this option allows you to fulfill that requirement. A screenshot for audit logs is shown here:

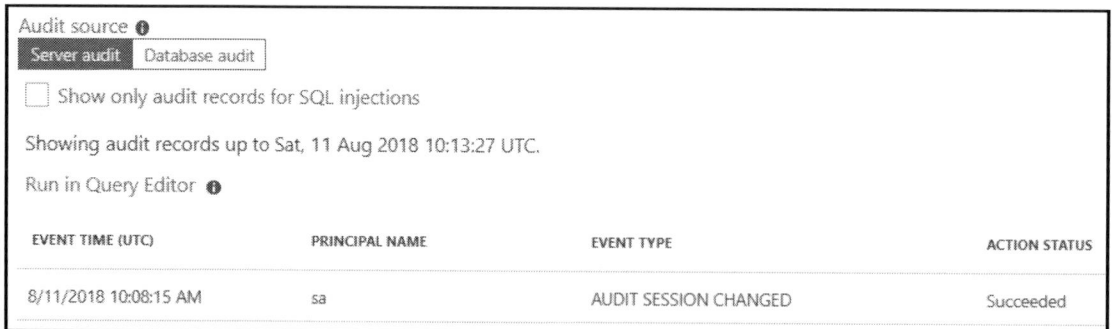

Before we proceed to dynamic data masking, let's run a simple query. Selecting the top 100 rows on the table `SalesLT.Customers` will return all information on the first 100 customers from the table. Here we have various types of data, and we may not want everyone with access to the database to see everything. Let's take a phone number, for example. Note that in the following screenshot, we can see that running the query will return the phone column:

```
SELECT TOP (1000) [CustomerID]
      ,[NameStyle]
      ,[Title]
      ,[FirstName]
      ,[MiddleName]
      ,[LastName]
      ,[Suffix]
      ,[CompanyName]
      ,[SalesPerson]
      ,[EmailAddress]
      ,[Phone]
      ,[PasswordHash]
      ,[PasswordSalt]
      ,[rowguid]
```

Results | Messages

anyName	SalesPerson	EmailAddress	Phone	PasswordHash
e Store	adventure-works\pamela0	orlando0@adventure-works.com	245-555-0173	L/Rfwxzp4w7RWmEgXX+/A7cXae
ssive Sports	adventure-works\david8	keith0@adventure-works.com	170-555-0127	YPdtRdvqeAhj6wyxEsFdshBDNXxk
iced Bike Components	adventure-works\jillian0	donna0@adventure-works.com	279-555-0130	LNoK27abGQo48gGue3EBV/UfYS
lar Cycle Systems	adventure-works\jillian0	janet1@adventure-works.com	710-555-0173	ElzTpSNbUW1Ut+L5cWfR7MF6nB
politan Sports Supply	adventure-works\shu0	lucy0@adventure-works.com	828-555-0186	KJqV15wsX3PG8TS5GSddp6LFFV
ic Exercise Company	adventure-works\linda3	rosmarie0@adventure-works.com	244-555-0112	OKT0scizCdlzymHHOtyJKQiC/fCILS
iated Bikes	adventure-works\shu0	dominic0@adventure-works.com	192-555-0173	ZccoP/jZGQm+Xpzc7RKwDhS11Y
Cycle Emporium	adventure-works\josé1	kathleen0@adventure-works.com	150-555-0127	Qa3aMCxNbVLGrc0b99KsbQqiVgw

The dynamic data masking blade will provide information on all the masking rules currently applied and recommendations for rules that you also may want to consider for masking. Note that the SQL administrator is excluded from data masking, and that you can add additional users to be excluded. A screenshot of dynamic data masking is shown here:

🖫 Save	✕ Discard	➕ Add mask	♥ Feedback	

Masking rules

MASK NAME	MASK FUNCTION
You haven't created any masking rules.	

SQL users excluded from masking (administrators are always excluded) ❶

SQL users excluded from masking (administrators are always excluded)	✓

Recommended fields to mask

SCHEMA	TABLE	COLUMN	
SalesLT	Address	AddressID	ADD MASK
SalesLT	Address	AddressLine1	ADD MASK
SalesLT	Address	AddressLine2	ADD MASK
SalesLT	Customer	FirstName	ADD MASK
SalesLT	Customer	LastName	ADD MASK

Load more

To add a new rule, we need to provide the **Schema**, **Table**, **Column**, and **Masking field format**. The **Masking field format** will allow you to control what masked data looks like in a query result. An example of how to add the phone column for data masking is shown here:

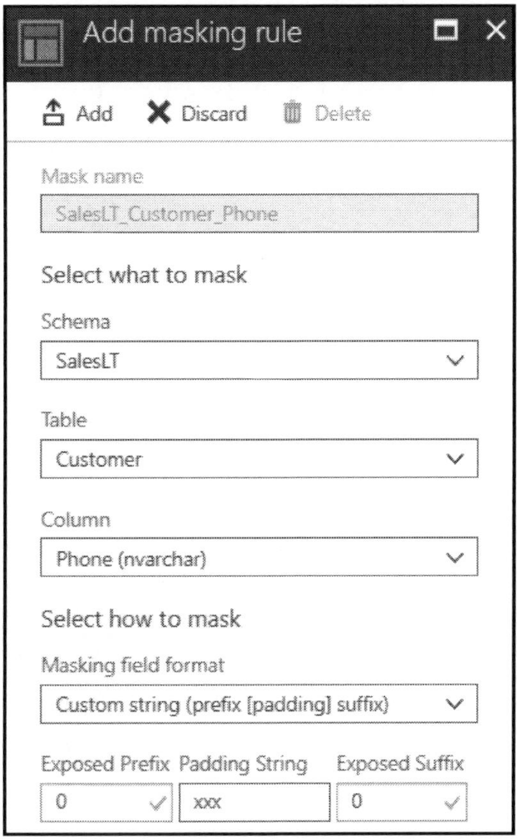

Once the data masking rule is applied, we can run the query again. As you can see in the following screenshot, the result will be different when the masking rule is applied, and the phone column will then return xxx for all values:

```
SELECT TOP (1000) [CustomerID]
      ,[NameStyle]
      ,[Title]
      ,[FirstName]
      ,[MiddleName]
      ,[LastName]
      ,[Suffix]
      ,[CompanyName]
      ,[SalesPerson]
      ,[EmailAddress]
      ,[Phone]
      ,[PasswordHash]
      ,[PasswordSalt]
      ,[rowguid]
```

Results | Messages

yName	SalesPerson	EmailAddress	Phone	PasswordHash
Store	adventure-works\pamela0	orlando0@adventure-works.com	xxx	L/Rlwxzp4w7RWmEgXX+/A7cXaePEPcp+KwQhl2lJL7w
ive Sports	adventure-works\david8	keith0@adventure-works.com	xxx	YPdtRdvqeAhj6wyxEsFdshBDNXxkCXn+CRgbvJltknw=
ed Bike Components	adventure-works\jillian0	donna0@adventure-works.com	xxx	LNoK27abGQo48gGue3EBV/UrfYSToV0/s87dCRV7uJk=
Cycle Systems	adventure-works\jillian0	janet1@adventure-works.com	xxx	ElzTpSNbUW1Ut+L5cWlfR7MF6nBZia8WpmGaQPjLOJ
ltan Sports Supply	adventure-works\shu0	lucy0@adventure-works.com	xxx	KJqV15wsX3PG8TS5GSddp6LFFVdd3CoRftZM/tP0+R4=
Exercise Company	adventure-works\linda3	rosmarie0@adventure-works.com	xxx	OKT0scizCdlzymHHOtyJKQiC/fCILSooSZ8dQ2Y34VM=
ed Bikes	adventure-works\shu0	dominic0@adventure-works.com	xxx	ZccoP/jZGQm+Xpzc7RKwDhS11YFNybwcPVRYTSNcn
cle Emporium	adventure-works\josé1	kathleen0@adventure-works.com	xxx	Qa3aMCxNbVLGrc0b99KsbQqiVgwYDfHcsK9GZSUxcT

Using dynamic data masking, we can control user access to data and prevent them seeing confidential information. For example, if we have billing information and contact information in the same table, we may want to provide access to the table to different users but allow them to see different information. We can allow our sales department to see an email or phone number, but want to prevent them from seeing credit card information. On the other hand, we don't want to prevent everyone from seeing credit card information and want to allow this information to be accessed by the finance department. Dynamic data masking is ideal for this scenario, wherein users can have access to the same table but see different sets of information.

Transparent data encryption (**TDE**) is used for encrypting databases in rest mode. This feature is available for on-premises versions of SQL Server but requires an implementation that isn't so simple. For Azure SQL Databases, this feature is turned on automatically for newly created databases. This wasn't always the case, and for older databases you can turn it on simply by switching the TDE option on. As simple as that, databases (and all backups) are encrypted at rest. Transparent database encryption is shown in the following screenshot:

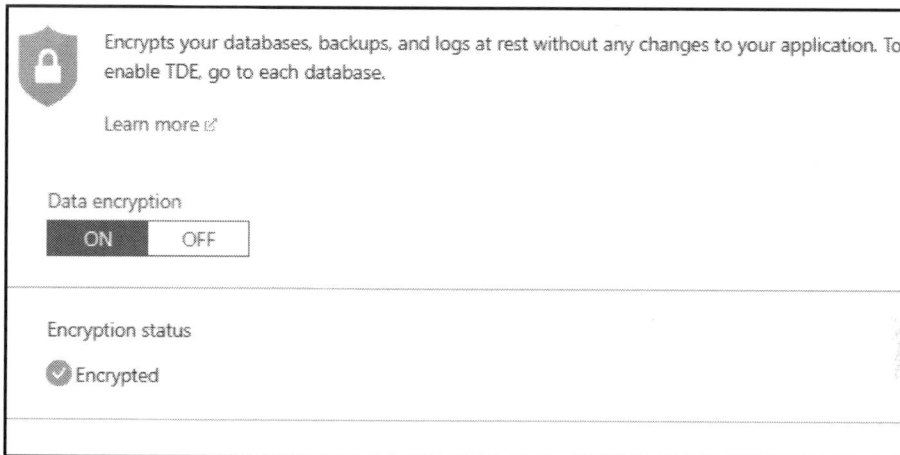

Monitoring and troubleshooting Azure SQL Database

MONITORING options for Azure SQL Databases is very similar to options for other Azure resources. Options available for **MONITORING** are **Alerts (Classic)**, **Metrics (preview)**, and **Diagnostic settings**. All of these features are available for Azure Virtual Machines and Azure Web Apps, and these were covered in previous chapters.

SUPPORT + TROUBLESHOOTING options bring us a few features that are specific to Azure SQL Databases. Features such as **Resource health** and **New support request** are present, as for other Azure resources. New features are **Performance overview**, **Performance recommendations**, **Query Performance Insight**, and **Automatic tuning**.

Performance overview gives us an overview of query performance. Here we can find information on resource consumption by queries. Overview gives us insight into aggregated consumption for queries per resource type. Resource type can be DTU, CPU, and IOPS. This aggregation will show queries which create the biggest resource cost, but as this is aggregated consumption, it can be the result of the query being executed often and not of the query spending resources in a single run. A list of queries which take more time to execute can be found under the **Long running queries** tab. This information can help us improve performance, as queries that are often executed and queries that take a long time to execute are spending lot of resources. Editing these queries can improve performance and save money in the long run as well. A graph showing CPU consumption in the **Performance overview** category is shown here:

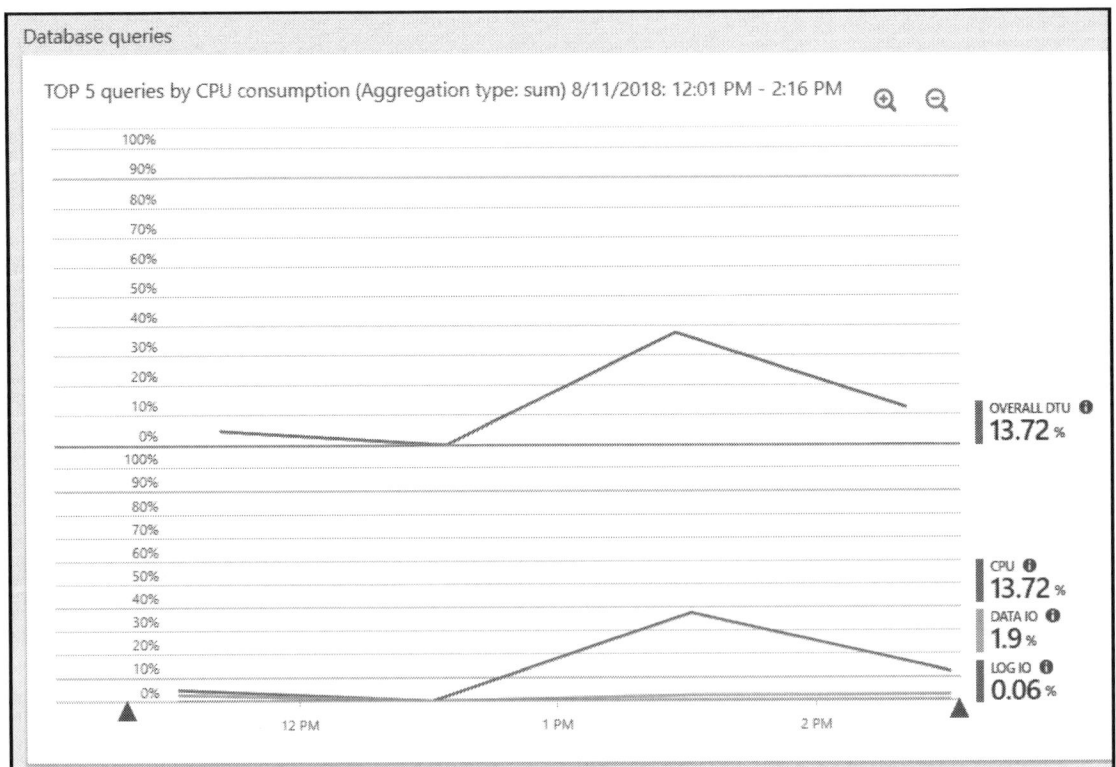

Under performance list, we can see **Recommendations** based on performance history for our database. It will give us a list of **Recommendations**, along with the options to automatically apply these recommendations. In the **Performance recommendation** blade, we can see both new **Recommendations** and recommendations already applied, shown as follows:

Recommendations

ACTION		RECOMMENDATION DESCRIPTION		IMPACT	

We analyzed your database and found that your database was created recently. At this time, we don't have any recommendations.

Tuning history

ACTION		RECOMMENDATION DESCRIPTION		STATUS		TIME	

There are currently no operations to display. Once you apply a recommendation, its status will be displayed here.

Query Performance Insight gives us very similar options to performance overview. The difference is that you can customize and edit graphs and dashboards in **Query Performance Insight**. You can change different metrics and time periods that will be displayed, helping you to observe performance over longer periods of time. The default blade for **Query Performance Insight** is shown here:

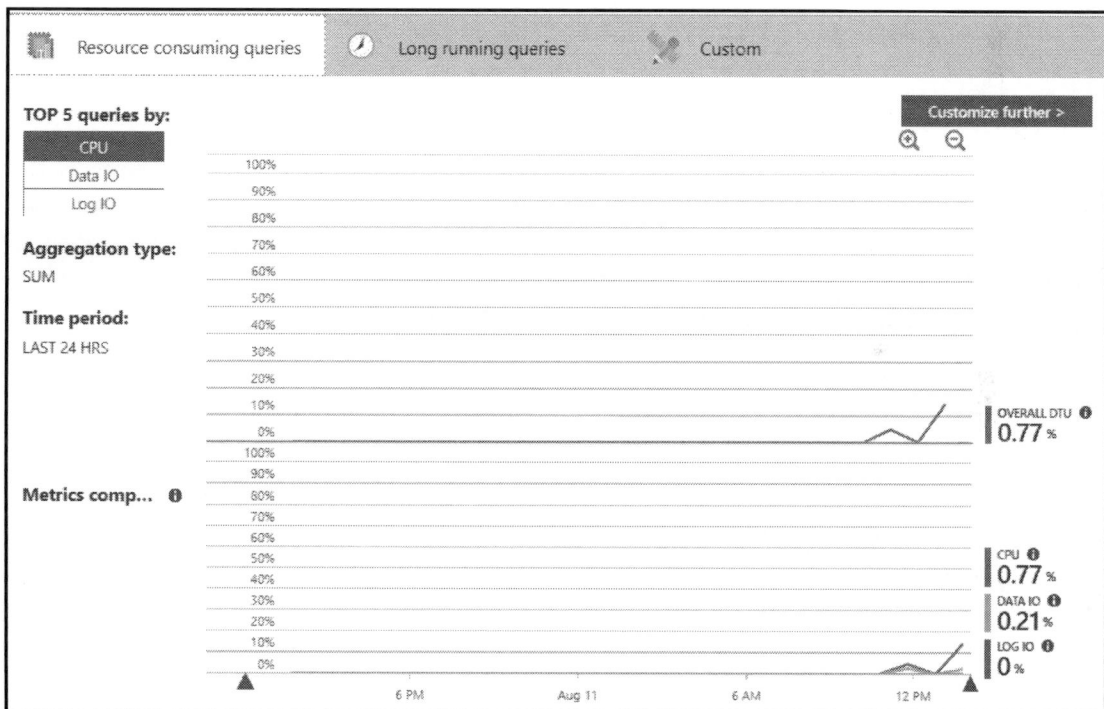

Automatic tuning options is a dream come true for all database administrators. This option will use built-in intelligence, observing performance over time and applying machine learning to solutions to improve the performance of the database. The option can be automatically enabled on a server or subscription level. Further, it can be set on and off for individual databases. Settings available for automatic tuning are **FORCE PLAN**, **CREATE INDEX**, and **DROP INDEX**. If enabled, automatic tuning will analyze the performance and automatically apply changes that will improve performance. Examples of automatic tuning settings are shown here:

Inherit from: 🛈

| Server | Azure defaults | Don't inherit |

🛈   The database is inheriting automatic tuning configuration from the server. You can set the configuration to be inherited by going to: Server tuning settings

⚠   The database is inheriting settings from the server, but the server is in the unspecified state. Please specify the automatic tuning state on the server.

Configure the automatic tuning options   🛈

OPTION	DESIRED STATE	CURRENT STATE
FORCE PLAN	ON OFF **INHERIT**	**OFF** Inherited from server
CREATE INDEX	ON OFF **INHERIT**	**OFF** Inherited from server
DROP INDEX	ON OFF **INHERIT**	**OFF** Inherited from server

Azure SQL Database backup

A very important task for any database administrator is backup. This option is automatically enabled in Azure SQL Database. When a new database is created, geo-redundant storage is created in the process and backups are performed in this storage. This feature is provided automatically and free of charge. For Azure SQL Database, SQL Server backup technology is used to create full, differential, and transaction backups. Transaction backups are performed every 12 hours and differential backups every 5–10 minutes, depending on database size and activity. This allows us to have a point-in-time restore by restoring the last full backup before the point selected, all differential backups between the full backup and the point selected, and, finally, all transnational backups between the last differential backup and the point selected.

The retention period for the backup depends on the database tier and can be from 7–35 days. There is also the option to enable **long-term retention backup (LTRB)** and keep backups for up to 10 years. The default backup is the option provided with no additional charge, but LTRB uses additional storage that is charged extra. However, there are situations in which we are required to keep a backup for a longer period of time and this option can be useful. Also, the price of storage is low, so this doesn't create a big addition to your bill.

Another option directly connected to backups is database export. This allows you to keep an additional copy of your database in separate storage. This backup can be used to restore a database on a new server or another subscription. Export will create a BACPAC file that contains schema and data.

Other data services in Azure

SQL Server in VM and Azure SQL Database are just a fraction of the Azure data platform offering.

When we talk about RDBMS in IaaS, we really don't have any restrictions. We can create any type of VM with a number of different operating systems and install anything we want, such as Oracle, MySQL, PostgreSQL, and so on. There are also a number of images that include this software pre-installed. The same thing goes for NoSQL databases: we can install anything on our VM, or we can even choose an image that includes MongoDB, CouchDB, and many others.

When talking about RDBMS in the PaaS model, we have also different options such as **MySQL**, **PostgreSQL**, **SQL data warehouses**, and others. Running NoSQL as PaaS also offers different options, including **Azure Cosmos DB** or **MongoDB**.

Azure data platform is extended with analytic services in Azure that also have multiple options for both IaaS or PaaS models.

Overall, Microsoft Azure offers different options for data and analytics, whether you're migrating existing solutions or building a new cloud solution. You can choose between different IaaS and PaaS services and combine them for specific scenarios to get the best possible results.

A screenshot showing some of the database and analytics options in Azure follows:

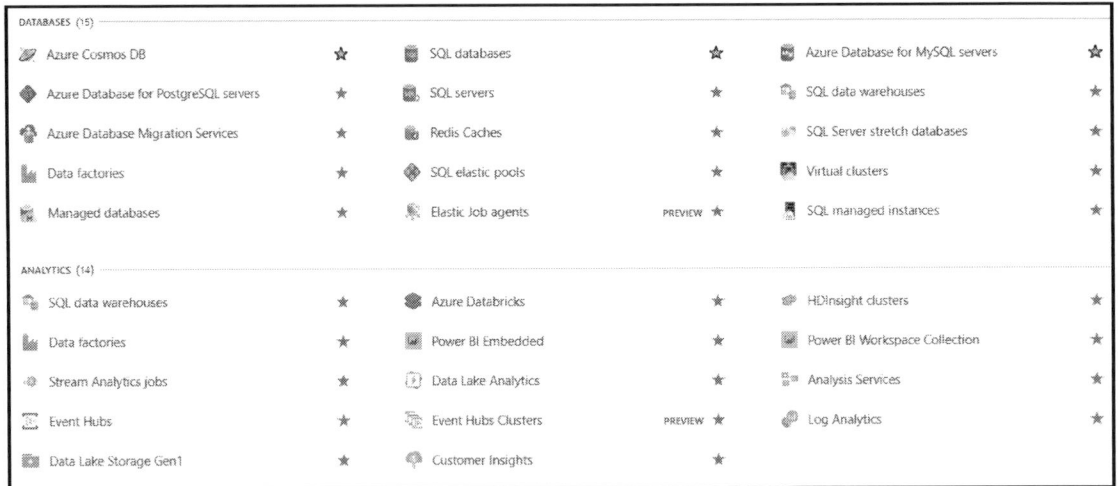

DATABASES (15)

Azure Cosmos DB	☆	SQL databases	☆	Azure Database for MySQL servers ☆
Azure Database for PostgreSQL servers ★		SQL servers ★		SQL data warehouses ★
Azure Database Migration Services ★		Redis Caches ★		SQL Server stretch databases ★
Data factories ★		SQL elastic pools ★		Virtual clusters ★
Managed databases ★		Elastic Job agents PREVIEW ★		SQL managed instances ★

ANALYTICS (14)

SQL data warehouses ★		Azure Databricks ★		HDInsight clusters ★
Data factories ★		Power BI Embedded ★		Power BI Workspace Collection ★
Stream Analytics jobs ★		Data Lake Analytics ★		Analysis Services ★
Event Hubs ★		Event Hubs Clusters PREVIEW ★		Log Analytics ★
Data Lake Storage Gen1 ★		Customer Insights ★		

Summary

The Azure data platform offers multiple options when deciding to use both IaaS and PaaS. Running databases in IaaS offers more control, but requires more maintenance and administration as well. DaaS has many features which make a database administrator's life easier, but it lacks support to run certain features and legacy applications. The bottom line is that we need to decide how we want to proceed and assess the ideal option for our scenario based on the options required by our solution and offered by different data services.

Once data is in the cloud, Azure offers many analytics options which can help us to extend our solution. Again, we can choose between different IaaS and PaaS services to select the best fit for us.

In previous chapters, we discussed how to set up applications and data in Azure. Creating and designing new applications is great, but not always an option. In most cases, the journey starts with moving existing solutions from on-premises to the cloud. In the next chapter, we are going to explain options available for migrating our existing applications and databases to Azure.

Questions

1. Database in Azure can be run as...
    1. IaaS
    2. PaaS
    3. Both

2. Azure Virtual Machine with SQL is different from VM without SQL because of...
    1. SQL server configuration
    2. Amount of memory and CPU
    3. Its name

3. Azure SQL Database is also called...
    1. Database as a Service
    2. SQL as a Service
    3. Data as a Service

4. The Azure SQL Database tier can be measured in...
    1. DTUs
    2. vCores
    3. Both

5. You can run a query on Azure SQL Database with...
    1. SQL Server Management Studio
    2. Query Editor in Azure Portal
    3. Both

6. To connect to Azure SQL Database, you need to...
    1. Add an IP address to a firewall rule
    2. Allow an IP in VNet
    3. Allow an IP in the master database

7. To create an Azure SQL Database replica, you can use...
    1. Database backup
    2. Database export
    3. Geo-replication

8. To create a highly available Azure SQL Database, you need to create a...
    1. Failover group
    2. Failover cluster
    3. Always-On

9. To mask columns in Azure SQL Database, you use...
    1. Transparent data encryption
    2. Dynamic data masking
    3. Data classification

10. To detect potential threats to your database, you use...
    1. Vulnerability assessment
    2. Advanced threat protection
    3. Both

6
Azure Storage, Backup, and Site Recovery - Moving your Data to Azure

In this chapter, we will focus on migrating data to Azure. We'll start with Azure Storage as one of the most important services in Azure. Everything begins with Storage and it's important to understand how it's used. We'll discuss how to use Azure Storage for backup and how to migrate your workloads to the cloud. Further, we'll discuss how to use Azure Backup and **Azure Site Recovery** (**ASR**) to speed up your journey and migrate data to Azure.

The following topics will be covered in this chapter:

- Azure Storage
- Azure Backup
- Azure Site Recovery

Technical requirements

For this chapter, you'll need:

- An Azure subscription
- A local server running Windows Server 2012 R2 or later
- A Hyper-V Server
- A local instance of SQL Server 2012 or later

Azure Storage

Azure Storage is a service that plays a very important part in Microsoft Azure. Almost all Azure services use storage in one form or another. In some cases, it's obvious that storage is used, in others it's a service in the background we don't realize even exists.

For example, if we create a new VM, virtual disks are created in the process. These disks are stored in Azure Storage. If managed disks are used, storage is created in the background and not visible. If we don't use managed disks, storage created in the process is shown among resources, since managing storage is our responsibility when managed disks are not used.

Similar to this, when any PaaS resource is created, storage is created in the background. In most PaaS cases, storage is not directly visible, but we can see the amount of storage available and used in the resource blade. For example, Azure SQL database or Azure App Service plan have a certain amount of resources available depending on the tier. We don't have direct access to storage management but we can see information about storage space.

But Azure Storage can be used as stand alone service and managed independently. In order to explain this service, let's start with creating a new Azure Storage account.

Creating an Azure Storage account

In order to create an Azure storage account, we need to provide a **Name**, **Deployment model**, **Account kind**, **Location**, **Replication** policy, **Performance**, **Secure transfer required**, **Subscription**, and **Resource group**. **Subscription**, **Location,** and **Resource group** are the usual settings needed for all Azure resources.

The name must be unique within Azure as it's used to form an URL for your storage account. The URL is formed by adding the storage account name in front of the standard DNS suffix. For example, naming the storage account `packtdemo` would create the URL `packtdemo.core.windows.net` and therefore the storage account name must be unique.

The **Deployment model** allows us to choose between **Resource manager** and **Classic** model. As the **Classic** model is outdated and using **Resource manager** is recommended, I advise you choose **Resource manager** whenever creating a new resource.

Performance allows us to choose between **Standard** and **Premium** storage. This is basically choosing between HDD and SSD, but will also impact the price of your storage. **Premium** storage comes with SSD and significantly better performance, but the price increase is equally significant.

Secure transfer required allows us to choose between enabling and disabling this option. Enabling will require all incoming requests to our storage to be done over HTTPS and automatically blocking any requests coming over HTTP. The feature is very similar to **Allow only HTTPS** in Azure web apps. As this feature is security related, I recommend enabling this option.

A screenshot with Azure Storage account options is shown here:

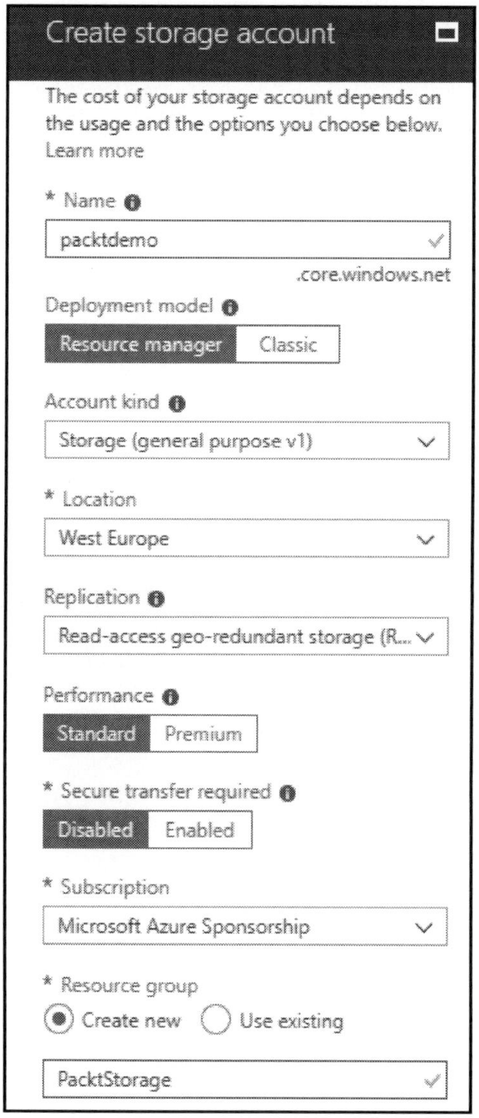

Now we come to a couple of settings that are related only to the Azure Storage account. Even through the performance option is also related directly to storage, we can see the option to choose storage performance in other services too, such as VMs or even some PaaS resources. Options unique to the Storage account are account kind and replication.

Account kind allows us to choose between three options:

- **Storage (general purpose v1)**
- **StorageV2 (general purpose v2)**
- **Blob storage**

General purpose v2 storage supports all features that are supported by general purpose v1, and brings some newer features. It's recommended you use general purpose v2, especially if you want to use the latest APIs and features such as access tier, that allows you to use hot and cold storage.

Hot and cold storage allows you to choose what kind of access tier you want to use based on the data you are storing. Hot costs more per GB stored but transactions to storage are lower. Cold costs less per GB stored but transactions to storage come with higher prices. This makes the cold access tier more suitable for archive and the hot access tier for active storage. What's great about this feature is that you can switch between access tiers and change from one to another at any time.

An upgrade from general purpose v1 to general purpose v2 can be made at any time (but not the other way around) in case you already have a storage account in v1 and want to benefit from features of v2. However, there are some cases in which you need to use v1 as the only option. For example, when classic deployment is needed (general purpose v2 is only supported in resource manager), or where you need to use an older storage service REST API.

A Blob storage account supports the same features as general purpose v2 when it comes to block blobs, but are limited only to block blobs; they don't support page blobs. As the price is very similar, it's recommended you use general purpose v2 storage as this comes with the same price but more options.

Options for account kind are shown in the screenshot here:

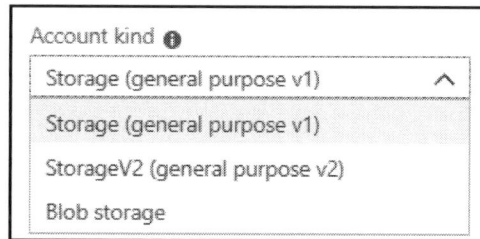

Account kind ⓘ

Storage (general purpose v1)	∧
Storage (general purpose v1)	
StorageV2 (general purpose v2)	
Blob storage	

Replication comes with three options, which are the same as account kind. We can choose between:

- **Locally-redundant storage (LRS)**
- **Geo-redundant storage (GRS)**
- **Read-access geo-redundant storage (RA-GRS)**

LRS is based on a strategy similar to availability set and availability zones for VMs. Additional copies of data are kept across the Azure Datacenter to provide durability and redundancy in case of hardware faults or updates. It's designed to provide SLA of 99.999999999% (11 9s). All data is kept inside a single Datacenter, and possible failover is triggered automatically.

GRS is designed in a very similar fashion, with the difference being that copies are in different Azure Datacenters which are, thousands of miles away from the original Datacenter. Because of this, additional durability is in place with an SLA of 99.99999999999999% (16 9s) . Redundant copy is available for access only when automatic failover is triggered.

RA-GRS is designed in the same way as GRS, but with the difference that redundant copy is available for read, even when failover isn't activated.

Replication options are shown in following screenshot:

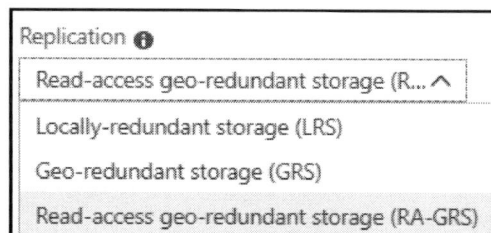

Replication ⓘ

Read-access geo-redundant storage (R...	∧
Locally-redundant storage (LRS)	
Geo-redundant storage (GRS)	
Read-access geo-redundant storage (RA-GRS)	

Additional options for the Azure Storage account are virtual networks and data lake storage v2.

If we enable **Virtual networks**, we can select an existing VNet (or create a new one) and select a **Subnets**. This will join our storage to the selected subnet on the selected VNet and assign a private IP address to our storage, allowing us to access storage over a private network rather then over the internet. Data lake storage v2 is in preview, and can be enabled only if a few requirements are met. We need to choose general purpose v2 storage, it's available only in a limited number of Azure Datacenters, and preview must be pre-approved. These options are shown in the following screenshot:

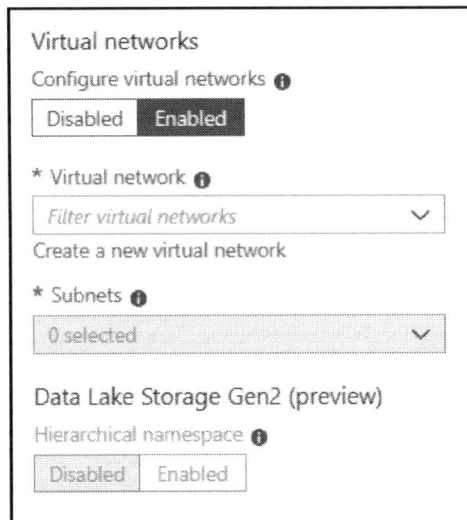

Virtual networks

Configure virtual networks ⓘ

| Disabled | **Enabled** |

* Virtual network ⓘ

| *Filter virtual networks* | ⌄ |

Create a new virtual network

* Subnets ⓘ

| 0 selected | ⌄ |

Data Lake Storage Gen2 (preview)

Hierarchical namespace ⓘ

| Disabled | Enabled |

> Note that account kind, replication, and performance will impact the price of Azure Storage. Location is also a factor as not all resources cost the same in all Azure Datacenters, but this doesn't have as much impact as the other three options.

Deployment of the Azure Storage account is fast and is usually done in under one minute.

Azure Storage settings

Once the Azure Storage account is created, we can use different options to manage it. Some of the options are similar to the options available to other Azure resources, so let's focus on the Azure Storage account unique options.

The first option under **Settings** is **Access keys**. **Access keys** are used to authenticate access to your Azure Storage account. They are usually used to enable access from applications, so you can find connection strings here along with access keys. There are two access keys available, and you can regenerate them if you think the original keys have been stolen or compromised.

Cross-origin resource sharing (CORS) allows you to define trusted domains. Web browsers implement security restrictions that prevent applications from calling APIs in a different domain. CORS provides ways for the original domain to securely access an API from another domain.

Configuration allows us to change some of the settings that are available when creating the Storage account. Under this option, we can upgrade storage from general purpose v1 to v2, we can change performance, and replication settings, and enable or disable secure transfer requirements.

Azure Storage is automatically encrypted and protects data at rest. Automatic encryption is done using using Microsoft Managed Keys for Azure blobs, tables, files and queues. However, the encryption option allows us to bring our own key and encrypt storage with that key instead.

Shared access signature (SAS) provides an access key that lasts a limited time. We can use this key to provide temporary access to our storage and can define how long this access is going to last. After the key expires, it can't be used again.

Under **Firewall** and **Virtual network** settings, we can change networking and access settings for our storage. We can attach storage to VNet (and subnet) or change the VNet storage it's associated with. Using firewall, we can block access to our storage to anyone who isn't coming from a trusted IP address. We can white list our on-premises IP addresses or other trusted IP addresses to allow Azure Storage access only from these addresses and to prevent anyone else from gaining access.

Properties, **Locks**, and **Automation scripts** are options available to all Azure resources.

The next set of options is related to blob service. Here we have **Blobs**, **Custom domains**, **Soft delete**, **Azure CDN**, and **Azure search**.

Blobs allow you to see the current list of blobs in the storage account and perform actions such as creating a new blob or deleting an existing one. Further, you can access a blob and see the list of files inside the blob and perform actions on files such as download or delete.

Custom domain allows you to use a custom domain with your storage account. Instead of using the provided DNS, you can set up CNAME on your custom domain and point it to your storage to start using the custom domain.

Soft delete allows you to set up a retention policy for your storage. If enabled, the default retention policy is seven days but this can be change to up to 365 days. **Soft delete** will give you ability to recover any deleted blobs. This extends to blobs that are deleted as result of overwrite, so you can recover deleted blobs or older versions of blobs.

Azure CDN and **Azure search** are options to link these Azure services to your storage account. **Azure CDN** is used to cache storage content in order to increase performance and minimize latency. **Azure search** is a fully managed cloud search service that provides a better user experience.

The following options allow us to manage the file service, table service, and queue service. For each of these services, we can see a list of existing file services in the storage account and we can perform different operations such as **Delete existing service**, **Create a new one** or **Set up access policies**.

Migrating a database to the cloud

Once we have our Storage account, we can start loading data. This can be any type of file, we can use storage as a staging phase in which we prepare uploaded files before they are actually used, or we can upload files that are directly used by our applications.

Over the years, I've seen many organizations using Azure Storage as a backup location for on-premises SQL databases. This is a convenient way to start our cloud journey as we get relatively cheap storage that is offsite and encrypted.

Once databases are stored to cloud, the next step would be to use backups to restore a database in Azure and start using them either as IaaS or PaaS.

Let's see how we can back up our database directly to Azure Storage.

Backing up a database to storage

In order to back up the database to Azure Storage, first we need to open **SQL Server Management Studio (SSMS)**, select the database we want to back up, and then select **Tasks | Back Up...**. The first step is shown in this screenshot:

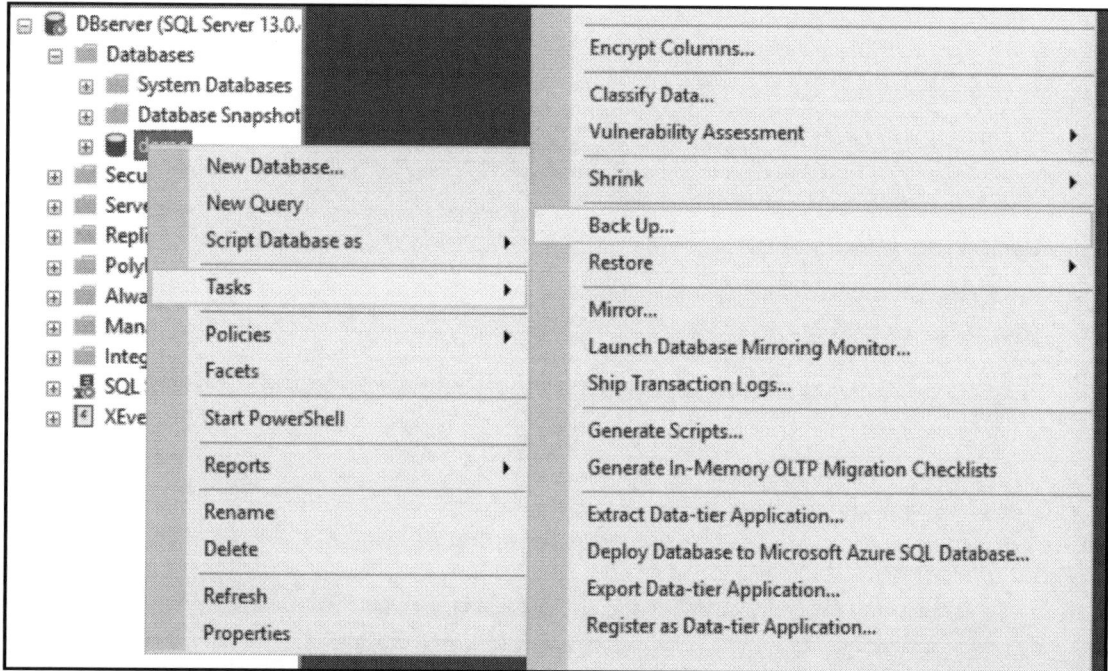

New windows will open with options to select the **Database** (this will already be selected if we selected a proper database in the first step, but can be changed or we can select multiple databases), **Backup type** (usually a full backup is recommended) and finally, **Destination**. The default option is **Disk,** and we need to change this to an **URL**. A screenshot of these options is shown here:

After selecting the **URL** as the destination, we must select add in order to provide the path. This will open a new window in which we need to provide our Azure account information in order to access our Azure subscription. After this is done, we have access to our Azure subscription from SSMS and can select our storage account and blob where the backup will be stored. As **Shared Access Signature (SAS)** is used to perform the backup, we must create a new SAS and provide a date of expiration. Setting up a destination for the backup is shown in this screenshot:

Finally, we click **OK** and the backup is performed. Time to perform the backup depends on bandwidth, database size, and storage type. In this case, the storage type is usually standard, as storing backups to premium storage is overkill and we would be paying a premium service for an archive. After the backup is completed, we can see the file information in the Azure portal under the storage account in the blob we selected. An example of the file information in the Azure portal is shown here:

After the backup is performed, we can use this backup to restore the database in Azure. However, full backup can be only restored on an SQL Server running on an Azure Virtual Machine (IaaS). In order to restore a backup in the Azure SQL Database (PaaS), we must use BACPAC. BACPAC contains data and metadata of the SQL database. The process to backup BACPAC to Azure Storage is similar to the process of creating a full backup of the database.

Migrating a database to Azure SQL

Creating backup and restoring it is not the only option on how to migrate the database to Azure. This process can be done without using a backup, directly migrating the database to Azure.

In order to do this, the first step is to select the database, click on bold Tasks and select the option to **Deploy Database to Microsoft Azure SQL Database in SSMS**. The first step is shown in this screenshot:

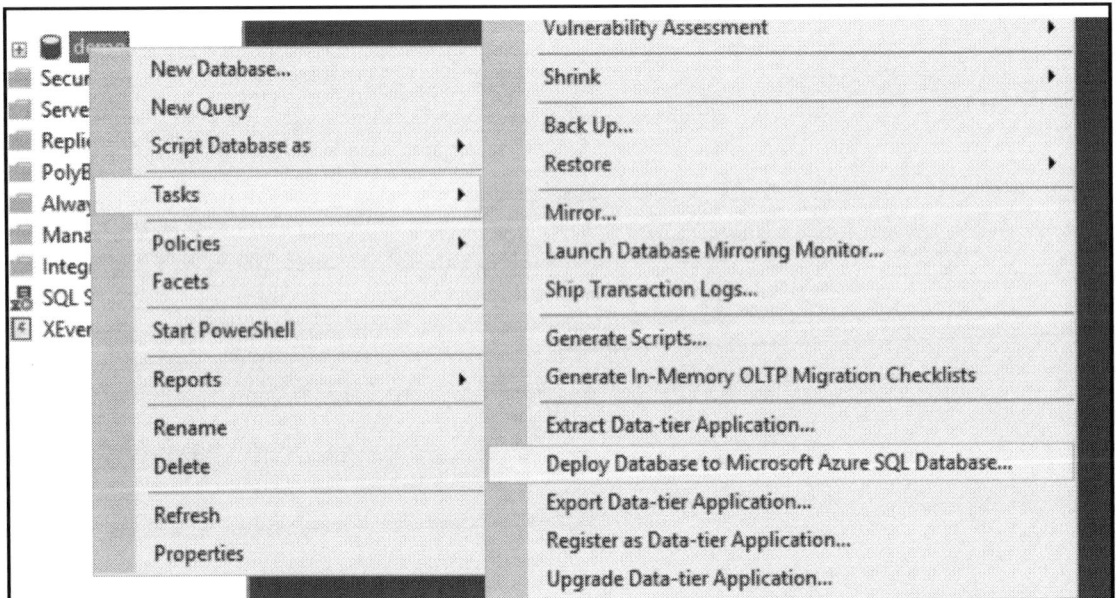

The second step is to connect to your Azure SQL Server. In order to do this, we select
Connect... in the new window that opened after selecting the options in the first step. This
window is shown in this screenshot:

Specify Target Connection

Specify the name of the instance of SQL Server or the Microsoft Azure SQL Database server that will host
the deployed database, name the new database, and then click Connect to login to the target server.

Server connection:

| | Connect... |

New database name:

| demo |

Microsoft Azure SQL Database settings

Edition of Microsoft Azure SQL Database:

Maximum database size (GB):

Service Objective :

Other settings

Temporary file name:

| C:\Users\mustafa\AppData\Local\Temp\2\demo-20180825104053.bacpac | Browse... |

In order to connect to the Azure SQL database, we need to provide the server URL, username, and password. Make sure that the public IP address of your server is added to the firewall rule of your Azure SQL Server, otherwise you will not be able to connect. An example of connection options is shown in this screenshot:

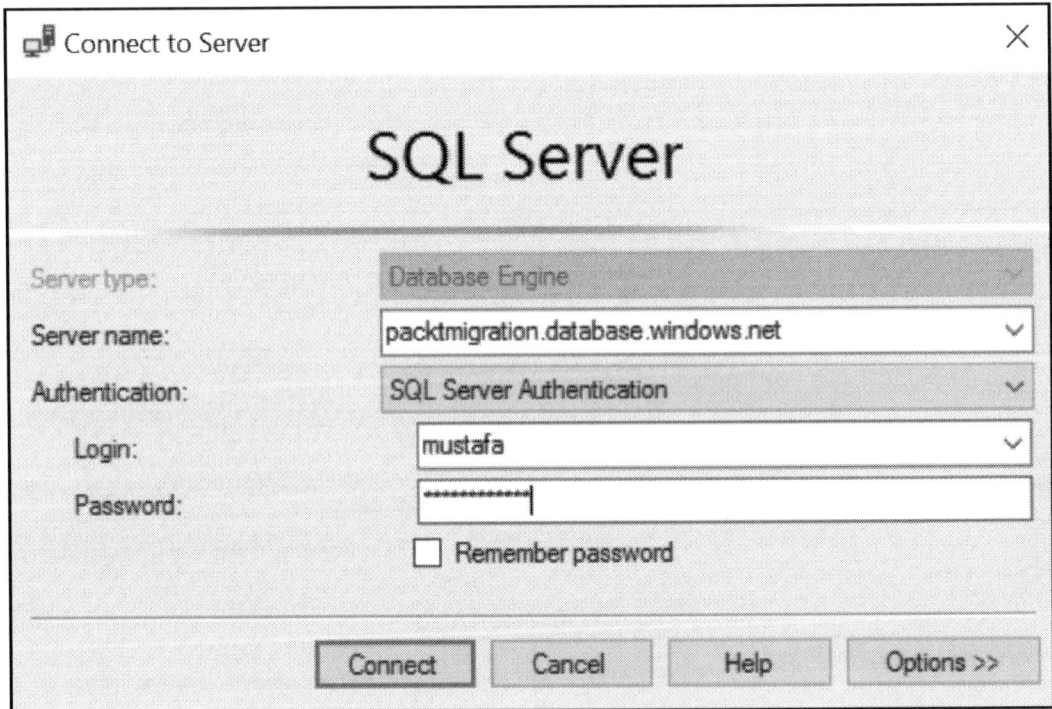

After a connection is established, we are back to the window from the previous step. Finally, we must provide the database tier for the Azure SQL database that will be used for migration (a new database is created). An example of the database size option is shown here:

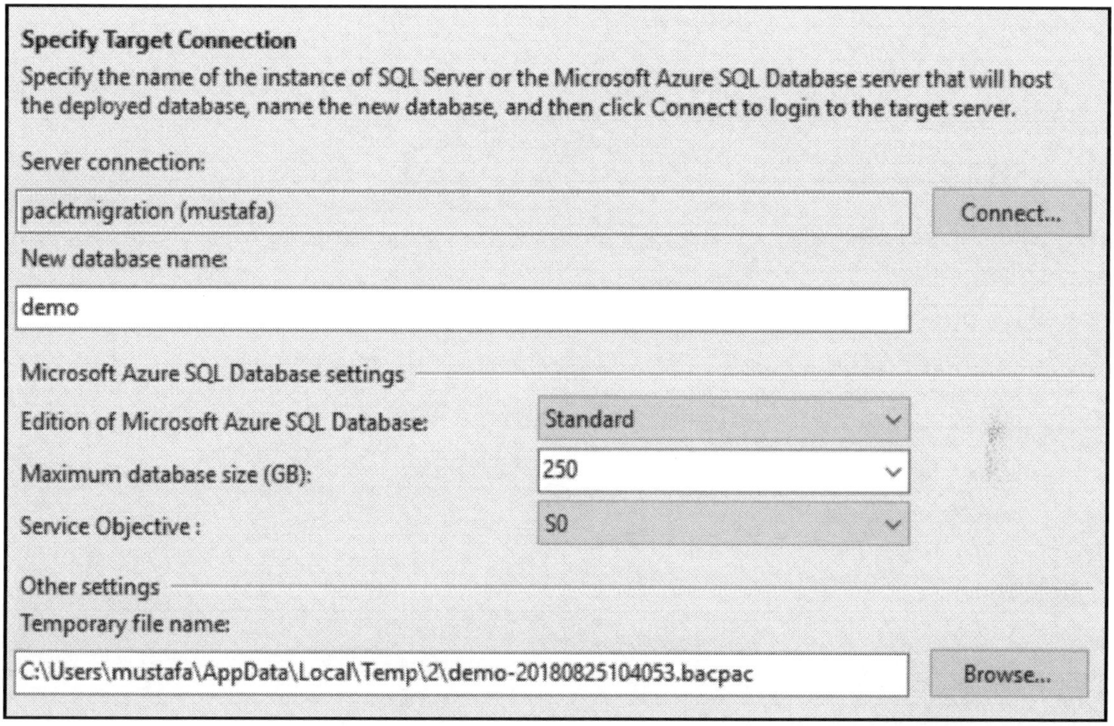

Specify Target Connection

Specify the name of the instance of SQL Server or the Microsoft Azure SQL Database server that will host the deployed database, name the new database, and then click Connect to login to the target server.

Server connection:

```
packtmigration (mustafa)                                    Connect...
```

New database name:

```
demo
```

Microsoft Azure SQL Database settings

Edition of Microsoft Azure SQL Database: Standard   ⌄

Maximum database size (GB):   250   ⌄

Service Objective :   S0   ⌄

Other settings

Temporary file name:

```
C:\Users\mustafa\AppData\Local\Temp\2\demo-20180825104053.bacpac    Browse...
```

After the process is completed, we will receive a message about successful tasks. the time needed to complete migration can depend on many factors such as database size, bandwidth, and Azure SQL database tier. Note that selecting too small a tier (if we are migrating a large database) will result in an error as the performance of the target database can be insufficient to handle the workload needed to perform the migration of a large database. A screenshot of a successful migration is shown here:

Name	Result
Exporting data from database	Success
Exporting data	Success
Processing Export.	Success
Processing Table '[dbo].[Users]'.	Success
Importing database	Success
Creating deployment plan	Success
Initializing deployment	Success
Verifying deployment plan	Success
Analyzing deployment plan	Success
Importing package schema and data into database	Success
Updating database	Success
Importing data	Success
Processing Import.	Success
Disabling indexes.	Success
Processing Table '[dbo].[Users]'.	Success
Enabling indexes.	Success
Refreshing Object Explorer	Success

Operation Complete

Summary:

After migration is completed, we can connect to the Azure SQL server with SSMS and find the database that is migrated, as shown here:

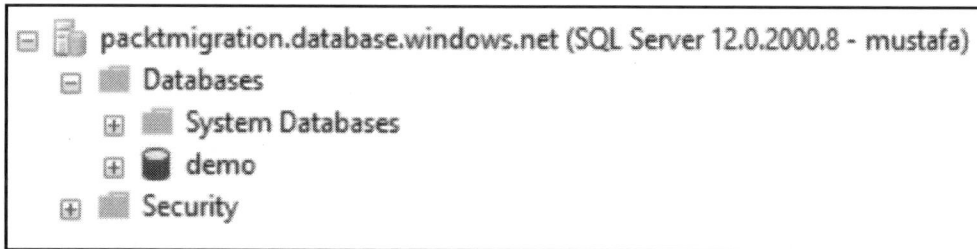

In some cases, migration will fail even when the proper Azure SQL database tier is selected. This is due to database incompatibility with Azure SQL database. For example, when using Azure SQL database, a clustered index is required (recommended for on-premises). If the database that is migrated, doesn't contain clustered indexes, migration will fail. Luckily, there is a tool that can help us perform assessment that will tell us about possible issues and problems on our database.

Database assessment

To create an assessment of our database and make sure it's ready for migration, we can use Microsoft Data Migration Assistant. This is tool is free and can be downloaded from the Microsoft Download Center.

After you install this tool, you can start a new project. Select **Assessment**, provide the **Project name**, and **Source server type**, and **Target server type**,. For source, select **SQL Server** and for target, select **Azure SQL Database**. An example for a new project is shown here:

The second step is to select assessment options. You can select to check compatibility and feature parity. Compatibility will check your database features and provide if there are any blocking issues or deprecated features preventing migration. Feature parity will check if there are any features or functions that are not supported. For example, an Azure SQL database doesn't support **SQL Server Reporting Service (SSRS)**, so if your application is using SSRS, this can cause an issue. I recommend selecting both options, as shown here:

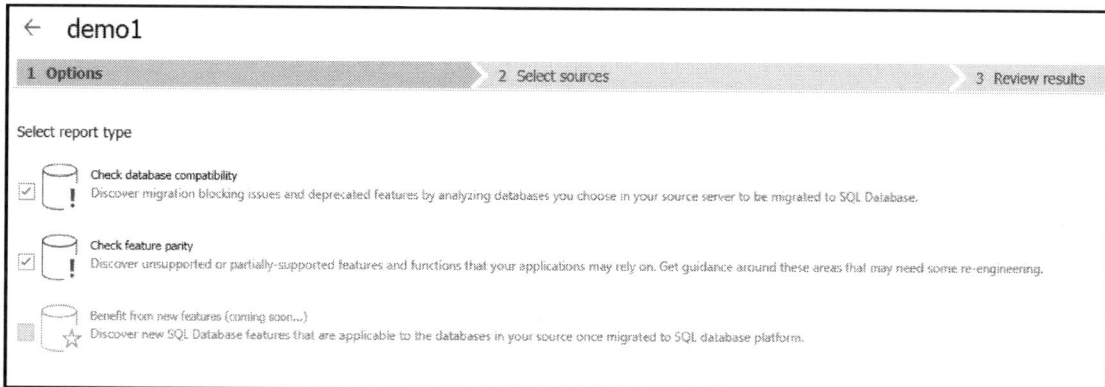

After selecting what to check, we need to provide a source that will be checked. In order to make an assessment, this tool needs access to the database, so we must provide the SQL Server, credentials, and database. Selected databases will be shown in the list along with the SQL Server version, as shown here:

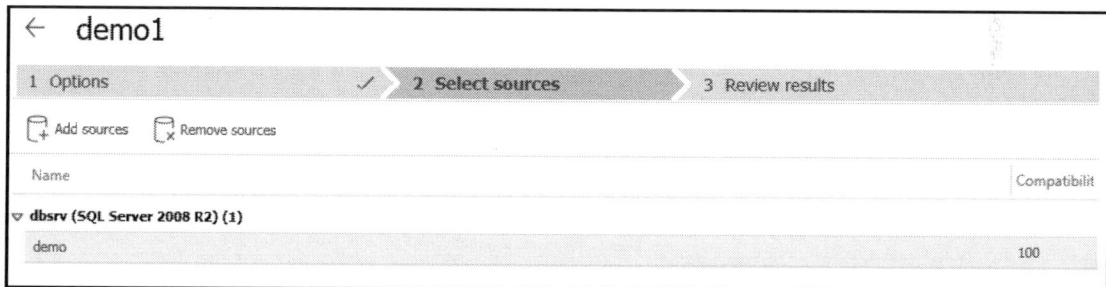

The time needed to perform assessment depends on database size and complexity, and it can take from a couple of minutes to a couple of hours. After assessment is completed, we'll receive two reports. The first report is on feature parity, and an example is shown here:

Target Platform
Azure SQL Database

dbsrv / SQL Server 2008 R2

Feature parity (3)

Recommendation	Databases	Windows authentication not supported in Azure SQL Database
▽ **Unsupported features (3)**		Details
Windows authentication not supporte...	N/A	Impact
Azure SQL Database doesn't support...	N/A	This server is in Windows authentication mode, and Windows authentication is not supported in SQL Azure.
SQL Server Reporting Services is not s...	N/A	Recommendation
▷ Partially-supported features (0)		Due to Azure SQL Database's cloud architecture, any Windows authentication used in a source database should be handled using SQL Azure.
		Azure SQL Database supports Azure Active Directory or SQL Azure authentication.
		If considering using Azure Active Directory, make sure Azure Active Directory is well configured, or else use SQL Azure authentication.
		More info
		SQL Database Authentication and Authorization: Granting Access

The second report is on database compatibility. With a little luck, and if the maintenance of the database was performed regularly, you will get a report shown in the following example, showing there are no compatibility issues preventing you from migrating your database to Azure SQL Database:

Target Platform

Azure SQL Database

demo / SQL Server 2008 R2   Compat 100   Size 3.00 MB

Compatibility 140 (0)	Compatibility 130 (0)	Compatibility 120 (0)	Compatibility 110 (0)	Compatibility 100 (0)

There are no compatibility issues with your database.

One of the possible compatibility issues is a clustered index. It was recommended you have a clustered index for each table in the database but with an Azure SQL database, this is a requirement. Another example are CLR functions that are not supported in an Azure SQL database.

An assessment tool can be used to make an assessment, not only for migration to Azure SQL Database but to other versions of SQL Server. So, if you are planning on migrating a database to a newer version of SQL Server (in Azure or on-premises), this tool can make assessment for these migrations as well.

Microsoft Data Migration Assistant can be used to perform the migration of database as well. Note that the difference between this migration and migration through SSMS is that here the Azure SQL database must be created (empty Azure SQL database) prior to migration.

As a third option for migration, there is the Azure Database Migration Service. This migration is in fact a data sync option as a database and schema must exist before running this service. Azure Database Migration Service allows you to link source and target database and copy data from the source to the target for a complete database or for selected tables.

Azure Recovery Service

Another service to help migration to the cloud is the Azure Recovery Service. This service contains features that can help us move data to the cloud:

- Azure Backup
- Azure Site Recovery

Both services aren't only used to move data to the cloud but to protect both Azure and on-premises resources. Their primary purpose is in fact to protect resources but once we have data in the cloud, this data can be used to perform migration.

Creating a recovery service vault

In order to start using the Azure recovery service, we must create a **Recovery Services vault**. All usual parameters are needed: **Name**, **Subscription**, **Resource group**, and **Location**. Note that **Location** is very important if you want to protect Azure resources. You will not be able to protect resources that are in the same location as the recovery services vault. A screenshot showing an example of parameters for recovery services vault is given here:

Enabling Azure Backup

Once the recovery services vault is created, we can start configuring. As mentioned, we have two different services and both services can be used to protect resources in Azure and on-premises.

Let's start with enabling Azure Backup on Azure resources. If we select that we want to protect workloads in Azure under the Azure Backup configuration, options for protections are **Virtual machine**, **Azure FileShare (Preview)**, and **SQL Server in Azure VM (Preview)**. Let's select **Virtual machine** and continue. An example of Azure resources for Azure Backup is shown here:

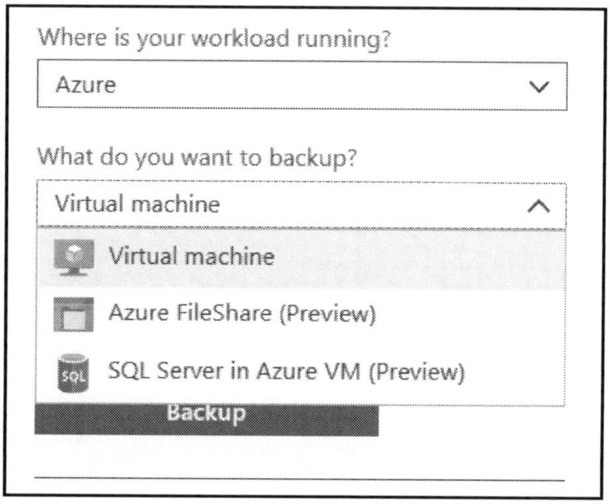

Where is your workload running?

Azure ∨

What do you want to backup?

Virtual machine ∧

🖥 Virtual machine

▢ Azure FileShare (Preview)

🗄 SQL Server in Azure VM (Preview)

Backup

A list of resources available will be automatically provided. As **Virtual machine** are selected, this will be a list of Azure VMs. If **Azure FileShare (Preview)** was selected, this would be a list of Azure Storage accounts containing FileShare. We select the **Virtual machine** that we want to back up, as shown in the following screenshot:

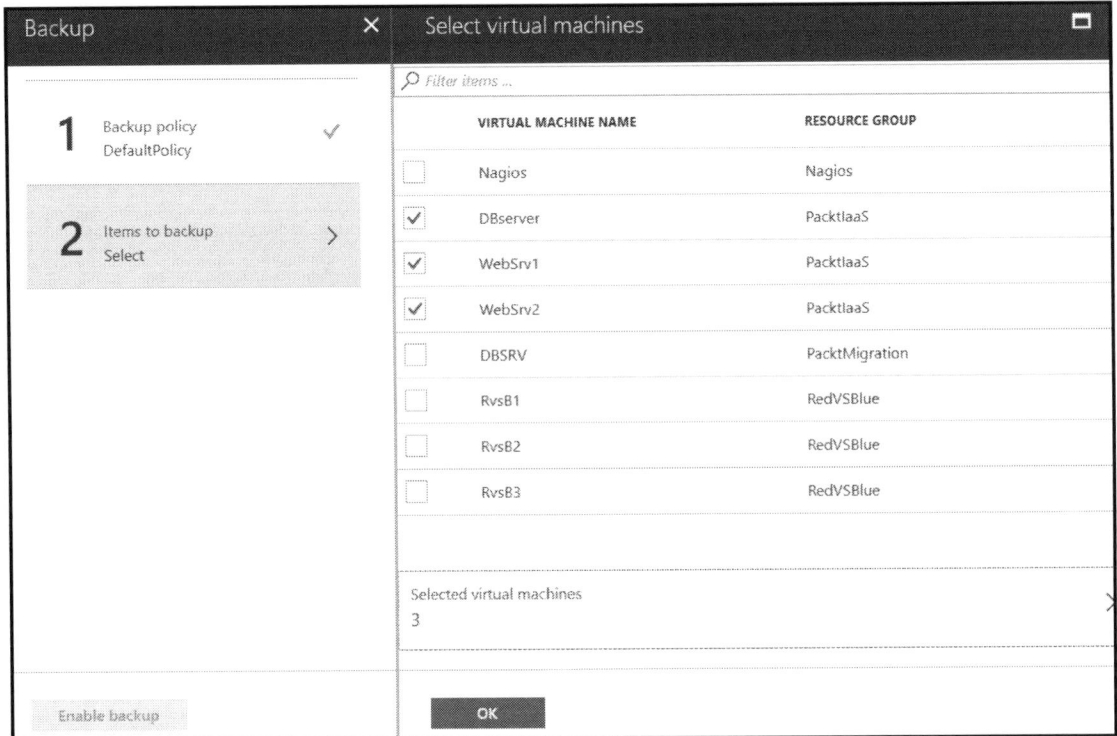

After backup is enabled, we can see a list of protected VMs under backup items. The list will also show the **STATUS**, the **TYPE** of protected resources, and other useful information as shown here:

Backing up on-premises resources

Using Azure Backup to protect on-premises resources requires a little more work. After selecting on-premises resources in the Azure Backup configuration, we get a different list from the one when we selected Azure resources. We can choose between **Files and folders**, **Hyper-V Virtual Machines**, **VMware Virtual Machines**, **Microsoft SQL Server**, **Microsoft SharePoint**, **Microsoft Exchange**, **System state**, and **Bare Metal Recovery**.

After configuration in the Azure portal, we need to install the Recovery Service Agent, which will allow us to register on-premises resources in the recovery services vault. A screenshot of the Recovery Service Agent is shown here:

To proceed with registration, we must provide **Vault Credentials**. **Vault Credentials** are provided in the form of a file that can be downloaded from the recovery services vault. After the **Vault Credentials** are provided, the Recovery Service Agent will automatically load backup vault information, as shown here:

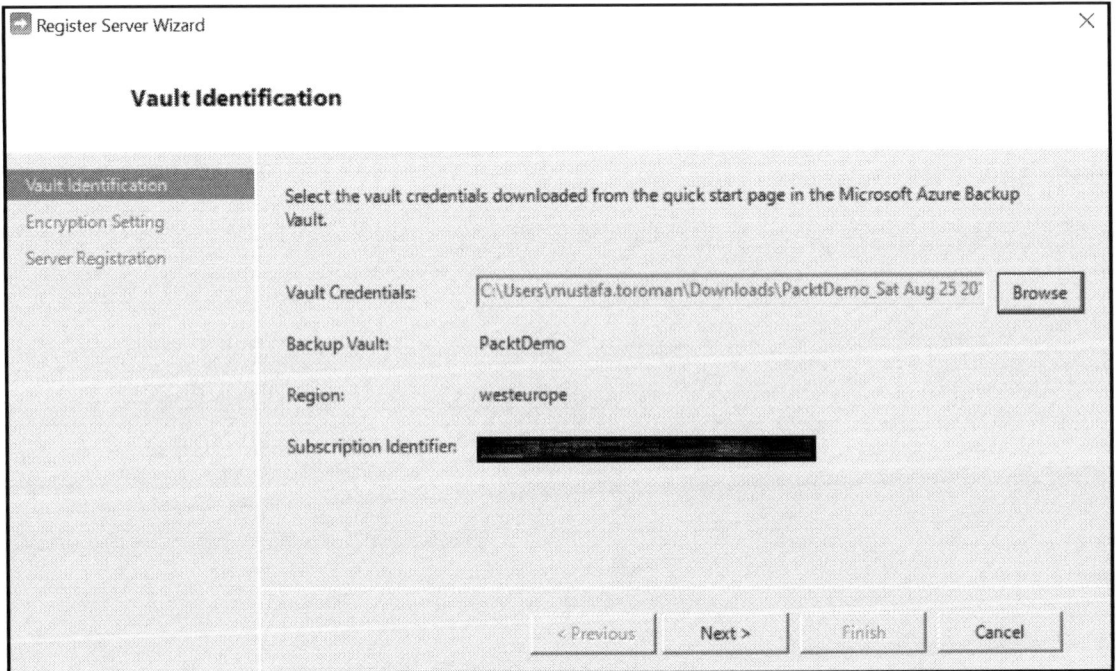

The following step is to provide a passphrase that will be used to encrypt and decrypt the backup. A passphrase must be a minimum of 16 characters and will be stored in the location of your choice. Make sure that you know where your passphrase is located. Otherwise, you will not be able to restore any of your backups, if needed. The process to create a passphrase is shown here:

Encryption Setting

Vault Identification

Encryption Setting

Server Registration

Backups are encrypted to protect the confidentiality of your data.

Generate or type a passphrase to encrypt and decrypt backups from this server.

Enter Passphrase (minimum of 16 characters)

| ************************************* | (36) | | Generate Passphrase |

Confirm Passphrase

| ************************************* | (36) |

Enter a location to save the passphrase

| C:\Users\mustafa.toroman\Desktop | ▾ | Browse |

⚠ If your passphrase is lost or forgotten, the data cannot be recovered. Microsoft Online Services does not save or manage this passphrase. It is strongly recommended you save your passphrase to an external location like a USB drive or network drive.

| < Previous | Next > | Finish | Cancel |

Once the server is registered in the recovery service vault, we can use Microsoft Azure Backup software on the target server (this can be installed on the client OS as well) to configure what and when we are going to back up. We can see the status of current jobs and perform other actions as shown here:

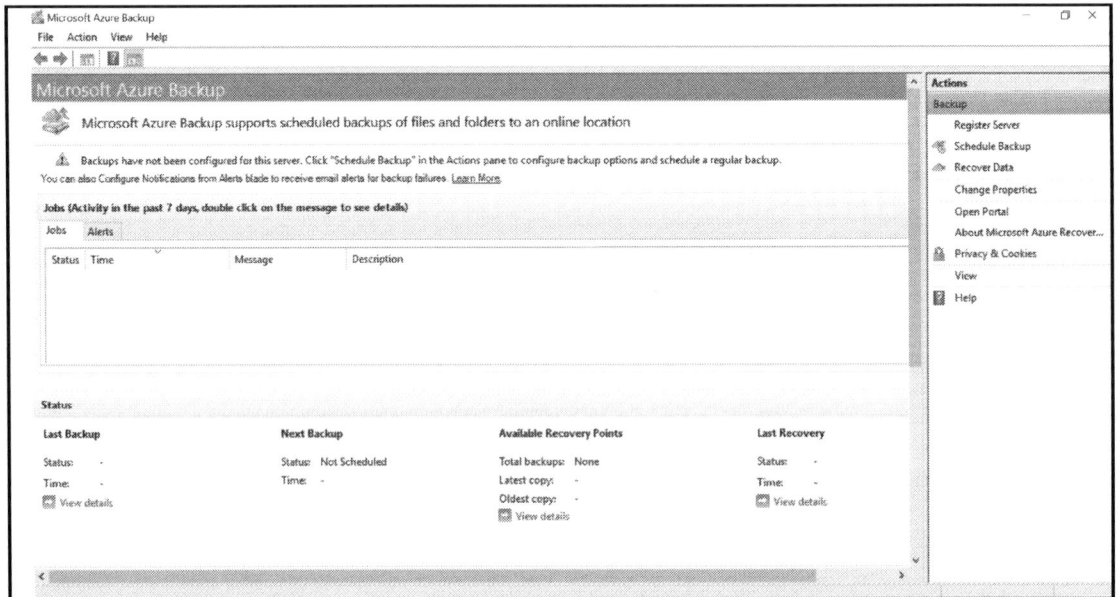

To configure the backup job, we need to provide what we are going to back up. We can select an entire drive, or select specific files and folders as shown here:

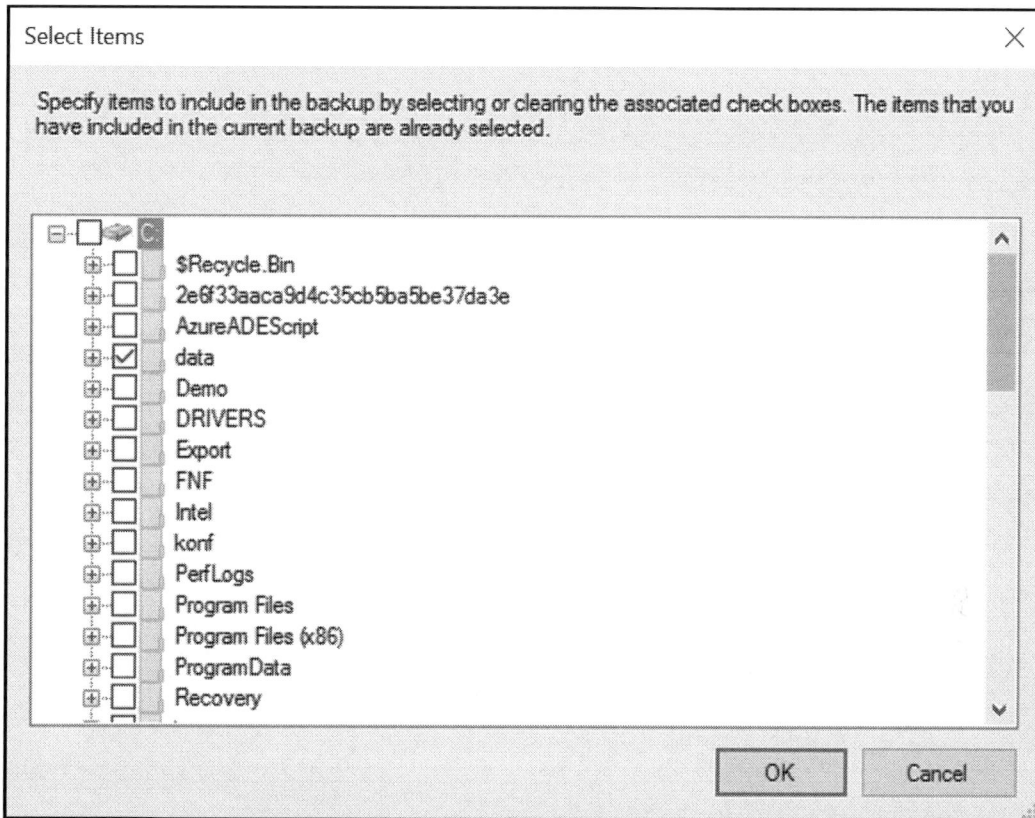

After selecting what to back up, we need to define when and the schedule when backup is going to be performed. We can select a weekly or daily backup (maximum is three times a day). An example of a schedule is shown here:

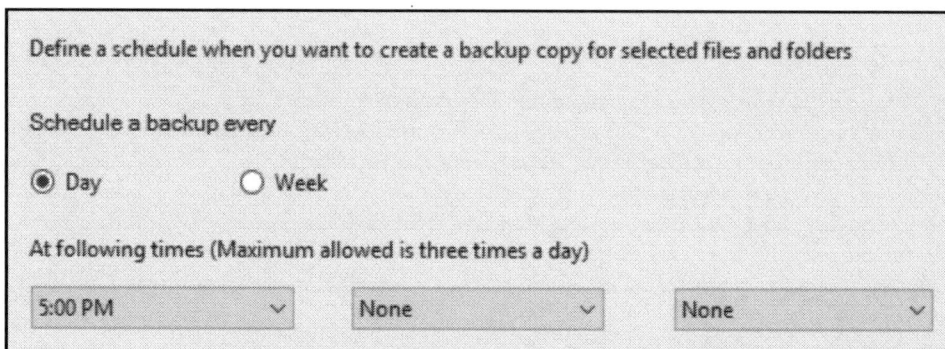

After the schedule, we need to provide a retention policy. A retention policy defines how long our backups are going to be available and can be configured on a weekly, monthly and yearly basis. A default retention policy is shown here:

The last option is to configure how the initial backup is going to be performed. As an initial backup usually means that a large amount of data is going to be backed up, we need to define if this is going to be performed directly over the network (possibly creating overload), or in stages by copying parts of data to Azure Storage and then copying data to the recovery vault. An example of options is shown here:

Time to perform the initial backup depends on the size of data and the network bandwidth. After the initial backup, backups are performed as delta (copying only changes) and should not take long to complete. Note again that keeping the passphrase is very important, backups are encrypted and you will not be able to restore any data without the passphrase used to encrypt.

Azure Site Recovery

ASR is not a backup solution but a **disaster recovery** (**DR**) site in the cloud. Having a DR site was never easier and never cheaper than having one in Azure. Most traditional DR sites involve equipment identical (or at least very similar) to the site that is protected, and cost around 80% of price of the original site. On the other hand, ASR is charged per protected node and for storage where data is stored, so comes very cheap. If recovery is activated in Azure, then compute prices is added for VMs. This way you are paying only for protection and compute prices only when failover occurs. If we create an on-premises DR site, we must pay for the hardware needed to run DR even when failover isn't in place but only used as protection.

ASR can also be used to perform the migration of VMs from on-premises to the cloud. As protecting Azure VMs is fairly simple, we will skip to protecting on-premises VMs and show how to protect local resources and use ASR to perform migration.

Configuring ASR for on-premises resources

To start creating disaster recovery in Azure, we must start by configuring ASR in the recovery services vault. Three steps are involved:

1. Prepare infrastructure
2. Replicate application
3. Manage recovery plans

After we select to **Prepare infrastructure**, a new blade will open. Here we have couple of options that we need to define. First, we need to select if we want to protect Azure or **On-premises** resources. As I want to demonstrate how to use ASR for migration, I'll select **On-premises**. The next option is to define where we want to replicate our resources, and the options available are Azure or another site.

We need to define if the infrastructure that we want to protect is virtualized, and if it is, we select between Hyper-V and VMware. If we are using Hyper-V, we need to define whether we are using SC VMM or not. A screenshot of the protection goal blade is show here:

| Prepare infrastructure | × | Protection goal | ▢ |
| PacktDemo | | PacktDemo | |

These are long running tasks done on-premises.

1 Protection goal
Select　　　　　　　>

2 Deployment planning
Select　　　　　　　>

3 Source
Prepare　　　　　　　>

4 Target
Prepare　　　　　　　>

* Where are your machines located?

> On-premises ⌄

* Where do you want to replicate your machines to?

> To Azure ⌄

* Are your machines virtualized?

> Yes, with Hyper-V ⌄

* Are you using System Center VMM to manage your Hyper-V hosts?

> No ⌄

The second step will lead you to **Deployment planning**. Here we can download a tool to estimate requirements for ASR in our on-premises infrastructure. This step isn't required but it's recommended as insufficient capacity can lead to replication issues. A deployment planner can be downloaded directly from the Azure portal as shown here:

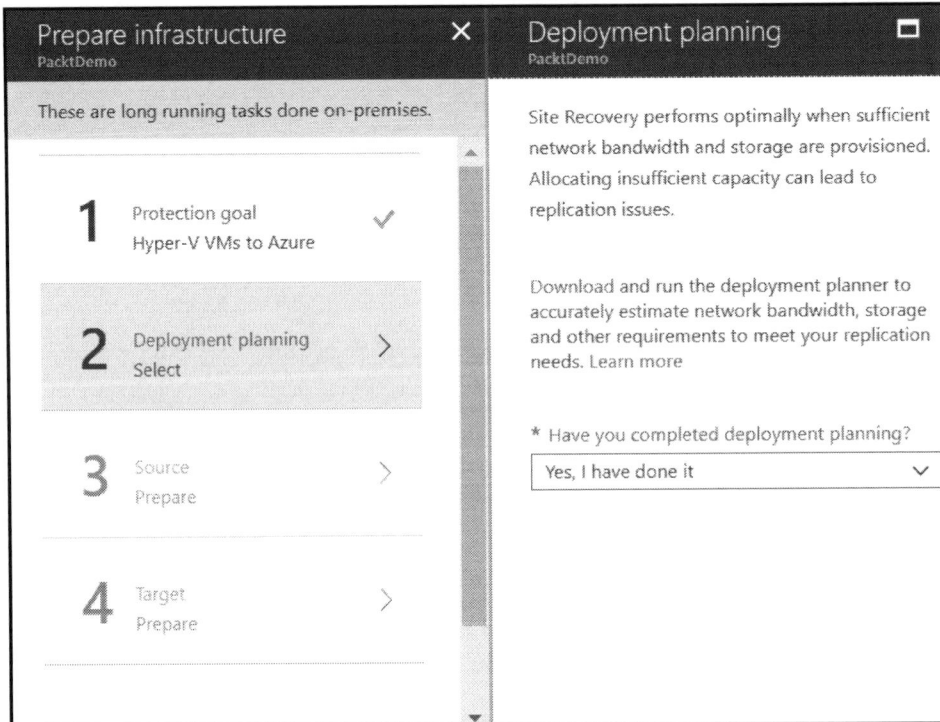

If the capacity is in order, we can proceed to **Source** preparation. We need to create a Hyper-V site and register a Hyper-V server that should be included in the replication, as shown here:

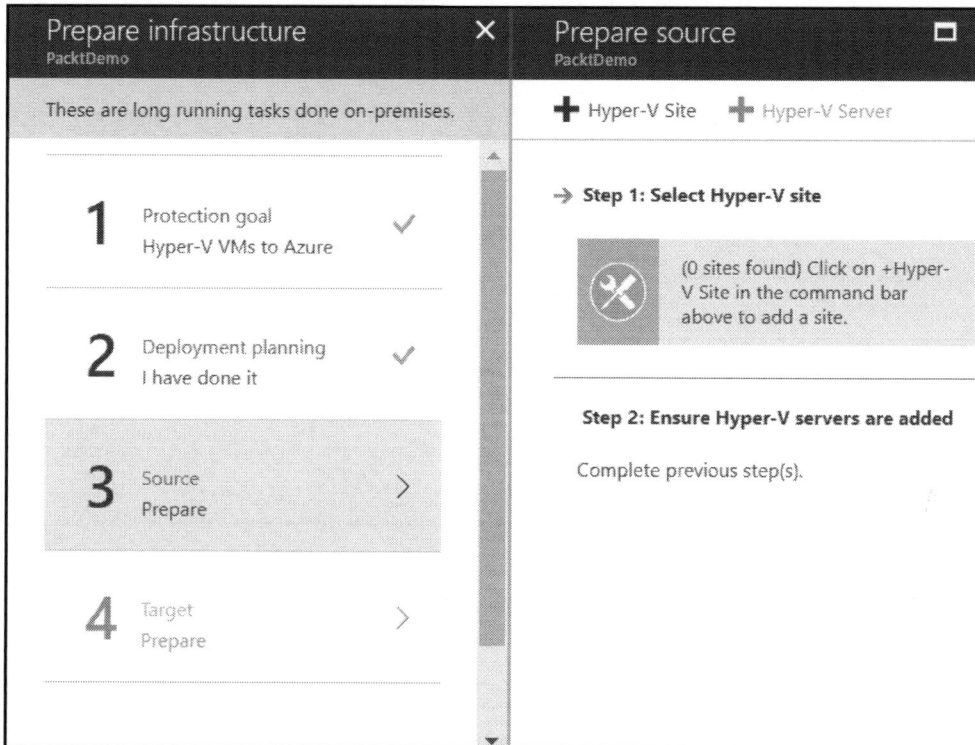

After we create a new site, we need to download and install agents on all Hyper-V hosts that we want to protect on that site. Installation of this agent is similar to the backup agent (we need the vault credentials that can be downloaded from the recovery services vault) and after we have finished, we will have Hyper-V hosts available under our site. Note that after installation, it can take 15 to 30 minutes before Hyper-V hosts are visible in the Azure portal. A successfully registered site and host are shown here:

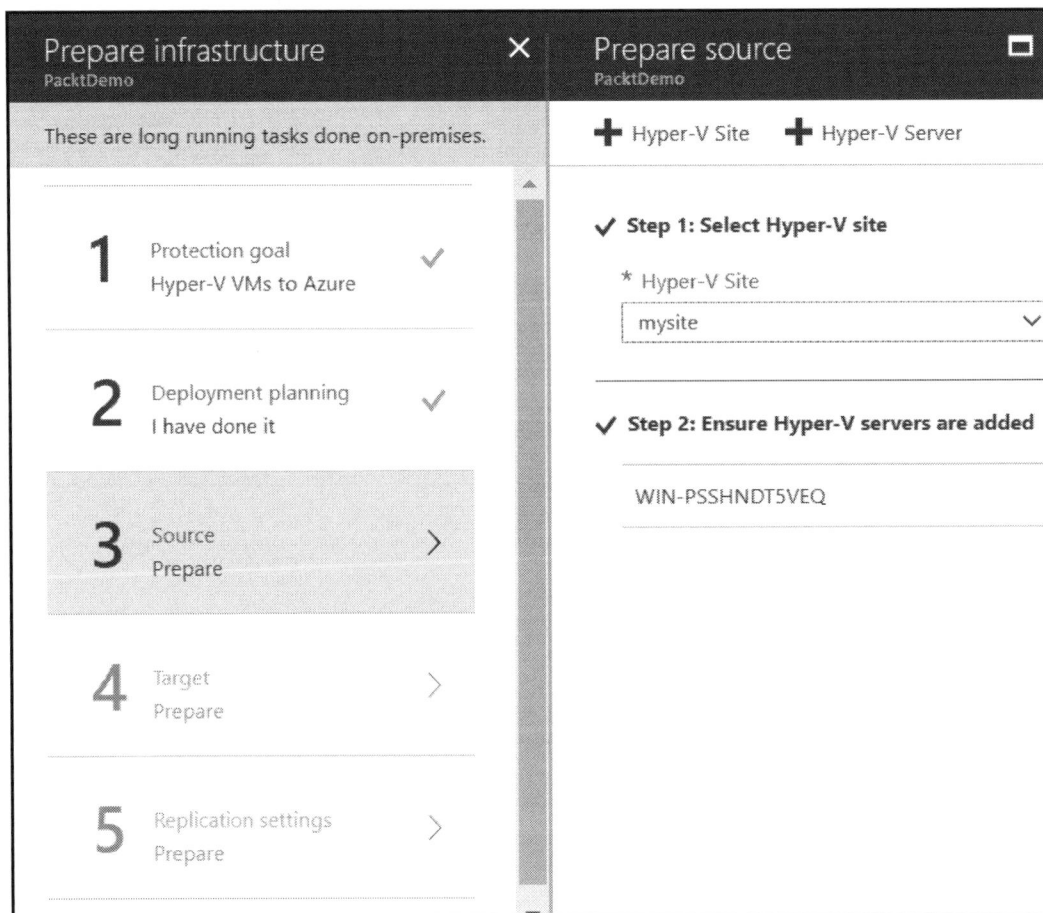

After we set up the **Source** environment, we need to prepare the **Target** as well. We need to select the Azure **Subscription**, and deployment model, and prepare Azure infrastructure. Under infrastructure, we need to provide at least one storage account and one VNet for the target environment. The storage account must be provided for the VM disks and VNet is used in case DR is triggered and VMs must be restored to Azure (VM must be connected to VNet). The **Target** configuration is shown here:

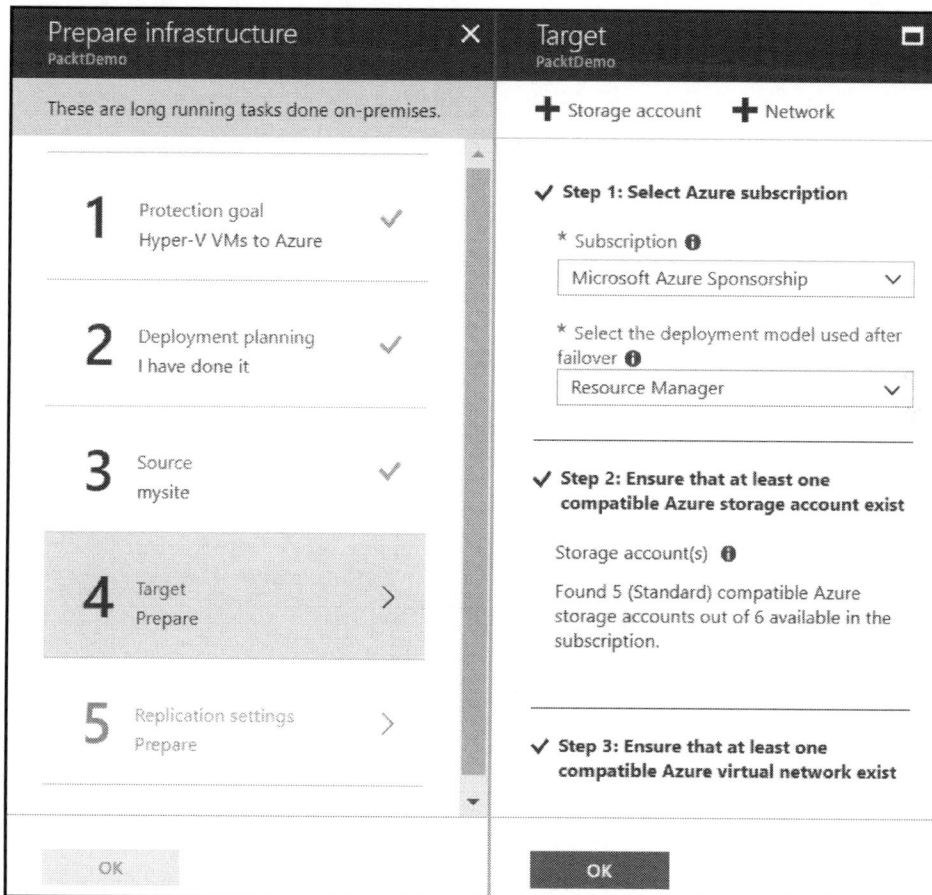

The last step in infrastructure preparation is to create a replication policy. We need to define rules for frequency, recovery points retention, and some other settings. I recommend leaving everything on default settings except **Copy frequency** that may be changed based on the roles of the servers that are protected. You can also create multiple policies and apply them according to your requirements. You probably don't need to replicate a web server as often as a database or file server and can use a different replication policy based on the roles of the protected server. An example of a default replication policy is shown here:

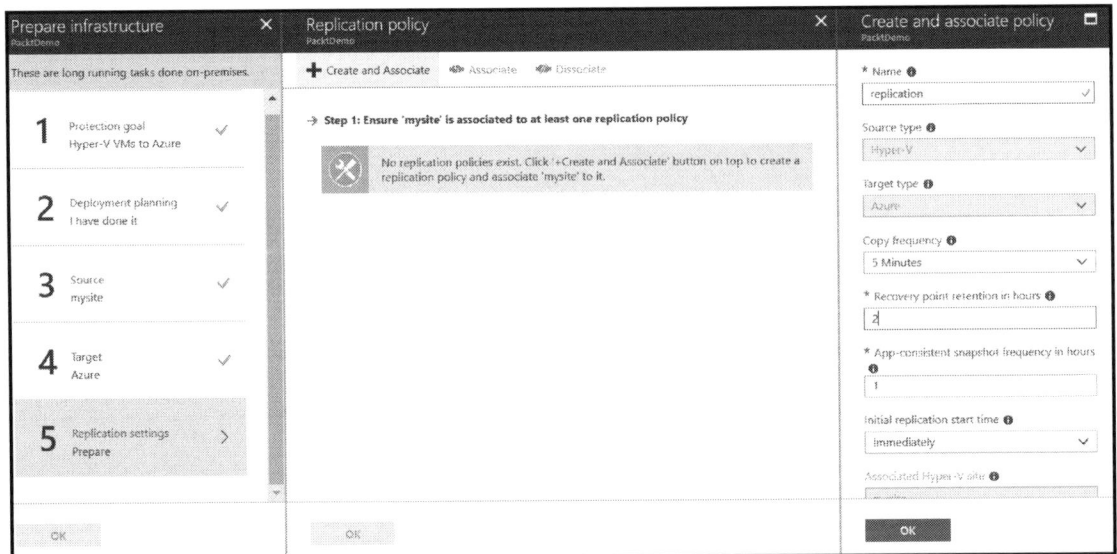

Based on the previous steps, we can add multiple sources to a single key vault. In the same key vault, we can have registered Azure resources, multiple Hyper-V sites, VMware sites, or physical servers.

After we prepare the infrastructure for ASR, we need to define what we are going to replicate and when. We need to select a source (**Azure** or **On-premises**) and select an appropriate location registered in recovery services vault. An example of **Source** selection is shown here:

After we select **Source**, we need to select the **Target** as well. Required parameters are the Azure **Subscription**, resource group, deployment model, storage, and network settings. The resource group will be used as the location where the VMs will be created in case of failover.

The same goes for the virtual network, it will be used only if failover is in place and VMs need to be created in Azure. Storage is used to place VM disks (VHDs) but it will be used even when failover isn't in place, as data must be stored even when VM is not running. An example of **Target** settings is shown here:

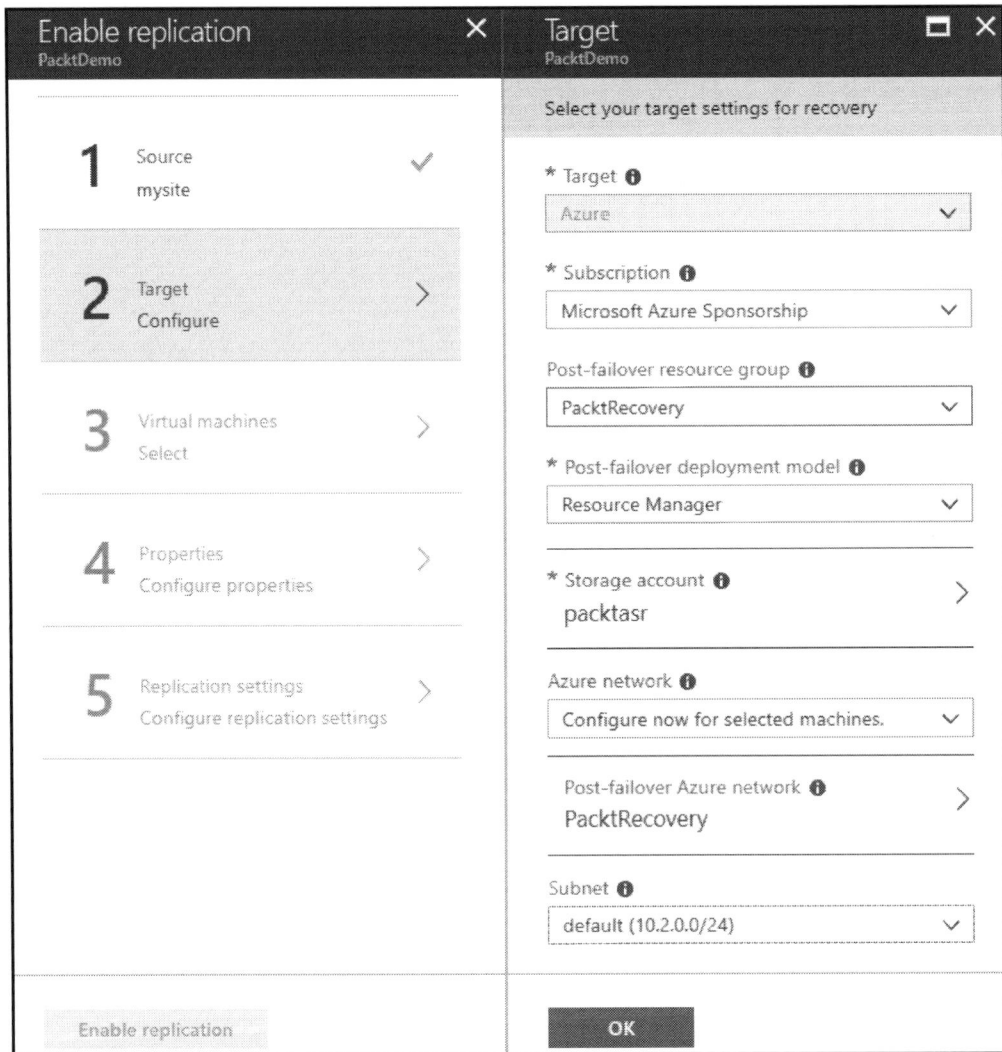

The **Source** and **Target** are in place and now we need to select what will be protected. This is done in two steps. The first will be to select **Virtual machines** in the previously selected site that we want to protect, as shown here:

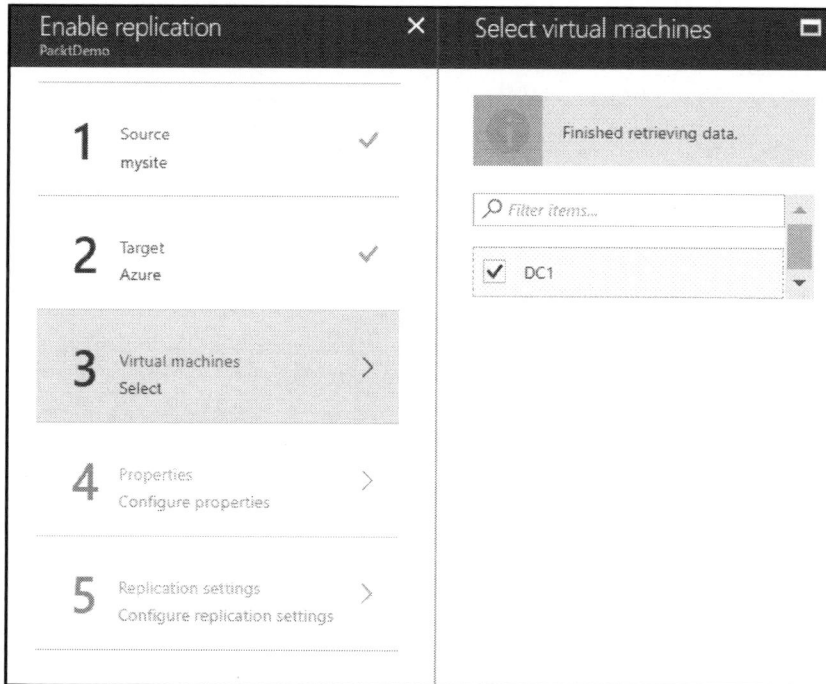

After the **Virtual machines** that will be protected are selected, we must provide additional settings for these VMs. Settings that are required are the operating system for our VM, and disks that we want to replicate. An example is shown here:

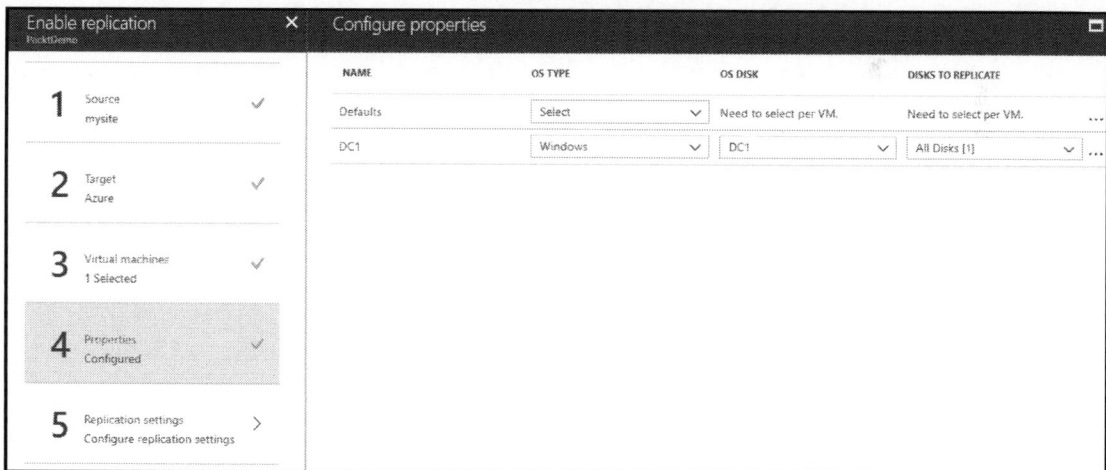

One of the last steps is to select a replication policy that will be applied. As we can have multiple policies created, we can assign one that best fits the roles and settings of the VMs that are protected. An example of **Replication settings** is shown here:

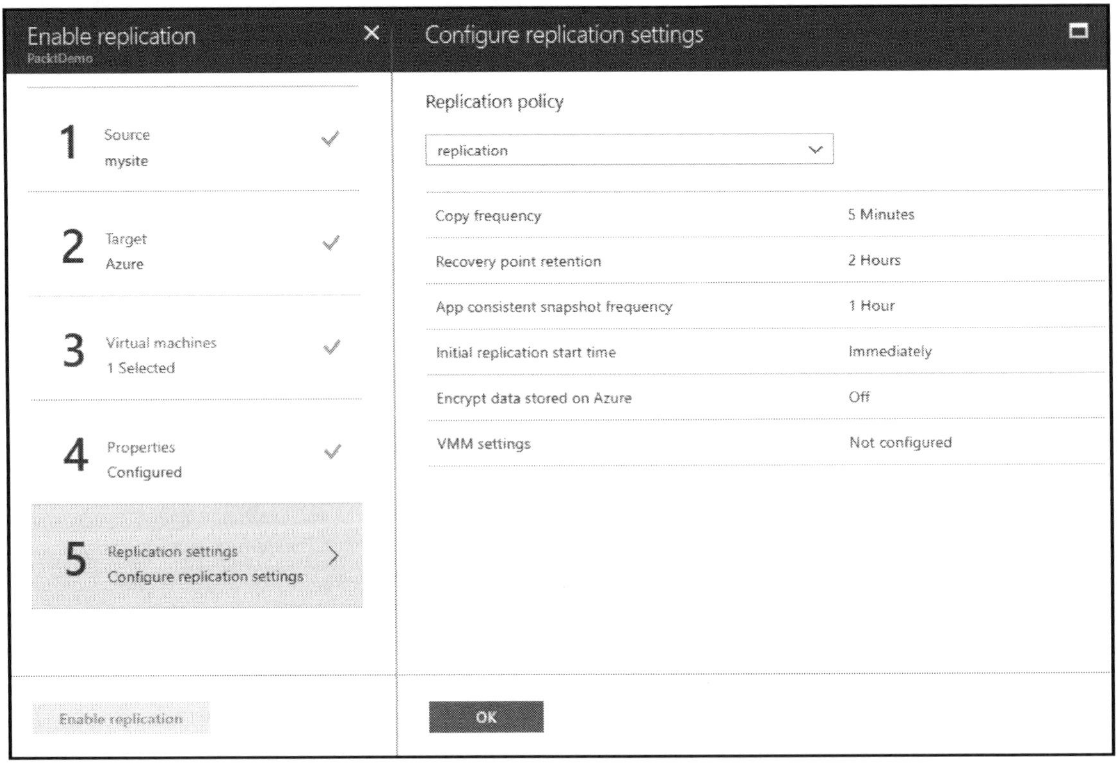

Finally, everything is in place and by clicking **OK**, we can enable replication and start the protection of our VMs. The last step is shown here:

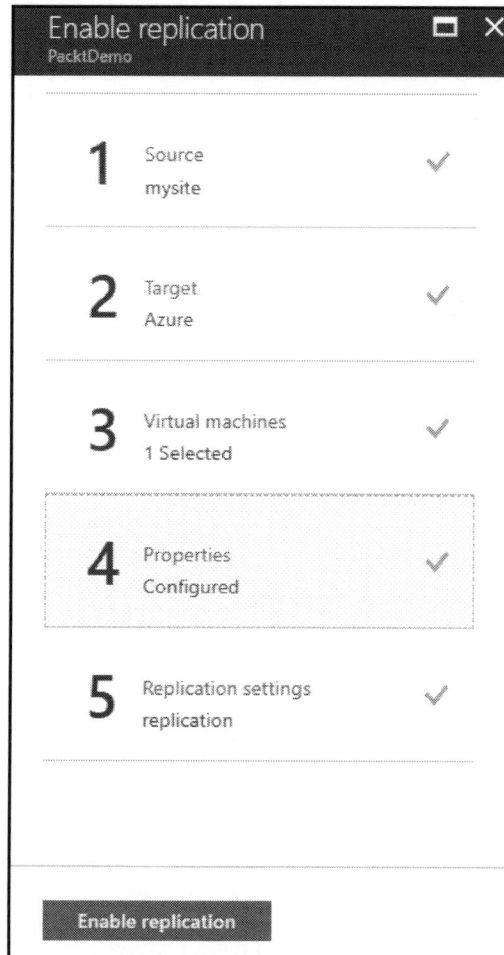

Using ASR as a migration tool

After replication is completed, you can see the status of replicated VMs under the protected items in the recovery services vault. You can use the same blade to monitor the replication process and see the percentage of replicated items. Time needed to complete initial replication depends on network bandwidth, storage settings, and the size of data that will be replicated. An example of a successful replication is shown here:

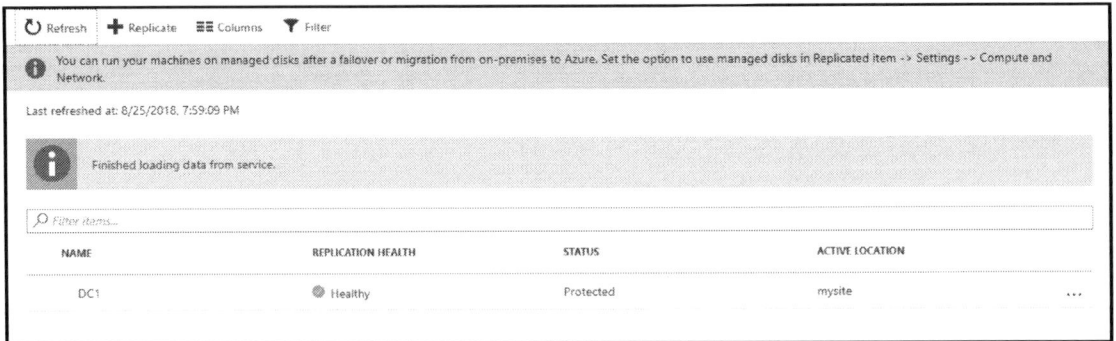

If we select any of the VMs under replicated items, we can find additional information on health, events, and options for failover (planned failover, failover, and test failover) as shown here:

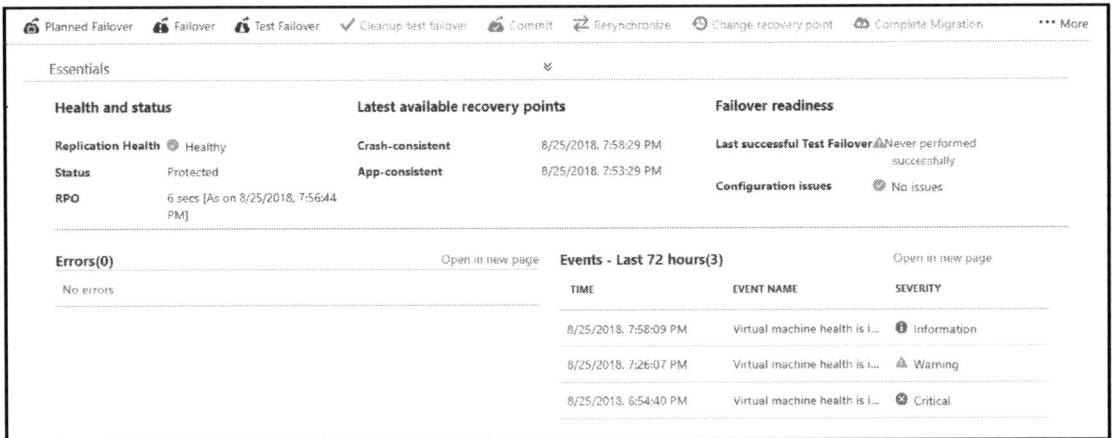

There is a difference on different failovers and how they affect the primary VM. For example, a test failover will create a VM instance in Azure but will not affect the on-premises (primary) VM in any way. On the other hand, a planned failover and failover will create a new VM instance in Azure, declare it primary, and can even turn off the on-premises VM.

Another thing that can be found in this blade is a diagram of the infrastructure involved, showing you how all components involved in the process are connected. A diagram for the Hyper-V site is shown in this screenshot:

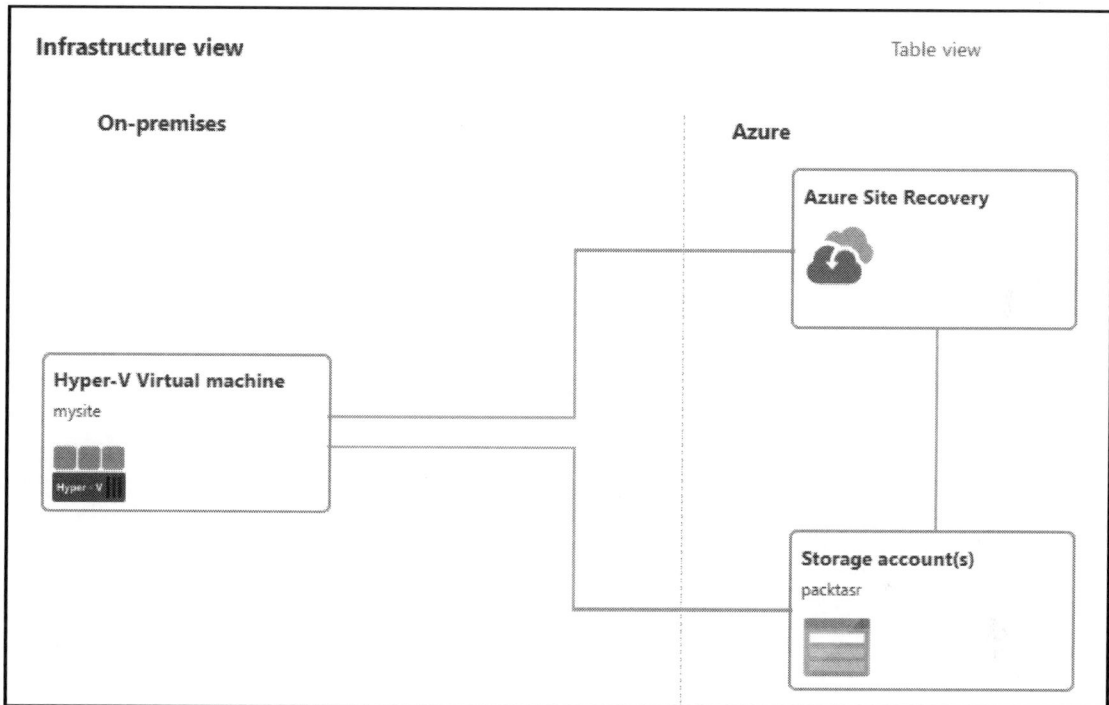

Failover and migrating the VM

As the purpose of our replicating our VM is to migrate it to the cloud, let's move on and show how to perform this task.

First, we will need to perform the failover of our VM. Here we need to select a **Recovery Point** we want to use, as we have multiple recovery points. Time needed for failover to complete depends on the size of the VM that will be created, amount of disks, and the size of data on these disks. An example for failover settings is shown here:

After failover completes, the VM will be running, and Azure and you can manage it as any other Azure VM. Note that this VM will not be using managed disks. This is because ASR replicates disks to storage and creates copies of on-premises VHD. When failover occurs, VHDs are used for our VM and attach to it but as result disks are not managed. However, you can perform migration to managed disks when needed. If you plan to migrate this VM completely, I strongly recommend performing migration to managed disks. The VM after failover is shown here:

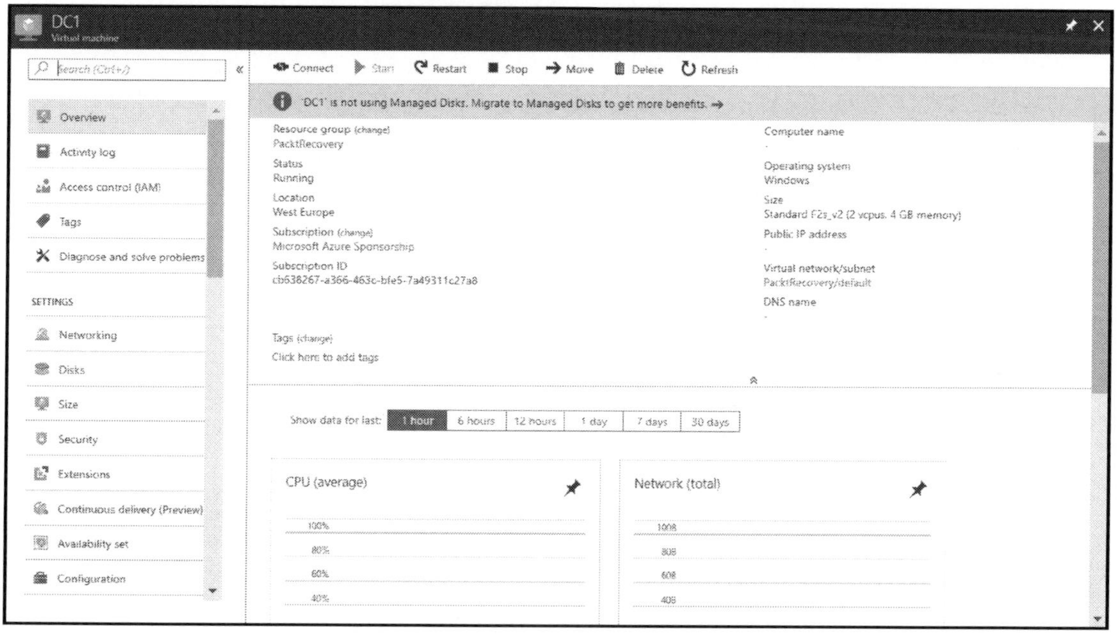

After we complete failover, the VM is running in Azure but it's still connected to the on-premises VM. We can perform failback at any time and the VM is listed under the replicated items in the recovery services vault. To complete migration and have the VM running only as an Azure VM, we need to perform a complete migration step. This will remove the association of our VM from the on-premises VM and the recovery service vault, as shown here:

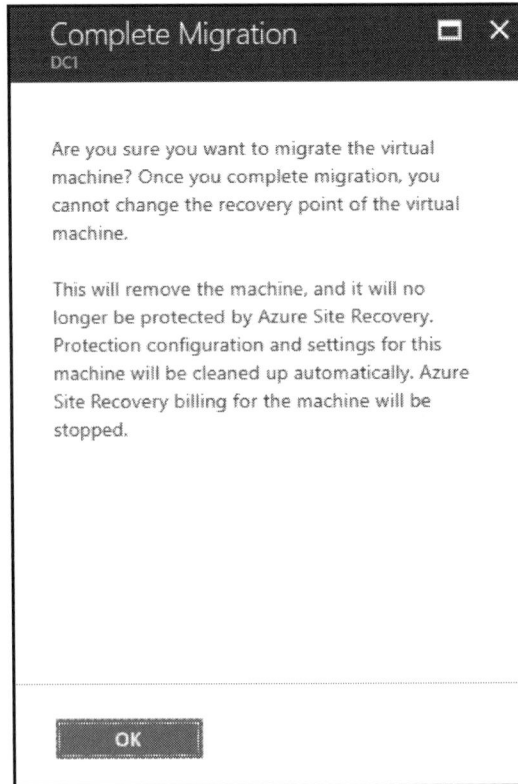

Complete Migration
DC1

Are you sure you want to migrate the virtual machine? Once you complete migration, you cannot change the recovery point of the virtual machine.

This will remove the machine, and it will no longer be protected by Azure Site Recovery. Protection configuration and settings for this machine will be cleaned up automatically. Azure Site Recovery billing for the machine will be stopped.

OK

Other options

Finally, our VM is migrated to the cloud and running in Azure. Migrating with ASR allows us to minimize the downtime of our services but isn't the only option.

AzCopy allows us to copy data from on-premises to the cloud as well, and can be used as a migration tool for all sorts of files. Another option is to use PowerShell to upload VHDs to Azure and use them to deploy the Azure VM.

Azure import/export job is used to transfer a large amount of data to Azure. Imagine you have disks with 4 TB of data. Copying that over internet would take a lot of time. With Azure import/export job, you can create a job in Azure, copy that to physical disks and ship them to the Azure Datacenter. Disks will be then available to you in the Azure portal and you can use this data in the cloud. The process can go in the other direction as well and you can export data from Azure and ship it to yourself.

Summary

After we introduced basic Azure services, both IaaS and PaaS, we explained the process of moving data to Azure. Microsoft offers extended options on how to assess if our data is cloud-ready, and also offers multiple tools to move data from on-premises to Azure. As the cost of inbound traffic is 0 and only outbound traffic from Azure is charged, we can see where Microsoft wants data to go.

The next step in the Azure journey is a hybrid cloud that will help us use on-premises resources we already have, and extend them with all the benefits the cloud has to offer. This scenario is the reality for most companies as most of them are already invested in local resources. Ignoring existing resources is not an option and we can leverage the Azure offering by extending existing resources with a hybrid cloud. In Chapter 7, *Hybrid Cloud with Azure – Extending Local Workloads to the Cloud*, we'll discuss how to create a secure connection between Azure and local infrastructure, and use Azure as a hybrid cloud.

Questions

1. An Azure Storage account can be deployed as...
    1. Resource manager
    2. Classic
    3. Both

2. To have maximum SLA, the Storage account should be...
    1. Locally redundant
    2. Geo-redundant
    3. Both

3. The Storage account tier can be...
    1. Standard
    2. Premium
    3. Both

4. Can a local database be backed up to the Azure Storage account?
    1. Yes
    2. No

5. Can a local database be deployed directly to Azure SQL database?
    1. Yes
    2. No

6. To use ASR, you need to create...
    1. Azure Storage account
    2. Recovery services vault
    3. Azure Backup

7. With Azure Backup, you can protect...
    1. Azure resources
    2. On-premises resources
    3. Both

8. With ASR, you can protect...
    1. Azure Virtual Machines
    2. On-premises virtual machines
    3. Both

9. To migrate a VM protected with ASR to the cloud, you must...
    1. Replicate the VM
    2. Perform failover
    3. Start the VM in Azure

10. To migrate a large amount of data to Azure, we must use...
    1. AzCopy
    2. PowerShell
    3. Azure import/export job

7
Hybrid Cloud with Azure - Extending Local Workloads to the Cloud

The hybrid cloud is an important part of the cloud journey, helping us to combine Azure (or any other cloud) with on-premises resources. In this chapter, we'll discuss how to configure the environment and the connections between the Azure and local infrastructure in order to take advantage of the best from both worlds—local and cloud infrastructure.

The following topics will be covered in this chapter:

- Hybrid clouds
- Connecting virtual networks to on-premises
- On-premises data gateways
- Azure Stack

Technical requirements

For this chapter, you'll need:

- An Azure subscription
- A local server running Windows Server 2012 R2 or later
- A VPN (firewall) device supporting an S2S connection

Hybrid clouds

Migrating completely to the cloud is not an option for many organizations. Even though the cloud offers multiple benefits, there are many scenarios to consider.

For example, if a company invested in local infrastructure, it would be hard to just abandon all that and move everything to the cloud. When creating a local data center, we need to invest in server rooms, networking, servers, storage, and software licenses. There is no business justification to abandon all investments and start investing in the cloud.

Another scenario is when we are not allowed to move specific services. In this case, compliance with the law can stop us from moving something out of a local data center. For example, some countries don't allow you to keep a user's personal information outside of that country. If an Azure data center is not available in your region, this may be a blocker and you may have to keep data in your local data center.

In both cases, when something is preventing us from using all of the cloud's services, we can benefit from what the cloud offers by setting up a hybrid cloud. This allows us to use cloud services along with local infrastructure, allowing us to create powerful combinations of the best from both wolds.

For example, we can set up database in a local data center (if we're not allowed to migrate a database or we have a brand new database server) and set up cloud services that will use a local database in the background. This especially applies to the Azure data analytics platform, which offers multiple powerful services that can provide you with fast data processing and still retain data locally.

There is a third scenario in which you can use services from multiple cloud providers and benefit from what each of them has to offer. Again, we need to set up a hybrid cloud scenario to secure communication and exchange resources between services you are using in each cloud.

The best way to set up security and keep your data safe in the hybrid cloud is to create a direct connection between Azure and the local infrastructure.

Connecting the local network and Azure Virtual Network

In order to connect local infrastructure and Azure, we need to create a connection between the local network and Azure Virtual Network. This connection can be either **Point-to-Site (P2S)** or **Site-to-Site (S2S)**. As P2S allows access to Azure Virtual Network from a single computer, it's not ideal for a true hybrid cloud, but more as point of access for remote workers.

To set up a true hybrid cloud, we need to create an S2S connection that will allow full communication between our local network and Azure Virtual Network. By doing so, we extend our local network to Azure and can access resources in Azure the same way as we would access resources in a local environment.

Creating an S2S connection can be done in two ways: using a VPN and using ExpressRoute. A VPN will provide communication encryption between two networks. ExpressRoute goes one step further and provides a dedicated connection between a local network and Azure Virtual Network. A dedicated connection provides more reliability, faster speeds, lower latency, and higher security, but it must be purchased as a separate service provided by the ISP.

Establishing a connection between a local network and Azure Virtual Network is a two-step process. First, we need to create and configure Azure resources, and in the second step we need to configure our local firewall. In the local environment, we need a VPN (firewall) device that supports creating S2S connections and public IP addresses. Note that all devices, with S2S option, do not support S2S connection with Azure.

Creating a S2S Connection

To create an S2S connection between Azure Virtual Network and our local network, first we must create two Azure resources: a virtual network gateway and a local network gateway.

Creating a virtual network gateway is done in a single blade. The information we need to provide is the **Name**, **Gateway type**, **VPN type**, **SKU**, **Virtual network**, **Gateway subnet address range**, **Public IP address**, **Subscription**, and **Location**. The **Name**, **Subscription**, and **Location** are the usual parameters.

The first option is to select the **Gateway type**. This can be either **VPN** or **ExpressRoute** (as we explained earlier). If **VPN** is selected, we need to choose whether the VPN type is policy- or route-based. (This option will probably depend on the settings of your local network.) The next step is to select an **SKU** that will decide the bandwidth and number of connections available. The option for active-active mode can be enabled or disabled. This mode allows you to create a redundant connection that will be observed as a single one from a traffic point of view. In other words, you need to create two S2S connections on your on-premises device, which will route traffic to the same virtual network. Traffic will be routed though both connections unless one becomes unavailable, and then traffic is routed through the S2S connection that is still available.

Active-active mode is not only used for highly available connections, but for better performance as well. You need to select a **Virtual network** that is available. Available networks will depend on the subscription and location that are selected. After the virtual network is selected, you need to provide a range for the gateway subnet. If such a subnet doesn't exist, it will be created automatically (unless there is no free address space on the network; then the process will fail). Note that there is no resource group needed. A virtual network gateway will be created in the same resource group in which the virtual network is located.

Next, you need to create or select an existing **Public IP address** that will be used for the connection. This IP is needed to establish a connection to your local network and will be used in the configuration for the local firewall in order to accept a connection from Azure. I recommend using a static IP address as you don't want to change the configuration in case the IP address changes.

An example of a virtual network gateway configuration is shown next:

Creating a virtual network gateway takes from 30 to 90 minutes. This is one of the resources in Azure that takes the longest time to deploy.

The ARM template for the deployment of an Azure virtual network gateway is provided here:

```
{
"$schema":
"http://schema.management.azure.com/schemas/2015-01-01/deploymentTemplate.j
son#",
"contentVersion": "1.0.0.0",
"parameters": {
"name": {
"type": "string"
},
"location": {
"type": "string"
},
"sku": {
"type": "string"
},
"gatewayType": {
"type": "string",
"defaultValue": "Vpn",
"allowedValues": [
"Vpn",
"ExpressRoute"
]
},
"vpnType": {
"type": "string",
"defaultValue": "RouteBased",
"allowedValues": [
"RouteBased",
"PolicyBased"
]
},
"existingVirtualNetworkName": {
"type": "string"
},
"newSubnetName": {
"type": "string"
},
"subnetAddressPrefix": {
"type": "string"
},
"newPublicIpAddressName": {
"type": "string"
}
},
"resources": [
```

```
{
"apiVersion": "2017-06-01",
"name": "[parameters('name')]",
"type": "Microsoft.Network/virtualNetworkGateways",
"location": "[parameters('location')]",
"dependsOn": [
"Microsoft.Network/virtualNetworks/PacktVnet/subnets/GatewaySubnet",
"[concat('Microsoft.Network/publicIPAddresses/',
parameters('newPublicIpAddressName'))]"
],
"properties": {
"gatewayType": "[parameters('gatewayType')]",
"ipConfigurations": [
{
"name": "default",
"properties": {
"privateIPAllocationMethod": "Dynamic",
"subnet": {
"id": "[resourceId('PacktIaaS',
'Microsoft.Network/virtualNetworks/subnets',
parameters('existingVirtualNetworkName'), parameters('newSubnetName'))]"
},
"publicIpAddress": {
"id": "[resourceId('PacktIaaS', 'Microsoft.Network/publicIPAddresses',
parameters('newPublicIpAddressName'))]"
}
}
}
],
"vpnType": "[parameters('vpnType')]",
"sku": {
"name": "[parameters('sku')]",
"tier": "[parameters('sku')]"
}
}
},
{
"apiVersion": "2018-04-01",
"type": "Microsoft.Network/virtualNetworks/subnets",
"name": "[concat(parameters('existingVirtualNetworkName'), '/',
parameters('newSubnetName'))]",
"location": "[parameters('location')]",
"properties": {
"addressPrefix": "[parameters('subnetAddressPrefix')]"
}
},
{
"apiVersion": "2017-08-01",
```

```
"type": "Microsoft.Network/publicIPAddresses",
"name": "[parameters('newPublicIpAddressName')]",
"location": "[parameters('location')]",
"properties": {
"publicIPAllocationMethod": "Dynamic"
}
}
]
}
```

After the deployment of the virtual network gateway is completed, we can proceed and create a local network gateway. A local network gateway is used to input information on your local firewall and network. You need to the provide the public **IP address** of your local firewall and the **Address space** of the local network (or gateway subnet of your local network, depending on the firewall). You also need to provide a **Subscription**, **Location**, and **Resource group**. The **Location** should be the same as the one that is used for the virtual network gateway and virtual network. I recommend placing them in the same resource group for easier management. Example settings for the local network gateway are shown here:

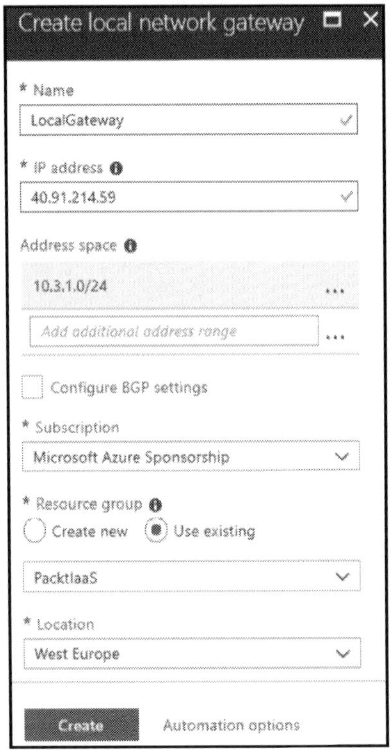

The ARM template for the deployment of a local network gateway is provided here:

```
{
"$schema":
"http://schema.management.azure.com/schemas/2015-01-01/deploymentTemplate.j
son#",
"contentVersion": "1.0.0.0",
"parameters": {
"localNetworkGatewayName": {
"type": "string"
},
"location": {
"type": "string"
},
"gatewayIpAddress": {
"type": "string"
},
"addressPrefixes": {
"type": "array"
}
},
"resources": [
{
"name": "[parameters('localNetworkGatewayName')]",
"type": "Microsoft.Network/localNetworkGateways",
"apiVersion": "2017-06-01",
"location": "[parameters('location')]",
"properties": {
"localNetworkAddressSpace": {
"addressPrefixes": "[parameters('addressPrefixes')]"
},
"gatewayIpAddress": "[parameters('gatewayIpAddress')]"
}
}
]
}
```

Deploying a local network gateway is relatively fast compared to a virtual network gateway, and deployment should complete in under 5 minutes.

Configuring Azure settings for S2S

After the virtual network gateway and local network gateway are created, we can proceed to configuration. In the virtual network gateway, we select **Connection type** options under **Settings**. You'll see that **Settings** has options for configuration, connections, and point-to-site connections.

As we are going to concentrate on S2S connections, we only use the connections blade and add a new connection. We need to provide a **Name** as usual. The options for the **Virtual network gateway**, **Subscription**, **Resource group**, and **Location** are locked and can't be changed, as they depend on the **Virtual network gateway** that is used to create a connection. Parameters that we need to provide are the **Connection type** and **Shared key (PSK)**. The **Connection type** options are **VNet-to-VNet**, **Site-to-Site (IPsec)**, and **ExpressRoute**. We are going to select the option for **Site-to-Site (IPsec)** as we want to connect to a local network. For the **Shared Key (PSK)**, I recommend it be as complex as possible because security can depend on this. Sample settings for a new connection are shown here:

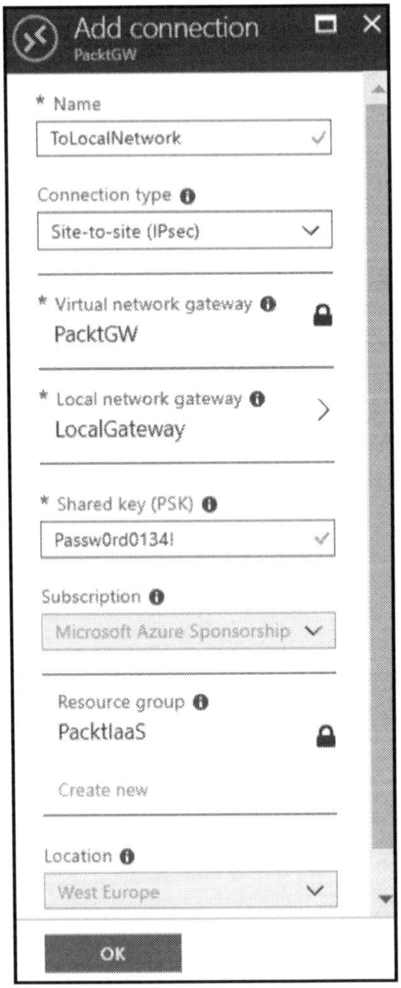

Creating a connection is only the first step; we also need to configure settings for our local network. After the initial creation, the status of the connection will be unknown, as shown in the following screenshot:

NAME	STATUS	CONNECTION TYPE	PEER
ToLocalNetwork	Unknown	Site-to-site (IPsec)	LocalGateway

Configuring a local firewall for S2S

Configuration of a local firewall depends on the vendor and type of device. Under created connection, there is an option to download configurations for some devices. You can select a few different vendors (for example, **Cisco** and **Juniper**), and also depending on the **Device vendor**, **Device family**, and **Firmware version** to download specific configuration. Only a few devices are available to download directly from the Azure portal. In Microsoft's documentation you can find more devices, and some vendors have a section on Azure S2S configuration on their websites. A screenshot of the configuration downloading process is shown next:

After the connection is configured on both sides, the status will change to **Connected**, as shown:

NAME	STATUS	CONNECTION TYPE	PEER
ToLocalNetwork	Connected	Site-to-site (IPsec)	LocalGateway

This will allow you to connect to any resource in the Azure Virtual Network directly from the local network with a secure, private connection. In some cases, you don't want to expose your resources for public access, so this is the only approach to connect to your resources.

In other cases, and this is probably most common practice, services are accessed publicly, but management is done over a private network. For example, access to a website is allowed over HTTP or HTTPS over the internet, but access to databases or an RDP connection to virtual machines is only allowed over a private network.

Configuring services in a hybrid environment

Once we have established a connection between the local network and Azure, we can start using services in both environments, as if these are single site or network. However, there are a few things that we need to keep in mind.

If we have a domain set up in the local environment and want to use the same domain in the cloud, it's a good idea to have one domain controller running in the Azure Virtual Network. Even when we have an S2S connection established, occasional interrupts in connection can be expected. By having one DC running in the cloud, we can ensure that services in Azure can use all features and run independently when interruptions occur.

When running SQL Server and using **Always On Availability Groups**, you can use Azure to extend the service and add one replica in the cloud. As we previously mentioned, there are two modes for running Azure: resource manager and classic. The classic model supports adding a replica in Azure through a wizard, and it's relatively easy to set up.

The resource manager requires use of T-SQL commands to add a replica in Azure resource manager mode, but it's a little more complicated. But as the resource manager is a recommended mode, I suggest using the resource manager, as classic is bound to be dropped at some point and you'll have to set up the resource manager eventually anyway.

Another thing to consider is Azure Hybrid Benefit, which allows you to use existing on-premises licenses in Azure. With software assurance, you can use licenses for Windows server and SQL Server, and deploy Azure resources with a significant discount.

The data center location is very important when establishing a connection between the local network and Azure. If you are located on one continent and the Azure data center (in which the virtual network is deployed)is in another, you will experience network latency and lag. Choosing the closest geographical location is the best possible option.

If you experience network latency and lag or have performance issues, ExpressRoute is the service you need to consider. It does come at a price, but it has an enterprise-grade connection with the best possible reliability, speed, and security.

Connecting virtual networks across Azure

A virtual network gateway can be used to connect different Azure Virtual Networks. But as you pay for a virtual network gateway, I recommend a different approach. To connect Azure Virtual Networks to another Azure Virtual Network, we can use **peering**. Peering, in general, is the interconnection of separate networks for the purpose of exchanging traffic networks. Options for peering are available under **Settings** in the virtual network blade. If we choose to create a new peering, we need to provide a **Name** and select if we are going to connect to a **Resource manager** or **Classic** virtual network. As **Resource manager** is recommended, we'll explain this process. If **Resource manager** is selected, we can either provide an ID for a resource or use a drop-down menu to select our Azure **Subscription** and the **Virtual network** we want to connect to.

Some additional options are available for forwarded traffic and a remote gateway if needed. Example peering settings are shown in the following screenshot:

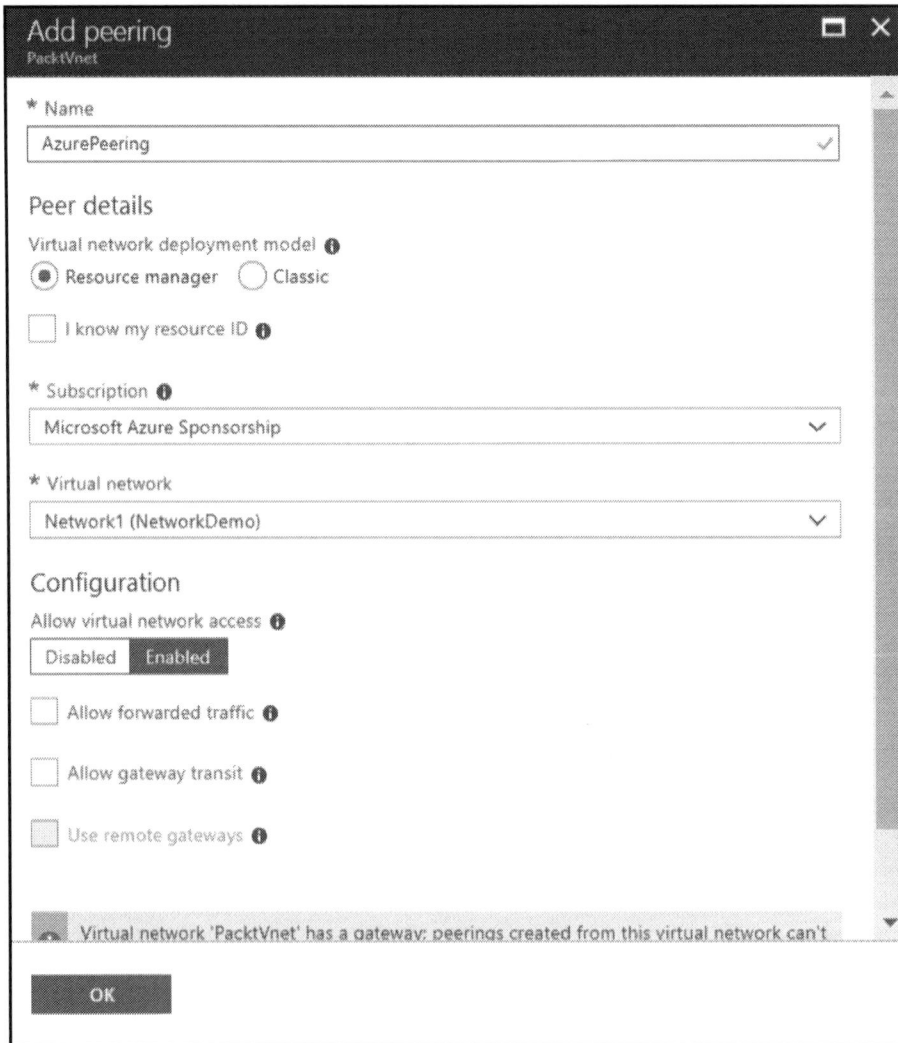

On-premises data gateway

In some cases, all the requirements to create S2S connections to Azure are not met, but we still need to connect to local resources. For example, we need to connect to a local database, but the VPN device we have locally doesn't support a connection to Azure.

In this case, we can use an on-premises data gateway to allow Azure services to use a local database in a secure way.

An on-premises data gateway acts as a bridge and allows us to access local data with Azure services. Services currently supported are Power BI, Microsoft Flow, PowerApps, Azure Analysis Services, and Azure Logic Apps. Logic apps can be used to pass this data to other services as well.

Supported connectors are:

- BizTalk Server 2016
- Filesystems
- IBM DB2
- IBM Informix
- IBM MQ
- MySQL
- Oracle Database
- PostgreSQL
- SAP Application Server
- SAP Message Server
- SharePoint Server
- SQL Server
- Teradata

Setting up an on-premises data gateway is a two-step process; we need to install the agent locally and configure the gateway in Azure next.

Local installation

To start the installation process, we need to sign in with an account that has access to an Azure subscription. Usually, to access an Azure subscription, you use either a Microsoft Live account or a work/school/O365/AAD account. In this case, we cannot use a Microsoft Live account because only a work account is allowed. The sign-in form is shown here:

After the sign-in process is completed, we need to provide a **New on-premises data gateway name** and a **Recovery key (8 character minimum)**. The recovery key is used if you need to restart the service or change its configuration:

Once deployment is completed, you will see a **Status** page and some additional configuration. You can change the **Service Settings**, **Network** settings, and **Connectors**, or launch **Diagnostics** if you're having an issue with the service. In order to access these settings again, you need to use a recovery key:

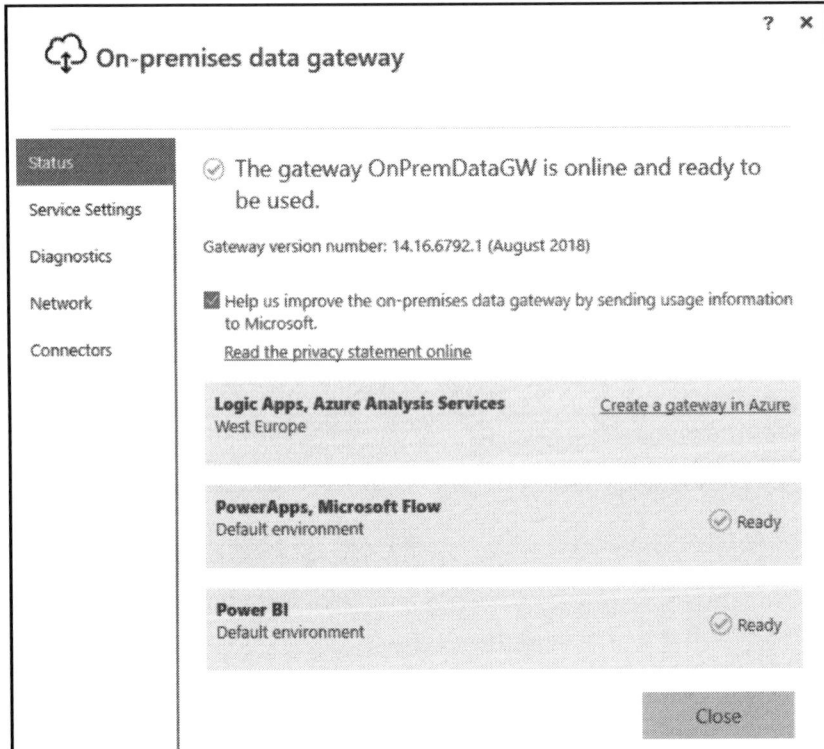

Cloud service

After installation on a local server is done, we need to configure a gateway in Azure as well. Parameters we need to provide are the **Resource Name**, **Subscription**, **Resource group**, and **Location**. Based on other information, available gateways will be available for selection under **Installation Name**:

After deployment is completed, we can use an on-premises data gateway to connect Azure to the local server. The number of services that can use this kind of connection is limited, but we can use logic app to extend the connection to other services as well. Configuring the logic app to use an on-premises data gateway allows us to extend this connection to other services in a single logic app flow and access the same data. The connection is limited, but it can help in certain scenarios in which S2S is not an option.

Azure Stack

Microsoft is probably the only cloud provider that has the option for true hybrid cloud. Most cloud providers include some sort of hybrid cloud, allowing you to combine on-premises and cloud services. In most cases, with IaaS, we have the option of running everything we have on-premises in the cloud with little to no effort. Migrating local resources to the cloud is an option everyone in the cloud business is offering.

Azure Stack is the only option which allows you to have things the other way around and to run cloud services in your local data center. With Azure Stack, you can run IaaS and even PaaS in your own environment. Basically, Azure Stack is an extension of Azure in a local environment, and it uses the same fabric that the public version of Azure is using, but on a much smaller scale. It comes in a pre-configured box that must be bought from one of the authorized vendors and uses the same "real" fabric Azure uses. It supports the same models and deployment tools that the public version of Azure supports. All applications and services deployed in Azure will run in the Azure Stack, and all applications and services deployed in Azure Stack will run in Azure. The model is developed once and deployed anywhere.

There are a few scenarios in which Azure Stack may be considered. The first is one we already mentioned when we discussed hybrid cloud options: when we have regulatory requirements to keep data in our local data center or within our own country. Even with the hybrid cloud, in this scenario we must use SQL Server. With Azure Stack, this is not the case anymore; we can use Azure SQL databases and take advantage of PaaS even when retaining the database locally.

Latency and connectivity can be an issue when handling large datasets. Azure Stack is a solution with which we can process data locally and then aggregate it in Azure for further analytics, sharing common application logic across both.

Another example would be systems that are disconnected, or partly disconnected, and have connections to the internet occasionally. With Azure Stack, we can provide cloud applications in environments like airplanes or ships that don't have an internet connection all the time. An airline could create a cloud application for customers, and customers could access such an application when the airplane is offline. Once an internet connection is established, a data sync can be performed and everything updated.

In certain scenarios, a company can have multiple locations, and some of these locations can be required to be offline. Cloud applications were not an option in this scenario before, but with Azure Stack all locations can use the same application even when using the cloud. Some locations may use an application in public Azure and some of them may use Azure Stack, but they have all the same features and capabilities.

Azure Stack may be an interesting option for Microsoft partners that may want to host Azure Stack in their data center and offer Azure services in their country. If companies or government agencies are required to keep data in their country, hosting providers could use Azure Stack to run Azure services in that country for such organizations.

Fabric, model, and deployment tools are not only things that Azure and Azure Stack share. Azure portal is another thing that is very similar in both cases. Azure Stack comes with two versions of portal: user and administration. The former is used for consuming and creating resources, similar to what we have in the public Azure portal, and is later used to configure quotas and limitations for users and tenants. The administration part of the portal is especially interesting for those who decide to use Azure Stack to host Azure services locally and offer them to others, as this will allow them to control limitations and spending for each customer.

You can compare the design of Azure and the Azure Stack portal in the next two screenshots, the first being **public Azure** and the second **Azure Stack**. As you can see, the design is very similar and the difference is the name in the top-left corner:

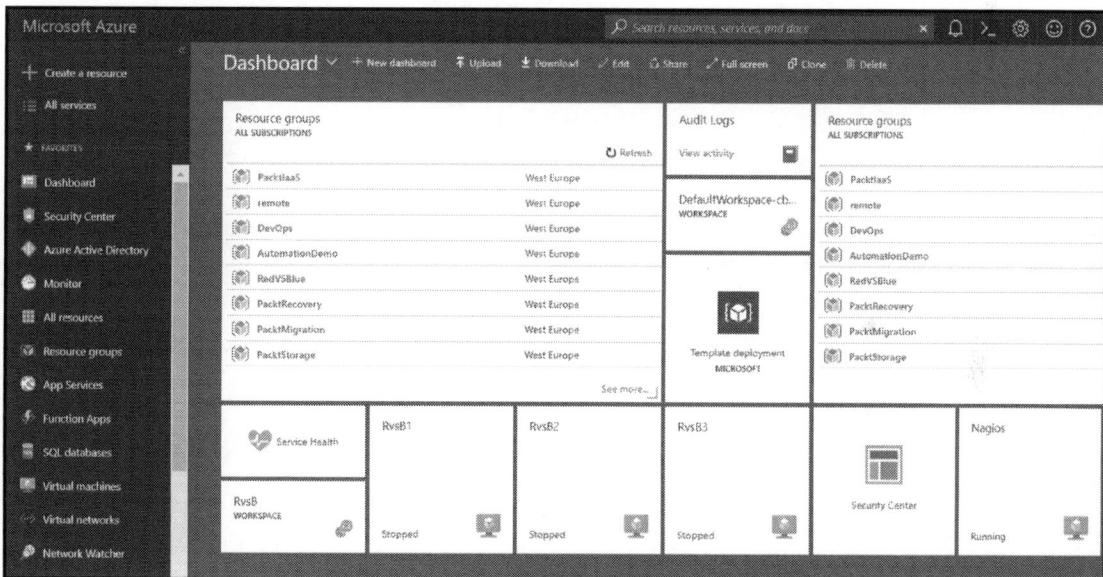

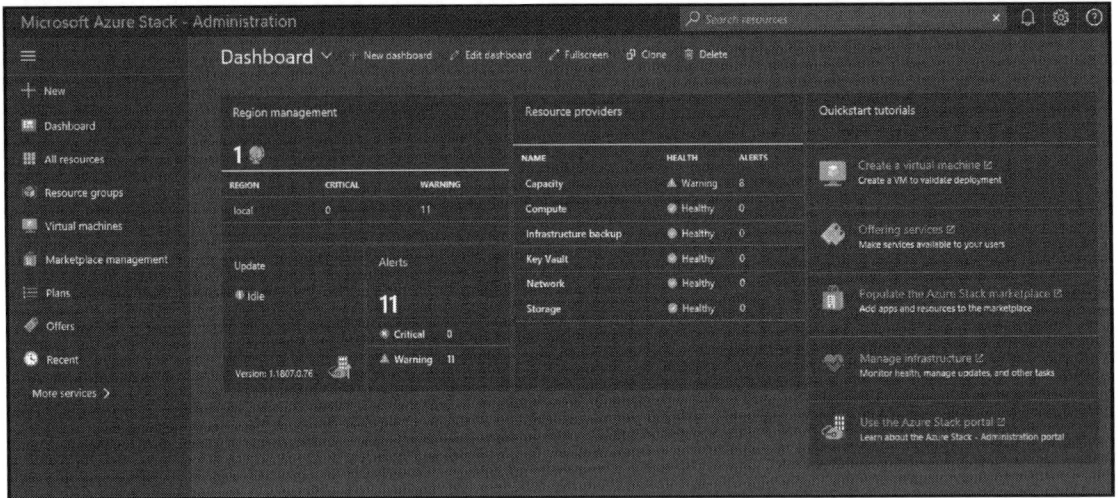

Summary

As explained, the hybrid cloud is a reality for most organizations, whether it's because of regulations or investment in local infrastructure. We already covered how to migrate or extend services to the cloud, and a very important part of this is managing identities in the cloud. Data is important, but managing who can access that data is just as important. In extending local infrastructure to the cloud, we can set up a replica of the domain controller and use the Active Directory to manage identities and delegate access, but this only extends to IaaS.

To manage this with PaaS, we must use Azure Active Directory, which is often called Identity as a Service. In the next chapter, we'll discuss Azure Active Directory, how to use it, and even extend local identities to Azure Active Directory.

Questions

1. The hybrid cloud is often only an option because of...
    1. Regulations
    2. Investment
    3. Both

2. We can connect a local network and Azure using...
    1. Site-to-Site
    2. ExpressRoute
    3. Both

3. Azure resources needed for S2S...
    1. A virtual network gateway
    2. An on-premises data gateway
    3. Both

4. A local network gateway holds the configuration of a...
    1. Virtual network
    2. Local network
    3. Both

5. A VPN device configuration can be downloaded from the Azure portal.
    1. True
    2. True, but for a limited number of devices
    3. False

6. The recommended mode for S2S connection is...
    1. Resource manager
    2. Classic
    3. Both

7. To ensure that you can use local identities in the hybrid cloud, you must deploy...
    1. Domain controller in disaster recovery
    2. Domain controller in Azure
    3. Always on availability group

8. An on-premises data gateway can be used with...
    1. All Azure Services
    2. A limited number of Azure Services
    3. A single Azure Service

9. Azure Stack is...
   1. An extension of Azure in your local data center
   2. An extension of your local data center in Azure
   3. An extension of Azure in another public cloud

10. Azure Stack offers...
    1. IaaS
    2. PaaS
    3. Both

8
Azure Active Directory - Identity in the Cloud

We already have applications and data in Azure, and the connection between our local network and Azure is up and running. But what about authentication and authorization? How can we manage permissions and access for our users? The answer to all these questions is an **Azure Active Directory (AAD)** that allows us to set up a cloud-based identity authentication which, along with **Azure role-based access control (RBAC)**, allows us to authenticate users and allow them access to specific resources.

The following topics will be covered in this chapter:

- The Azure Active Directory
- Syncing local AD with AAD
- Managing users and applications in AAD

Technical requirements

For this chapter, you'll need the following:

- An Azure subscription
- A local server running a Windows Server 2012 R2 or later, with the domain controller role installed

The Azure Active Directory

AAD is a cloud-based directory and identity management service that provides application access management and identity protection. It's often referred to as IaaS.

We already mentioned this, but let's review it anyway. AAD is at the top level of the Azure management chain and it's directly tied to the tenant. Under the tenant, we can have multiple subscriptions, under subscriptions multiple resource groups, and under resource groups multiple resources.

A single account can have access to multiple tenants but each tenant is isolated. When a user signs in, the default directory and tenant is selected. Only resources that are under subscriptions under that tenant are available. In order to manage resources in another tenant, we must switch the directory.

AAD comes in four tiers:

- Azure Active Directory Free
- Azure Active Directory Basic
- Azure Active Directory Premium P1
- Azure Active Directory Premium P2

Azure Active Directory Basic offers cloud-centric application access and self-service identity management solutions with group-based access management, self-service password reset for cloud applications, and the AAD Application Proxy.

The premium tiers offer additional features and enterprise-grade management tools such as dynamic groups, self-service group management, and Microsoft identity management (P1) or identity protection and privileged identity management (P2). Azure Active Directory Premium P2 contains all the features of P1 plus identity protection and privileged identity management.

Here, we are going to focus on features that are covered by the Azure Active Directory Free tier. The free tier is limited to 500.000 directory objects and supports a limited set of features but allows for user/group management, syncing on-premises directories to Azure, and basic security reports. It will be sufficient to provide general images and to introduce AAD. Including all features provided by all AAD tiers would probably result in a separate book and would be too much to cover when discussing Azure administration in general.

Creating a new directory

Even though AAD will probably exist if an Azure subscription is in place, let's start by creating a new AAD (a new tenant).

To create a new directory, we need to provide an **Organization name**, **Initial domain name**, and **Country or region**. Note that the initial domain name will be used to form an initial domain using `yourdomain.onmicrosoft.com`. The domain must be unique and can be customized for your custom domain later. An example of the settings is shown in the following screenshot:

Creating a new directory takes about 1 minute. After the new directory is created, you need to switch directories in order to manage it. Note that the directory name is located under your profile. To change the directory, click on the **Directory** menu to the left of your profile and select directory from the list; it will open, as shown here:

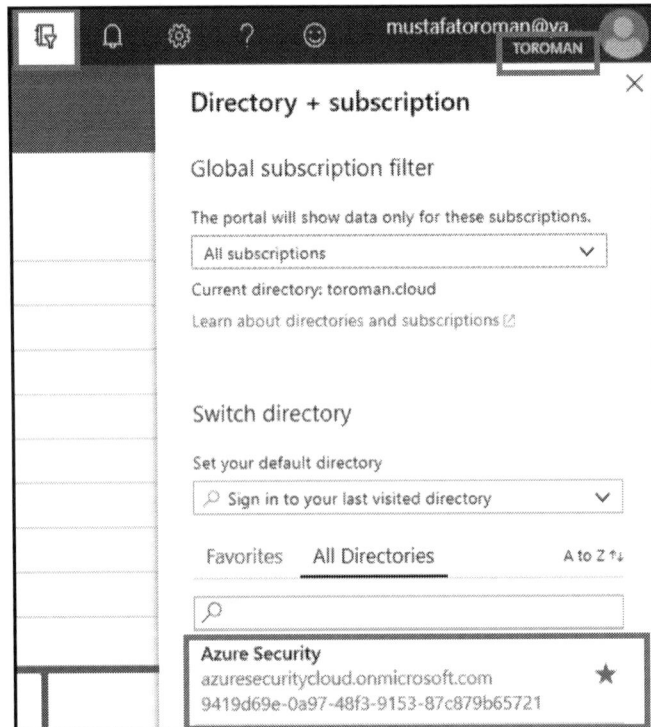

After you switch the directory, you will be in a new tenant. If you created a new directory, the tenant will be empty and no subscriptions will be assigned. To start creating Azure resources, you must create a new subscription under this tenant. The only thing that you can manage in an empty tenant is AAD. The **Overview** and **Manage** options for Azure Active Directory Free are shown in the following screenshot:

Customizing your domain

The first thing we need to customize is the domain name. In order to add a custom domain to your directory, you need to enter a **Custom domain name**, which is actually a public domain that you own. For example, I'm going to use my domain, `azuresecurity.cloud`:

After the custom domain is added, the domain needs to be verified, or to be more precise, domain ownership needs to be verified. In order to verify domain ownership, you need to input a **TXT** or **MX** record into your domain name register. An example for the **TXT** records is shown here:

After you input records and press the **Verify** button, you might receive an error. DNS records may need up to 72 hours to propagate changes. The time depends on the DNS you're using but usually, it doesn't take more than 30 minutes to propagate changes. If the changes aren't propagated yet, you'll receive error, as shown in the following screenshot:

After changes are propagated and verification passes, you'll receive a message stating that verification has passed. You'll be offered two additional options—make this domain primary, and download Azure AD Connect. We'll ignore Azure AD Connect for now, but I recommend making the custom domain primary. This way, the custom domain will become the primary and the preferred domain suffix. Instead of the default username being `username@yourdomain.onmicrosoft.com`, it will become `username@yourdomain.com`. As in the preceding example, instead of `username@azuresecuritycloud.onmicrosoft.com`, the new username will be `username@azuresecurity.cloud`. A screenshot showing a verified custom domain is shown after you've done this:

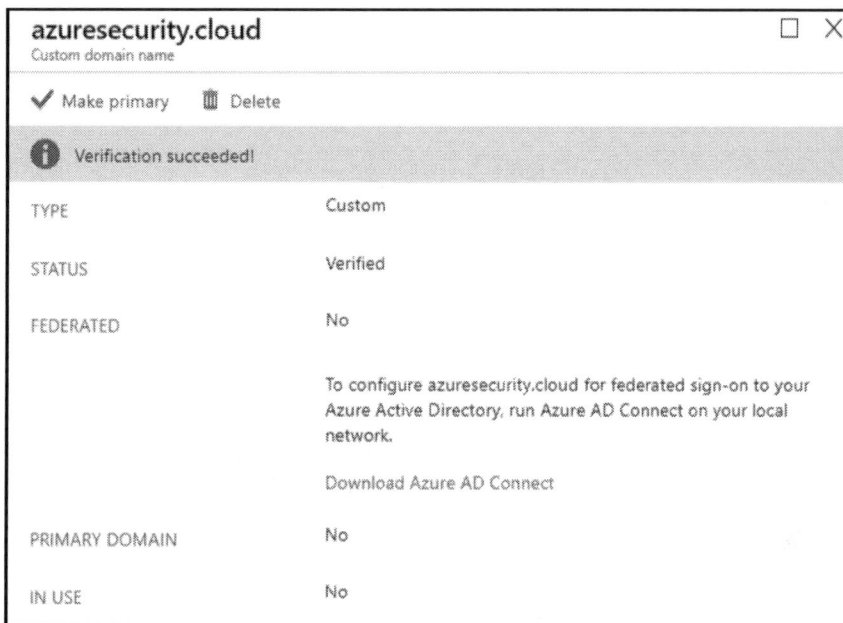

Syncing AAD with on-premises AD

We have a new directory in place; we can start adding users and assigning them access rights. But there is a good chance that we already have an identity solution in an on-premises environment and that users already have one identity in place. Providing users with an additional identity can cause issues and confusion. Users will have problems detecting when to use which account, and if the same or a similar account is created, users will start typing in the password for the wrong account...

Fortunately, with AAD, we can use Azure AD Connect, and that will allow us to sync accounts from on-premises AD to Azure and allow users to use the same account for everything. This will make things easier for everyone; users will not have to think about which account they will use (as it's the same account) and admins will have less issues to resolve (less accounts to manage and less users blocking their account with wrong password attempts).

Additionally, with Azure AD Connect, we can implement **single sign-on** (**SSO**), which will allow users to access Azure and on-premises resources with the single sign-in process. The user is asked to enter their credentials once, and the same credentials are used to access everything that the user has access to.

In order to start syncing with the local AD, we need to go to the Azure AD Connect blade in AAD. Here, we can see the current sync status. If sync isn't enabled yet, you will also have the download link for the Azure AD Connect client, as you can see here:

Installing Azure AD Connect

Azure AD Connect must be installed on a server in your on-premises environment. It's recommended that you use a server without a domain controller role but with access to a domain controller. A server with Azure AD Connect must have access to the internet as it will need the internet to sync information between on-premises AD and AAD. All traffic going over Azure AD Connect is encrypted and secure.

The installation wizard is very intuitive and explains every step of the process; you just need to follow the guidelines (and understand the local AD structure). A screenshot of the first screen in the installation process, explaining what the tool will do, is shown here:

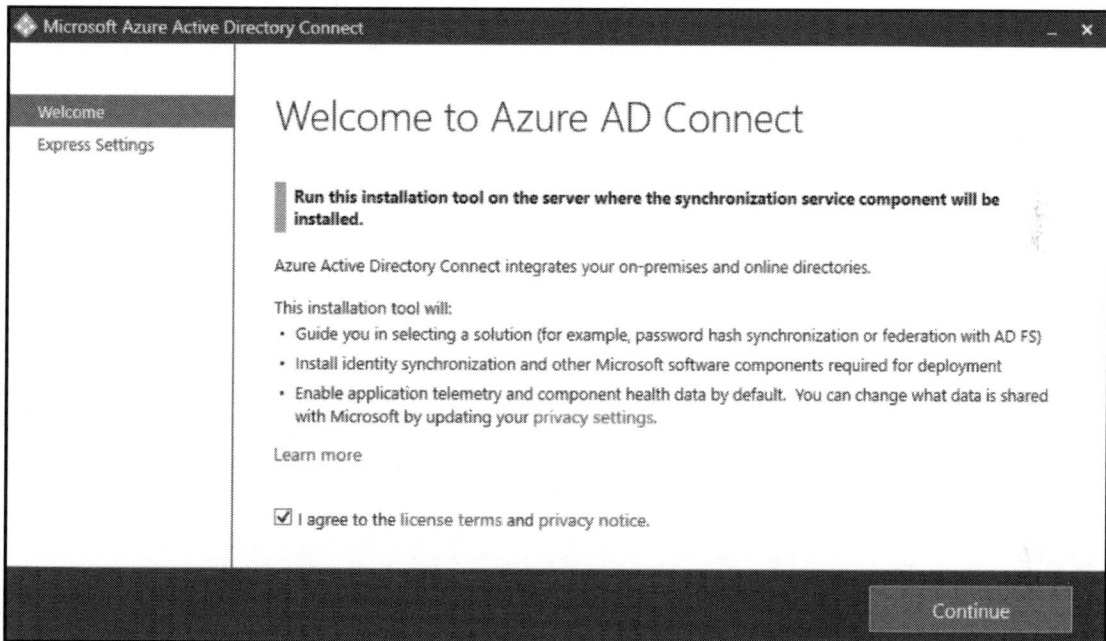

The first choice you need to make is whether you want to use express or custom settings. If you select **Use express settings**, all features are determined in advance. The installation will use the default installation path, install SQL Express, and use the default options for syncing, such as password hash sync, sync all attributes, or sync all identities across AD forest.

An example of the Azure AD Connect express settings is shown here:

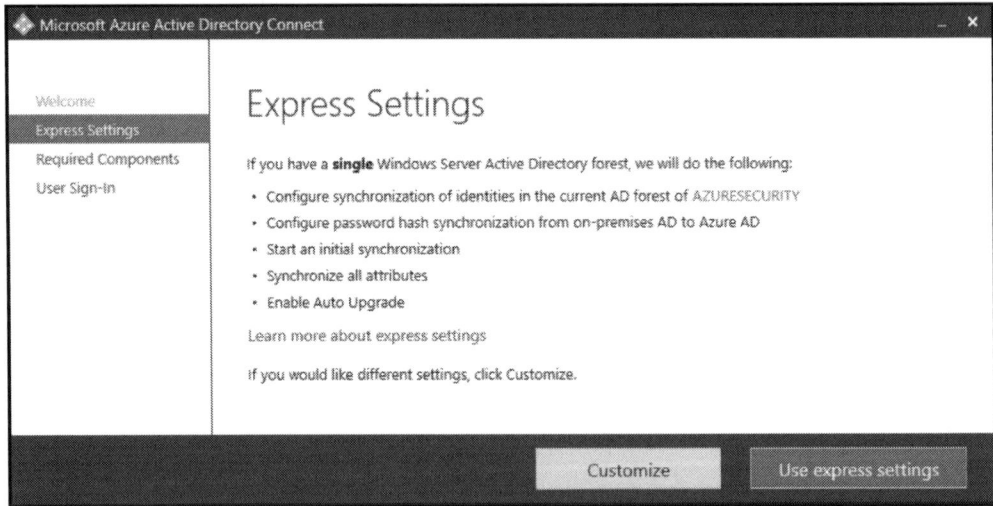

If you decide on using **Customize** options, some features such as the installation path, SQL Server instance, and sync groups can be set. For example, you can use an existing instance of SQL Server or you can choose to sync only specific user groups. Also, a new service account will be created for the sync process with express settings; in custom settings, you can choose an existing service account. An example of custom settings is shown in the following screenshot:

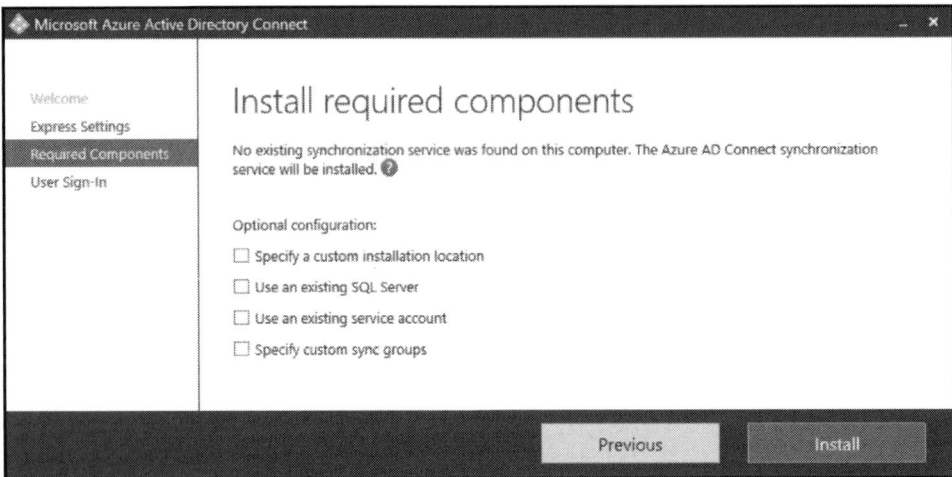

After choosing the settings, you need to provide accounts that will enable sync. First, you need to provide AAD credentials that have global administration rights. I recommend creating a separate account for this and not tying it to your personal account. If an admin leaves the company, there is a good chance that the account will be deactivated and the sync will stop. A screenshot of entering an AAD account is shown here:

The second account you need to provide is an AD DS enterprise administrator account. The same goes for the local account as for the Azure one: try using a service account dedicated to this service, and not a personal admin account. A screenshot of entering an AD DS account is shown here:

Finally, you'll get to a screen where you need to confirm the installation. It will again state all of the actions that will be taken and allow you to enable the sync process to start right after configuration is completed. You can see the confirmation screen in the following screenshot:

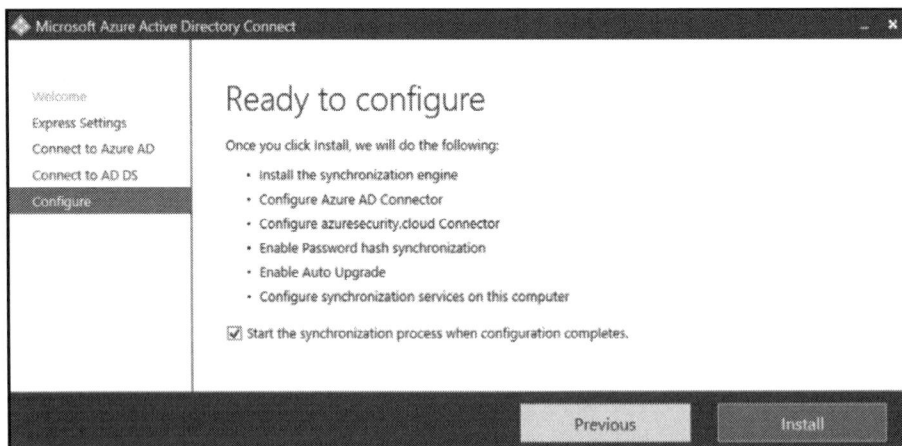

After the installation completes, you will be provided with a status report with recommendations as to what else should be done. For example, in my domain, Active Directory Recycle Bin is not enabled. The process will detect this setting and suggest that you enable it, as shown in the following screenshot:

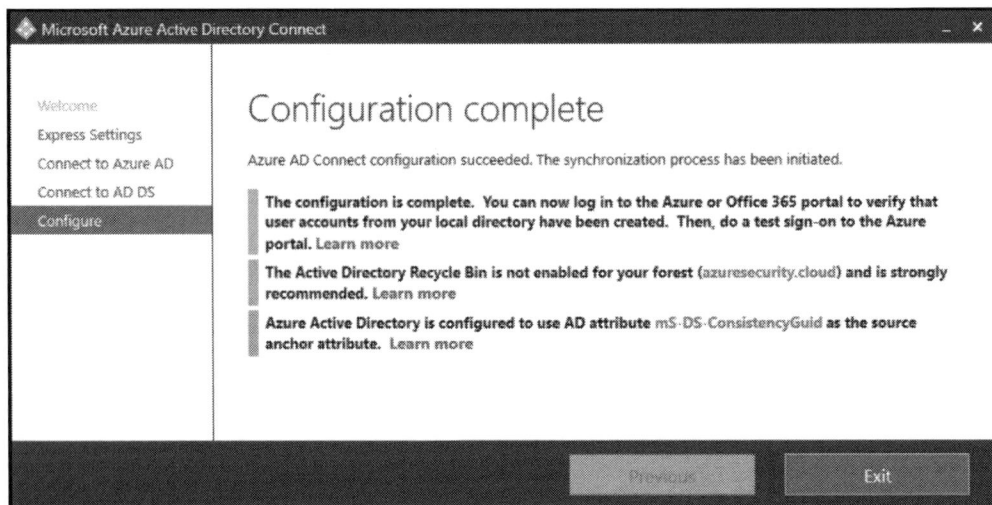

In the Azure Portal, under the **Azure AD Connect** blade, you will see the new status. The link for Azure AD Connect is gone and you can see that sync is enabled and that the `Last sync` was `Less than 1 hour ago`. Depending on the on-premises environment, you can also have a federation, SSO, and some other settings. An example of a synced directory is shown in the following screenshot:

SYNC STATUS

Sync Status	Enabled
Last Sync	Less than 1 hour ago
Password Hash Sync	Enabled

USER SIGN-IN

Federation	Disabled	0 domains
Seamless single sign-on	Disabled	0 domains
Pass-through authentication	Disabled	0 agents

ON-PREMISES APPLICATIONS

Looking to configure remote access for on-premises applications? Head to Application Proxy

HEALTH AND ANALYTICS

Monitor your on-premises identity infrastructure and synchronization services in the cloud. Azure AD Connect Health

Managing AAD

After the sync is completed, all synced users will be present in AAD. In AAD, accounts can be from two different sources: AAD and Windows Service AD. Accounts with a Windows Server AD source are accounts that have been synced from the local Active Directory. AAD accounts exist only in AAD and these accounts are created in Azure. There is a third type of account, that is, a Microsoft Account. These accounts are actually Microsoft Live Accounts that can be added to your AAD.

The **USER TYPE** in AAD can be a `Member` or a `Guest`. Members are accounts in AAD (with your domain name) and guests are accounts that are coming from other AAD or Microsoft Live Accounts. The only exception is that a Microsoft Live Account can be a member of your AAD when that account was used to create AAD. The same thing applies to external AAD accounts (AAD accounts from outside your tenant); these can only have member status when that account is used to create a new tenant. An example of a member list is shown in the following screenshot:

NAME		USER NAME	USER TYPE	SOURCE
AA	aad	aad@azuresecurity.cloud	Member	Azure Active Directory
AD	Adnan Dragnic	adnan.dragnic@azuresecurity.cloud	Member	Windows Server AD
DB	Dino Buljubasic	dino.buljubasic@azuresecurity.cloud	Member	Windows Server AD
DS	Dzemail Selmanovic	dzemail.selmanovic@azuresecurity.cloud	Member	Windows Server AD
EM	Edin Muharemagic	edin.muharemagic@azuresecurity.cloud	Member	Windows Server AD
MT	Mustafa Toroman	mustafa.toroman@azuresecurity.cloud	Member	Windows Server AD
MT	mustafatoroman@yahoo.com Toron	mustafatoroman@yahoo.com	Member	Microsoft Account
OD	On-Premises Directory Synchronizat	Sync_DC1_a2fb1d47c674@azuresecurityclou...	Member	Windows Server AD
RS	Rijad Smajlovic	rijad.smajlovic@azuresecurity.cloud	Member	Windows Server AD
TK	Tarik Karic	tarik.karic@azuresecurity.cloud	Member	Windows Server AD

Creating a new user

Accounts with an AAD source are accounts that have been created in Azure. I mentioned that, for Azure AD Connect, you should use a service account for syncing. Note that this account must have a global admin role. An example of how to create such an account is shown here:

User □ ✕

Azure Security

* Name ❶

| AAD | ✓ |

* User name ❶

| aad@azuresecurity.cloud |

Profile ❶ ＞
Not configured

Properties ❶ ＞
Default

Groups ❶ ＞
0 groups selected

Directory role ＞
User

Create

The default user role (when creating a new AAD user) is **User**. This option can be changed to Admin during creation or after the user has been created.

Managing user options and permissions

After the user has been created, you have the option to manage the user and assign different roles and permissions. Along with **Manage** options, you have an activity section where you can monitor and audit a user's activity. An example of a user profile is shown in the following screenshot:

One of the most important management options is role assignment. Under **Directory role**, you can select multiple predefined roles that can be assigned to a user. Each role comes with an explanation, as shown here:

Directory roles   ✕

Choose admin roles that you want to assign to this user.
Learn more about directory roles >

ROLE	DESCRIPTION
Application administrator	Can create and manage all aspects of app registrations and enterprise apps.
Application developer	Can create application registrations independent of the 'Users can register applications' sett...
Billing administrator	Can perform common billing related tasks like updating payment information.
Cloud application administrator	Can create and manage all aspects of app registrations and enterprise apps except App Pro...
Cloud device administrator	Full access to manage devices in Azure AD.
Compliance administrator	Can read and manage compliance configuration and reports in Azure AD and Office 365.
Conditional access administrator	Can manage conditional access capabilities.
Customer LockBox access approver	Can approve Microsoft support requests to access customer organizational data.
Dynamics 365 administrator	Can manage all aspects of the Dynamics 365 product.
Exchange administrator	Can manage all aspects of the Exchange product.
Global administrator	Can manage all aspects of Azure AD and Microsoft services that use Azure AD identities.
Guest inviter	Can invite guest users independent of the 'members can invite guests' setting.
Information Protection administrator	Can manage all aspects of the Azure Information Protection product.

Select

Users can be added to groups to simplify management. For example, we can assign multiple roles to groups, and by assigning a user to a group, the user will automatically be assigned all roles assigned to the group the user is a member of. Groups can be assigned and synced, similar to accounts. Assigned groups originate in AAD and are synced using Windows Server AD. Examples of groups assigned to users in AAD are as follows:

Registering an application in AAD

In order to use AAD as an authentication method for an application, you need to register the application in AAD. This will create two objects in your AAD: an application object and a service principal.

To register a new application, we need to go to **Application registration** in the AAD blade and select **New Application Registration**. Information that we need to provide includes the application **Name**, **Application type** (**Web app / API** or **Native**), and **Sign-on URL** (I'm using localhost as an example):

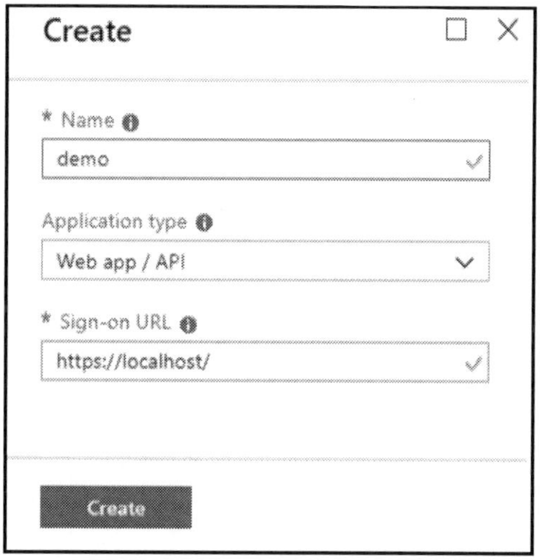

Creating the application is only the first step as you need additional configuration to use this registration. In the first screen that will open after the application has been created, there are two very important sections: **Application ID** and **Object ID**. These will be used later in order to identify the application with AAD. In other words, the application uses the ID to contact AAD and gathers information on whether the user is authorized to access the application. Which ID, application, or object is used for authentication depends on the authentication method. An example of this is shown in the following screenshot:

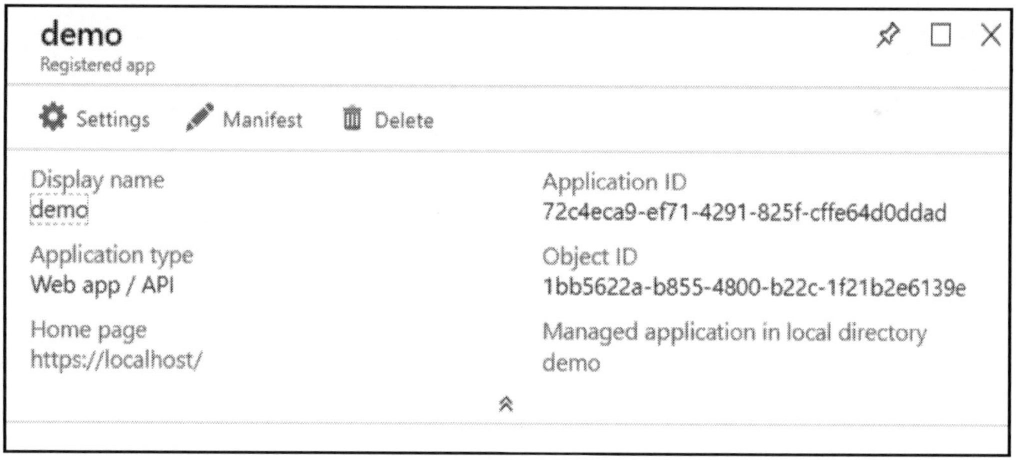

In order to provide access to a registered application, we need to configure permissions and keys. To provide permissions to the application, we must set the required permissions under **Required permissions** in the **Settings** blade. You need to be very careful here as you may fall into a trap when using too many permissions.

I have often seen people giving all possible permissions to applications that only required basic authentication. If too many permissions are assigned, this can be exploited and presents high security risks. An example permissions blade is shown in the following screenshot:

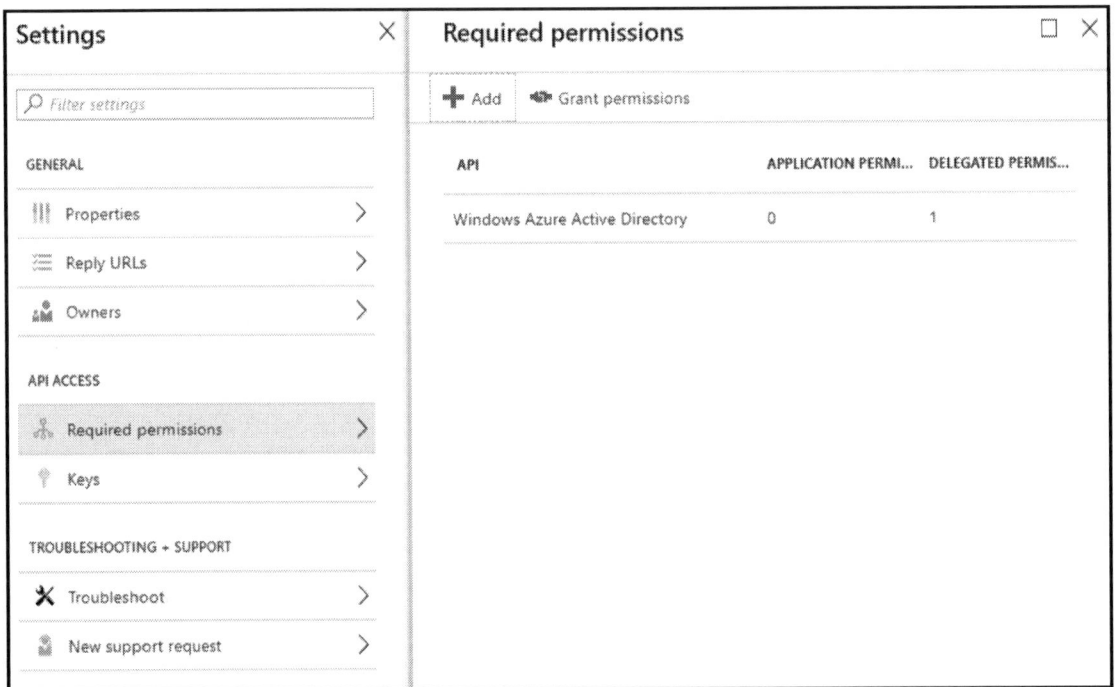

Settings	✕	Required permissions	☐ ✕
🔍 *Filter settings*		➕ Add ⊕ Grant permissions	
GENERAL			
┇┇┇ Properties	›	**API** **APPLICATION PERMI...** **DELEGATED PERMIS...**	
⌰ Reply URLs	›	Windows Azure Active Directory 0 1	
⩫ Owners	›		
API ACCESS			
⚶ Required permissions	›		
⚱ Keys	›		
TROUBLESHOOTING + SUPPORT			
✘ Troubleshoot	›		
⚱ New support request	›		

Once we have the ID and permissions in place, the last thing we are missing is the key. The application will use the ID and key to authorize access to AAD. To add a new key, we must provide a **DESCRIPTION**, **EXPIRES** (expiration time), and **VALUE** for the key. The expiration time can be **in 1 year**, **in 2 years**, or **Never expires**. I strongly recommend not using **Never expires** as this is another possible security risk. The **VALUE** for the key is not the actual key; this value will be encrypted and then a new value will be provided. After entering all values, click **Save**. An example of adding a new key is shown as follows:

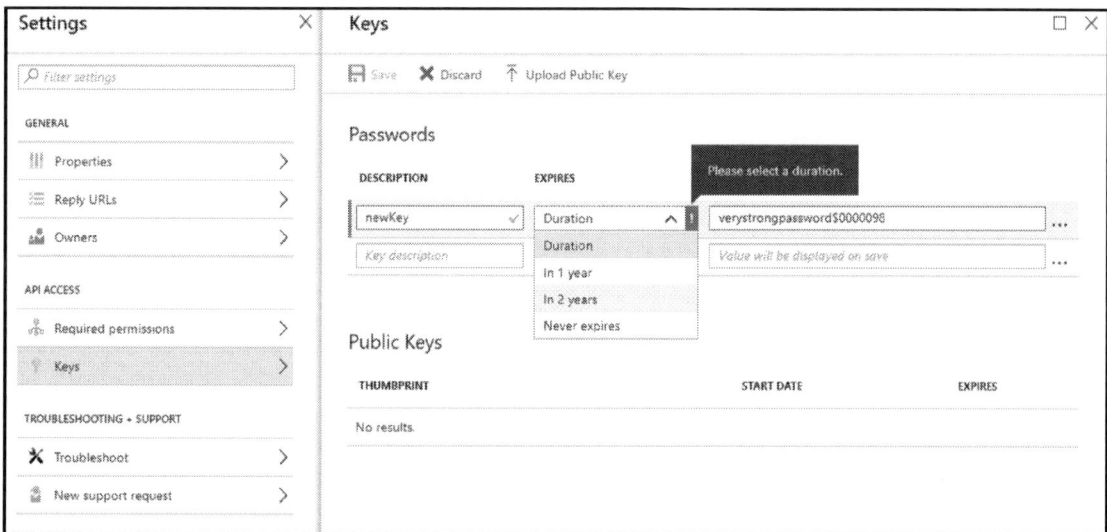

After saving, a new value for the key will be provided. Make sure to copy this value as this is the only time you will be able to collect it. Once you leave this blade, you will not be able to retrieve this value. An example generated key is shown in the following screenshot (note the warning at the top of the blade):

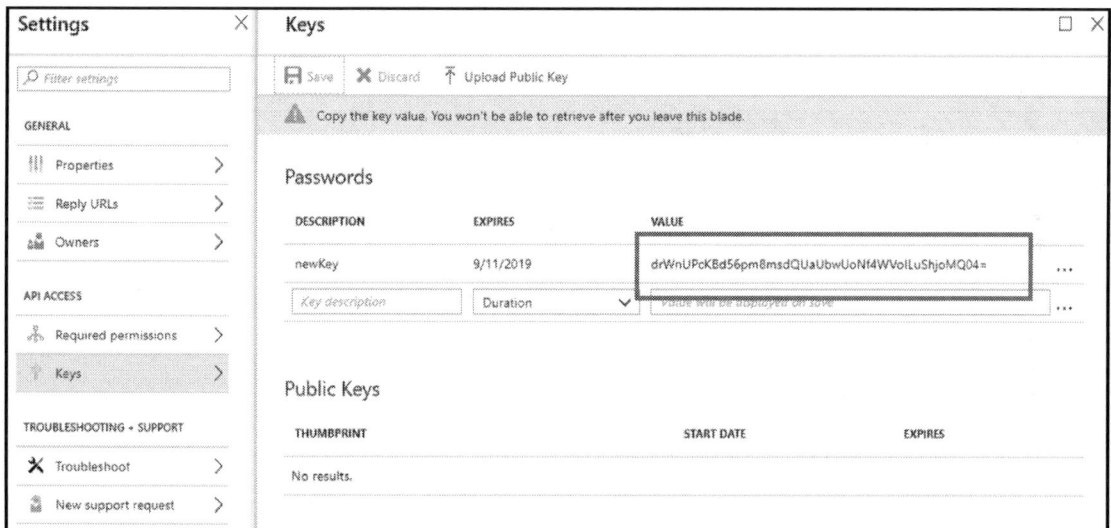

Applications, using IDs and keys registered in AAD, will be able to communicate with AAD. These applications don't have to be hosted in Azure; this can be done for an on-premises application or in some other cloud.

Note that when using Azure Web apps, you can achieve a similar goal by using **Authentication/Authorization** in the Web app blade. This option will automatically create all of the necessary objects and provide the Web app with an ID and key. Minimum permissions will be created, which is a good thing, but if you need to provide an application with more permissions, you need to do this manually.

We already mentioned that in this process, two objects will be created: an application object and a service principal.

Now would be good time to talk about the concept of multi-tenancy. Multi-tenant applications allow users from multiple tenants to use the same application and resources. For example, we can develop an application for customers and host it in our own subscription (and our tenant). Then, we can set access for the application for multiple customers and allow them to use their own AAD for authentication and authorization. In this concept, users coming from multiple tenants are using the same application and the same resources. If a multi-tenant approach is used, the application would have one application object in the home tenant and multiple service principles—one for each directory. Basically, an application object has a one-to-one relationship with the application and a one-to-many relationship with service principles.

Role-based access control

We already mentioned RBAC and how it can help with the management and administration of cloud resources. RBAC allows you to use AAD accounts to set up different roles and permissions on different levels of the Azure tenant. In order to provide user administration rights in the tenant, we must use the AAD blade. These rights are not transferred further. Under the tenant, we can have multiple subscriptions, and subscription engagement is done separately for each subscription.

Assigning a user to admin (or some other role) will automatically provide them with the same role on all resource groups and resources under that subscription. If we assign a role to a user on the resource group level, the role will be automatically provided for all resources in that resource group. Providing a role access to a single resource, will give the user access only to that resource.

During the process of assigning permissions on any of these levels (subscription, resource group, resource), we use the same option: **Access Control (IAM)**. Here, we select a **Role**, assignment type, and user. Instead of users, you can also use groups or service principals. An example of how to add a new Contributor to your subscription/resource group/resource is shown in the following screenshot:

You can select multiple predefined roles, create custom roles, or assign users to multiple roles. If a user is assigned multiple roles that are in conflict, the highest role will be applied.

For example, the **Reader** role allows you to only see information about resources, and you can't make any changes. If the **Reader** role is assigned along with the **Contributor** role (which allows you to make changes), the **Contributor** role will be applied.

A screenshot of the available roles is shown here:

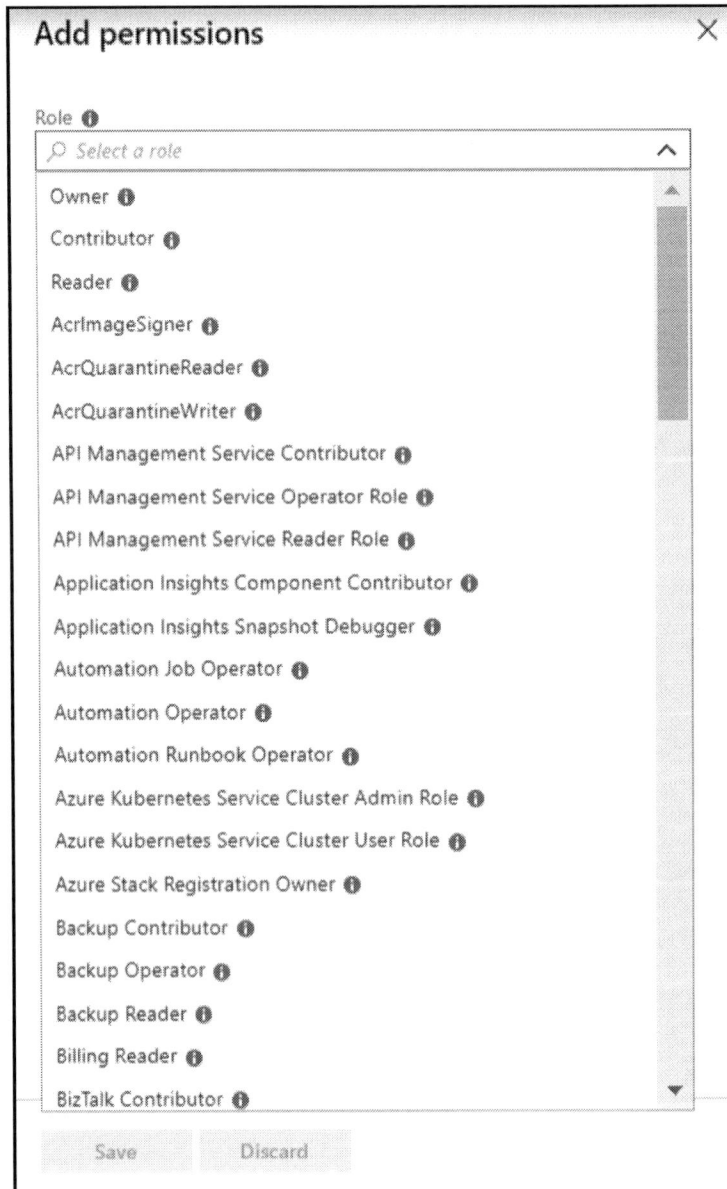

Add permissions ✕

Role ⓘ

🔍 *Select a role* ⌄

Owner ⓘ

Contributor ⓘ

Reader ⓘ

AcrImageSigner ⓘ

AcrQuarantineReader ⓘ

AcrQuarantineWriter ⓘ

API Management Service Contributor ⓘ

API Management Service Operator Role ⓘ

API Management Service Reader Role ⓘ

Application Insights Component Contributor ⓘ

Application Insights Snapshot Debugger ⓘ

Automation Job Operator ⓘ

Automation Operator ⓘ

Automation Runbook Operator ⓘ

Azure Kubernetes Service Cluster Admin Role ⓘ

Azure Kubernetes Service Cluster User Role ⓘ

Azure Stack Registration Owner ⓘ

Backup Contributor ⓘ

Backup Operator ⓘ

Backup Reader ⓘ

Billing Reader ⓘ

BizTalk Contributor ⓘ

Save   Discard

As mentioned previously, groups can be assigned roles on any level. In this case, all users that are members of that group will be assigned that role automatically.

Service principles are often used to set up access for applications that need the ability to change or create something. For example, a service principle is often used to allow Azure DevOps to access your subscription during the release process and to create or edit resources that are needed for deployment.

Summary

AAD provides authentication and authorization in Azure. Along with RBAC, it allows you to control who can do what and where. These tools are your first line of defense when managing and securing your cloud resources.

Now, we will concentrate on what else we need to secure in Azure and how can we protect our data and other resources. Securing Azure is different from securing our on-premises infrastructure and requires a different mindset. In Chapter 9, *Azure Security and Administration*, we will discuss how to harden Azure security and what is available to protect us.

Questions

1. An AAD is on top of a...
    1. Tenant
    2. Subscription
    3. Resource group

2. An account can be part of multiple tenants:
    1. Yes
    2. No

3. AAD can contain Microsoft Live Accounts:
    1. Yes
    2. No

4. AAD can be synced with Windows Server AD:
    1. Yes
    2. No

5. The Azure Active Directory Free tier has a limit of...
    1. 5,000 objects
    2. 500,000 objects
    3. 5,000,000 objects

6. To set up a custom domain...
    1. You can choose any domain
    2. You must own the domain
    3. You must use `.onmicrosoft.com`

7. To verify your custom domain, you must use...
    1. MX records
    2. TXT records
    3. Either
    4. Both

8. Using RBAC, you can assign roles for...
    1. A subscription
    2. A resource group
    3. A resource
    4. All of the above

9. Roles can be assigned to...
    1. Users
    2. Groups
    3. Both

10. To set up AAD sign-in from the application, you must...
    1. Register the application in AAD
    2. Create an AAD group for the application
    3. Both

9
Azure Security and Administration

Security is often one of main reasons why many organizations are postponing their move to the cloud. There are too many unknown factors; people don't understand how security is set up and often don't trust anyone with their data. "If it leaves our data center, then I don't know what is happening to it" is something I have heard often over the years.

The truth is that your data is probably far more secure in Azure than it could ever be in your local center. In this chapter, I'll try to explain how security in Azure is set up and remove any doubts about cloud security.

The following topics will be covered in this chapter:

- Azure Active Directory multi-factor authentication
- Azure Network Security
- Azure Firewall
- Data encryption
- Azure Key Vault
- Azure Security Center
- Advanced threat protection
- Just-in-Time access

Technical requirements

For this chapter you'll need the following:

- An Azure subscription
- PowerShell
- Azure PowerShell

Demystifying cloud security

So, how secure is Azure really? Let's start by saying very secure.

Microsoft is investing heavily in Azure, and particularly in Azure Security. Azure has extensive compliance offerings, including HIPAA, FFIEC, PCI DSS, ISO 9001, and ISO 27001, just to name a few.

Azure Security starts with physical security. Data center has dedicated security staff around the clock; everything is covered by cameras and alarms, and there are several layers of perimeter checks.

To enter the Azure data center, you need to pass several checkpoints and provide valid authentication and authorization. Authentication is done on multi-factor levels, and besides providing a PIN or password, you must pass biometric and card reader checks as well.

Everything within data centers is encrypted and secure. All data is encrypted at rest, and even if someone manages to steal a disk containing your data, it would be unusable. All data transferring is also encrypted per industry standards.

Another important part of data security is redundancy to ensure that data is never lost. The default redundancy in Azure is 3 (three). When you create a new resource, Azure VM for example, a disk is created with three copies. This ensures that data is always available, and even if one disk fails, there are an additional two copies. Redundant 3 is present even with backup power generators; if one fails, there are two additional backups.

And even Microsoft is heavily involved in Azure Security; it's not enough to put your data into Azure for it to be safe. The partnership with Microsoft takes care of one part of security and provides various tools and services to help you stay secure. However, you are responsible for how you implement these tools and put them to use.

Securing your identity

Securing your identity is a very important part of IT security. Most data breaches happen as a result of social engineering or phishing attacks. So, in most cases, leaked credentials are responsible for breaches.

Azure Active Directory offers a few tools to improve security, and one that stands up is **multi-factor authentication** (**MFA**). MFA requires users to provide additional security authentication after signing in. After a user provides a username and password, additional action is required to prove their identity. Many different tools can be used for additional checks, like biometric readers or card readers, but the most popular tool is a mobile device. After signing in, a user receives a notification on their mobile device and needs to provide additional confirmation. Notifications can be in the form of a phone call (the user needs to provide a code during the call), a text message (a user receives a code that needs to be provided during login), or an application (connected to the user account and requires confirmation that the user is trying to log in).

When MFA is enabled, leaked credentials are less of a concern, as stealing a username and password is not enough to access data anymore. Access to a user's mobile device is required to authorize your sign-in attempt, and this makes data breaching much harder.

Enabling multi-factor authentication

Enabling MFA in Azure Active Directory is simple and fast. In Azure Active Directory, under **User management** you need to select **Multi-Factor Authentication**. An example is shown in the screenshot:

A new window will open in which all MFA is done. Here, you can set up individual user settings or do bulk updates for multiple users. Under **Service settings**, you can also edit what options are available for MFA and choose between a phone call, text message, mobile app, or token. To enable a single user for MFA, select the user and click **Enable** in the settings on the right side, as shown:

MFA is free for users with the global administrator role. So, there is no excuse for not adding an additional layer of security for admins as a leaked admin account can do far more damage than a regular user. However, if you want to enable MFA for all users, then an additional license is required. MFA comes with Azure Active Directory Premium, but can be licensed as a standalone service per user or per login.

Other identity security options

Azure Active Directory offers other services that can help you increase security.

Other service such as conditional access or privileged identity management can help us increase security and prevent unauthorized access. We can use audit logs and risky sign-ins to review who tried to access services and data and when. There are extensive Azure Active Directory logs that can be used for audits as well. Most of these features come with AAD Premium and aren't available with a basic or free license.

Securing the network

The next step in staying secure is securing our network resources. Leaving a network unprotected can result in data breaches or service denial. Even the Azure networking stack comes with lots of security features, such as default DDOS protection or network security groups; sometimes this is not enough and we need to take additional steps.

Azure Firewall

Azure Firewall is a managed, cloud-based network security service that protects Azure Virtual Network resources. It is Firewall as a Service with built-in high availability and scalability.

With Azure Firewall, you can create, enforce, and log application and network connectivity policies. Static public IP addresses for your virtual network resources allow outside firewalls to identify traffic originating from your virtual network. The service is integrated with Azure Monitor for logging and analytics.

Preparing the environment

Azure Firewall requires you to be connected to a subnet named AzureFirewallSubnet. We can create a new Azure VNet and a new subnet in the process of creating new Azure Firewall. But as I already have the VNet that I want to use, I'll add a new subnet to `PackVnet`, which was previously created.

An example of how to add a new subnet for Azure Firewall is shown in the following screenshot:

Home > Resource groups > PacktIaaS > PacktVnet - Subnets > Add subnet

Add subnet
PacktVnet

* Name

> AzureFirewallSubnet ✓

* Address range (CIDR block) ⓘ

> 10.1.3.0/24

10.1.3.0 - 10.1.3.255 (251 + 5 Azure reserved addresses)

Network security group
None ›

Route table
None ›

Service endpoints

Services ⓘ

0 selected ⌄

Subnet delegation

Delegate subnet to a service ⓘ

None ⌄

OK

Creating an Azure Firewall

To create a new Azure Firewall, we need to provide a **Subscription**, **Resource group**, **Name**, and **Location**. Additionally, we need to provide a **Virtual network** and **Public IP address**. In both cases, we can **Use existing** resources or **Create new** ones. Note that for the existing virtual network, `AzureFirewallSubnet` must exist. Example parameters are shown in the screenshot:

After the deployment is finished, Azure Firewall is ready for use and we can start the configuration. For now, take note of the **Private IP address** (remember it or write it down), as we are going to need it in the next few steps.

The Azure Firewall blade is shown in the following screenshot:

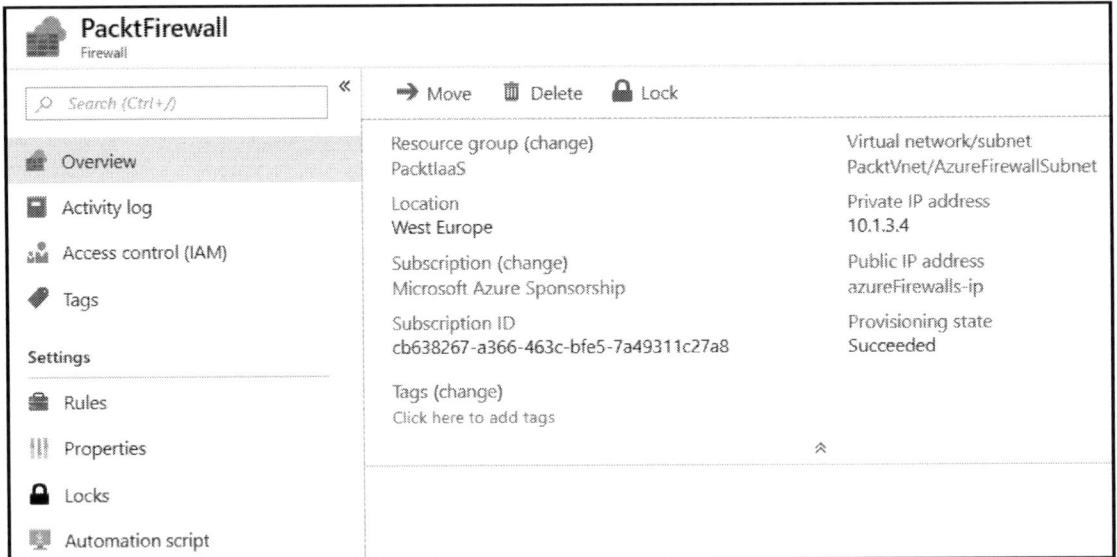

To deploy Azure Firewall, we can use ARM templates as well.

Here is the ARM template to deploy a new Azure Firewall:

```
{
    "$schema":
"http://schema.management.azure.com/schemas/2015-01-01/deploymentTemplate.j
son#",
    "contentVersion": "1.0.0.0",
    "parameters": {
        "location": {
            "type": "string"
        },
        "resourceGroup": {
            "type": "string"
        },
        "azureFirewallName": {
            "type": "string"
        },
        "vnetName": {
            "type": "string"
        },
        "vnetAddressSpace": {
            "type": "string"
        },
```

```
            "subnetAddressSpace": {
                "type": "string"
            },
            "publicIpAddressName": {
                "type": "string"
            },
            "subnetId": {
                "type": "string"
            }
        },
        "variables": {
            "networkApiVersion": "?api-version=2018-08-01"
        },
        "resources": [
            {
                "apiVersion": "2018-08-01",
                "type": "Microsoft.Network/publicIpAddresses",
                "name": "[parameters('publicIpAddressName')]",
                "location": "[parameters('location')]",
                "sku": {
                    "name": "Standard"
                },
                "properties": {
                    "publicIPAllocationMethod": "Static"
                },
                "tags": {}
            },
            {
                "apiVersion": "2018-07-01",
                "type": "Microsoft.Network/azureFirewalls",
                "name": "[parameters('azureFirewallName')]",
                "location": "[parameters('location')]",
                "dependsOn": [
                    "[resourceId(parameters('resourceGroup'),
'Microsoft.Network/publicIpAddresses', parameters('publicIpAddressName'))]"
                ],
                "properties": {
                    "ipConfigurations": [
                        {
                            "name": "IpConf",
                            "properties": {
                                "subnet": {
                                    "id": "[parameters('subnetId')]"
                                },
                                "publicIPAddress": {
                                    "id":
"[resourceId(parameters('resourceGroup'),
'Microsoft.Network/publicIpAddresses', parameters('publicIpAddressName'))]"
```

```
                           }
                      }
                 }
            ]
        },
        "tags": {}
    }
  ]
}
```

Azure Route Table

Now we want to create a route table that will direct all traffic through Azure Firewall. To create a new Azure Route Table, we need to provide a **Name**, **Subscription**, **Resource group**, and **Location**. Optionally, we can enable or disable **BGP route propagation**. An example of how to create a new route table is shown in the following screenshot:

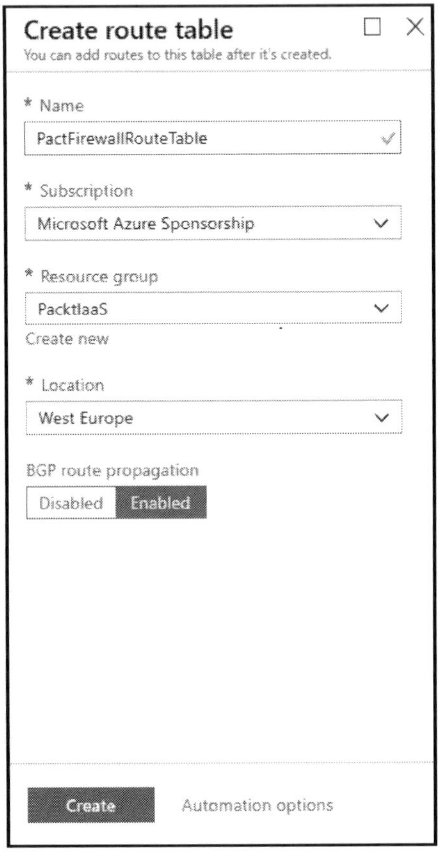

After the route table is created, we need to associate it with a subnet and create a route. Under the **Subnets** option in the route table blade, select **Associate**, as shown:

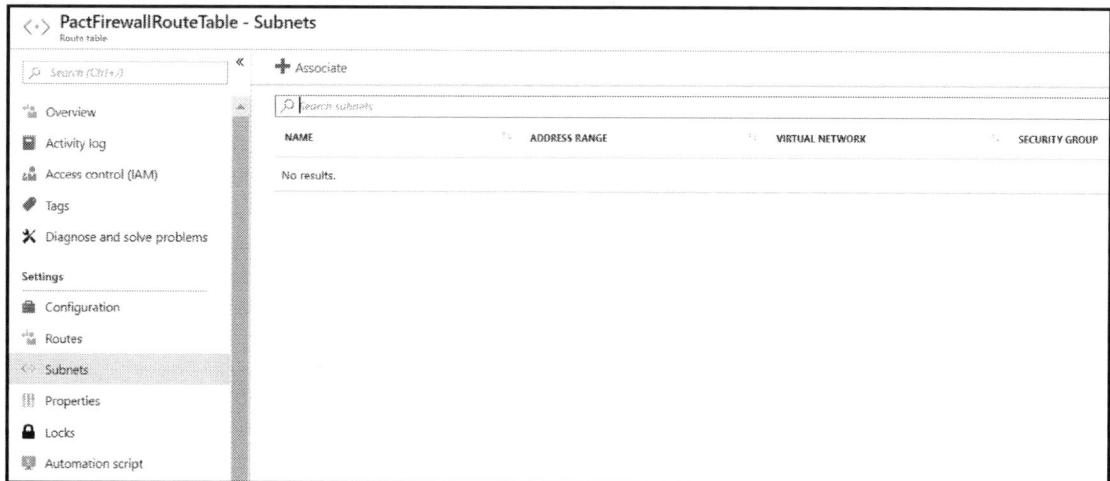

To associate a route table with a subnet, we need to provide a **Virtual network** and **Subnet** in that network. In the following example, the **Virtual network PacktVnet** is selected and the **Subnet** is **default**:

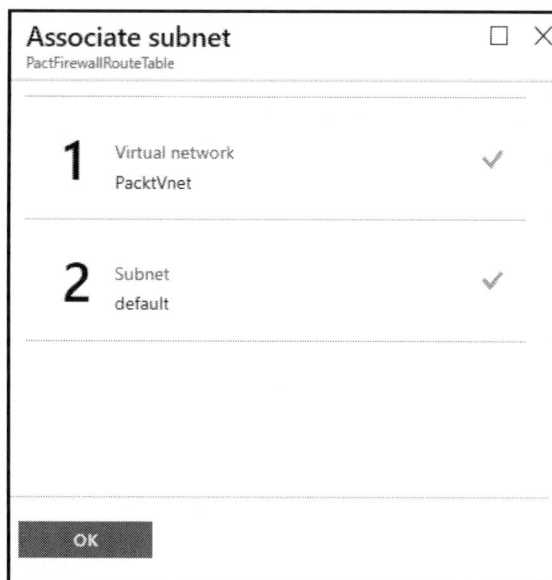

Finally, we need to add a route. We need to provide a **Route name**, **Address prefix**, **Next hop type**, and **Next hop address**. For the **Next hop type**, we need to select **Virtual appliance**. Azure Firewall is a Firewall as a Service, but it still falls under this category. To create a similar effect, we could use any virtual appliance in which we would use third-party firewalls in IaaS mode. Under **Next hop address**, we enter the private IP address of our Azure Firewall (I previously mentioned that you needed to remember this address). An example of route settings is shown in the following screenshot:

All traffic from the default subnet in the `PacktVnet` virtual network is now routed to our Azure Firewall. We can proceed and create rules on what will be allowed or denied.

Configuring Azure Firewall

Under **Rules** in the Azure Firewall blade, we have three options: **NAT rule collection**, **Network rule collection**, and **Application rule collection**. Depending on what we want to achieve, we can use NAT rules to rewrite the source address. We can use network rules to define traffic from what source is allowed to go to what target, or with application rules we can define FQDNs that are allowed or denied. An example of the **Rules** blade in Azure Firewall is shown here:

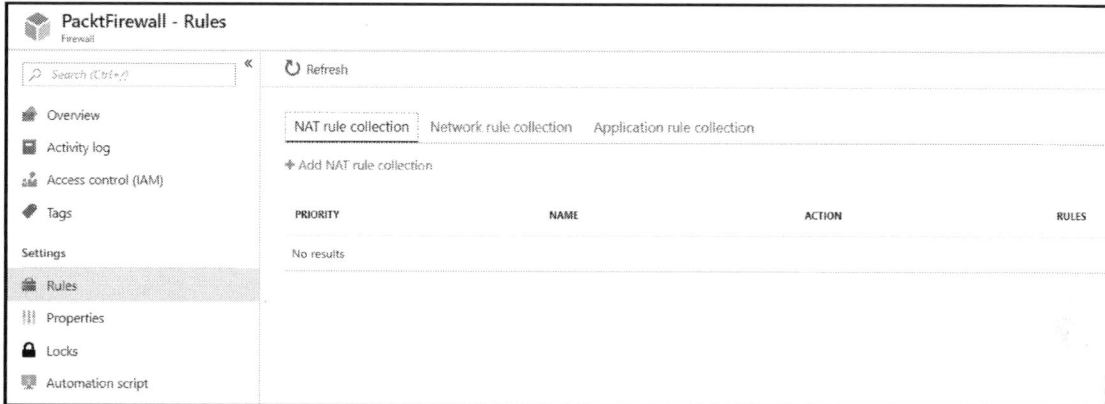

Let's create a rule that will allow for traffic from the default subnet to VSTS. First, we need to provide a **Name**, **Priority**, and **Action** (**Allow** or **Deny**). Then we need to define **SOURCE ADDRESSES**, a **PROTOCOL:PORT**, and **TARGET FQDNS**. Optionally, we can add tags to our rule. For the **SOURCE ADDRESSES**, I'll add a subnet, as I want VSTS to be reached from anywhere on the subnet. You can use a smaller scope of IP addresses if you want to restrict where FQDN can be reached from.

The protocol will be HTTP and HTTPS and the **TARGET FQDNS** is
`*.visualstudio.com`. An example of a new application rule is shown here:

Note that you can have more than one rule in a collection and you can create all rules that apply to a specific service in a single collection. This makes it easier to manage and maintain Azure Firewall rules.

If everything is configured correctly, you can go to VM, located in the default subnet, and open any browser. You should be able to access any VSTS collection, but nothing else will be allowed.

Other network security options

Besides using default Azure components such as NSG, route tables, or even Azure Firewall, there are a number of third-party firewalls that are available as virtual appliances. Virtual appliances are set up as Azure VMs, and most industry leaders in network security are available in Azure. Managing virtual appliances has two components: managing Azure VM and managing firewalls. We already talked about managing Azure VMs, and managing firewalls depends on the manufacturer and isn't any different than managing those firewalls on-premises.

Other than that, we can collect logs from our network resources with Azure Monitor and Log Analytics to help us audit and troubleshoot Azure Network. There is another tool that can help us monitor Azure Network, which is called Network Watcher. Azure Network Watcher provides tools to monitor, diagnose, view metrics, and enable or disable logs for resources in an Azure virtual network.

With Azure Network Watcher, we can monitor endpoints, network flow, hops, VPNs, and everything else network-related. It's a great tool, as it allows us to graphically display our network schema and locate issues in an easier way.

Encryption

Another important step in security is encryption. We want our data to be encrypted always—in rest and transit. Everything is redundant to ensure there is no data is lost, and even with three copies of that, all of them encrypted, we have the option to create additional redundancy with geo-replication and other settings.

All resources in Azure are encrypted at rest by default. But sometimes we need additional security to ensure data is more protected. For example, disks for our Azure VMs are encrypted inside the Azure data center, and even if the disk was accessed without authorization, no one could read data on that disk. But what if the disk was downloaded? In this case, the disk could be used. Data could be read or attached to another VM, or a VM could be created with that disk.

We can apply additional encryption and make our resources more secure by using **Azure Key Vault**.

Azure Key Vault

Azure Key Vault is used to store secrets, keys, and certificates. It's a centralized management solution for holding, distributing, and controlling secrets, keys, and certificates. Secrets in Azure Key Vault can be called during deployment so you can prevent passwords from being shown in plain text. Keys can be used to encrypt storage and disks. You can use certificates in Azure Key Vault and assign them to services during deployment to secure SSL and TLS.

Azure Key Vault greatly reduces the chances that secrets may be accidentally leaked, increases the security of your resources at rest by using keys to encrypt, and increases security in transit by assigning certificates.

Creating an Azure Key Vault

To create a new Key Vault, we need to provide a **Name**, **Subscription**, **Resource Group**, and **Location**. We can optionally change the **Pricing tier**, assign **Access policies**, and provide **Virtual Network Access**. The tier comes with two options: **Standard** and **Premium**. The only difference is that **Premium** supports **hardware security modules (HSMs)**. The default policy assigned is to grant all access to the person creating the vault. You can additionally add policies as needed at any time, either during creation or later. **Virtual Network Access** is granted to all networks in your subscription by default, but you can edit this and grant access to specific networks only. An example of the default settings is shown here:

Creating an Azure Key Vault is relatively fast and should be completed in under one minute. Note the **DNS Name**, as this will be used later. An example of an Azure Key Vault blade is shown in the following screenshot:

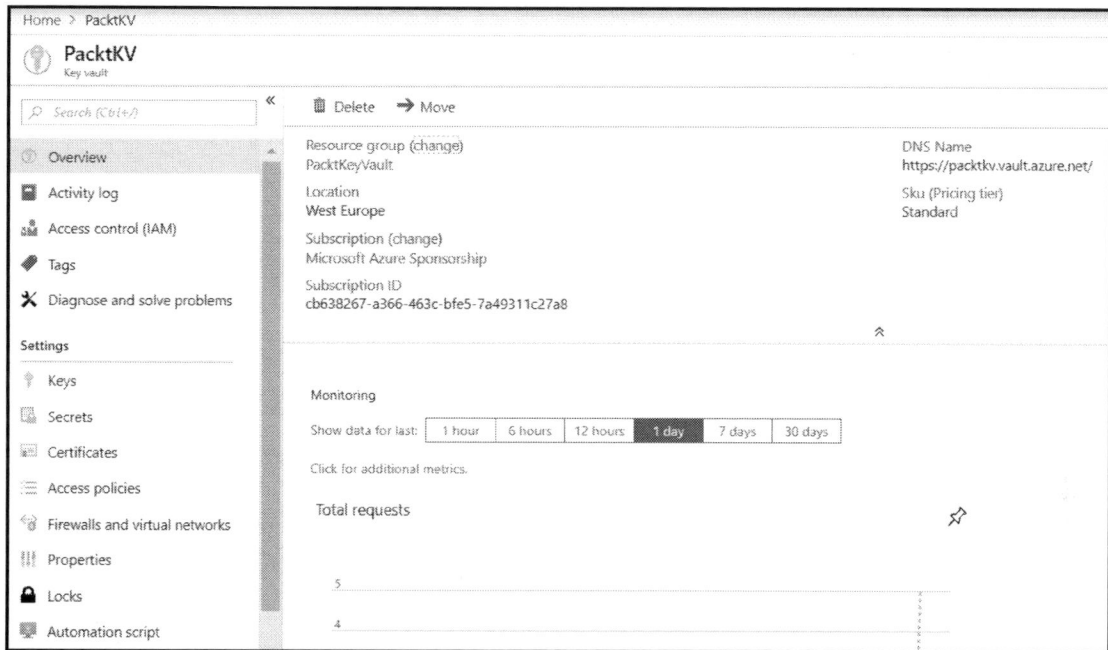

To deploy Azure Key Vault, you can use the following ARM template:

```
{
    "$schema":
"http://schema.management.azure.com/schemas/2014-04-01-preview/deploymentTe
mplate.json#",
    "contentVersion": "1.0.0.0",
    "parameters": {
        "name": {
            "type": "String"
        },
        "location": {
            "type": "String"
        },
        "sku": {
            "defaultValue": "Standard",
            "allowedValues": [
                "Standard",
                "standard",
                "Premium",
```

```
                "premium"
            ],
            "type": "String",
            "metadata": {
                "description": "SKU for the vault"
            }
        },
        "accessPolicies": {
            "defaultValue": [],
            "type": "Array",
            "metadata": {
                "description": "The access policies defined for this
vault."
            }
        },
        "tenant": {
            "type": "String"
        },
        "enabledForDeployment": {
            "type": "Bool"
        },
        "enabledForTemplateDeployment": {
            "type": "Bool"
        },
        "enabledForDiskEncryption": {
            "type": "Bool"
        },
        "networkAcls": {
            "type": "Object",
            "metadata": {
                "description": "The network firewall defined for this
vault."
            }
        }
    },
    "resources": [
        {
            "type": "Microsoft.KeyVault/vaults",
            "name": "[parameters('name')]",
            "apiVersion": "2016-10-01",
            "location": "[parameters('location')]",
            "properties": {
                "enabledForDeployment":
"[parameters('enabledForDeployment')]",
                "enabledForTemplateDeployment":
"[parameters('enabledForTemplateDeployment')]",
                "enabledForDiskEncryption":
"[parameters('enabledForDiskEncryption')]",
```

```
            "accessPolicies": "[parameters('accessPolicies')]",
            "tenantId": "[parameters('tenant')]",
            "sku": {
                "name": "[parameters('sku')]",
                "family": "A"
            },
            "networkAcls": "[parameters('networkAcls')]"
        }
    }
]
}
```

Adding keys and secrets

After the Key Vault is created, we can add secrets and keys.

Let's first add a key that we'll use for encryption later. Keys can be generated, imported, or restored from backup. An example of how to add a new key is shown here:

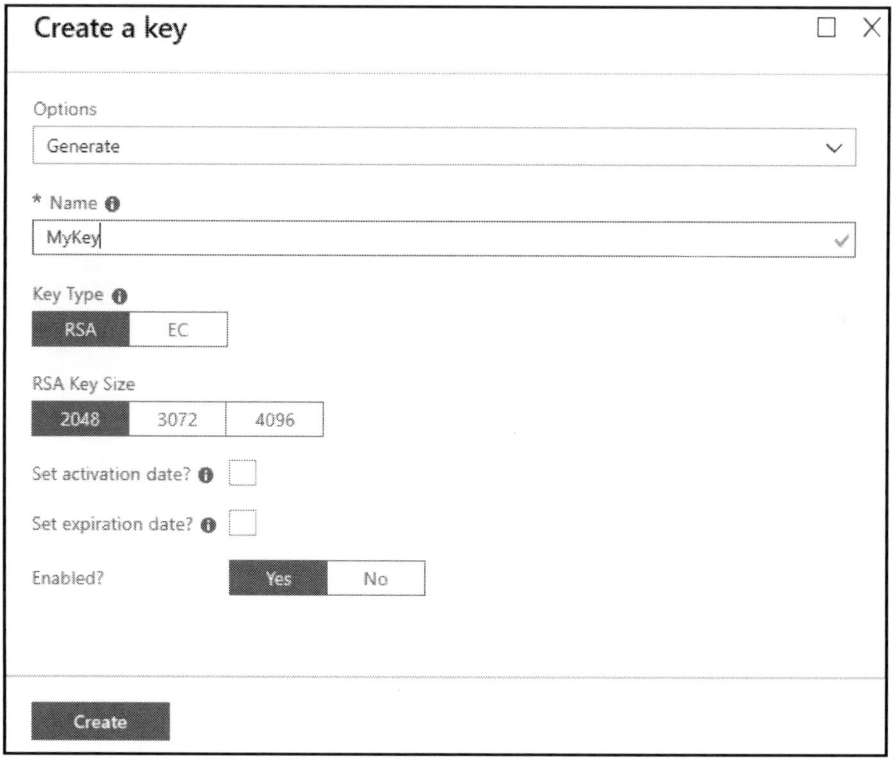

Secrets can be used to provide passwords when creating resources. When you are creating resources using an ARM template, you need to provide a password. To prevent the password from being shown as plain text, you can use secrets in Key Vault to provide a value for the password and prevent this. Secrets can be manually created or imported from the certificate. In this example, we can see how to add a new secret manually:

Similar to these two examples, you can add certificates. Certificates can be generated or imported. Note that if you want to use these certificates for publicly available applications, you must use a valid certificate issued by a public certification authority.

Encrypting the storage account

As mentioned, most resources are encrypted by default, and the same goes with the Azure Storage Account. However, you have the option to use your own key to encrypt storage. To use your own key, you must select **Use your own key**, which will allow you to select the Key Vault and the key that will be used for encryption. An example is shown in the following screenshot:

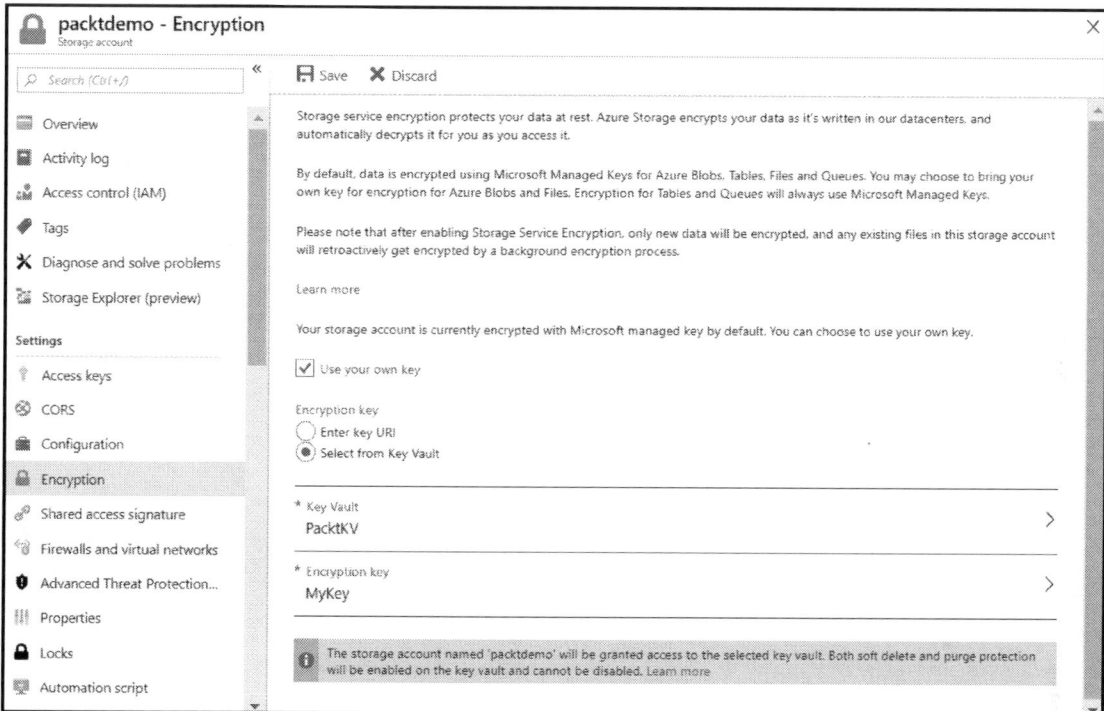

The time it takes to encrypt storage depends on the amount of data in the storage account. For smaller storage, it's a matter of seconds, but with large storage accounts it can take hours until the process is completed. If you are encrypting large storage accounts in a production environment, try doing this outside of working hours as it may impact performance.

Encrypting databases

Azure SQL Databases are encrypted with TDE. This option is now enabled by default when creating a new Azure SQL Database. If you have older databases, created before this became a default option, it's enough to change the option to **ON** and save. The **Transparent database encryption** options in the Azure SQL Database blade are shown here:

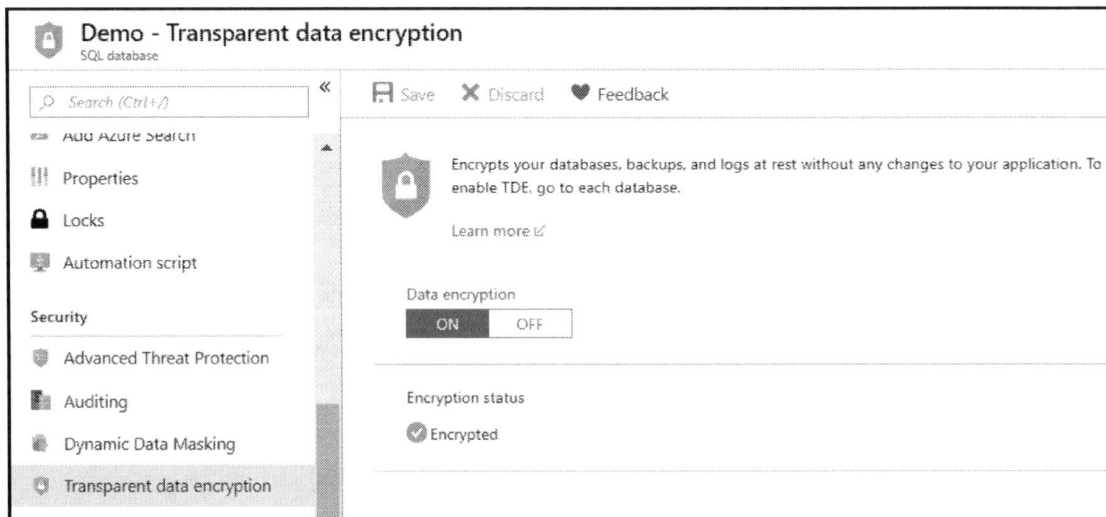

When TDE is enabled for Azure SQL Database, data and backups are encrypted at rest. But if you download or export a backup, this will no longer be the case. To have a database encrypted even after leaving Azure data center, we can use our own key for encryption. To do so we'll need to use Azure PowerShell.

Installing Azure PowerShell

PowerShell is a command-line shell and scripting language based on the .NET Framework. It's used by system administrators to automate tasks and manage operating systems.

Azure PowerShell is a PowerShell module that allows us to automate and manage Azure resources.

To install Azure PowerShell, we need to have Windows PowerShell installed. Luckily, Windows PowerShell comes pre-installed on Microsoft OS from Windows 7 (Client OS) and Windows Server 2012 R2 (Server OS).

To install Azure PowerShell, we need to run the following command:

```
Install-Module -Name AzureRM
```

Next, we need to import the module:

```
Import-Module AzureRM
```

If the module is already installed, we can update it with:

```
Update-Module -Name AzureRM
```

After we have successfully imported the module, we can connect to Azure with:

```
Connect-AzureRmAccount
```

Using your own key for Azure SQL Database encryption

To use our own key for Azure SQL Database TDE, we must execute a few commands.

First, we need to sign our Azure Active Directory identity in to our Azure SQL server:

```
$dbRG = 'PacktPaaSDB';
$dbServer = 'packt';
$server = Set-AzureRmSqlServer -ResourceGroupName $dbRG -ServerName
$dbServer -AssignIdentity
```

Second, we must grant Key Vault permission to our server:

```
$dbRG = 'PacktPaaSDB';
$dbServer = 'packt';
$KeyVaultName = 'PacktKV';
Set-AzureRmKeyVaultAccessPolicy -VaultName $KeyVaultName -ObjectId
$server.Identity.PrincipalId -PermissionsToKeys get, wrapKey, unwrapKey
```

Third, we add the Key Vault key to the server and set the TDE protection level:

```
$dbRG = 'PacktPaaSDB';
$dbServer = 'packt';
$rgName = 'PacktKeyVault';
$KeyVaultName = 'PacktKV';
$keyEncryptionKeyName = 'MyKey';
$keyEncryptionKeyUrl = (Get-AzureKeyVaultKey -VaultName $KeyVaultName -Name
$keyEncryptionKeyName).Key.kid;

<# Add the key from Key Vault to the server #>
Add-AzureRmSqlServerKeyVaultKey -ResourceGroupName $dbRG -ServerName
$dbServer -KeyId $keyEncryptionKeyUrl
```

```
<# Set the key as the TDE protector for all resources under the server #>
Set-AzureRmSqlServerTransparentDataEncryptionProtector -ResourceGroupName
$dbRG -ServerName $dbServer -Type AzureKeyVault -KeyId $keyEncryptionKeyUrl
<# To confirm that the TDE protector was configured as intended: #>
Get-AzureRmSqlServerTransparentDataEncryptionProtector -ResourceGroupName
$dbRG -ServerName $dbServer
```

Finally, we turn on the TDE:

```
$dbRG = 'PacktPaaSDB';
$dbServer = 'packt';
$dbName = 'Demo'
Set-AzureRMSqlDatabaseTransparentDataEncryption -ResourceGroupName $dbRG -
ServerName $dbServer -DatabaseName $dbName -State "Enabled"
```

All parameters in Azure PowerShell script can be edited. To execute this on any Azure SQL Database using any Key Vault, change the names of the parameters accordingly.

Encrypting VM disks

A similar thing can be applied to Azure VMs. Disks are encrypted by default and data is protected at rest. But as mentioned, when a disk is exported or downloaded, it's no longer protected. Using Key Vault, we can set additional encryption to our Azure VM disks and protect data in any situation. If we open disks in any of our Azure VMs, we can see that the disk is not encrypted, as shown:

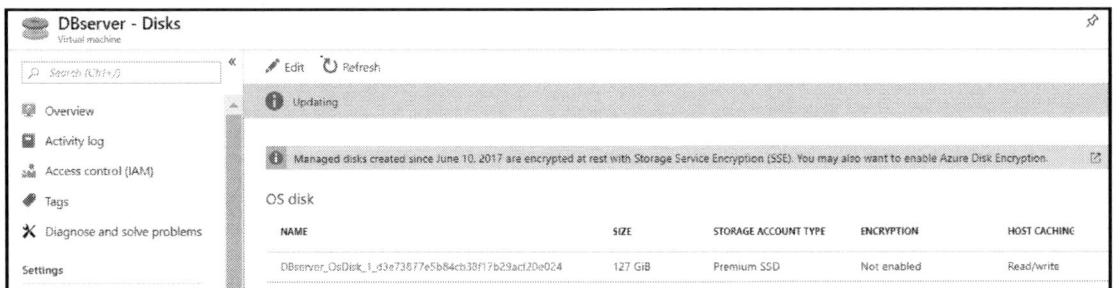

To enable disk encryption, first we must enable the Key Vault for disk encryption:

```
Set-AzureRmKeyVaultAccessPolicy -VaultName 'PacktKV' -ResourceGroupName
'PacktKeyVault' -EnabledForDiskEncryption
```

Now we can enable disk encryption:

```
$VMRG = 'PacktIaaS';
$VMname= 'DBserver';
$rgName = 'PacktKeyVault';
$KeyVaultName = 'PacktKV';
$KeyVault = Get-AzureRmKeyVault -VaultName $KeyVaultName -ResourceGroupName
$rgname;
$diskEncryptionKeyVaultUrl = $KeyVault.VaultUri;
$KeyVaultResourceId = $KeyVault.ResourceId;

 Set-AzureRmVMDiskEncryptionExtension -ResourceGroupName $VMRG -VMName
$vmName -DiskEncryptionKeyVaultUrl $diskEncryptionKeyVaultUrl -
DiskEncryptionKeyVaultId $KeyVaultResourceId;
```

The command will run in 5-15 minutes, depending on the size of the disk. After we receive a message that it's completed, we can check the disk status again and see that encryption is enabled:

Azure Security Center

Azure Security Center provides a central place for security management and advanced threat protection across Azure and the hybrid cloud. With security center, we can apply security policies across workloads, limit exposure to threats, and detect and respond to attacks. It comes in two tiers, free and standard. The free tier is enabled by default, and it provides a security policy, continuous security assessment, and actionable security recommendations to protect Azure resources. The standard tier extends to private or hybrid cloud workloads and adds advanced threat detection. Advanced threat detection uses built-in behavioral analytics and machine learning to identify attacks and zero-day exploits to reduce exposure to any type of attack.

Azure Security Center overview

The **Overview** dashboard in the Azure Security Center blade provides an instant summary of the security status of your Azure and non-Azure workloads, enabling you to discover and assess the security of your workloads and to identify and mitigate risks. We can see different metrics that allow us to instantly identify any security risks and see recommendations on what needs to be improved in our subscription based on best practices. An example of the **Overview** dashboard in Azure Security Center is shown in the screenshot:

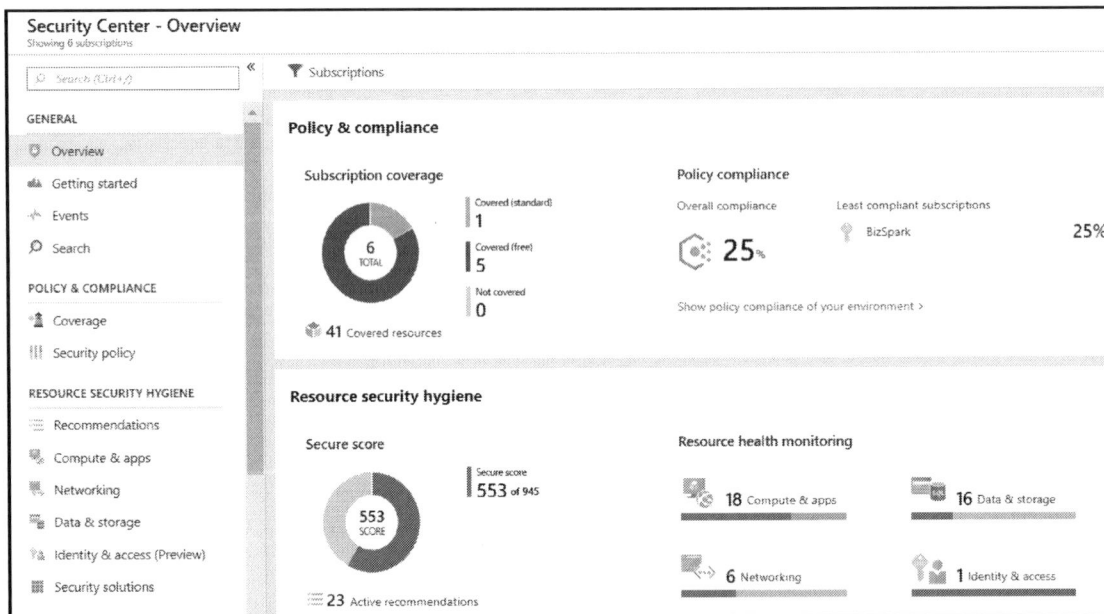

Azure Security Center is a complex service with a lot of options. As with many other services, it deserves a book of its own and it would be hard to cover all options in a single chapter. We are going to concentrate on the most important ones that will help you instantly increase your security.

Azure Security Center recommendations

Azure Security Center analyzes your security settings and compares them to best practices. Based on this, you can see recommended changes that need to be implemented under **Security Center - Recommendations**. Recommendations are divided into four categories—**Compute & apps**, **Data & storage**, **Networking**, and **Identity & access (Preview)**. All resources can have three statuses: green, orange, and red. Green shows that all security best practices are enabled and that the resource is secure; orange represents recommendations that should be implemented but aren't critical; and red shows recommendations that present high security risks and should be implemented immediately. We can also see our security score based on what is implemented and what remains to be resolved as a possible security risk. The **Security Center - Recommendations** blade is shown in the following screenshot:

Let's take the **Compute** section as an example. Here, we can find a list of all security issues that are related to compute resources (**Vms and Computers**, **App services (Preview)**, and **Cloud services**). In this list of recommendations, we can see descriptions of issues and how many resources are affected by these issues. In the example here, we can see at the top of the list that 8 out of 10 VMs don't have endpoint protection enabled and that this is classified as red:

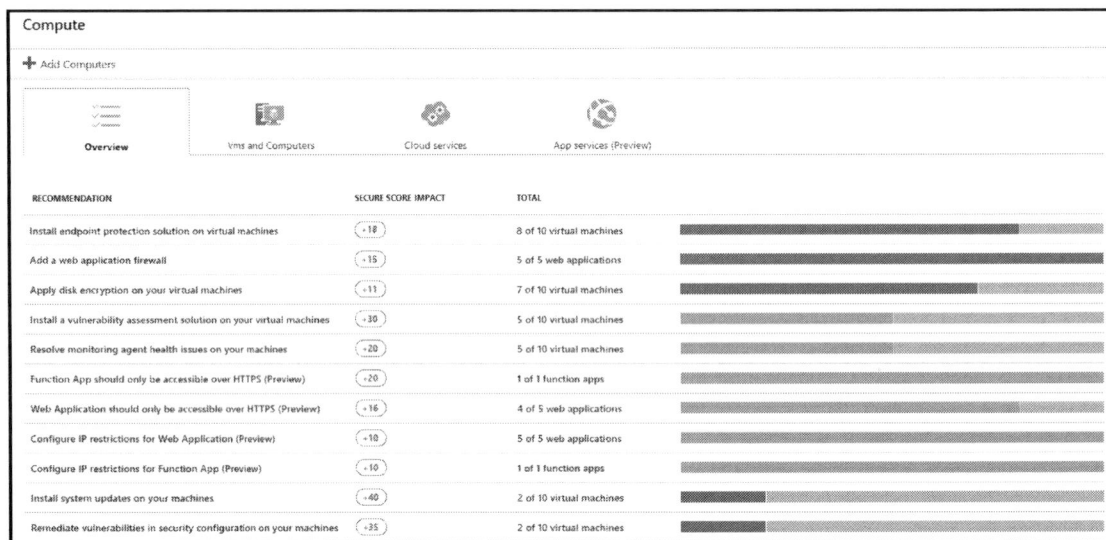

Compute			
➕ Add Computers			
Overview	Vms and Computers	Cloud services	App services (Preview)

RECOMMENDATION	SECURE SCORE IMPACT	TOTAL	
Install endpoint protection solution on virtual machines	+18	8 of 10 virtual machines	
Add a web application firewall	+15	5 of 5 web applications	
Apply disk encryption on your virtual machines	+11	7 of 10 virtual machines	
Install a vulnerability assessment solution on your virtual machines	+30	5 of 10 virtual machines	
Resolve monitoring agent health issues on your machines	+20	5 of 10 virtual machines	
Function App should only be accessible over HTTPS (Preview)	+20	1 of 1 function apps	
Web Application should only be accessible over HTTPS (Preview)	+16	4 of 5 web applications	
Configure IP restrictions for Web Application (Preview)	+18	5 of 5 web applications	
Configure IP restrictions for Function App (Preview)	+10	1 of 1 function apps	
Install system updates on your machines	+40	2 of 10 virtual machines	
Remediate vulnerabilities in security configuration on your machines	+35	2 of 10 virtual machines	

Enabling endpoint protection

As an example, let's click on this recommendation and resolve it. A new blade will open
with a list of VMs that don't have endpoint protection. We can select specific VMs or all of
them, and can opt to install endpoint protection. Installation will start, and after it is
completed, we'll see that the recommendation is resolved:

Endpoint Protection not installed on Azure VMs			
▼ Filter ⬇ Install on 8 VMs			
VIRTUAL MACHINE	STATE	SEVERITY	
✔ DBSRV	Open	❶ High	...
✔ DBserver	Open	❶ High	...
✔ DC1	Open	❶ High	...
✔ RvsB1	Open	❶ High	...
✔ RvsB2	Open	❶ High	...
✔ RvsB3	Open	❶ High	...
✔ WebSrv1	Open	❶ High	...
✔ WebSrv2	Open	❶ High	...

Similar to this, we can resolve most security center recommendations. We click on the
recommendation and follow the steps. However, some recommendations can't be resolved
in this way and require additional steps. In this case, you will be taken to documentation
that describes the issue and provides steps to resolving it.

Azure Security Center Alerts

Alerts are another part of Azure Security Center; these are very helpful and allow you to detect possible issues. The security alerts section allows you to track and see when unauthorized access to your resources was attempted. In the overview of alerts in Azure Security Center, you can see a list of possible attacks on your resources and see when they happened, as shown in the following screenshot:

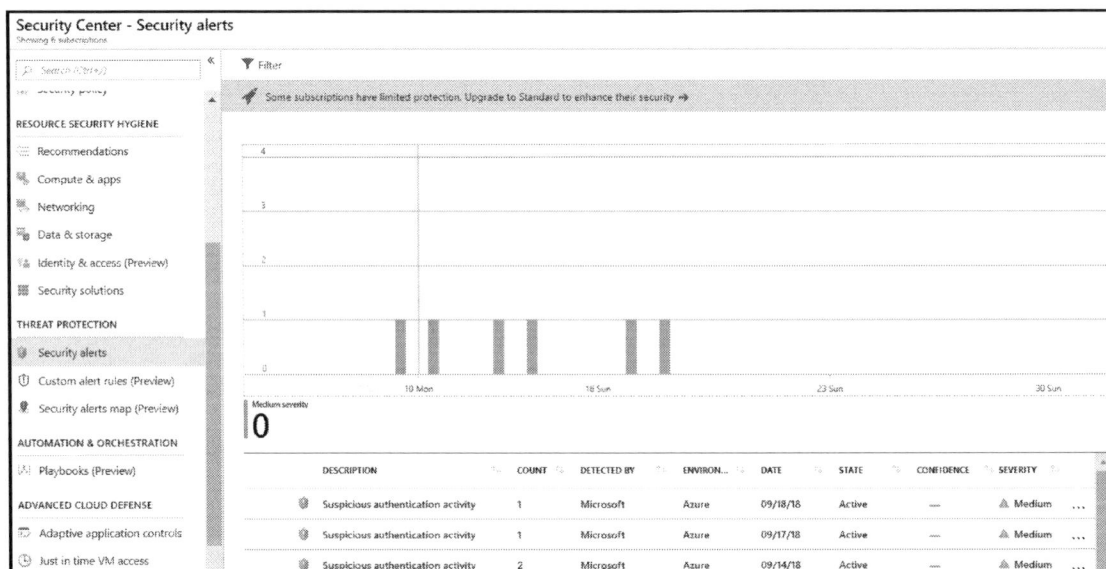

If we select any alerts, we will see more information such as a date, what credentials were used, the number of login attempts, and other information. Under **Geo and Threat Intelligence Information**, we can see from where an attack took place, giving us a detailed geographical location of the attack origin. Based on the login information and geo-location, we can detect if this was a legitimate user or a brute-force attack on our resources. If we have a valid user attempting this three times from a known location, we can assume this was a user who has simply forgotten their password.

If we have 50 attempts from unknown user(s) from unknown location(s), we can assume it was a brute-force attack. Under **Remediation steps**, we have instructions on how to prevent similar attacks in the future. A sample of suspicious authentication activity is shown here:

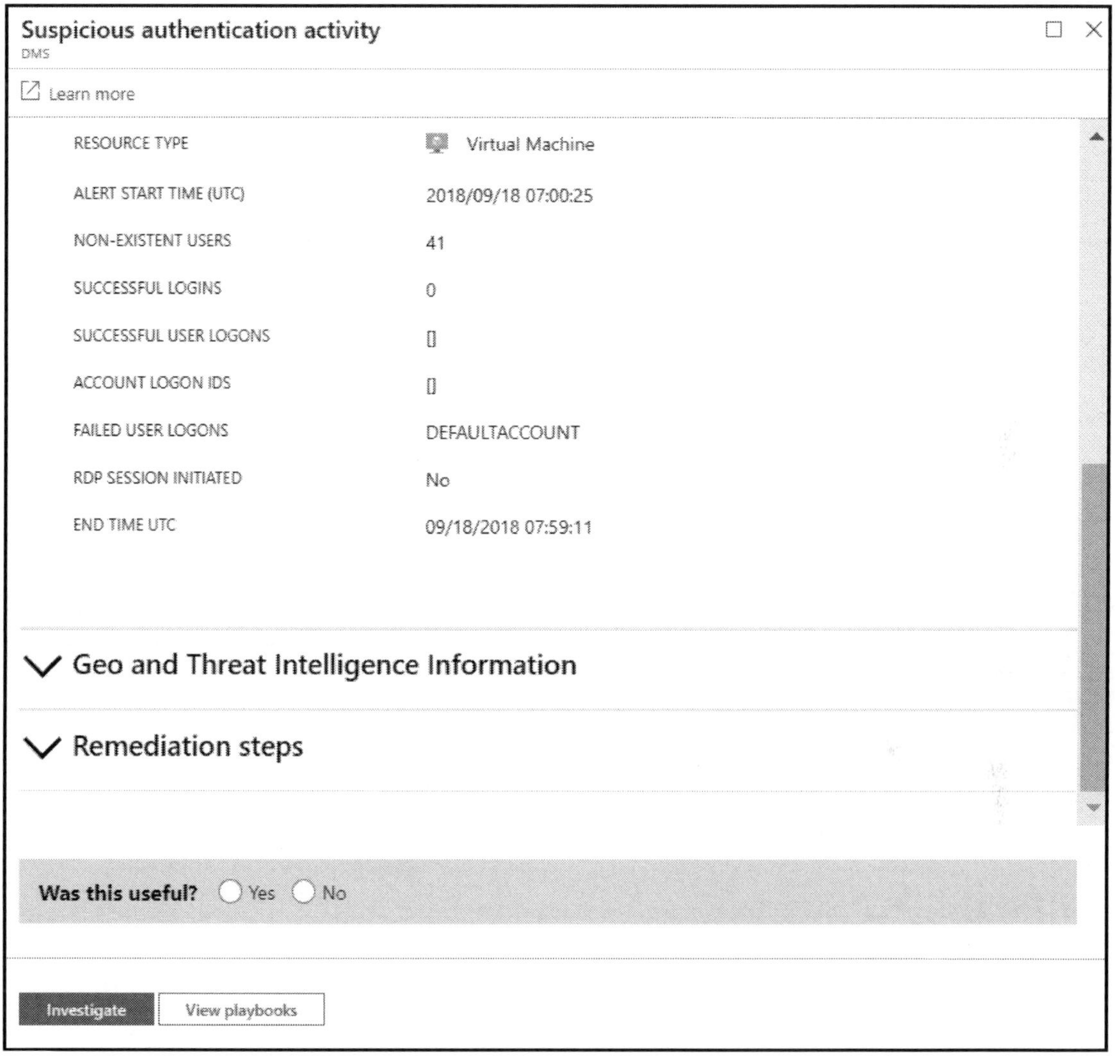

Suspicious authentication activity	□ ✕
DMS	

◻ Learn more

RESOURCE TYPE	🖥 Virtual Machine
ALERT START TIME (UTC)	2018/09/18 07:00:25
NON-EXISTENT USERS	41
SUCCESSFUL LOGINS	0
SUCCESSFUL USER LOGONS	[]
ACCOUNT LOGON IDS	[]
FAILED USER LOGONS	DEFAULTACCOUNT
RDP SESSION INITIATED	No
END TIME UTC	09/18/2018 07:59:11

∨ Geo and Threat Intelligence Information

∨ Remediation steps

Was this useful? ◯ Yes ◯ No

Investigate	View playbooks

At the bottom, we have two additional actions—**Investigate** and **View playbooks**. **Investigate** allows us to review details about incidents with more details. **View playbooks** allows us to create (or use an existing) logic app that will take action if similar events happen in the future. With a logic app, we can design steps and actions that will prevent attacks. For example, if login with an invalid user is attempted more than three times, it will add an NSG rule that will prevent access to a resource for the next 48 hours. An example of investigation details is shown in the following screenshot:

Just-in-Time access

One of the best features in Azure Security Center is Just-in-Time access. Just-in-Time access prevents access to Azure VMs unless it's been specifically requested. By default, all management ports are closed, and you need to request access from specific IP address(es) for a short period of time to enable such access.

To set up Just-in-Time access on Azure VM, go to the Just-in-Time access blade in the **Security Center** and select one or more VMs from the list, as shown:

After you select the VM(s) that will have Just-in-Time access enabled, a new blade will open. Here we must define ports that will be closed by default and enabled only on request. The default ports are SSH (22), RDP (3389), and WinRM (5985 and 5986), but you can remove and add any port you want. An example of the default settings is shown in the following screenshot:

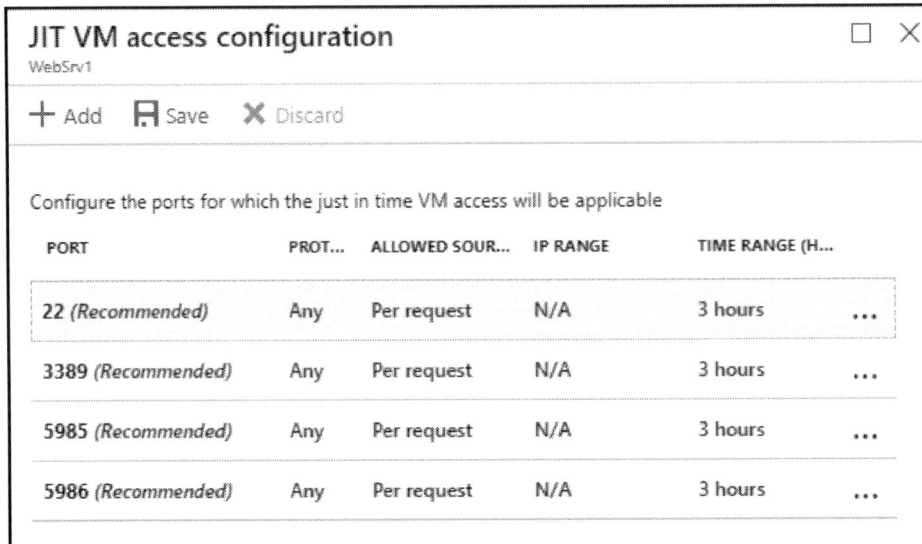

JIT VM access configuration WebSrv1				□ ✕	
+ Add 🖫 Save ✕ Discard					
Configure the ports for which the just in time VM access will be applicable					
PORT	**PROT...**	**ALLOWED SOUR...**	**IP RANGE**	**TIME RANGE (H...**	
22 *(Recommended)*	Any	Per request	N/A	3 hours	...
3389 *(Recommended)*	Any	Per request	N/A	3 hours	...
5985 *(Recommended)*	Any	Per request	N/A	3 hours	...
5986 *(Recommended)*	Any	Per request	N/A	3 hours	...

After Just-in-Time access is enabled, the option to connect to the VM will not be available. To access the VM, you must request access in Azure Security Center. Here, you need to define which port you want to open, from which IP address(es) it will be able to connect, and for how long (from 1 to 3 hours). An example of the request blade is shown here, where we can see how to open the RDP port from the current IP address for one hour:

Request access
WebSrv1

Please select the ports that you would like to open per virtual machine.

PORT	TOGGLE	ALLOWED SOURCE IP	IP RANGE	TIME RANGE (HOURS)
▼ WebSrv1				
22	On / **Off**	**My IP** / IP Range	*No range*	3
3389	**On** / Off	**My IP** / IP Range	*No range*	1
5985	On / **Off**	**My IP** / IP Range	*No range*	3
5986	On / **Off**	**My IP** / IP Range	*No range*	3

Open ports

With Just-in-Time access, you are controlling who can access your VMs, when, and from where. Unauthorized access is brought to a minimum and your VMs are protected. Another amazing thing is that with Azure Security Center in the standard tier, you can register and protect resources in private and hybrid clouds. This option is not limited only to Azure VMs, but can be enabled for on-premises VMs as well.

Summary

Microsoft takes Azure Security very seriously. Lot of steps are taken to ensure your resources are protected and safe in Azure. In addition to this, Microsoft offers lots of additional services that we can use to improve security further. To be secure and achieve maximum, it takes combines effort from Microsoft and us, and we need to take advantage of the security services that Azure has to offer in addition to what Microsoft is already doing to secure our data and services. Besides security features that are declared as security services (such as Key Vault or security center), there are lots of security features that services have built in (such as Azure SQL Firewall or network security groups).

As we are getting toward the end, we are going to review what we have learned. In the last chapter, we are going to talk about services we already discussed and the best practices when using them. Infrastructure-as-Code is a very important part of cloud computing, and we're going to talk about tools that will allow us to work with Azure by automating tasks. Using the Azure portal is a great way to learn about Azure, but if you want to take full advantage, Infrastructure-as-Code is what you want to use.

Questions

1. Everything in Azure is redundant and has how many copies?
    1. One
    2. Two
    3. Three

2. Most data breaches are caused by...
    1. Brute-force attacks
    2. Leaked credentials
    3. Viruses

3. MFA stands for...
    1. Multi-factor authentication
    2. Multi-factor authorization
    3. Multi-factor activation

4. MFA can be configured to use:
    1. Phone calls
    2. Text messages
    3. A mobile app
    4. All of the above

5. Azure Firewall is...
    1. Infrastructure as a Service
    2. Firewall as a Service
    3. Both

6. Azure resources can be encrypted using...
    1. An Azure-provided key
    2. A custom key
    3. Both

7. To use custom keys, we must use...
    1. Azure Security Center
    2. Azure Key Vault
    3. Both

8. Azure Security Center provides...
    1. Security management
    2. Advanced threat protection
    3. Both

9. Azure Security Center can be used to protect...
    1. Azure resources
    2. On-premises resources
    3. Both

10. Just-in-Time access provides...
    1. Control over management access for our VMs
    2. Live monitoring of access to VMs
    3. Both

10
Best Practices

In this final chapter, we are going to review what we have learned so far and highlight some best practices. Some simple tips can help you set up things right from the start and save you a lot of trouble down the road. Best practices will help you in administration and troubleshooting, as you'll be able to track things better and notice mistakes easier. We'll add some security tips and how to avoid the most common mistakes. We are going to use **infrastructure as code (IaC)** as a tool that will help us in our daily tasks in Azure. Using Azure Portal is simple and great to learn things, but to use Azure to its full capacity, we must use ARM templates, Azure PowerShell, or Azure CLI. Finally, to expand IaC, we are going to discuss configuration as code and introduce **Desired State Configuration (DSC)** and Azure Automation.

The following topics will be covered in this chapter:

- Azure best practices
- Infrastructure as code
- ARM templates
- Azure PowerShell
- Azure CLI
- Configuration as code
- Desired State Configuration
- Azure Automation

Technical requirements

For this chapter, you'll need the following:

- An Azure Subscription
- PowerShell

- Azure PowerShell
- The Azure CLI

Azure best practices

There are a lot of small things that you need to pay attention to, otherwise you may end up having issues in the long run. When you're managing a single subscription and a small number of resources, it may look simple and not important to create some ground rules. But as the number of subscriptions and resources starts increasing, you may find chaos and it may be too late to turn back. In these situations, it's hard to correct mistakes and get back on the right path.

Naming convention

It's very important to set the naming convention for subscriptions, resource groups, and resources. Your first subscription will probably have a name similar to `Pay-as-you-go`. And if you have a single subscription, it's not a big deal. But what if you end up with 5, 10, or 100 subscriptions, and all of them are named `Pay-as-you-go`? These subscriptions will have different subscription IDs and you can use this information to separate them, but it will be difficult and confusing. Subscriptions can be renamed and you should definitely use this option. You can organize subscriptions in different ways and it depends on your requirements regarding how you are going to do this. It can be based on departments, applications, environments, and so on.

For example, you can have multiple subscriptions per department. This will help you separate cost and consumption and see how much each department is spending on resources. In this case, you may want to rename subscriptions to something like `HumanResources`, `Finances`, `IT`, and so on. If you have different environments for each department for production, testing, and development, you can add the environment to the subscription name and have something like `HumanResources-prod`, `HumanResources-test`, and `HumanResources-dev`.

You can apply similar principles for naming resource groups, again depending on your requirements. Let's say we use a single subscription, and want to add the department, environment, or application to the resource group name. In this case, we'll have resource groups named like `IT-helpdesk-prod`. Or, if we have a subscription per department, the resource group would be named something like `helpdesk-prod`.

But, when you have multiple subscriptions and all of the subscriptions are listed in the resource group view, with some resources that have similar names, it can get confusing, and it's good idea to include the subscription name in the resource group name anyway. For example, you can have the subscriptions `Finance` and `HR`, and both of them have applications named `Employees`. If you name both resource groups using product and environment, both production resource groups will be named `Employees-prod`. They would be in different subscriptions, but when all resource groups in all subscriptions are listed, things can get confusing. In this scenario, it can be beneficial to include the complete path in the resource group name that will include the subscription name as the front part of the resource group name.

For resources, it's good to have some kind of naming convention as well. Design can depend on different things, but I recommend using all available variables to avoid confusion. For example, let's say that our IT department has its own subscription and uses an application named `helpdesk`. The application requires two VMs (web and database server) and has production, development, and testing environments. In this case, we would have six VMs being used by the same application, for different purposes and environments. In cases like this, it's good to use parameters such as subscription, environment, product, resource type, and resource purpose. So, VM names for a production environment would be something like `it-helpdesk-prod-VM-web` and `it-helpdesk-prod-VM-db`. There is also a scenario where you have multiple VMs with the same role, such as multiple web servers behind a load balancer. In this scenario, it's good to add numbers to the name and have something like `it-helpdesk-prod-VM-web-01`, `it-helpdesk-prod-VM-web-02`, and so on.

Public endpoints

It's generally a good idea to avoid exposing public endpoints if it's not required, especially when we talk about management and administration. Exposing the endpoint of your Web App is something you probably want to do, but why expose the database? It will only cause additional security risks and increase the chance of your data being breached. The same goes for management; exposing RDP, SSH, or any other port that can be used to manage and administrate your resources should be avoided.

In case we have a database in IaaS, the best practice is to allow access to the database over port 1433, only inside Azure Vnet, or even limit access to a specific subnet. Use NSGs and **Application Security Groups (ASGs)** to set up access and allow access only when it's needed. For example, we can use an NSG and an ASG to set up access to a database, but only when traffic is coming from a specific subnet (use an NSG) and only when coming from a server that is part of the web server group (use an ASG). This isn't limited to port 1433 and MS SQL Server; you can apply this approach on any other database you are using in IaaS and whatever port these databases are using, such as 1521 for Oracle, 50000 for IBM DB2, 3306 for MySQL, or any custom port you define.

Databases in PaaS, the Azure SQL Database, and other database PaaS options, offer firewall protection. With firewall protection, you can limit the IP addresses from which you can connect to the database. Make sure that you keep the firewall up to date and remove any unnecessary IP addresses. Also, there is one option in the Azure SQL database firewall that may create additional risk. There is an option to **Allow access to Azure services** to connect to your Azure SQL Database, as shown here:

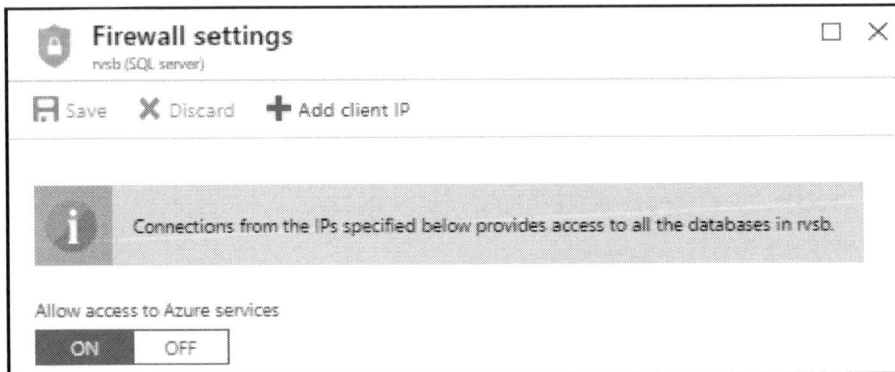

This option is **ON** by default and it may look like it makes sense to leave this enabled. Most people would think "Yeah, sure, I want my services in Azure to be able to connect to my database". But this option only checks whether a connection to the database is coming from Azure; it does not check whether the connection is coming from your subscription or even your tenant. Leaving this option **ON** allows someone to create an Azure account and try to access your database, as firewall rules will not apply if the connection is coming from Azure.

Connecting to the database will still require the username and password, but this creates an opportunity. In this case, it's very good for us that Microsoft requires credit card information when creating a trial subscription as any account can be tracked to the owner. If someone managed to access the database, this way, the person can be tracked, but you may want to disable this option to prevent any unauthorized access in the first place.

A similar approach can be taken for other backend services that shouldn't be exposed publicly. These can be anything from databases, different connectors, and business logic, to various APIs. Don't expose anything that doesn't need to be exposed. In IaaS scenarios, use NSGs and ASGs to restrict access. When using PaaS, there are different approaches that can be taken. As we mentioned previously, an Azure SQL database has a firewall. For a Web App, we can use an isolated App Service Plan, that allows access only over an Azure Virtual network. Similar to this approach, most PaaS services can be connected to Azure VNet and we can set up access to services from inside our Azure Virtual Network. Then, NSG and ASG rules can be applied to these services as well.

Limiting access to the management ports of Azure VMs is another thing that we need to pay attention to. For example, exposing RDP access to your VM over the internet can have big consequences. I tested leaving the default RDP port open and tracked access attempts with Azure Security Center. Over a single month, there were over 150,000 unauthorized attempts to access the VM. Most of these attempts were using administrator, admin, sysadmin, and root (over 80% of attempts were using these four usernames) as a username, so it's a good thing that you are not allowed to use these names for your Azure VMs.

There are several ways you can restrict access to the management of Azure VMs:

- Disable public access for management ports and manage Azure VMs over secure connections. This can be P2S, S2S, or Azure ExpressRoute. By using a secure connection, you are limiting management access to authorized users from trusted locations.

- If you cannot use a secure connection, restrict access to trusted public IP addresses. Use NSGs to limit access to Azure VMs that are to be accessed only from IP addresses that are pre-allowed. An example of how to restrict access with NSGs is shown in the following screenshot:

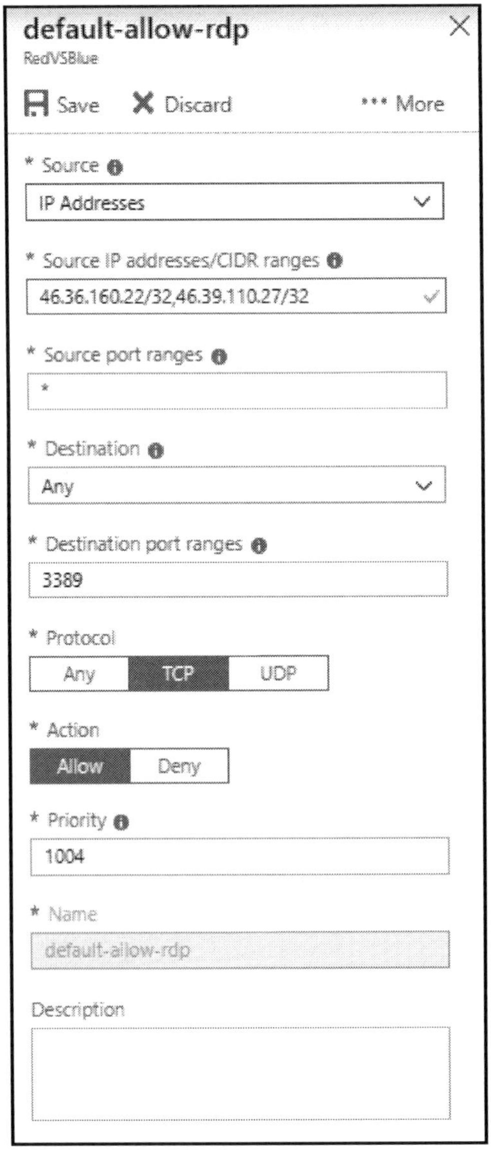

- Use Just in Time Access for Azure VM access. Setting up Just in Time in Azure is simple and fast. When this option is enabled, you need to create a request for access from a predetermined IP address and only for a limited time. This way, access is blocked unless a specific request is created to allow management access. An example of a request to open an RDP port for single hour for user's current IP address is shown here:

Please select the ports that you would like to open per virtual machine.

PORT	TOGGLE		ALLOWED SOURCE IP		IP RANGE	TIME RANGE (HOURS)	
▼ RvsB1							
22	On	Off	My IP	IP Range	No range	◯▬▬▬▬▬	1
3389	On	Off	My IP	IP Range	No range	◯▬▬▬▬▬	1
5985	On	Off	My IP	IP Range	No range	◯▬▬▬▬▬	1
5986	On	Off	My IP	IP Range	No range	◯▬▬▬▬▬	1

Other things to consider

Besides naming standards or endpoint security, there are a lot of little things we need to pay attention to:

- Use PaaS whenever possible. Microsoft Azure offers a number of options, but IaaS will, in general, be more expensive. There are cases where you have no option, but using PaaS will keep the cost of your subscription down.
- Use monitoring and logging services. Each Azure Service has some sort of logging, monitoring, and alerting feature. Try expanding these services with services such as Azure Monitor, Azure Network Watcher, or Log Analytics. These tools can help you track issues and performance over time.
- Use Azure Advisor to apply some best practices. Azure Advisor analyzes resources in a subscription, compares settings to best practices, and gives recommendations that need to be implemented to increase performance or cut cost.
- Similar to Azure Advisor, Azure Security Center offers recommendations to increase the security of your resources. Security Center compares your current security settings and, in combination with security events, creates recommendations to increase security.

- Encrypt data. Even though most Azure services have default encryption, that encryptions is at rest. To secure our data after export or backup, we need to apply additional encryption.
- Encrypt connections and use HTTPS. Securing is pointless if data is exposed in transit, so we need to consider this as well.
- Check Azure Service Health if you have issues. This can save you hours of troubleshooting. You will be able to notice performance issues or whether a service is unavailable, and automatically connect to Azure to see what is wrong. It can be an issue with Azure on the global or data center level, and it can save time checking if this is the case as the first step.
- Configure auto scaling when possible. One of the advantages Azure offers is that you pay only for what you use. Auto scaling, if set up properly, will increase the size/number of instances when the workload increases, and decreases the size when the workload decreases. This can save a lot of money over time.
- Use Azure Active Directory authentication whenever possible. Most services can be set up to use a different form of authentication or enable you to create local accounts only for that specific service. It's hard to audit or keep track of access in this case. Using AAD accounts will give you more insight and make tracking much easier.
- Enable auditing on services. Some services, such as Azure SQL, have an audit feature built in. Enable this when possible or use Log Analytics to log everything.
- Design for resiliency whenever possible. Having a redundant service can cost a lot of money and in some cases even double our cost. However, having a redundant service in another Azure data center can increase availability for your services. In case there is an issue with a service, regardless of whether it's an issue with your service or on the Azure data center level, you can failover to a redundant copy.
- Always plan for failure. This isn't only an Azure or cloud-related best practice—planning for failure is an IT best practice. Try to predict different scenarios and what would happen if the service fails. Then, try to fix possible issues and prevent failure.
- Try enabling multi-factor authentication. As this can increase cost, it ins't always possible, and the budget might prevent you from accomplishing this. In this case, enable MFA at least for administrators; MFA for administrators is free.
- Install endpoint protection on Azure VMs. Endpoint protection will provide real-time protection and prevent malicious or unwanted software from being installed and potentially harming your system.

- Install the latest patches for Azure VMs. Regular patch installation has a double effect: security patches will increase security and other updates can increase performance.
- Analyze performance regularly. Having auto-scaling in place is sometimes not enough. Try to monitor the performance of your resources manually when possible. You can spot performance issues or you can see that some services are not utilized. You can make your service perform better and save money.

Infrastructure as code

IaC is a very important part in Azure best practices. Using Azure Portal is simple and excellent for creating a single resource and learning, but if we want to create complex environments, IaC is what we want to use. For example, for creating a single Azure VM, Azure Portal is a good choice. It takes 3-5 minutes to go through the New VM wizard and complete all of the steps. But what if we need to create new VMs on a daily basis or create tens or even hundreds of them? In this case, we would probably want to use some kind of automation to simplify our work, and this is exactly where IaC comes in. To work with Azure, we have a few options available:

- ARM templates
- Azure PowerShell
- Azure CLI

We have already mentioned ARM templates. ARM templates are JSON files that hold information about Azure resources and can be used for deployment (or editing/updating existing resources).

To answer what Azure PowerShell is, we need to answer what PowerShell is first. PowerShell is a task-based, command-line scripting language based on the .NET framework. It is used to automate tasks and manage operating systems and processes from the command line. Azure PowerShell is a PowerShell module that provides a set of `cmdlets` (commands) that allow us to manage Azure resources.

Azure CLI, or Azure **command-line interface (CLI)**, is Microsoft's cross-platform command-line tool for managing Azure resources. It supports macOS, Linux, and Windows, and provides the same experience whatever platform you choose. The first version of Azure CLI 1.0 was also called X-Plat CLI and was written in JavaScript. It was initially created to support Azure Service Management APIs, and Azure Resource Management support was added later. Azure CLI 2.0 was built for ARM from the start and was written in Python.

Installing tools

In this section, we'll be discussing various tools, via which you can begin different installations.

ARM templates

ARM templates don't really require anything, but you can use various tools to help you manage them. As they're JSON files, you can create one using any text editor, but it would be much easier to use an **integrated development environment** (**IDE**). My recommendation would be either Visual Studio or Visual Studio Code. Using Visual Studio or Visual Studio Code, you can connect to a repository and set up version control, which will allow you to track changes in templates over time. However, we can deploy with ARM templates, calling APIs or from Azure Portal without any additional tools.

Azure PowerShell

To install Azure PowerShell, we need Windows PowerShell installed first. Luckily, in the client OS, it's already pre-installed on Windows 7 and newer, and for the server OS on Windows Server 2008 R2 and newer. So, all we are missing is the Azure PowerShell module. To install the Azure PowerShell module, we need to run PowerShell and execute the following:

```
Install-Module -Name AzureRM
```

You will receive a message that will ask you to install the module from PSGallery, so select **Yes** or **Yes to all**. After you install the module, we need to import it with this command:

```
Import-Module AzureRM
```

Finally, we can sign in with the following command:

```
Connect-AzureRmAccount
```

This will open a window where we need to input our credentials and authorize access to our subscription.

As a new version of Azure PowerShell is released every three weeks, you need to keep it updated. To install the latest version, we need to run this:

```
Update-Module -Name AzureRM
```

Azure CLI

Installing the Azure CLI depends on the platform that we're using.

For Windows, we need to download the installer from `https://aka.ms/ installazurecliwindows` and simply run the installer like so:

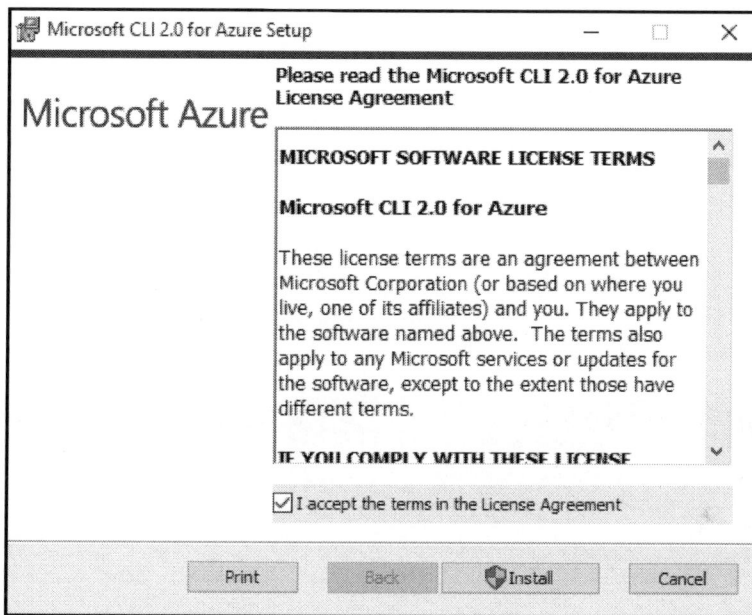

To install it on macOS, we need to run this command:

```
brew update && brew install azure-cli
```

Installing on Linux depends on the distribution. For example, on a distribution with `yum` (such as RHEL or CentOS), we need to run three commands.

First, we import the Microsoft repository key:

```
sudo rpm --import https://packages.microsoft.com/keys/microsoft.asc
```

Second, we create the repository information:

```
sudo sh -c 'echo -e "[azure-cli]\nname=Azure
CLI\nbaseurl=https://packages.microsoft.com/yumrepos/azure-cli\nenabled=1\n
gpgcheck=1\ngpgkey=https://packages.microsoft.com/keys/microsoft.asc" >
/etc/yum.repos.d/azure-cli.repo'
```

Finally, we run the installation:

```
sudo yum install azure-cli
```

Installation may depend on the platform, but after the installation process has completed, running Azure CLI commands is the same on all platforms. To log in to Azure with the Azure CLI, we need to run this:

```
az login
```

This will display a message (shown here) and open a new browser session, where you need to authorize access to Azure:

```
C:\>az login
Note, we have launched a browser for you to login. For old experience with device code, use "az login --use-device-code"
```

All commands in the Azure CLI start with `az`. To get more information, you can run this:

```
az --help
```

You will get the following output:

```
C:\>az --help

Group
    az

Subgroups:
    account             : Manage Azure subscription information.
    acr                 : Manage Azure Container Registries for private registries within Azure.
    acs                 : Manage Azure Container Services.
    ad                  : Manage Azure Active Directory Graph entities needed for Role Based Access
                          Control.
    advisor             : Manage Azure Advisor.
    aks                 : Manage Azure Kubernetes Services.
    ams                 : Manage Azure Media Services resources.
    appservice          : Manage App Service plans.
    backup              : Manage Azure Backups.
    batch               : Manage Azure Batch.
    batchai             : Manage Batch AI resources.
    billing             : Manage Azure Billing.
    bot                 : Manage Microsoft Bot Services.
    cdn                 : Manage Azure Content Delivery Networks (CDNs).
    cloud               : Manage registered Azure clouds.
    cognitiveservices   : Manage Azure Cognitive Services accounts.
    consumption         : Manage consumption of Azure resources.
    container           : Manage Azure Container Instances.
    cosmosdb            : Manage Azure Cosmos DB database accounts.
    deployment          : Manage Azure Resource Manager deployments at subscription scope.
    disk                : Manage Azure Managed Disks.
    dla                 : (PREVIEW) Manage Data Lake Analytics accounts, jobs, and catalogs.
    dls                 : (PREVIEW) Manage Data Lake Store accounts and filesystems.
    dms                 : Manage Azure Data Migration Service (DMS) instances.
    eventgrid           : Manage Azure Event Grid topics and subscriptions.
    eventhubs           : Manage Azure Event Hubs namespaces, eventhubs, consumergroups and geo
                          recovery configurations - Alias.
    extension           : Manage and update CLI extensions.
    feature             : Manage resource provider features.
    functionapp         : Manage function apps.
    group               : Manage resource groups and template deployments.
    identity            : Managed Service Identities.
    image               : Manage custom virtual machine images.
    iot                 : Manage Internet of Things (IoT) assets.
    iotcentral          : Manage IoT Central assets.
    keyvault            : Manage KeyVault keys, secrets, and certificates.
    lab                 : Manage Azure DevTest Labs.
    lock                : Manage Azure locks.
    managedapp          : Manage template solutions provided and maintained by Independent Software
                          Vendors (ISVs).
    maps                : Manage Azure Maps.
    monitor             : Manage the Azure Monitor Service.
    mysql               : Manage Azure Database for MySQL servers.
    network             : Manage Azure Network resources.
    policy              : Manage resource policies.
    postgres            : Manage Azure Database for PostgreSQL servers.
    provider            : Manage resource providers.
    redis               : Manage dedicated Redis caches for your Azure applications.
    relay               : Manage Azure Relay Service namespaces, WCF relays, hybrid connections, and
                          rules.
    reservations        : Manage Azure Reservations.
    resource            : Manage Azure resources.
    role                : Manage user roles for access control with Azure Active Directory and service
                          principals.
    search              : Manage Azure Search services, admin keys and query keys.
    servicebus          : Manage Azure Service Bus namespaces, queues, topics, subscriptions, rules
                          and geo-disaster recovery configuration alias.
    sf                  : Manage and administer Azure Service Fabric clusters.
    snapshot            : Manage point-in-time copies of managed disks, native blobs, or other
                          snapshots.
    sql                 : Manage Azure SQL Databases and Data Warehouses.
    storage             : Manage Azure Cloud Storage resources.
    tag                 : Manage resource tags.
    vm                  : Manage Linux or Windows virtual machines.
    vmss                : Manage groupings of virtual machines in an Azure Virtual Machine Scale Set
                          (VMSS).
    webapp              : Manage web apps.
```

You can combine `--help` with any of the commands in the list to get more information on a specific command.

Creating Azure resources with IaC

To better understand how ARM templates, Azure PowerShell, and the Azure CLI work, let's see a simple example and create an Azure Web App with each tool.

Creating an Azure Web App with ARM templates

With ARM templates, we need two JSON files. The first file defines what needs to be created and the second file contains parameters that are defined during deployment. So, basically, the first file holds information on what needs to be created (in our example, App Service Plan and Web App), and the second file holds information on where, the size of the service, name, and so on.

This is the template file:

```
{
"$schema":
"https://schema.management.azure.com/schemas/2015-01-01/deploymentTemplate.
json#",
"contentVersion": "1.0.0.0",
"parameters": {
"webAppName": {
"type": "string",
"metadata": {
"description": "Base name of the resource such as web app name and app
service plan "
},
"minLength": 2
},
"sku":{
"type": "string",
"defaultValue" : "S1",
"metadata": {
"description": "The SKU of App Service Plan, by defaut is standard S1"
}
},
"location": {
"type": "string",
"defaultValue": "[resourceGroup().location]",
"metadata": {
"description": "Location for all resources."
}
}
},
"variables": {
"webAppPortalName": "[concat(parameters('webAppName'))]",
```

```
"appServicePlanName": "[concat( parameters('webAppName'),'-
AppServicePlan')]"
},
"resources": [
{
"apiVersion": "2017-08-01",
"type": "Microsoft.Web/serverfarms",
"kind": "app",
"name": "[variables('appServicePlanName')]",
"location": "[parameters('location')]",
"comments": "This app service plan is used for the web app and slots.",
"properties": {},
"dependsOn": [],
"sku": {
"name": "[parameters('sku')]"
}
},
{
"apiVersion": "2016-08-01",
"type": "Microsoft.Web/sites",
"kind": "app",
"name": "[variables('webAppPortalName')]",
"location": "[parameters('location')]",
"comments": "This is the web app, also the default 'nameless' slot.",
"properties": {
"serverFarmId": "[resourceId('Microsoft.Web/serverfarms',
variables('appServicePlanName'))]"
},
"dependsOn": [
"[resourceId('Microsoft.Web/serverfarms',
variables('appServicePlanName'))]"
]
}
]
}
```

This is the parameter file:

```
{
"$schema":
"https://schema.management.azure.com/schemas/2015-01-01/deploymentParameter
s.json#",
"contentVersion": "1.0.0.0",
"parameters": {
"webAppName": {
"value": "packt-demo-arm-webapp-01"
},
"sku": {
```

```
"value": "S1"
},
"location": {
"value": "[resourceGroup().location]"
}
}
}
```

Save both files. Now, let's create a resource group for deployment. Create a new empty **Resource group** named `packt-demo-arm`. Open **Template deployment** and select the **Custom template**. Under **Edit template**, load the template file and under **Edit parameter**, load the parameter file. Select **Subscription** and **Resource group** for **packt-demo-arm** (if you didn't create it previously, you have the option to do so here). All other fields should be automatically loaded from the parameter file, like in this example (remember to accept **TERMS AND CONDITIONS**):

After the deployment has completed, you should find the App Service Plan and Web App, as shown in the following screenshot:

packt-demo-arm-webapp-01	App Service	West Europe
packt-demo-arm-webapp-01-AppServicePlan	App Service plan	West Europe

We can use this same ARM template to deploy new Web App simply by changing the resource name or tier in the parameter file; we don't have to go through the deployment wizard in Azure portal for each deployment. This can save a lot of time if we need to deploy multiple Web Apps.

Creating an Azure Web App with Azure PowerShell

To create the same resources with Azure PowerShell, we need to execute a single script that will create a resource group, App Service Plan, and Web App. The script starts with parameters and then executes three `cmdlets` to create everything we need for deployment. Make sure you are connected to Azure in Azure PowerShell:

```
$ResourceGroupName = "packt-demo-ps"
$webappname="packt-demo-ps-webapp-01"
$location="West Europe"
New-AzureRmResourceGroup -Name $ResourceGroupName -Location $location
New-AzureRmAppServicePlan -Name $webappname -Location $location -
ResourceGroupName $ResourceGroupName -Tier Free
New-AzureRmWebApp -Name $webappname -Location $location -AppServicePlan
$webappname -ResourceGroupName $ResourceGroupName
```

After executing the script, you should receive the following output:

```
GitRemoteName               :
GitRemoteUri                : https://packt-demo-ps-webapp-01.scm.azurewebsites.net
GitRemoteUsername           : $packt-demo-ps-webapp-01
GitRemotePassword           : System.Security.SecureString
State                       : Running
HostNames                   : {packt-demo-ps-webapp-01.azurewebsites.net}
RepositorySiteName          : packt-demo-ps-webapp-01
UsageState                  : Normal
Enabled                     : True
EnabledHostNames            : {packt-demo-ps-webapp-01.azurewebsites.net, packt-demo-ps-webapp-01.scm.azurewebsites.net}
AvailabilityState           : Normal
HostNameSslStates           : {packt-demo-ps-webapp-01.azurewebsites.net, packt-demo-ps-webapp-01.scm.azurewebsites.net}
ServerFarmId                : /subscriptions/cb638267-a366-463c-bfe5-7a49311c27a8/resourceGroups/packt-demo-ps/providers/Microsoft.Web/serverfarms/packt-demo-ps-webapp-01
Reserved                    : False
LastModifiedTimeUtc         : 10/9/2018 7:50:31 AM
SiteConfig                  : Microsoft.Azure.Management.WebSites.Models.SiteConfig
TrafficManagerHostNames     :
ScmSiteAlsoStopped          : False
TargetSwapSlot              :
HostingEnvironmentProfile   :
ClientAffinityEnabled       : True
ClientCertEnabled           : False
HostNamesDisabled           : False
OutboundIpAddresses         : 40.114.210.78,40.114.239.62,40.114.231.39,13.80.106.127,40.114.212.109
PossibleOutboundIpAddresses : 40.114.210.78,40.114.239.62,40.114.231.39,13.80.106.127,40.114.212.109,40.114.236.249,40.114.238.127,13.80.108.215
ContainerSize               : 0
DailyMemoryTimeQuota        : 0
SuspendedTill               :
MaxNumberOfWorkers          :
CloningInfo                 :
SnapshotInfo                :
ResourceGroup               : packt-demo-ps
IsDefaultContainer          :
DefaultHostName             : packt-demo-ps-webapp-01.azurewebsites.net
SlotSwapStatus              :
HttpsOnly                   : False
Identity                    :
Id                          : /subscriptions/cb638267-a366-463c-bfe5-7a49311c27a8/resourceGroups/packt-demo-ps/providers/Microsoft.Web/sites/packt-demo-ps-webapp-01
Name                        : packt-demo-ps-webapp-01
Kind                        :
Location                    : West Europe
Type                        : Microsoft.Web/sites
Tags                        :
```

If we go to Azure Portal, we should find a new resource group and new items inside it:

☐ 📦 packt-demo-ps-webapp-01	App Service plan	West Europe
☐ ⊚ packt-demo-ps-webapp-01	App Service	West Europe

To start a new deployment, we simply change the parameter values and execute again. We can quickly deploy multiple websites by just changing the name of the Web App and deploying sites in the same resource group. For example, if I needed to deploy four instances of the same site in the same resource group, I could just change the value of `$webappname` and change the numbers at the end to `packt-demo-ps-webapp-01`, `packt-demo-ps-webapp-02`, `packt-demo-ps-webapp-03`, and `packt-demo-ps-webapp-04`. Instead of going through the wizard in Azure Portal each time, I can run the script by changing a single value.

To clean up deployment, you can execute a command that will delete the resource group, along with all the resources inside that resource group:

```
$ResourceGroupName = "packt-demo-ps"

Remove-AzureRmResourceGroup -Name $ResourceGroupName -Force
```

You should receive output like this, and can verify in Azure Portal that the resource group doesn't exist anymore:

```
PS C:\Windows\system32> $ResourceGroupName = "packt-demo-ps"
Remove-AzureRmResourceGroup -Name $ResourceGroupName -Force
True
```

Creating an Azure Web App with Azure CLI

Now, let's repeat the same process using the Azure CLI. You can see that the Azure CLI script structure is very similar to Azure PowerShell:

```
$webappname='packt-demo-cli-webapp-01'
$ResourceGroupName ='packt-demo-cli'
az group create --location westeurope --name $ResourceGroupName
az appservice plan create --name $webappname --resource-group
$ResourceGroupName --sku Free
az webapp create --name $webappname --resource-group $ResourceGroupName --
plan $webappname
```

After executing the script, you should receive a long output that ends like this:

```
"hostNames": [
    "packt-demo-cli-webapp-01.azurewebsites.net"
],
"hostNamesDisabled": false,
"hostingEnvironmentProfile": null,
"httpsOnly": false,
"id": "/subscriptions/331583a8-386b-4a0e-be78-67c97ddc8810/resourceGroups/packt-demo-cli/providers/Microsoft.Web/sites/packt-demo-cli-webapp-01",
"identity": null,
"isDefaultContainer": null,
"kind": "app",
"lastModifiedTimeUtc": "2018-10-09T08:21:45.473333",
"location": "West Europe",
"maxNumberOfWorkers": null,
"name": "packt-demo-cli-webapp-01",
"outboundIpAddresses": "104.214.237.135,51.144.123.73,23.97.221.250,51.144.120.21,51.144.126.188",
"possibleOutboundIpAddresses": "104.214.237.135,51.144.123.73,23.97.221.250,51.144.120.21,51.144.126.188,104.214.234.130,51.144.121.68,104.46.33.147",
"repositorySiteName": "packt-demo-cli-webapp-01",
"reserved": false,
"resourceGroup": "packt-demo-cli",
"scmSiteAlsoStopped": false,
"serverFarmId": "/subscriptions/331583a8-386b-4a0e-be78-67c97ddc8810/resourceGroups/packt-demo-cli/providers/Microsoft.Web/serverfarms/packt-demo-cli-webapp-01",
"siteConfig": null,
"slotSwapStatus": null,
"snapshotInfo": null,
"state": "Running",
"suspendedTill": null,
"tags": null,
"targetSwapSlot": null,
"trafficManagerHostNames": null,
"type": "Microsoft.Web/sites",
"usageState": "Normal"
}
```

If we go to Azure Portal, we should find the new resource group and new items inside it:

packt-demo-cli-webapp-01	App Service plan	West Europe
packt-demo-cli-webapp-01	App Service	West Europe

Similar to Azure PowerShell, to deploy again, we just need to edit the parameter values. To clean up deployment, you can execute a command that will delete the resource group, along with all the resources inside the resource group:

```
$ResourceGroupName ='packt-demo-cli'
az group delete --name $ResourceGroupName
```

You should receive an output message that the command is completed and verify in Azure Portal that the resource group doesn't exist anymore.

Deploying multiple resources

Each of these deployment methods can be used to deploy multiple resources in a single script. My personal favorite tool is definitely Azure PowerShell, but this is probably because of my system engineering background. I was using Windows PowerShell for years and find Azure PowerShell easiest to use. This doesn't mean that ARM templates or the Azure CLI are behind Azure PowerShell, and I think developers will find these other tools more familiar.

For an example on how to deploy multiple resources as simply as possible, I'll create an Azure PowerShell script that will deploy multiple websites in a single run. You can do similar things with other tools as well:

```
$ResourceGroupName = "packt-demo-ps-multiple"
$webappname="packt-demo-ps-webapp"
$location="West Europe"
$NumberOfWebApps= 4

New-AzureRmResourceGroup -Name $ResourceGroupName -Location $locationNew-
AzureRmAppServicePlan -Name $webappname -Location $location -
ResourceGroupName $ResourceGroupName -Tier Standard

$i=1

Do

{

New-AzureRmWebApp -Name $webappname'-0'$i -Location $location -
AppServicePlan $webappname -ResourceGroupName $ResourceGroupName

} While (($i=$I+1) -le $NumberOfWebApps)
```

In the preceding output, you'll receive a message for each resource created, and you can verify the deployment in Azure Portal. If the script executed successfully, you should see all of the resources, like this:

packt-demo-ps-webapp	App Service plan	West Europe
packt-demo-ps-webapp-01	App Service	West Europe
packt-demo-ps-webapp-02	App Service	West Europe
packt-demo-ps-webapp-03	App Service	West Europe
packt-demo-ps-webapp-04	App Service	West Europe

To clean up deployment, you can use the same command that we used previously:

```
$ResourceGroupName = "packt-demo-ps-multiple"
Remove-AzureRmResourceGroup -Name $ResourceGroupName -Force
```

We can use a similar approach when deploying any type of resource in Azure; for example, we can deploy multiple Azure VMs. Let's execute a similar script, this time deploying two web servers:

```
$ResourceGroupName = "packt-demo"
$location = "westeurope"
$vmName = "packtdemoVM"
$NumberOfServers= 2

New-AzureRmResourceGroup -Name $ResourceGroupName -Location $location

$i=1

Do

{

New-AzureRmVm -ResourceGroupName $ResourceGroupName -Name $vmName"-0"$i -
Location $location -VirtualNetworkName $vmName"-Vnet" -SubnetName $vmName"-
subnet" -SecurityGroupName $vmName"-nsg" -PublicIpAddressName $vmName"-IP-
"$i -OpenPorts 80,443,3389

} While (($i=$I+1) -le $NumberOfServers)
```

The script should deploy one virtual network, one subnet, and one NSG. These resources will be shared between VMs. We don't want to create unnecessary resources as this will enable VMs to communicate. For each VM, we'll create an NIC and disk. An example of the resources created by the script for two servers is shown here:

packtdemoVM-01	Virtual machine	West Europe
packtdemoVM-01	Network interface	West Europe
packtdemoVM-01_OsDisk_1_aaae7ea40cd441f5a9bdd7ad6e5a318c	Disk	West Europe
packtdemoVM-02	Virtual machine	West Europe
packtdemoVM-02	Network interface	West Europe
packtdemoVM-02_OsDisk_1_4427daa582784470868a9d46d21f602e	Disk	West Europe
packtdemoVM-IP-1	Public IP address	West Europe
packtdemoVM-IP-2	Public IP address	West Europe
packtdemoVM-nsg	Network security group	West Europe
packtdemoVM-Vnet	Virtual network	West Europe

We can now edit this script to deploy more servers, deploy to a new resource group or a new subnet, or change any number of parameters to influence the deployment results.

So, using this script, I could deploy and number of servers, from 1 to 100, or even more. Now, imagine that you need to deploy 100 VMs in Azure Portal with a wizard. Which task will take more time? I think we can recognize that using IaC for deployment has multiple benefits and can make our job significantly easier.

Configuration as code

IaC is only the first step in automation. After we deploy our servers with code, we still need to configure them. Configuring servers manually will probably take more time than deploying them. Luckily, there is the option for configuration as code to complete the configuration steps as well. There are many different tools for configuration, but we are going to explore Azure Automation as the Azure-native configuration as code tool.

Azure Automation can be used for automating and scheduling different tasks. When talking about configuration as code, Azure Automation uses DSC. DSC is a declarative management platform in PowerShell, used for the configuration, deployment, and management of systems.

Apply DSC with Azure Automation

To create a new Azure Automation account, we need to provide the **Name** for the account, **Subscription**, **Resource group**, and **Location**. Another option is to create **Run-as-account**. **Run-as-account** is a service principal that's used to authenticate to Azure when managing Azure resources through Azure Automation. I strongly recommend that you create this as it will be easier to manage with accounts in place. An example of creating an Azure Automation account is shown here:

With Azure Automation, you can perform various operations, schedule and run scripts, manage your resources, and so on. It's important to mention that you can manage both Azure and on-premises resources, as well as resources in other clouds. Here, we are going to concentrate on applying DSC to Azure VMs.

Managing DSC in Azure Automation is done under **State configuration (DSC)**. Here, we can manage **Nodes**, **Configurations**, and **Compiled configurations**, and access the **Gallery**. We are going to see each of these settings, except **Gallery**. **Gallery** contains a number of DSC scripts that you can use or edit, based on your requirements. An example of the **State configuration (DSC)** blade is shown in the following screenshot:

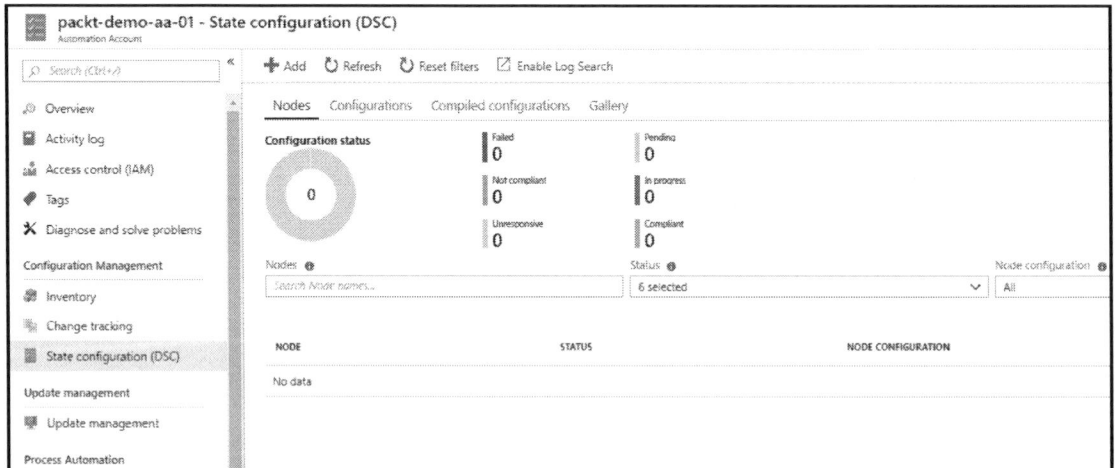

DSC uses a script that is applied on selected nodes. **Nodes** are VMs or groups of VMs. These VMs can be both Azure VMs or local VMs.

To start a new configuration, we need a DSC script. The script we are going to use ensures that the IIS role is installed on the server. Save the script locally and make sure that the name of the file is the same as the name of the configuration. In our case, the name should be `webserverDSC`:

```
configuration webserverDSC {
    Node WebServer {
        WindowsFeature IIS {
            Ensure = 'Present'
            Name = 'Web-Server'
            IncludeAllSubFeature = $true
        }
    }
}
```

Under **Configurations**, select **New configuration** and import the previously saved script:

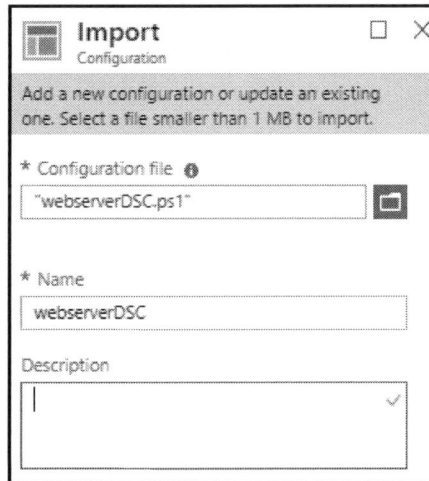

After the script has been imported, it needs to be compiled before we can proceed. Select the imported script and a new blade will open. Select **Compile** and wait for the compile to finish. The compile time will depend on the size of the script, but in this case, it shouldn't take more than 2-3 minutes. An example of the configuration blade is as follows:

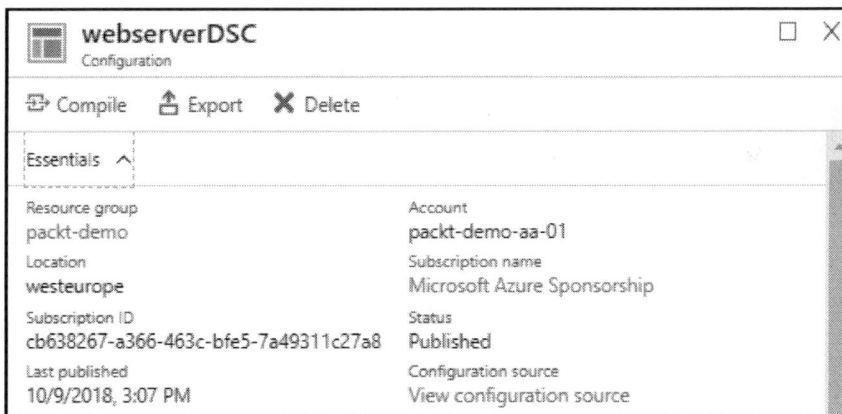

After the script has compiled, we can proceed and apply configuration to the nodes. Under **Nodes**, select **New** and a new blade will open. In the list of VMs, we can select the VMs we want DSC to be applied to. I'm going to select the VM I created with the last script in this chapter, **packtdemoVM-01**.

Under **Registration**, we can select a few options. We can select which **Registration key** will be used, **Node configuration name**, **Refresh frequency**, **Configuration Mode Frequency**, **Configuration Mode**, **Allow Module Override** or **Reboot Node if Needed**, and **Action after Reboot**. I'm going to select the new configuration we just created and leave the rest of the settings as the defaults. An example of node registration is shown here:

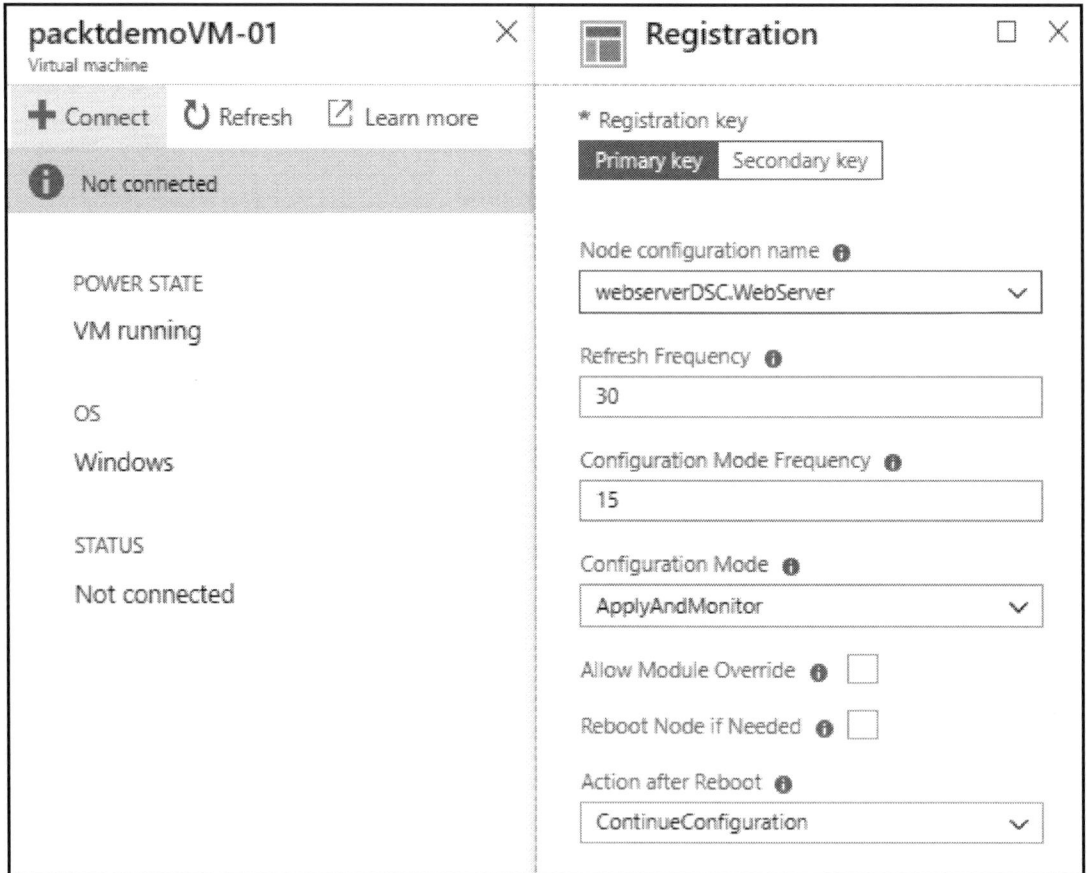

After registration is complete, we need to wait for the initial check and for configuration to be applied to our server. This can take some time, depending on the frequency selected and the complexity of DSC we want to apply. If you monitor the node blade, the added node will go from pending to in progress, until it finally reaches compliant. An example of a node with configuration applied is shown in the following screenshot:

After the node becomes compliant, we can verify that the configuration is applied. Go to the VM blade that we used in node registration and locate the public IP address. Open the browser and try reaching http://'youripaddress'. You should get the default IIS page, which will confirm that IIS is installed on the server:

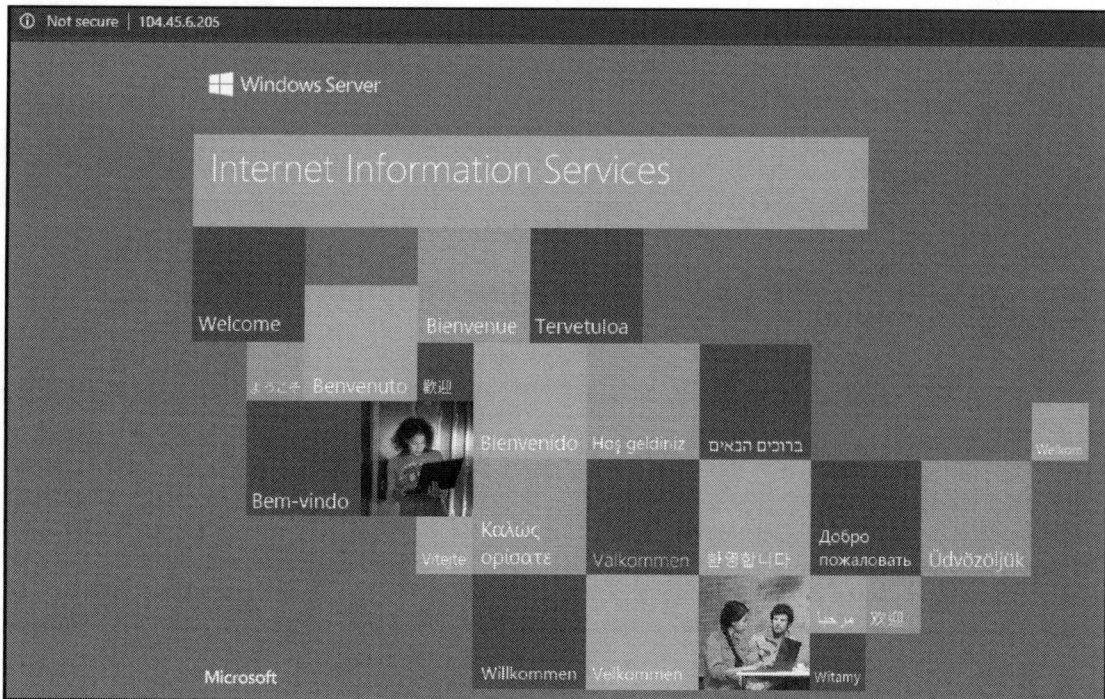

Summary

Microsoft Azure is a cloud with a lot of services and options. Combining these results in endless possibilities. We mentioned some of the best practices that can guide you to create productive and secure cloud environments. Based on these, you can expand and create your own rules and practices, depending on your services and requirements.

Although we have reached the end of this book, we have covered only a fraction of what Azure has to offer. Covering all of the available services would be just impossible in a single book, and if we wanted to provide a deep dive into each service, it would probably end up with a separate book for each service. This book was intended to provide you with an understanding of cloud design, cloud services, and best practices in the cloud, in order to give you a solid foundation of where you can start your cloud journey and build more, based on the knowledge gained here.

Learning Azure never stops, as new services and options are added daily. I've been using Azure for a long time and almost each time I open Azure Portal, I find something new. But, understanding new services is not an issue if you get a grasp on cloud patterns and best practices. If you understand the services you are currently using, understanding new features and services is not a problem and you will quickly find a way to use them to your advantage.

I hope you enjoyed this book and gained at least some knowledge from it!

Questions

1. The name of the resource should contain...
    1. As much information as possible
    2. As little information as possible
    3. Basic information

2. Public endpoints should be...
    1. Always exposed to internet access
    2. Exposed to internet access only when needed
    3. Never exposed to internet access

3. To control management access to Azure VMs, you can use...
    1. NSGs
    2. Just in Time access
    3. Both

4. Multi-factor authentication is...
    1. Free for all users
    2. Free for administrators
    3. Payed for all users
    4. Payed for administrators

5. IaC stands for...
    1. Infrastructure as code
    2. Infrastructure as configuration
    3. Information as code

6. An ARM template is a...
    1. Script
    2. JSON file
    3. TXT file

7. The Azure command-line tool is...
    1. Azure PowerShell
    2. Azure CLI
    3. Both

8. With IaC, we can...
    1. Deploy a single resource
    2. Deploy multiple resources
    3. Deploy only resources of the same type

9. DSC stands for...
    1. Desired State Configuration
    2. Digital Signature Configuration
    3. Desired Scaling Configuration

10. The steps to apply DSC in Azure Automation are...
    1. Import script, compile script, and register node
    2. Register script, apply to node, and compile configuration
    3. Register node, compile script, and apply configuration

Assessments

Chapter 1: Key Concepts of Cloud Computing

1. Which type of cloud requires an internet connection and allows anyone to sign up for service?
   Answer: Public cloud

2. Which cloud service model allows us most control over resources?
   Answer: IaaS

3. Which cloud service model requires the least management and administration?
   Answer: SaaS

4. Which cloud service model always gives us the latest features and updates?
   Answer: PaaS

5. What is responsible for separating the client environment from other clients in Azure?
   Answer: Azure fabric

6. What is the first access layer in Microsoft Azure?
   Answer: Azure tenant

7. What is the lowest granularity you can assign access to Azure resources?
   Answer: Azure resource

8. What is the recommended access level that should be assigned for Azure resources?
   Answer: Azure resource group

9. How is pricing calculated for Microsoft Azure?
   Answer: Per minute

10. ARM templates are part of what?
    Answer: Infrastructure as Code

Chapter 2: Azure Networking – Foundation of Azure IaaS

1. Which services are dependent on the Azure network in Microsoft Azure?
   Answer: Both
2. What defines the IP address range in Azure?
   Answer: CIDR
3. Service endpoints are used to connect which services to your virtual network?
   Answer: PaaS
4. The default DNS service in Microsoft Azure is...?
   Answer: Azure DNS
5. When can service endpoints be added?
   Answer: At any time
6. Private IP address in Azure can be...?
   Answer: Both
7. Public IP address in Azure can be...?
   Answer: Both
8. NSGs are...?
   Answer: Security rules that define traffic flow
9. What does an NSG define?
   Answer: Both
10. To what can an NSG not be assigned to?
    Answer: Virtual network

Chapter 3: Infrastructure as a Service – the First Layer of Cloud Computing

1. What is the oldest Windows Server version supported for Azure VMs?
   Answer: Windows Server 2008 R2 SP1
2. What can basic-tier VMs support?
   Answer: Lower IOPS
3. What are low-priority VMs intended to be used for?
   Answer: Batch processing
4. Size setting in the Azure Virtual Machine blade is used to...?
   Answer: Both

5. Runbooks can be used to perform?
   Answer: Both

6. Azure Load Balancer is used...?
   Answer: To distribute traffic across VMs in the backend pool

7. Placing VMs in the same availability set will result in...?
   Answer: VMs will be placed in a different rack

8. Scaling by creating additional instances of VM is called...?
   Answer: Scaling out

9. Scaling out is an example of...?
   Answer: Horizontal scaling

10. For scaling out of Azure VMs we use...?
    Answer: Scale set

Chapter 4: Azure App Service – Hosting Web Applications without a Server

1. Azure App Service is...
   Answer: PaaS

2. How much control do we have with an App Service Plan compared to virtual machines?
   Answer: Less

3. How much administration do we have with Azure App Service Plan compared to virtual machines?
   Answer: Less

4. App Service Plan is used to host...
   Answer: Web applications

5. Slots are used to...
   Answer: Host different versions of the application

6. An Azure App Service Plan's increased workload is handled by...
   Answer: Scaling out

7. The best monitoring tool for Azure Web Apps is...
   Answer: Application Insights

8. High availability for Azure Web Apps is achieved by...
   Answer: Traffic Manager

9. Traffic Manager supports...
   Answer: Both

10. An isolated and dedicated environment for Azure Web Apps is an...
    Answer: Azure ASE

Chapter 5: The Azure Data Platform

1. Database in Azure can be run as...
   Answer: Both
2. Azure Virtual Machine with SQL is different from VM without SQL because of...
   Answer: SQL server configuration
3. Azure SQL Database is also called...
   Answer: Database as a Service
4. The Azure SQL Database tier can be measured in...
   Answer: Both
5. You can run a query on Azure SQL Database with...
   Answer: Both
6. To connect to Azure SQL Database, you need to...
   Answer: Add an IP address to a firewall rule
7. To create an Azure SQL Database replica, you can use...
   Answer: Geo-replication
8. To create a highly available Azure SQL Database, you need to create a...
   Answer: Failover group
9. To mask columns in Azure SQL Database, you use...
   Answer: Dynamic data masking
10. To detect potential threats to your database, you use...
    Answer: Advanced threat protection

Chapter 6: Azure Storage, Backup, and Site Recovery – Moving your Data to Azure

1. An Azure Storage account can be deployed as...
   Answer: Both
2. To have maximum SLA, the Storage account should be...
   Answer: Geo-redundant
3. The Storage account tier can be...
   Answer: Both

4. Can a local database be backed up to the Azure Storage account?
   Answer: Yes

5. Can a local database be deployed directly to Azure SQL Database?
   Answer: Yes

6. To use ASR, you need to create...
   Answer: Recovery services vault

7. With Azure Backup, you can protect...
   Answer: Both

8. With ASR, you can protect...
   Answer: Both

9. To migrate a VM protected with ASR to the cloud, you must...
   Answer: Perform failover

10. To migrate a large amount of data to Azure, we must use...
    Answer: Azure import/export job

Chapter 7: Hybrid Cloud with Azure – Extending Local Workloads to the Cloud

1. The hybrid cloud is often only an option because of...
   Answer: Both

2. We can connect a local network and Azure using...
   Answer: Both

3. Azure resource needed for S2S...
   Answer: A virtual network gateway

4. A local network gateway holds the configuration of a...
   Answer: Local network

5. A VPN device configuration can be downloaded from the Azure portal.
   Answer: True, but for a limited number of devices

6. The recommended mode for S2S connection is...
   Answer: Resource manager

7. To ensure that you can use local identities in the hybrid cloud, you must deploy...
   Answer: Domain controller in Azure

8. An on-premises data gateway can be used with...
   Answer: A limited number of Azure Services

9. Azure Stack is...
   Answer: An extension of Azure in your local data center
10. Azure Stack offers...
    Answer: Both

Chapter 8: Azure Active Directory – Identity in the Cloud

1. An AAD is on top of a...
   Answer: Tenant
2. An account can be part of multiple tenants:
   Answer: Yes
3. AAD can contain Microsoft Live Accounts:
   Answer: Yes
4. AAD can be synced with Windows Server AD:
   Answer: Yes
5. The zure Active Directory Free tier has a limit of...
   Answer: 500,000 objects
6. To set up a custom domain...
   Answer: You must own domain
7. To verify your custom domain, you must use...
   Answer: Either
8. Using RBAC, you can assign roles for...
   Answer: All of the above
9. Role can be assigned to...
   Answer: Both
10. To set up AAD sign-in from the application, you must...
    Answer: Register the application in AAD

Chapter 9: Azure Security and Administration

1. Everything in Azure is redundant and has how many copies?
   Answer: Three
2. Most data breaches are caused by...
   Answer: Leaked credentials
3. MFA stands for...
   Answer: Multi-factor authentication
4. MFA can be configured to use:
   Answer: All of the above
5. Azure Firewall is...
   Answer: Firewall as a Service
6. Azure resources can be encrypted using...
   Answer: Both
7. To use custom keys, we must use...
   Answer: Azure Key Vault
8. Azure Security Center provides...
   Answer: Both
9. Azure Security Center can be used to protect...
   Answer: Both
10. Just-in-Time access provides...
    Answer: Control over management access for our VMs

Chapter 10: Best Practices

1. The name of the resource should contain...
   Answer: As much information as possible
2. Public endpoints should be...
   Answer: Exposed to internet access only when needed
3. To control management access to Azure VMs, you can use...
   Answer: Both
4. Multi-factor authentication is...
   Answer: Free for administrators
5. IaC stands for...
   Answer: Infrastructure as code

6. An ARM template is a...
   Answer: JSON file

7. The Azure command-line tool is...
   Answer: Both

8. With IaC, we can...
   Answer: Deploy multiple resources

9. DSC stands for...
   Answer: Desired State Configuration

10. The steps to apply DSC in Azure Automation are...
    Answer: Import script, compile script, and register node

Other Books You May Enjoy

If you enjoyed this book, you may be interested in these other books by Packt:

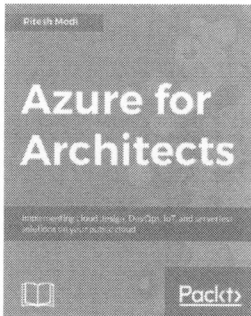

Azure for Architects
Ritesh Modi

ISBN: 978-1-78839-739-1

- Familiarize yourself with the components of the Azure Cloud platform
- Understand the cloud design patterns
- Use enterprise security guidelines for your Azure deployment
- Design and implement Serverless solutions
- See Cloud architecture and the deployment pipeline
- Understand cost management for Azure solutions

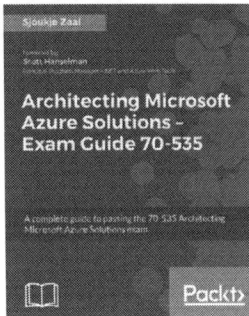

Architecting Microsoft Azure Solutions - Exam Guide 70-535
Sjoukje Zaal

ISBN: 978-1-78899-173-5

- Use Azure Virtual Machines to design effective VM deployments
- Implement architecture styles, like serverless computing and microservices
- Secure your data using different security features and design effective security strategies
- Design Azure storage solutions using various storage features
- Create identity management solutions for your applications and resources
- Architect state-of-the-art solutions using Artificial Intelligence, IoT, and Azure Media Services
- Use different automation solutions that are incorporated in the Azure platform

Leave a review - let other readers know what you think

Please share your thoughts on this book with others by leaving a review on the site that you bought it from. If you purchased the book from Amazon, please leave us an honest review on this book's Amazon page. This is vital so that other potential readers can see and use your unbiased opinion to make purchasing decisions, we can understand what our customers think about our products, and our authors can see your feedback on the title that they have worked with Packt to create. It will only take a few minutes of your time, but is valuable to other potential customers, our authors, and Packt. Thank you!

Index

A

Application Security Group (ASG) 54, 332
ARM templates
  for Azure Load Balancer 100
  using 59, 69
AzCopy 238
Azure Active Directory
  about 266, 295
  application, registering 282, 283, 284, 285, 286
  creating 267, 268
  custom domain, adding 269, 270
  managing 277
  permissions, managing 280, 281
  syncing, with on-premises AD 271
  tiers 266
  user options, managing 280, 281
  user, creating 278
Azure AD Connect
  installing 273, 274, 275, 276, 277
Azure App Service Plan
  about 118
  creating 119, 120, 121, 143, 144
Azure Backup
  enabling 213, 214
  on-premises resources, backing up 215, 216,
    217, 218, 220
Azure CLI 339
Azure Firewall
  about 295
  configuring 297, 303
  creating 297
  deploying 298
  environment, preparing 295
Azure Key Vault
  about 305
  creating 306, 307

  deploying 307
  secrets, adding 309
Azure Load Balancers
  about 91
  ARM template 100
  configuring 94, 96, 97, 99, 100
  creating 92
Azure network services 59
Azure networking
  basics 36
Azure portal
  reference 14
Azure PowerShell
  about 338
  installing 312
Azure Recovery Service 211
Azure Resource Manager (ARM) 13, 31, 32
Azure resources
  creating, with Infrastructure as code (IaC) 342
  deploying 348, 349, 350
  pricing 29, 30
Azure Route Table
  creating 300, 301
Azure Security Center Alerts 320, 322
Azure Security Center
  endpoint protection, enabling 319
  overview 315, 316
  recommendations 317, 318
Azure settings
  configuring, for S2S 249
Azure Site Recovery
  about 222
  configuring, for on-premises resources 222, 225,
    226, 227, 228, 229, 231, 233
  failover, performing of VM 236
  using, as migration tool 234
  VM, migrating 237, 238

Azure SQL Database encryption
  key, using for 313
Azure SQL
  database, migrating to 202, 203, 205, 207
Azure Stack 260
Azure Standard Management (ASM) 12
Azure Storage account
  creating 192, 193, 194
  encrypting 311
  options 196
  replication options 195
  types 195
Azure Storage
  about 192
  database, backing up to 199, 200, 201
  settings 197, 198
Azure subscription model 22, 24
Azure subscription
  types 24, 25, 26
Azure Traffic Manager
  configurations 148, 150
  creating 146
  settings 148, 150
Azure Virtual Machine Scale Set
  about 102
  ARM template 109
  creating 102, 105, 106
  managing 107
Azure virtual machine
  advanced options 78, 79, 80, 81
  basic information 75, 76
  creating 45, 47, 48, 49, 74, 75
  deploying 74
  managing 82
  monitoring 84, 87, 89
  operations 84, 87, 89
  settings 82, 84
  sizes 76, 77
Azure virtual network (Azure VNet)
  about 36
  creating 36, 37, 39
  options 39, 40, 41, 42, 43
Azure Virtual Network
  local network, connecting with 243
Azure Web App high availability 145

Azure Web Apps
  about 118
  API 136
  Application Insights 138, 139, 141
  certificates 131, 134
  creating 121, 122
  creating, with ARM templates 342, 344
  creating, with Azure CLI 347
  creating, with Azure PowerShell 345, 346
  custom domain 131
  deployment settings 123, 124, 125
  development tools 136
  general settings 127
  managing 123
  mobile 136
  monitoring 137
  running 151
  scaling 132, 134
  settings 129, 130
Azure
  best practices 330
  considerations 335, 336, 337
  data services 187
  database options 155
  history 12, 13
  virtual networks, connecting across 253

B

best practices, Azure
  naming convention 330, 331
  public endpoints 331, 332, 333, 334, 335

C

cloud computing
  benefits 18, 19, 20, 21
  concepts 7, 8
  hosted 8, 9
  hybrid 8
  private 8
  private cloud 8
  public 10, 12
cloud security
  demystifying 292
cloud service models
  about 15, 16

cons 18
pros 18
cloud
database, migrating to 198
command-line interface (CLI) 337
configuration as code
about 350
DSC, applying with Azure automation 351, 352,
353, 354, 355
Cross-origin resource sharing (CORS) 197

D

database assessment
creating 207, 208, 210, 211
database transaction unit (DTU) 167
database
backing up, to Azure Storage 199, 200, 201
encrypting 312
migrating, to Azure SQL 202, 203, 205, 207
migrating, to cloud 198
disaster recovery (DR) 222
DNS 52

E

Elastic Cloud Compute (EC2) 12
encryption 305

G

general data protection regulation (GDPR) 177

H

hardware security modules (HSMs) 306
hosted cloud
about 8, 9
versus private cloud 10, 11
hybrid cloud 8, 242
hybrid environment
services, configuring 252

I

IaaS
versus PaaS 27, 29
identity security
options 295

identity
securing 292
Infrastructure as code (IaC)
about 15, 337
ARM templates 338
Azure CLI 339, 340
Azure PowerShell 338
Azure Resources, creating 342
tools, installing 338
integrated development environment (IDE) 338
IP address
private IP address 51
public IP address 52, 58
types 50, 51

J

Just-in-Time access 322, 324, 325

K

key
using, for Azure SQL Database encryption 313

L

local firewall
configuring, for S2S 251
local network
connecting, with Azure Virtual Network 243

M

multi-factor authentication (MFA)
about 293
enabling 293, 294
multiple resources
deploying 350

N

naming convention 330
network interface card (NIC) 50
network security groups 53, 54, 55, 56, 57
network security
options 304
network
securing 295

O

on-premises AD
  AAD, syncing with 271
on-premises data gateway
  about 255
  cloud service 258
  local installation 256, 257, 258
on-premises resources
  ASR, configuring for 222, 225, 226, 227, 228,
    229, 230, 231, 233

P

PaaS
  versus IaaS 27, 29
Point-to-Site (P2S) 243
private cloud
  about 8
  versus hosted cloud 10, 11
private IP address 52
public cloud
  about 8, 10
  key concepts 11
public endpoints 331, 332, 333
public IP address 51, 58

R

recovery service vault
  creating 212
Remote Server Administration Tools (RSAT) 91
role-based access control (RBAC) 13, 286, 287

S

S2S connection
  Azure settings, configuring for 249
  creating, between Azure Virtual Network and
    local network 243, 244, 246, 248, 249

local firewall, configuring for 251
service level agreement (SLA) 91
services
  configuring, in hybrid environment 252
Shared access signature (SAS) 197
Site-to-Site (S2S) 243
SQL Server Management Studio (SSMS) 170
SQL Server, as IaaS
  about 156
  Azure Virtual Machine, creating with SQL image
    156, 158, 160
  high availability, for SQL Server in Azure Virtual
    machine 164
  SQL Server, managing in Azure Virtual Machine
    162, 163
SQL Server, as PaaS
  about 165
  Azure SQL Database backup 186
  Azure SQL Database security 177, 179, 180,
    182
  Azure SQL Database, creating 165, 167, 168
  Azure SQL Database, managing 169, 170, 172
  Azure SQL Database, monitoring 183, 184
  Azure SQL Database, troubleshooting 183, 184
  highly available Azure SQL Database, creating
    173, 174, 175
stock keeping unit (SKU) 93

T

transparent data encryption (TDE) 183

V

virtual machine scale set (VMSS) 134
virtual networks
  connecting, across Azure 253
virtual private network (VPN) 10
VM disks
  encrypting 315

23899623R00221

Printed in Great Britain
by Amazon